YOU'LL NEVER WALK ALONE

LIVERPOOL
FOOTBALL CLUB

EST·1892 ®

LIVERPOOL IN EUROPE

**STEVE HALE and IVAN PONTING
with STEVE SMALL**

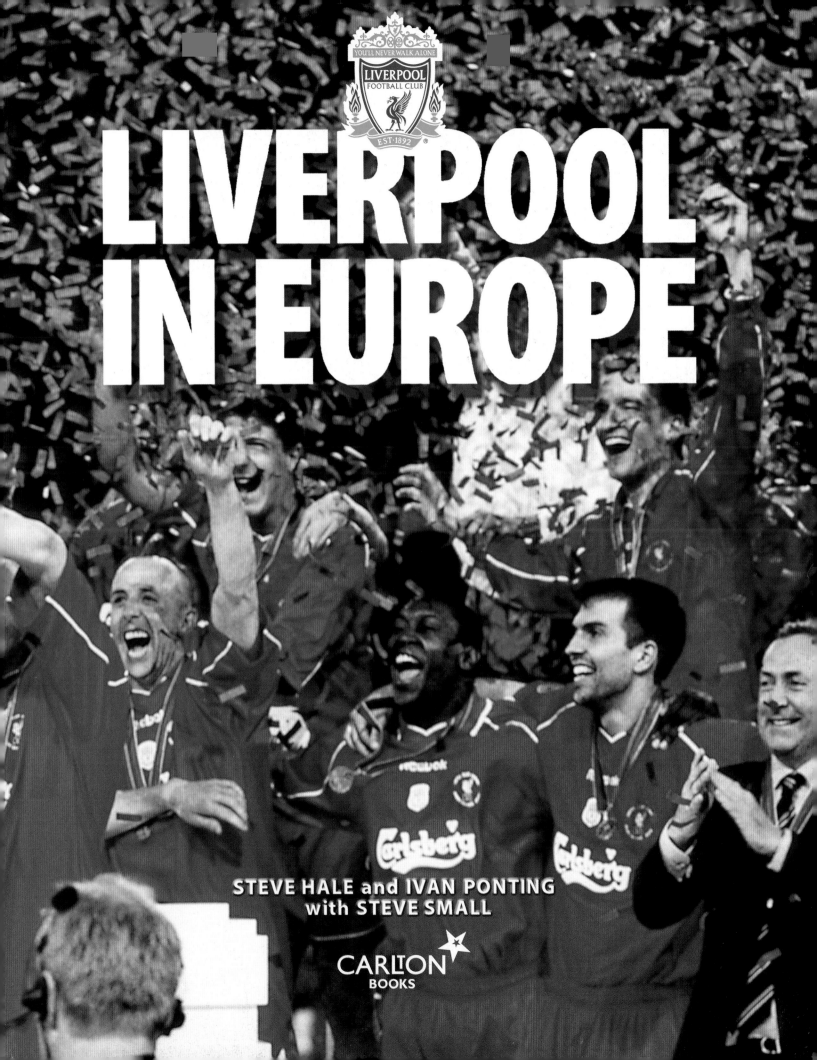

LIVERPOOL IN EUROPE

STEVE HALE and IVAN PONTING
with STEVE SMALL

CARLTON
BOOKS

ACKNOWLEDGEMENTS

The author and photographer wish to thank the
following: Pat, Rosie and Joe Ponting; Steve Small; the
late Eddie Marks; Ian Callaghan; Alan Kennedy; David
Johnson; Ian Rush; Tommy Smith; Ron Yeats; Ron
Moran; Roy Evans; Simon, Mary, Josh and Kyle Barrett;
Chris and Jo Forster; Colin Hunt and Karen Kenny of the
Liverpool Post and Echo; Frank Loughlin; Mark
Trowbridge at Allsport/Getty Images; Andy Cowie at
Colorsport; Fred, John and Derek, the lads on the press
photographers' door at Anfield.

First published in 1992 by
GUINNESS PUBLISHING
33 London Road, Enfield
Middlesex, EN2 6DJ

This edition published by:
CARLTON BOOKS LIMITED, 2001
20 Mortimer Street,
London W1T 3JW

Printed in Italy

ISBN: 1-84222-477-8

Managing Art Director: Jeremy Southgate
Design: Steve Small
Jacket Design: Bobby Birchall

10 9 8 7 6 5 4 3 2 1

CONTENTS

FOREWORD by Ian Callaghan MBE

Ian Callaghan has played in more European matches for one club than any other British footballer. Indeed, his total of 88 outings has been outstripped only by his former Anfield team-mate, Ray Clemence, who faced Continental opposition 77 times as a Red and then on a further 27 occasions after joining Tottenham Hotspur. Ian's figure, which includes one game as a substitute, was compiled between 1964 and 1978. In addition, he set Liverpool's all-time appearance record with 843 starts (plus five substitutions) in major domestic and European competition during his 18-year Anfield career.

From nights of unimaginable glamour in the world's grandest venues to uncomfortable interludes at primitive grounds in the back of beyond, the European experience has been an immeasurably rich one for everyone connected with Liverpool FC.

When it all started in 1964 it was a huge adventure, a giant step into the unknown; down the years it became part of our routine. But no matter how often we set off on a European campaign, it always created a special buzz around Anfield, a feeling that once again anything could happen.

As I sift through my memories, it comes home to me how privileged I was to be part of it for so long. In particular, I shall never forget the great Bill Shankly leading us into that remarkable first season, starting gently in Iceland and culminating in the fireworks of Milan. Ahead, of course, were trophies to be lifted on unforgettable occasions, none more glorious than the emotional night in Rome when finally we laid claim to the European Cup.

Yet Europe has meant considerably more to Liverpool and its players than trophies on the sideboard. Apart from the refreshing change from the weekly round of League football, it taught us so much in terms of technique and tactics, and the lessons we learned helped us immensely on the domestic scene. Certainly it broadened me, both football-wise and socially, and I shall be eternally grateful for the opportunity.

As to my one-club record of 88 European appearances, I hadn't thought about it until it was mentioned by the author of this book, Ivan Ponting, whom I have known since helping with research for his earlier volume, *Liverpool Player by Player*. He pointed out that it was the product of playing for the Reds through 14 consecutive seasons in Europe, which reinforces to me my good fortune in serving such a wonderful club for so long.

Normally, I am not one for looking back; these days I get as much satisfaction from winning a trophy at the golf club as I did from receiving medals during my career as a footballer. But so rich and colourful is the history of Liverpool in Europe that it deserves to be commemorated. So now, with the club back on the winning trail following the magnificent achievement of Gérard Houllier's marvellous new team in lifting the UEFA Cup in 2001, it's the perfect time for a second edition of this volume.

Last season I saw more of Liverpool than at any time since I finished playing, and it was an uplifting experience. The old passion and excitement were back and, sitting in the stands, I was delighted that the young supporters, to whom past successes must mean very little, were able to savour great times of their own.

Gérard has done an unbelievable job and, we hope, he has only just begun. The lads who lifted three trophies in 2000/01 will remember the taste of success and be eager for more. Certainly they could not have had better preparation for the Champions League challenge which lies ahead at the time of writing.

Appropriately, the majority of the pictures between these covers have been taken by Liverpudlian Steve Hale, who had the original idea for the book and who has been photographing the Reds since the mid 1960s. The story is a stirring one; I hope you enjoy it.

Ian Callaghan
August 2001

INTRODUCTION

AS a soccer-obsessed schoolboy growing up on Merseyside in the late 1950s, Steve Hale was not alone in being gripped by a dream of epic dimensions. Countless youthful imaginations were fired by the fantasy of playing for Liverpool or Everton, of mingling with the heroes of the day and, most vivid of all, of scoring dramatic goals that won championships and cups. Steve's flight of fancy, however, was a little more detailed than most. He saw himself shooting the winner in the closing minutes of the European Cup Final against Real Madrid; the location was not specific but it was definitely romantic, a world away from the familiar, down-to-earth surroundings of Anfield and Goodison.

Now Steve was not a bad footballer; he excelled for the school team, worked hard at his abiding passion, and had faith that one day he would make the grade. He didn't, and it seemed that his castle in the air, that ecstatic vision of glory on the European stage, had crumbled irrevocably, a brutal casualty of growing up. A practical lad at heart, he didn't fret, instead forging a successful career in photography, a move that was to lead him to a kind of fulfilment.

The original European Cup, held in perpetuity by Real Madrid, who fired the imagination of the young Steve Hale.

Cut to Paris in the spring of 1981. Liverpool had reached their third European Cup Final, and now they faced . . . Real Madrid. Throughout that season, fancifully perhaps, Steve had sensed an inevitability about the progress of the two teams towards their meeting in the French capital. When the time came he was there, in position behind the goal, a trifle more on edge than for the average working engagement. He had covered European finals before, but this was different. In truth, the match was a disappointment, a case of two good sides cancelling each other out as they sparred unavailingly for the glittering prize. But that all counted for nothing as, on 81 minutes, Steve Hale's supreme moment materialised from an unlikely source.

Alan Kennedy, Liverpool's good-natured, gritty left-back, seemed to come from nowhere as he bore down on the Spanish goal with the ball at his feet. From a narrow angle he unleashed his shot; the camera clicked; the net bulged; the joyous Wearsider took off towards the fans behind the goal. Steve jumped up and followed him, the professional lensman's instincts taking over. But as he returned to his place there was time for a few quiet seconds to himself, seconds in which he reflected that his dream had come true, albeit not quite in the manner he had envisaged as a short-trousered Europhile with stars in his eyes. After all those years, he HAD 'shot' the winner for Liverpool against Real Madrid.

But what was it about the European Cup, and Real Madrid in particular, that had so captivated the impressionable little fellow from Fazakerley? In fact, it was something indefinable – magical, if you like – about the Continent's premier club competition. Mention of such names as Red Star Belgrade, Honved and Fiorentina just oozed mystery and glamour to a youngster used to watching the likes of Bolton, Blackburn and, yes, even Liverpool and Everton, week in and week out.

At that time, of course, television had yet to sabotage the mystique of Europe through over-exposure, poking at every speck of action and analysing it to death. Back then, the fans had to rely on newspapers and occasional crackly radio reports to satisfy their craving for information; it all seemed tantalisingly out of reach, thus increasing the allure. Steve was hungry for every scrap of knowledge he could assimilate, being captivated by the Continentals' stylish kit and their slick, cutaway boots that seemed so graceful in comparison with the long shorts and clodhoppers still fashionable in the British game. His dad was a *Daily Mirror* reader who, all too often, returned home from his bakery shift and settled back to read the sports pages, only to find a gaping hole, his Euro-daft son having snipped out a picture of Fontaine, the French goal ace, or Vava, Atletico's deadly Brazilian.

But in Steve's circle of friends, THE team was Real Madrid. They talked of such men

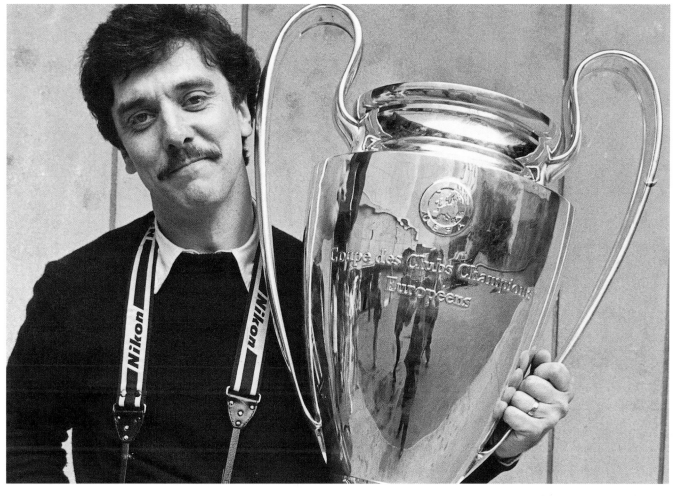

As proud as if he'd won it himself, photographer Steve Hale with the European Cup after he had shot the winner against Real Madrid in 1981.

as di Stefano, Puskas and Gento in reverent tones; they were the ultimate stars, the pure beauty of their football symbolised by their all-white strip. Of course, replica kits were not produced in the 1950s – how many cash-strapped parents wish they were not available today? – but mothers were badgered to assemble white T-shirt, shorts and long socks, so that their offspring could ape the aristocrats of Bernabeu on the backstreets of Liverpool. Eventually, as a result of constant nagging, an uncle took Steve to Old Trafford, where Manchester United were playing Red Star. The atmosphere of the occasion fed his obsession, gripped his emotions, and from that day Real Madrid's fate was sealed . . .

Now many years have passed and he is a photographic veteran, having covered five World Cups, but still the boy in Steve Hale thrills to the appeal of a big European night at Anfield. On such occasions, right up until his retirement in 2001, from the moment he got out of bed in the morning, there was a feeling of barely suppressed excitement around the house. A freelance who worked from home, he might have been developing in the dark-room, completing invoices, whatever, but always he felt that certain tingle and his mind was on the evening ahead. After an early dinner, he headed for the ground, parked on the far side of Arkles Lane and walked up to Anfield. At that point it was still quiet on the streets among the terraced houses, but there was something in the air. The hum of the gathering crowd began to pick up as he passed through the gates and he felt butterflies in the pit of his stomach.

It was never just a question of 'Can we win?' It was the whole occasion. There's a cocktail of smells about any night match that, in some way, was all the more noticeable to Steve when a European encounter was in the offing. He admits that there might have been a hint of self-delusion, yet swears that the hot-dogs were more pungent, the

smoke more acrid, the whiff of liniment a little stronger. Often it was cold and damp, the lights dazzling out of the blackness above, adding compellingly to the scene.

Soon came the moment when the teams ran out, and to Steve that was always special. Immediately he would glance at the visitors, scouring their ranks for star players. What could they do? Was there an embryo Cruyff or a nascent Eusebio among them? Was it going to be a night of theatre? He lives in Menorca now but, despite changes in football that make his heart ache, the degradation of the great game by money and greed, Steve, like millions of others, will never tire of it.

Come 2000/01, having endured an enforced absence from the Continental scene in the most traumatic of circumstances and then suffered a succession of disappointing campaigns, Liverpool returned to the high table of European soccer. Gérard Houllier's men lifted the UEFA Cup in spine-tingling fashion, then made ready to embark with spirits high on the trail of Champions League glory, another rich chapter in the great adventure pioneered by Bill Shankly and company in 1964/65.

This book, developed from a long-cherished idea of Steve's, chronicles the Reds' progress through his evocative pictures, taken during a third of a century on the road, and through comprehensive reportage. As well as analysis, scene-setting and interviews with some of the characters most closely involved in the drama, there are descriptions of the action and full statistics from each of the Reds' 187 European matches to date, which have included so many heady highlights. For sheer romance, the first campaign takes some beating, featuring widely different encounters against the gentlemanly Icelanders of Reykjavik and the formidable, passionate Italian champions, Inter Milan. There follows high endeavour but ultimate disappointment in the Cup Winners' Cup Final against Borussia Dortmund at Hampden Park; triumph in the UEFA Cup in both 1973 and 1976; the Reds' first European Cup victory in Rome in 1977; further successes in 1978, 1981 and 1984; the horror of Brussels a year later; and the exhilarating Houllier-inspired renaissance at the dawn of the 21st century.

As author, I have benefited from the wisdom of numerous players, including Ian Callaghan (to whom I am indebted for his gracious foreword), Alan Kennedy, David Johnson, Tommy Smith, Ron Yeats, Ian Rush, Ron Moran and Roy Evans, all of whom have been generous with their time.

Also rating more than their mention on the acknowledgements page are Steve Small and the late Eddie Marks, Scousers and avid Liverpool fanatics both. Not only has Steve made such an expert job of designing this book in both its editions, he has been a stimulating source of suggestions and, as befits a friend of nearly 40 years' standing with whom I still conduct arguments that date back to the school playground, he has never baulked at telling me when he thought I was wrong. In addition this time around, because prior commitments dictated that I was unable to add new chapters to *Liverpool In Europe,* he has stepped forward to supply the words which sit beside the dramatic images of the Reds' most recent campaigns.

Undoubtedly the saddest aspect of the project for me has been the fact that another good pal, Eddie Marks, did not live to experience Liverpool's rebirth as a major force on the Continental scene or to contribute to this second edition. Back in 1992, Eddie checked the facts and figures with a ferocious but cheerful attention to detail that proved indispensable, and acted as the ultimate arbiter on all matters of record relating to the club and its history. He chortled knowingly when I promised not to investigate too closely the circumstances surrounding his possession of the UEFA Cup Final corner flag that had taken up residence in his study, and he would have relished involvement in this updated chronicling of his beloved Reds' triumphs. Alas, Eddie died in 1996, a tragic loss to his friends, including many at Anfield where he was a familiar figure, but most of all to his family: wife Viv and daughters Vanessa and Lynsey.

How he would have revelled in Liverpool's glorious resurgence under Gérard Houllier, in the dazzling brilliance of new stars such as Steven Gerrard and Michael Owen, and in the promise, surely, of more success to come in the first decade of the new millennium.

This book, then, is dedicated to the memory of Eddie Marks.

Ivan Ponting
August 2001

Above: **A double-decker for the treble heroes. For the first time in 17 years, the Reds parade the spoils of European victory around their home city.**

Right: **Eddie Marks: a Red from the cradle to the grave.**

Above: The only words of English in the programme for Liverpool's first European tie. The courteous and friendly tone of the message from Reykjavik's president was typical of the generous hospitality extended to the Merseysiders throughout their stay in Iceland.

Chapter One

OH INTER 1-2-3, GO BACK TO ITALY!

Opposite: **Ready for the European challenge: Bill Shankly, who described his Inter Milan counterpart Helenio Herrera as 'a remarkable little fellow, a cut-throat man who always wants to win.' He might have been talking about himself.**

IT began with the players searching vainly for igloos, and it ended with a gigantic firework party in which the Reds were reduced, unceremoniously and rather scandalously, to the role of Guy Fawkes. Yet Liverpool's first Continental campaign came close, so very close, to landing the most glittering European prize of them all.

Looking back now, in the light of subsequent Champions' Cup triumphs in Rome (twice), at Wembley and in Paris, it is easy to underestimate the stirring achievements of 1964/65. But that is to ignore the magnitude of the task thrust upon Bill Shankly's men as they faced serious overseas competition for the first time. Remember that this was two years before Jock Stein's Celtic broke new ground for British clubs by lifting the great trophy, and three before Matt Busby attained his 'holy grail' by leading Manchester United to the first English triumph.

Liverpool, only two seasons after languishing in the Second Division for the best part of a decade, were suddenly entrusted with carrying their country's banner into battle against some of the finest sides in the world. The way they coped is, in its way, as glorious as anything that was to follow.

To kick off their European odyssey, however, the Reds could hardly have been handed a less demanding encounter. In the first round they were drawn against the amiable amateurs of Reykjavik, the Icelandic champions. These hitherto unknown opponents proved to be utterly naive in a footballing sense, refreshingly gracious and chivalrous in every other way; indeed, they might have hailed from a different planet to the seasoned, cynical opposition who lurked in the later stages of the competition.

Due to play the away leg first, Liverpool started out for Iceland on the Sunday after drawing two apiece at Anfield with West Ham United in the FA Charity Shield. Their strength was depleted by the unavailability of star Scottish centre-forward Ian St John, who was recovering from appendicitis, and fellow marksman Alf Arrowsmith, who damaged a knee so badly against the Hammers that he never regained a regular place. That injury to the man whose goals played a major part in winning the 1964 League title, and therefore qualifying for the European Cup, shed a sad sidelight on an

Left: **Not so hospitable: Ian St John in ruthless mood as he nets Liverpool's second goal of the night against Reykjavik at Anfield. The Scot's strike extended the aggregate lead to 7-0; by the end of the evening the score stood at 11-1.**

otherwise happy trip. Alf, a friendly, honest Mancunian who took his frequent joshing from Scouse team-mates in good part, was to miss some of Liverpool's most rousing successes before seeing out his career with Bury and Rochdale, his destiny a poignant, cautionary reminder of sport's uncertainty.

However, those fortunate enough to be Reykjavik-bound were in high spirits as they arrived at the Ayrshire holiday camp where they were due to kill a few hours before the flight. Immediately, the mood was lightened still further as Bill Shankly opened the door at the front of the team bus, leaned out and rasped in characteristic tones: 'We're Liverpool Football Club and we're on our way to Iceland.' The camp gateman responded, with either piercing wit or supreme artlessness: 'Then I'm sorry, Sir, you're on the wrong road!' It was one of the rare occasions that Bill didn't get to deliver the punchline.

Newly kitted out in club blazers, flannels and ties - as Ron Yeats recalls: 'We didn't half look well' - they climbed aboard their plane at Prestwick and headed for the unknown. None of them had much idea what to expect from Iceland, and after the pilot

Saintly frustration: Ian St John is foiled by Anderlecht goalkeeper Trappeniers at Anfield. Come the final whistle, though, the Reds' centre-forward was amply satisfied, having scored in a memorable 3-0 victory.

had caused considerable excitement by announcing that he was skirting a live volcano - disappointingly, there was no red-hot lava on display - noses were pressed to windows as they neared their destination. Some were anticipating a land of igloos and Eskimos, but what met their eyes could hardly have been more different. They were confronted by a pleasant, everyday sort of city, clean of aspect, slow of pace, and with not a sledge or a husky in sight. The air was invigorating and their hosts hospitable, apparently delighted to be welcoming the great Liverpool FC, of whom they had heard so much.

Throughout the visit, the atmosphere was one of politeness and bonhomie, even extending into the match. Reykjavik were ecstatic just to take part in the European Cup, and they had no thoughts of progressing to the next round. It was enough, it seemed, just to run on to the field with such illustrious opponents, and to fete them at every available moment between their arrival and departure. The Reds won the game as they pleased, two of their five goals being scored by Gordon Wallace, who was on duty in place of St John. At that time he was on something of a roll, having netted twice in the Charity Shield, and there were high hopes for his future. Indeed Shankly, never prone to understatement, once described his callow countryman as the nearest thing he had seen to Tom Finney since the war. Sadly, the nimble marksman was a victim of brittle bones and, before long, was to slide out of the first-team reckoning.

In fact, Gordon was missing from the line-up for the return at Anfield, an occasion which saw the Kopites in their most expansive humour. Revelling in the novelty of their heroes' vast lead - they knocked in another six goals - the inimitable Scousers took to cheering every Reykjavik move and booing the Reds, Willie Stevenson and Ron Yeats being subjected to ironic chants of 'Off, Off, Off' after committing the most innocuous of fouls. 'Keeper Guddjonsson and Felixson, scorer of the visitors' lone goal, were cheered to the rafters, and it was entirely appropriate when the home team formed a guard of honour to clap the Icelanders off at the end.

The match was significant, too, in that it marked the final Reds' bow of former England winger Alan A'Court, a stalwart servant in the club's frustrating Second Division days but now supplanted by Peter Thompson. A goal for Alan would have crowned the night, but it wasn't to be.

After their relaxed baptism, Liverpool faced the true reality of European competition. Only a few weeks earlier, England had scraped a lucky draw at Wembley against a Belgium side containing seven men from Anderlecht, the Merseysiders' next opponents. Prophets of doom predicted summary elimination but a combination of Shankly's canny tactics and superb psychology, his team's fabulous fitness and their oft-unsung technique, were to see Liverpool through with something to spare.

Before the first leg at Anfield the manager told his men, outrageously, that Anderlecht were, not to put too fine a point on it, a load of rubbish. But his incredulous listeners had watched the Belgian international side, and knew what Paul Van Himst and company could do. Yeats remembers: 'The general reaction in the dressing room was "Bloody hell, what's he on about?"' Of course, after the three-goal victory, Shankly was quick to inform his charges: 'Congratulations, you've just beaten one of the finest teams in Europe,' adding for good measure that Gerry Byrne's eclipse of the tricky Stockman amounted to the best full-back display Europe had ever seen.

But Bill's kidology was not confined to extravagant words. It was against Anderlecht that he introduced Liverpool's all-red strip for the first time, after experimenting with Ron Yeats as a model. The skipper recalls: 'One day after training, he asked me to try on this new kit and run out of the tunnel. He stared hard at me and said: "Jesus Christ, son, you look eight feet tall. You'll frighten the living daylights out of them."'

As well as terrifying the Belgians, Shankly was out to confuse them, doing so by introducing Tommy Smith as a defender with a number ten on his back. The man whose name was to become a byword through the iron of both his tackle and his will was only 19 at the time. He reminisces: 'Ron Moran told me I would be playing, but I didn't believe him, even when I was included in the party. I thought I was there to carry the skips, but when I went to pick them up I was told to save my strength. I was to play alongside Ron Yeats, who was brilliant in the air and strong on his left side, but couldn't do much with his right. Bill Shankly told me to be Ron's right leg. So there we were, playing a back-four system years before Alf Ramsey came up with it. I put everything I had into it and during the game one of the Belgians said to me "You're out of your box" or words to that effect. I thought "Well, you're not going to win tonight, sunshine." They had plenty of flashy players, but they couldn't cope with us.'

With Smith helping to block up the middle and drawing dumbfounded markers out of position, wing-half Gordon Milne was freed to prompt the attack, which he did with relish. The work rate of front-men Roger Hunt and Ian St John was prodigious, and Yeats scored his first goal at Anfield. In the second leg Liverpool maintained command with one of their greatest defensive displays against some of the most beautiful, flowing attacks they had ever encountered. The unflagging Hunt grabbed a late winner to confirm their superiority and underline their arrival as a major power.

Next on the agenda were FC Cologne, formidable opposition who were to take the Reds to three tight, gruelling contests before the two teams were finally and agonisingly separated by the toss of a plastic disc.

After a goalless draw in Germany, the teams were to be stymied by the elements at Anfield on a night when hundreds of supporters flirted with disaster. Shortly before kick-off, with the ground packed and the players changed, a blizzard descended and the referee had little alternative but to call off the game. When the announcement was made, the crowd accepted the decision with good humour; indeed, a few went skating on the pitch and one opportunist wit seized numbers from the half-time scoreboard, holding them up in the manner of a skating judge.

The problems began when fans became jammed in the exits; a small wall gave way and dozens of people suffered crush injuries. Shops in Oakfield Road were used as

Brrr! Liverpool players inspect the Anfield turf before a blizzard descended, causing the postponement of the second leg against FC Cologne. Left to right are Willie Stevenson, Gordon Milne, Tommy Smith, Gerry Byrne, Chris Lawler, Roger Hunt and a shivering Ian St John.

casualty clearing stations while ambulances were awaited, and nearby residents rose to the occasion by digging out blankets and dispensing hot drinks. In the confusion over ticket vouchers for the rearranged game, it took two hours to clear the ground, and some supporters climbed over one-way turnstiles. As one put it: 'You needed to be a wrestler to get in and a hurdler to get out.'

The Germans did not take the postponement as stoically as the crowd, however. Despite the excellent efforts of famous ex-Manchester City goalkeeper Bert Trautmann as interpreter, there was dissension between the two clubs and Bill Shankly was accused of wanting the match postponed for no good reason. His reaction was unprintable.

In due course, a bruising, punishing second leg also proved goalless, and a replay was fixed for Rotterdam, a venue welcomed by Cologne as their fans would not have far to travel. At last there were goals, the Reds going two up and looking set to consolidate. But the Germans came back with typical fortitude, equalising and forcing the marathon tie into extra time.

When that proved inconclusive, it was time for what the tabloids were to dub 'Rotterdam Roulette'. Ron Yeats takes up the story: 'I was worried about the toss during the closing stages, I must have died a hundred times out there that night. I had already lost two tosses, at the start of both the game and extra time, and dreaded another reverse. I felt that football was a team game, yet here was I having to make a decision for the whole club. I certainly felt tremendous pressure, and if we had lost it would have ruined the whole season for me.'

In the event, the tension was to be stretched out beyond belief. The hooters and klaxons in the crowd fell silent as the disc - one side red for Liverpool, the other white for Cologne - looped into the air, only to stick on its end in the mud. Ian St John, one of a jostling crowd of players, officials and policemen clustered around the ceremony, held his head in sheer despair. On his rounds as a highly entertaining after-dinner speaker, Ron will now maintain that the disc was leaning towards the Germans' side, but actually it was pretty straight. Up it went again, and no sooner had it landed than Ron took off himself, jumping for joy at the outcome.

Quarter of a century on, he says: 'I did feel sorry for Cologne, who were devastated. Several of their players were in tears. But we should have won the match anyway.' That sentiment, predictably, was echoed by Bill Shankly, who thought perhaps it might have been fairer to have decided the result on corners. Not surprisingly, Liverpool would have won that way, too!

After such a cliff-hanger, it seemed inconceivable that even higher drama awaited on the European trail that season but, incredibly, it did. In the draw for the semi-finals, the Reds were paired with Internazionale of Milan, holders of the trophy after vanquishing the legendary Real Madrid and, some said, the best club side in the world. Surely, at last, Shankly and company had met their match. Of course, no one said such a thing in Bill's hearing, but there were few people outside Anfield who believed Liverpool could make history by becoming the first British club to reach the final. Inter had a defence with a reputation for near-impregnability, masterful attackers such as Luis Suarez and Sandro Mazzola, and some of the most fanatical supporters on the face of the earth. Yet they came to Anfield, and they were thrashed.

In retrospect, Liverpool's momentous first-leg performance was somehow inevitable. The previous Saturday they had won the FA Cup, overcoming Don Revie's Leeds United through an Ian St John strike in extra time; the mood of celebration was extended by right-back Chris Lawler's wedding on the Monday; by Tuesday, when they faced a footballing challenge that Bill Shankly found utterly irresistible, their leg-weariness had gone but they were still on a high.

Bill's beloved Anfield was already overflowing, a bubbling bowl of joy and anticipation, as his players arrived for the game and headed for the dressing room. They were confronted by the Italians, already changed and doing physical jerks in the corridors. Some men might have been intimidated; Shankly greeted the sight with indifference; his lads would show what THEY could do on the pitch.

But before the action could get under way, Shanks was to pull what was perhaps his supreme psychological stroke. He ensured that Inter would take the pitch first, and must have been delighted when they headed for the Kop end, to be greeted by the kind of roar that turns legs to water. Presumably cowed, the visitors turned tail and made for the Anfield Road goal, the cue for Ron Yeats to lead out his team to the accompaniment of a renewed wall of sound. Then Bill played his ace; out of the tunnel came Gordon Milne, who had missed the Leeds game through injury, and Gerry Byrne, Saturday's hero, who had played most of the final with a broken collar-bone. They were holding aloft the FA Cup, and as they set off on a circuit of the ground, the din grew progressively more deafening. To the Italians it must have seemed like they were up against all the hounds of hell; to the Reds it was an uplifting union with the most devoted followers in the land. After experiencing that, how could they fail?

Such a display of raw emotion called for an early flourish, and the players responded magnificently. After four minutes, Ian Callaghan, so quick and skilful, crossed the ball into the box; Roger Hunt spun like a scarlet top to hook a sensational volley into the corner of the net, then punched the air in the fashionable style pioneered by the Brazilian Altafini. Inter were both fluent and resilient, however, and soon, when poor Yeats slipped, they broke away to equalise. But Liverpool - with Byrne's deputy, faithful veteran Ron Moran, dealing competently with the mercurial Jair - were not to be denied. They regained the lead when Willie Stevenson took a free-kick, Roger Hunt flicked the ball on and the sprinting Cally appeared in space to clip the ball home from a narrow angle. Now the Reds were rampant; a thrilling Lawler strike was disallowed for offside before St John scored the third and Liverpool spurned enough chances to have doubled their tally. Looking back, those missed opportunities probably cost Shankly's team the European Cup.

But this was not a time for cavilling over what might have been; it was an occasion of pure, unadulterated glory. Ron Yeats proclaimed that any club team in the world would have perished at Anfield that night; Tommy Smith felt that even the Brazilian national side would have fallen. Ian Callaghan was equally happy, if characristical-

Could we have played? Bobble-hatted Bill Shankly joins Danish referee Frede Hansen *(centre)* and another official for an examination of the ice-bound surface on the morning after the game was postponed. The Liverpool boss was accused of wanting the match put off for no good reason. His reaction was unprintable!

ly more calm. Though little prone to dwell on his footballing triumphs, still he reflects with satisfaction on his goal: 'We had practiced that free-kick routine so much, but had never scored from it, despite coming close in several League games. Everything had to be just right and this time it was. To do it on such a night in such unbelievable atmosphere was very special. In some ways it was the most satisfying goal I ever scored.'

There were plaudits, too, from the other side. Inter's renowned coach, Helenio Herrera, said: 'We have been beaten before, but never defeated. Tonight we were defeated.' Something may have been lost in the translation, but his meaning was clear. He had a tribute for Roger Hunt, too, saying that his goal was typically Continental rather than British in execution. In his terms, that was the ultimate compliment. In fact, so overcome was Herrera by the events of Anfield that for part of the match he sat with his back to the action, not bearing to look as his side, his creation, was pulled apart. Their rivalry notwithstanding, Herrera and Shankly held each other in high regard and Bill said of his opposite number: 'He's a remarkable little fellow, a cut-throat man who always wants to win.' He might have been talking about himself.

The essence of that famous night was summed up, with simple but wicked humour, by the ever-inventive Kop choir. As their favourites poured forward late in the match, they sang, to the distinctive strains of *Santa Lucia*: 'Oh Inter 1-2-3, Go back to Italy!' After that, there was little left to say, or rather there wasn't until the second leg, which was equally memorable but for starkly contrasting reasons.

If Inter felt they had been subjected to gamesmanship, crowd intimidation and mockery on Merseyside, then the Milanese fans responded in kind - and then some. On touching down in Italy, the Reds were greeted by banners describing them as savages and drug addicts, the latter accusation a ludicrous reference to the boundless energy of Liverpool just three days after their wearing tussle with Leeds. It seems that the European champions had expected their hosts to roll over and die without a fight.

Thereafter, throughout their stay, the English party was subjected to outright hostility from all sides, including an orchestrated campaign of vilification in the press and libellous abuse on leaflets distributed by their opponents' unofficial fan club. Indeed, it seemed that Inter followers might even have divine support in their campaign of disruption. Having booked into a hotel on picturesque Lake Como, the unwelcome visitors found they were next door to a church in which the bells tolled loudly and lingeringly every hour around the clock. Dismayed at the possible effect on the players' sleep, Bill Shankly called on the local priest and asked for the ringers to take a break during the night. He informed the cleric that his men were preparing for 'the most important match in the world this year', and that they needed some peace. Whether or not the holy man was an Inter fan is not recorded, but he replied, straight-faced, that the bells had been ringing regularly for centuries and could not be stopped now for the convenience of Liverpool FC. Unabashed, Bill persisted, suggesting that at least the bells could be padded, but this imaginative proposal found no more favour than his first. The Reds' boss was forced to retire from the discussion, entirely disgusted, though in the event the team slept soundly, actually finding more difficulty on their second night when they were subjected to a cacophony of car horns, road drills and even a brass band.

Yet even that boorish behaviour paled into insignificance alongside the naked hate they encountered in the San Siro stadium. As the Reds took the field, they were spat upon by crazed Italian fans, a revolting experience that proved to be one of the milder horrors in store. Despite the employment of 2,000 armed guards to keep the crowd in check, bonfires were lit on the terraces and firework rockets were launched horizontally across the pitch. Mercifully, no one was maimed, although Bob Paisley was hit by a purple smoke bomb and his clothes were ruined.

It was in this seething, cauldron-like atmosphere that Liverpool set out to protect their two-goal lead. They had reasoned before the game that if they could reproduce anything like their first-leg form, there was no reason why they should not reach the final; but sickeningly, after a mere ten minutes of the most controversial action imaginable, they were convinced they didn't have a chance. To put it with a mildness that is scarcely appropriate, the Merseysiders were not happy with the referee, Spaniard Ortiz de Mendibil. They believed he blew for a foul every time they made a tackle, legal or not, a handicap that proved cumulatively demoralising. But more immediately devastating were his decisions to allow two goals inside 60 seconds, both in highly debatable circumstances.

The first blow fell when Willie Stevenson made what appeared to be a scrupulously fair challenge on Jair on the edge of the box, and from the resultant free-kick Corso bent the ball venomously past goalkeeper Tommy Lawrence. Afterwards the Liverpool camp claimed that Senor de Mendibil had raised his arm for an indirect kick, though television film reveals an indeterminate gesture that could be interpreted as no more than a mere flexing of the referee's muscles. But if that strike was contentious, the second was to provoke sheer outrage. After snuffing out an Inter attack, Lawrence was bouncing the ball when Peiro surprised him from behind. Without making bodily contact, the Italian poked the ball away from the unfortunate custodian, then chipped it into the empty net. The Reds protested vehemently but to no avail, Senor de Mendibil waving them away with the harassed air of a schoolteacher dismissing recalcitrant children from his presence. In fact, their claim - held with understandable passion in the circumstances - that the ball had been kicked from Lawrence's grasp was not verified by television evidence. Indeed, at the time, commentator David Coleman made it clear: 'I must say I think the referee was right. There was no foul.' Be that as it may, Liverpool had a strong case in that Continental officials customarily penalised the slightest challenge of any nature on a goalkeeper; why should this time be an exception?

Most deserving of sympathy in all this was Tommy Lawrence, one of the most underrated net-minders in British football. Yes, he might have been guilty of a momentary lapse of concentration, but who could honestly apportion blame in such an emotional, almost volcanic atmosphere? Tommy had played magnificently, if unobtrusively, throughout that European campaign, though scant praise was wont to come his way. Now was no time to make him a scapegoat. Certainly, no one could call him to task for Milan's second-half winner, a scorching shot from Facchetti after a thrilling move had ripped the Reds' defence to shreds. Amid all the recriminations, it was easy to forget that the Italians were a very fine team.

However, after their 17th cup match of the season had ended in their first defeat, Liverpool left San Siro feeling cheated, and serious allegations were made about the referee's neutrality. As the whole city went wild with jubilation, traffic came to a standstill and the short coach ride back to the hotel took more than an hour. Drivers leant out of their cars to wave flags, revellers danced in the streets and the Reds were taunted along every inch of their journey. Surveying those excessive scenes, Shankly told his players: 'All right, we've lost. But see what you've done. Inter Milan are the unofficial champions of the world and all those people are going mad because they've beaten Liverpool. That is the standard you have raised yourself up to.'

Liverpudlians were united in their belief that the odds had been unfairly stacked against them. Tommy Smith maintains: 'Such was the set-up, if we had scored six, they would have scored ten. At the bottom of our hearts we knew it was no use. I was so frustrated afterwards that I kicked the referee, but I got no reaction.' To Ron Yeats, the most agonising aspect was that Milan went on to win a poor final, 1-0 against Benfica on a mud-patch. 'That would have been our sort of pitch. We would have battered Benfica. It must have been our European Cup. Having said that, we suffered for our lack of know-how and froze a bit in that white-hot atmosphere. We went at them when we should have sat back and soaked up the pressure. It taught us a lot.'

Thus ended the Reds' first season in Europe. If others were to prove more fruitful, none would be more eventful or richer in experience. Now, at least, the Continent was in no doubt - Liverpool were on the march.

Round 1 - 1st leg
17 August 1964

REYKJAVIK 0

LIVERPOOL 5

Wallace 3, 60; Hunt 46, 88; Chisnall 57
H-T 0-1; Crowd 10,000

| LAWRENCE |
| BYRNE |
| MORAN |
| MILNE |
| YEATS |
| STEVENSON |
| CALLAGHAN |
| HUNT |
| CHISNALL |
| WALLACE |
| THOMPSON |

It took Liverpool just 180 seconds to score their first goal in European competition, Wallace netting with a mishit shot from a Hunt pass. From that moment, the Reds cantered to victory, although their superiority was not underlined until after the interval. Then Wallace, offering reciprocal service to his fellow marksman, set up a Hunt strike, and Chisnall hammered home after a Callaghan cross had been parried by the 'keeper. A Wallace header and a typically efficient piece of finishing by Hunt completed the rout. Reykjavik appeared overawed by their visitors, offering nothing by way of aggression or initiative, and Liverpool could not have been presented with an easier opening.

Alan A'Court, the former England winger who played his final senior game for Liverpool in the second leg against Reykjavik. What a shame that he didn't sign off with one last goal.

Gordon Wallace, scorer of Liverpool's opening European goal, who was once likened to Tom Finney by the eloquent Bill Shankly. Unfortunately, Gordon's career was to be marred by injuries.

Round 1 - 2nd leg
14 September 1964

LIVERPOOL 6

Byrne 13; St John 23, 74; Hunt 50;
Graham 65; Stevenson 67

REYKJAVIK 1

Felixson 35
H-T 2-1. Crowd 32,597

| LAWRENCE |
| BYRNE |
| MORAN |
| MILNE |
| YEATS |
| STEVENSON |
| CALLAGHAN |
| HUNT |
| ST JOHN |
| GRAHAM |
| A'COURT |

The return encounter with the sportsmanlike amateurs from Iceland proved to be one of Anfield's gentlest occasions. With the tie already safe, Liverpool cruised into a two-goal lead, courtesy of Byrne's booming 35-yarder and a fierce drive from St John, before the visitors earned the biggest cheer of the night with an adroitly dispatched goal by Felixson. The Reds' subsequent plunder, taken with panache but at practice-match pace, merely underlined the yawning chasm in class between the two sides. What a shame that popular, long-serving winger A'Court - making what proved to be his final senior appearance - could not have capped the Kop's night by scoring a goal.

Liverpool won 11-1 on aggregate.

Round 2 - 1st leg
25 November 1964

LIVERPOOL 3
St John 10; Hunt 43; Yeats 50

ANDERLECHT 0

H-T 2-0. Crowd 44,516

LAWRENCE
LAWLER
BYRNE
MILNE
YEATS
STEVENSON
CALLAGHAN
HUNT
ST JOHN
SMITH
THOMPSON

Here began the first true test of Liverpool's fitness to compete with the best in Europe, an examination from which Bill Shankly's men emerged with reputations hugely enhanced. The much-vaunted Belgian skills made negligible impact against the Reds' combination of vigour and finesse, and once St John had tucked away the opening goal, pouncing after the 'keeper failed to hold a Hunt shot, there was a gratifying inevitability about the rest of the proceedings. Hunt's precise drive just inside a post after being freed by St John, and Yeats' forceful header from a Stevenson free-kick - the skipper's first goal at Anfield - ensured that the final score reflected the balance of play.

Round 2 - 2nd leg
16 December 1964

ANDERLECHT 0

LIVERPOOL 1
Hunt 90
H-T 0-0. Crowd 60,000

LAWRENCE
LAWLER
BYRNE
MILNE
YEATS
STEVENSON
CALLAGHAN
HUNT
ST JOHN
SMITH
THOMPSON

Liverpool broke the hearts of their opponents and silenced a noisily partisan crowd with a superb display of tactical acumen. Content to protect their lead, the Reds packed their defence from the kick-off, frustrating the waspish home forwards and slowly but surely drawing their sting. On the rare occasions when Lawrence's goal was threatened, he responded magnificently, making two acrobatic saves from Van Himst and safely gathering several crosses under severe pressure. Anderlecht suffered their final indignity in injury time, when Hunt sprang the hitherto flawless Belgian offside trap to steer the ball home via a post.

Liverpool won 4-0 on aggregate.

Top: **The ubiquitous Ian St John pops up in front of the Reykjavik goal, but this time misses the target. The Kop took the Icelandic amateurs to their hearts, cheering their every move and good-naturedly booing the Reds.**

It's that man again: Ian St John *(above)* notches the first of Liverpool's three goals at home to Anderlecht. After playing down the Belgians' ability before the match, Bill Shankly later told his men: 'Congratulations, you've just beaten one of the finest teams in Europe.'

FC COLOGNE 0

LIVERPOOL 0
Crowd 40,000

LAWRENCE
LAWLER
BYRNE
MILNE
YEATS
STEVENSON
CALLAGHAN
HUNT
ST JOHN
SMITH
THOMPSON

For the second successive European match, the Reds turned in an immaculate defensive performance against a side containing a bevy of explosive attackers. Muller and company were shackled resolutely by the likes of Yeats and Smith, Lawrence made a succession of outstanding saves and every Liverpool player beavered ceaselessly. Even so, the Germans came close to scoring on several occasions, Thielen hitting a post after 22 minutes and a Lohr strike being disallowed for offside shortly after half-time. For the visitors, Thompson was the most threatening raider, and though an away goal rarely seemed likely, it was the Reds who wore smiles of satisfaction come the final whistle.

LIVERPOOL 0

FC COLOGNE 0
Crowd 48,432

LAWRENCE
LAWLER
BYRNE
MILNE
YEATS
STEVENSON
CALLAGHAN
HUNT
ST JOHN
SMITH
THOMPSON

In a direct reversal of the first-leg action, Liverpool besieged the Cologne goal but were frustrated by the inspired form of 'keeper Toni Schumacher. The courageous, acrobatic German denied his hosts repeatedly throughout a one-sided first half, then made an astonishing series of saves during a frenzied period of non-stop Reds attack - in which Thompson was exhilaratingly prominent - immediately after the break. In fact, the entire Cologne rearguard excelled, matching the Merseysiders for fitness and determination, and as the game grew old the Liverpool storm began to subside. Over the two encounters, honours were even and a draw was the fairest result.

Aggregate score 0-0.

The Germans' saviour: goalkeeper Toni Schumacher, whose breathtaking display at Anfield kept Cologne in the European Cup, plucks the ball from the toe of Ian St John.

Left: Everybody off: referee Frede Hansen leads the way to the dressing rooms after Liverpool's Anfield encounter with Cologne had fallen victim to snow.

Top right: Relief for the Reds: after Cologne had equalised, Belgian referee R Schaut rules out a strike by Lohr, paving the way for the dramatic toss-up that decided the tie.

Right: Tommy Lawrence is helpless to prevent Cologne's first goal, a deft header from Thielen, in the Rotterdam replay. Until that moment Liverpool had seemed to be coasting into the semi-final.

Round 3 - replay in Rotterdam
24 March 1965

FC COLOGNE 2
Thielen 39; Lohr 48

LIVERPOOL 2
St John 22; Hunt 37
H-T 1-2. Crowd 45,000

LAWRENCE
LAWLER
BYRNE
MILNE
YEATS
STEVENSON
CALLAGHAN
HUNT
ST JOHN
SMITH
THOMPSON

In the end this pulsating tie was decided by the whim of fate, but not before a third stirring encounter between two well-matched teams. Liverpool, with wingers Callaghan and Thompson probing adventurously, started the more positively, and deserved the lead given them by St John when he stabbed home a short cross from Hunt. Soon afterwards, a 12-yard header from the England striker cannoned against the bar and over the line, seemingly settling the outcome. However, the resilient Germans were swift to retaliate, Thielen converting a curling free-kick with a glancing header, then Lohr equalising with a low-level scorcher from 25 yards. Indeed, Cologne found the net a third time, but the effort was ruled out for an infringement, and the battle continued to rage. After 300 minutes of football had proved inconclusive, a toss-up settled the issue, provoking English joy and German despair.

Liverpool won on toss after extra time.

Spinning like a scarlet top, Roger Hunt *(below)* volleys the Reds
into a sensational early lead against Inter Milan at Anfield.
It was, according to Helenio Herrera, a typically Continental goal.

Semi-final - 1st leg
4 May 1965

LIVERPOOL 3

Hunt 4; Callaghan 34; St John 75

INTER MILAN 1

Mazzola 10
H-T 2-1. Crowd 54,082

| LAWRENCE |
| LAWLER |
| MORAN |
| STRONG |
| YEATS |
| STEVENSON |
| CALLAGHAN |
| HUNT |
| ST JOHN |
| SMITH |
| THOMPSON |

Liverpool gave one of the finest performances in their history to outplay the European Cup-holders. After surviving an early scare when Brazilian winger Jair slipped through their defence, Liverpool drew first blood through Hunt, who swivelled on the penalty spot to volley a bouncing cross from Callaghan into the corner of Inter's net. The Italians responded with some slick movements, and regained parity when Mazzola scored following a mistake by Yeats. Thereafter, the Reds dominated and the goal that put them back in front - Callaghan sidefooting home after working a slick free-kick routine with Stevenson and Hunt - was a supreme example of their fluency. Shortly afterwards, Lawler danced past two opponents and slammed the ball beyond 'keeper Sarti, only to be denied a goal by a debatable offside decision against a team-mate. In the second half Liverpool continued to turn the screw, but were not rewarded until St John drove home a rebound from a Hunt shot a quarter of an hour from time. Now Inter wilted and the shots rained in on Sarti; sadly for the Reds, as it was subsequently to prove, he kept them out, but on the night it hardly seemed to matter. Nothing could detract from the glory of Anfield's most glittering occasion.

Semi-final - 2nd leg
12 May 1965

INTER MILAN 3

Corso 8; Peiro 9; Facchetti 62

LIVERPOOL 0

H-T 2-0. Crowd 90,000

| LAWRENCE |
| LAWLER |
| MORAN |
| STRONG |
| YEATS |
| STEVENSON |
| CALLAGHAN |
| HUNT |
| ST JOHN |
| SMITH |
| THOMPSON |

It was the ultimate anti-climax. After the euphoria of the first leg came the bitter - some would say outrageous - experience of a defeat which Liverpool fans had barely conceived possible after watching their heroes thrash the Italians a week earlier. In the event, the Reds' two-goal lead was wiped out during one disastrous minute during the opening phase of this controversial match. First Corso netted with a viciously curving 20-yard free-kick, then Peiro kicked the ball away from Lawrence as the goalkeeper was bouncing it and clipped it into the empty net. In the first instance, Liverpool believed the free-kick to be unfairly awarded and, in any case, indirect; in the second, they contended that Lawrence had been fouled. As the game wore on, the Englishmen appeared inhibited by refereeing decisions which invariably went against them, and produced only the sketchiest of form. In contrast, Inter blossomed and, none could impugn the legitimacy of Facchetti's brilliant match-winner, a savage shot that climaxed a flowing four-man move. For Liverpool, it signalled a sour end to a memorable campaign.

Inter Milan won 4-3 on aggregate.

**Down and out at San Siro:
Tommy Lawrence, beaten
earlier by two controversial
strikes, remains grounded as
the ball rebounds from the net
following Inter Milan's winner,
a scorcher from Facchetti.**

Chapter Two

HEARTACHE AT HAMPDEN

WITH the unhappy events of Milan still emblazoned on their consciousness, Liverpool embarked on their second Continental campaign just a few months older, but incalculably wiser about the pitfalls that litter the path of innocents abroad. Having defeated Leeds United to win the FA Cup for the first time in their history, they took their place proudly and ambitiously in the European Cup Winners' Cup, a trophy they were to come agonisingly close to winning.

Indeed, for battling steadfastly against the might of Juventus, overcoming both Belgian brutality and Hungarian style, then emerging victorious from the unofficial championship of Britain after surviving a barrage of (empty) bottles hurled by a legion of inebriated Scots, they might have expected better fortune than came their way in the final. But on a filthy night at Hampden Park, those same playful fates that had conspired so undiplomatically to send them straight back to Italy so soon after the San Siro affair deserted them in their hour of need.

Yet that is to jump ahead too quickly; the tale of such a brave bid for glory deserves to unfold in sequence, beginning with Juventus. Although an expedition to the likes of Malta or Cyprus must surely - with all due respect to those countries' worthy but hardly daunting entrants - have offered gentler reacclimatisation to the demands of overseas competition, there is little doubt that Bill Shankly relished the confrontation with the Turin giants. Here was the chance his combative soul must have craved to exact swift retribution, if not on the very club who he maintained had benefited from a woefully one-eyed refereeing display, then at least on their compatriots. And now, armed with precious knowledge of the Italian game that he had gained the hard way, he was ready.

The away leg came first, and Liverpool disciplined themselves to ensure that they would not, could not, lose heavily. They had already proved, against Anderlecht and Cologne during the preceding term, that they could defend in depth and now did so again, limiting the Juventus forwards to few scoring chances. Indeed, but for a late, unstoppable long-shot - the type of effort that no team can legislate against - they would have returned to Anfield with a clean sheet. The home fans - a mere 23,000 were scattered around the huge Stadio Communale, emphasising the decidedly second-class status of the Cup Winners' Cup in many countries - had been offered little in the way of entertainment, but there was ample reason for the Reds to be satisfied as they trooped off the pitch and into their cavernous, echoing dressing room. Later there was an official banquet at which the two teams sat near each other but were prevented by the language barrier from making any but the most basic communication. Even so, the Liverpudlians could not help noticing that the Italians, usually subjected to a regimental routine in everything they did, were allowed off the leash on this occasion, a rare freedom of which they took hearty advantage.

Although, looking back, Ron Yeats declares that a single goal was never enough for visitors to take to Anfield, the second-leg task facing Shankly's men was considerable. After all, Juventus hadn't conceded in their six previous games; in fact, if Liverpool were to progress, they would have to be the first side that season to find the Italians' net - and do it twice without reply. Juventus - mindful of the high emotions still residing from the Inter Milan episode - appealed to UEFA to safeguard their players, and before the game it was announced to the crowd that 'the eyes of the footballing world are upon you.' As if affronted by a slur on their character, the Kopites roared back with 'We're the best behaved supporters in the land.' In truth, the Italians did little to endear themselves to their hosts, indulging frequently in shirt-pulling, off-the-ball elbowing and a whole unsavoury selection of dirty tricks, but the only violence was verbal - a rousing chorus of 'Mussolini's dead' after first-half goals by Chris Lawler and Geoff Strong had settled the tie. Geoff's strike was particularly memorable, many Anfield regulars claiming they had never witnessed a more fearsome shot in a lifetime of watching Liverpool.

So to Standard Liege, and two of the most physical encounters the Reds were ever to face in Europe. On Merseyside, ironically, the Belgians revealed that when they concentrated on football they were a clever, accomplished side. But too much energy was spent on fouls, one of the chief offenders being centre-forward Claessen, who was then in the middle of a six-month domestic ban. However, in Ron Yeats he met an immovable object and made the mistake, after one crunching challenge, of spitting in the face of the colossal

First of many: Chris Lawler heads the opener against Juventus at Anfield. The quietly-spoken Merseysider was to forge an enviable reputation as a free-scoring full-back in European competition.

Scot. In the next tackle, the former Aberdeen slaughterman ensured that Mr Claessen would not be repeating this particularly repulsive act, the Belgian limping off for lengthy treatment. So incensed were Liege after their 3-1 defeat that one of their top officials referred to Ron as 'a gangster'.

Inevitably the second leg turned out to be, in the words of Ian Callaghan, a battle from start to finish. 'The crowd was wildly partisan and very close to the pitch, seeming right on top of us. It was intimidating and we were all glad when it was over. Afterwards Shanks, who had warned us what to expect, complimented us on how well we had behaved in the face of constant provocation. I can only say that the referee did a marvellous job in extremely trying circumstances.' Sadly, when the action had ceased on the pitch, it continued in the tunnel, a scuffle breaking out between an angry Claessen and Yeats, whom he saw as his chief persecutor. Tommy Smith remembers thinking that the Liege number nine would have made a formidable centre-half: 'Most centre-forwards take punishment, but don't hand it out. He was an exception - and he could play a bit, too.'

In footballing terms, the 2-1 victory had been impressive, with Ian St John at his superb best, his combination of subtlety, spirit and work rate never seen to better advantage. It was fitting that he should cap such a display with a spectacular, full-length header that put the result beyond doubt.

Lawler strikes again: Chris nets the first of his pair at home to Standard Liege.
The Belgian side shouldered most of the blame for one of the most unpleasantly physical encounters Anfield has seen.

Having thus survived such a bruising ordeal, Liverpool were not sorry to be drawn against Honved, who represented another high-class hurdle but of an entirely different nature. The Hungarian Army side were renowned for producing pure, skilful football in the tradition of the legendary 'Magnificent Magyars' whose Wembley demolition of England 12 years earlier had changed the perceptions of all thoughtful Britons about their national game. Yet although coached by Josef Bozsik, one of the most eminent of the 1953 Hungarians, this Honved team did scant justice to such an august reputation. In Budapest they played prettily enough but Liverpool - with 'keeper Lawrence on his mettle - held firm, while at Anfield the Reds won far more easily than the 2-0 scoreline suggests. Ron Yeats recalls reading about these thoroughbred Hungarian footballers and wondering what to expect; in the event, he was to discover that they were hardly awesome opponents, and didn't travel well.

As their heroes coasted towards the end of the second leg, the Kop proclaimed: 'We'll be running round Europe with the Cup', a trifle prematurely, as it turned out. They were to be more accurate in their chant of 'Callaghan for England', although the locally-born winger never won the regular international recognition that many felt to be his due. While attempting to gain Alf Ramsey's ear, the Scousers might also have voiced the claims of Chris Lawler, the right-back who had just scored in his third successive European tie. That night, also, he hit the post twice and might have finished with five - and he wasn't a bad defender, either!

A rousing contrast to the stately Hungarians awaited in the next round. There Liverpool met head to head with Jock Stein's Celtic, developing impressively into the indomitable combination that, one year hence on a sunny night in Lisbon, would become the first British winners of the European Cup. The pre-match build-up made much of the contest between the Scots and Liverpool's Anglo-Caledonians, the likes of Lawrence, Yeats, Stevenson and St John. There has always been a feeling north of the border that men who head south for fame and fortune are mercenaries, pure and simple, and therefore to be despised. Usually such sour and blinkered sniping has the opposite effect to that intended, merely motivating the targets to greater efforts, and there is no evidence to suggest it was successful on this occasion.

But whatever the reason, Liverpool played like drains in the first leg at Parkhead, turning in what was arguably their weakest performance in European competition to date. Admittedly it was a bleak, inhospitable night, but Shankly's Reds were not whingers and were not about to blame the hard pitch and high wind for their discomfiture. More accurate was that Stein's 'Bhoys' hustled the visitors out of their stride, their vigorous, direct and skilful play deserving to earn them more than the single-goal advantage they took with them to Anfield. Severely out of sorts at the back, and with Phil Chisnall proving a pallid deputy for the injured Roger Hunt up front, Liverpool were nothing less than anaemic, and the Scottish press panned them gleefully. However, as the media were to learn over coming decades, writing off these Merseysiders was a risky business . . .

Buoyed by their first-leg victory, Celtic supporters invaded Liverpool en masse for the second leg. In the afternoon they roamed the city centre in vast, intimidating hordes, bringing the traffic to a halt in Church Street while several of their number bowed low in obeisance before a green and white bus. Already well lubricated after a day of abandoned imbibing, they poured into Anfield, their pockets bulging with supplies of the hard stuff to see them through the match.

When the action got under way, it was spirited, full-blooded fare, exactly what might be expected of an all-British cup tie. Though there were close calls at either end, the Reds enjoyed rather the better of the exchanges for the first hour without managing to snatch an equaliser, and excitement mounted unbearably. In fact, at one time it seemed that the stadium might be on the verge of spontaneous combustion. Smoke appeared to be rising steadily from the Kop, but growing fears of an imminent catastrophe were soon stilled; the 'smoke' was actually steam, given off by the mass of damp, tightly-packed bodies whose owners generated further heat by their constant swaying and chanting.

Eventually, the deadlock was broken by a Tommy Smith free-kick, before Geoff Strong

A hobbling hero: the injured Geoff Strong *(right)* **celebrates after nodding the semi-final winner against Celtic at Anfield. Gordon Milne shares the elation while Bertie Auld** *(left),* **Billy McNeill (head in hands) and Bobby Murdoch try to work out how a man with one good leg could have outjumped their defence.**

scored one of the most heroic and best-remembered goals that even Anfield has known. At the time, the former Arsenal striker, who had made himself well-nigh indispensable as a utility man with the Reds, was hobbling in the centre-forward position, apparently of little more than nuisance value after damaging his knee in the first half.   Geoff takes up the story: 'I was injured after heading the ball in midfield; I turned round and my knee just gave way. It kept on collapsing but I couldn't think of coming off in such an important game because the competition did not allow substitutes in those days. It turned out to be a good decision. I can remember Ian Callaghan crossing the ball, and I managed to jump off my good leg to head it. I suppose they had not marked me properly because I was limping. Anyway, the ball went in the corner of the net, the crowd went wild, and suddenly it all seemed worthwhile.'

That was the end of the scoring, but not of the drama. Not long before the final whistle, Celtic's Bobby Lennox had a 'goal' disallowed, a disappointment that was just too keen for the well-oiled multitude at the Anfield Road end to absorb. First a few bottles began arcing through the air on to the pitch, and Tommy Lawrence, still concentrating fiercely on the game, stood his ground manfully. Soon, though, the shower of glass became a deluge and the 'keeper was forced to take refuge outside the penalty box and the referee stopped the game while the pitch was cleared. It was a sorry scene, with spectators at the front being hit by missiles hurled by their friends at the back; nearly 50 people were treated for cuts and bruises, and many more fainted in the crush. Certainly, for those who campaigned for alcohol to be banned from football grounds, this presented an unarguable case. Wisely, the referee ended the action a little early, leaving Liverpool in the final. When the groundstaff cleared the terraces and pitch surrounds the next morning, there were some 4,000 bottles and cans lined up on the boundary walls. Ron Yeats, at least, saw the funny side: 'The man I envied was Tommy Lawrence. He must have made £200 from the empties!'

Ironically, after such a passionate encounter, it was to Scotland that the Reds travelled for the denouement of a successful season in which they had already won the League Championship. It rained steadily throughout the afternoon of the match, but that did little to douse the enthusiasm of the 20,000 supporters who headed north, never doubting that they were about to see Borussia Dortmund put to the sword. Sadly, a truly dismal evening was in prospect.

As kick-off time approached, Hampden Park itself, the hallowed headquarters of Scottish football, presented a gloomy aspect. A squally, wet wind swirled around the vast stadium, the desolate effect heightened by substantial slabs of vacant terracing. In such dreadful weather, with the game being televised live, most neutral Scots - if there were any left after the events of Anfield - elected to remain by their firesides. What they missed was a leaden, uninspiring encounter enlivened by one high-quality goal and a bizarre ending.

Liverpool had the balance of possession, with the Germans content to attack on the break, an approach that had paid dividends in their semi-final against the holders, West Ham United. In that tie, Lothar Emmerich's two late first-leg strikes had been crucial, and he it was who played an important part in the first and best goal of the final, setting up Sigi Held for a blistering strike. That might have been that, but even a below-par Reds side does not give up easily and, sure enough, they regained parity, despite a linesman's signal that the ball had been out of play before Peter Thompson crossed it for Roger Hunt to score. By then, though, there were Liverpool fans celebrating on the pitch, and it would have taken a courageous referee to disallow the goal. No matter, the force was now with Shankly's men, and they might have won with a minute left when Hunt missed a great chance. But what the groaning Kopites did not realise was that Roger had spent much of the past two days soaking a sore ankle in the sea at Largs, and his injury had deprived him of crucial mobility and confidence.

Thus the final dragged into extra time, during which the Merseysiders were to fall victim to either a stroke of genius or a cruel freak, depending on your viewpoint. When Tommy Lawrence's clearance cannoned towards towards Reinhardt Libuda on Borussia's right wing, there seemed little immediate danger; Tommy was scrambling to regain his ground and Ron Yeats was patrolling the six-yard box and well placed to deal with any threat on goal. However, Libuda didn't stop to analyse the options, he just hit the approaching ball from fully 35 yards out. It soared high into the night sky and could have gone anywhere; but, as if guided by radar, it curled above Lawrence and Yeats, then hit the far post before rebounding into the net off the desperate, straining centre-half. Was it a shot? Was it a cross? Did Libuda himself have the faintest idea? As the noise of German klaxons and trumpets rent the air, it really didn't matter. Nothing could alter the fact that Borussia were in front, and there they stayed to claim the trophy.

Ron now recalls the occasion as one of his unhappiest memories in a Liverpool shirt, although no one could blame him for such an extraordinary incident. He says: 'That goal was bad enough, but it wasn't just that. We didn't do ourselves justice on the night. We pounded them at times, but they weren't a bad side and came back at us. We all wanted to do especially well because it was in Britain, and we Scottish lads felt it a bit more keenly for being at Hampden.'

Poignantly, that was the closest Ron and most of his colleagues in Bill Shankly's first great Liverpool side were to come to winning an international prize at club level. Seven years on, when space for European silverware finally had to be found in the Anfield trophy cabinet, only Ian Callaghan, Tommy Smith and Chris Lawler remained from the class of '66.

A study in desperation: Ron Yeats stretches in vain to reach a cross-cum-shot from Borussia's Libuda. The German's speculative effort, from some 35 yards, floated over Ron's head and struck the inside of the far post before rebounding on to the giant centre-half's thigh and into the net. That extraordinary extra-time goal, which clinched the Cup for the Germans, remains one of the Liverpool skipper's most painful memories.

Preliminary round - 1st leg
29 September 1965

JUVENTUS 1
Leoncini 81

LIVERPOOL 0

H-T 0-0. Crowd 23,000

| LAWRENCE |
| STRONG |
| BYRNE |
| ARROWSMITH |
| YEATS |
| STEVENSON |
| CALLAGHAN |
| HUNT |
| ST JOHN |
| SMITH |
| THOMPSON |

In view of their recent trauma in Milan, the Reds could be relatively satisfied with a single-goal reverse on their return to Italy. This time they were blessed by impeccable refereeing, Hungarian Istvan Zsolt turning down three impassioned penalty appeals from Juventus. Indeed, when the bravery of Lawrence denied Menichelli after 80 minutes it seemed that Liverpool would return to Anfield with a clean sheet, but it was not to be. A minute later Leoncini picked up a loose ball in midfield and strolled forward before bulging the top corner of the visitors' net with a fierce drive. There was little likelihood of a response in the short time that was left and the tie remained finely balanced.

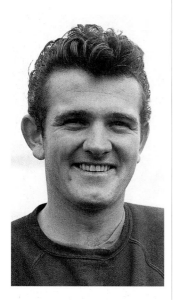

Preliminary round - 2nd leg
13 October 1965

LIVERPOOL 2
Lawler 19; Strong 24

JUVENTUS 0

H-T 2-0. Crowd 51,055

| LAWRENCE |
| LAWLER |
| BYRNE |
| STRONG |
| YEATS |
| STEVENSON |
| CALLAGHAN |
| HUNT |
| ST JOHN |
| SMITH |
| THOMPSON |

Backed by the Kop at its awe-inspiring best, Liverpool overcame the challenge of one of Europe's most accomplished sides. Already one goal to the good, Juventus might have doubled their lead early on but for Lawrence's perfectly judged dive at the feet of the marauding Menichelli. Undeterred, the Reds poured forward, and their ploy of countering the Italians' blanket defence by attacking from the back paid a rapid dividend as a Stevenson free-kick was nodded back across goal by Strong to Lawler, who headed home from close range. With the team from Turin still reeling from the setback, Liverpool took the lead with a strike of savage ferocity. Hunt's header was cleared to the edge of the box where Strong met it with such velocity that, although it was fired directly at 'keeper Anzolin, he managed only to touch it on to the bar and into the net. Thus Juventus were forced to emerge from their shell and, orchestrated by Del Sol, played some delightful football, but Shankly's men ran out worthy winners of a stirring tie.

Liverpool won 2-1 on aggregate.

Tommy Lawrence, one of the most underrated goalkeepers in British football, who pulled off crucial saves in both legs against Juventus. A testimony to the excellence of 'The Flying Pig' is that he kept a young man named Ray Clemence waiting in the reserves for two and a half years.

Round 1 - 1st leg
1 December 1965

LIVERPOOL 3
Lawler 2, 49; Thompson 72

STANDARD LIEGE 1
Storme 58
H-T 1-0. Crowd 46,112

| LAWRENCE |
| LAWLER |
| BYRNE |
| MILNE |
| YEATS |
| STEVENSON |
| CALLAGHAN |
| HUNT |
| ST JOHN |
| SMITH |
| THOMPSON |

Liverpool's clash with the Belgian Cup-winners remains as the sourest, most ill-tempered Anfield encounter in the club's European history. The fact that Liege were penalised for three times as many fouls as their hosts tells its own story, and it's ironic that when the visitors concentrated on pure football they pierced the Reds' defence with surprising alacrity; happily for the Kop, incensed by such physical excess, the Belgians let themselves down with profligate finishing. Liverpool, having taken an early lead through Lawler's header from a Thompson corner, had plenty of possession without looking penetrative until shortly after the interval, when Lawler struck again, netting from a St John knock-on. Liege promptly retaliated when Storme capitalised on a faulty back-pass from Yeats, and it was left to Thompson, the target for much of the rough stuff, to restore the two-goal lead with a low shot from the edge of the box.

Round 1 - 2nd leg
15 December 1965

STANDARD LIEGE 1
Claessen 42

LIVERPOOL 2
Hunt 51; St John 57
H-T 1-0. Crowd 30,000

| LAWRENCE |
| LAWLER |
| BYRNE |
| STRONG |
| YEATS |
| STEVENSON |
| CALLAGHAN |
| HUNT |
| ST JOHN |
| SMITH |
| THOMPSON |

The Reds kept their heads in the face of severe provocation to record a double triumph over opponents who, through their belligerence, failed to do justice to their undoubted talents. The Belgians, on huge cash promises if they reached the quarter-final, attacked from the off, but a composed Liverpool held firm and would have snatched a goal themselves had not Hunt been uncharacteristically inaccurate when presented with a splendid chance after 30 minutes. Soon afterwards, Claessen threw the tie wide open by netting through a forest of legs, only for the Merseysiders to regain control with two magnificent goals. First St John skipped past two tackles on the left flank before crossing for Hunt to slide the ball home, then Callaghan produced a dazzling run and cross which 'The Saint' met with a fearless diving header. Justice was well and truly done.

Liverpool won 5-2 on aggregate.

One that got away: Roger Hunt, normally Liverpool's most reliable finisher, miskicks in front of goal against Honved at Anfield. In truth the Hungarians, though they played neatly, never lived up to their reputation as soccer thoroughbreds and the Reds cruised into the semi-final.

Round 2 - 1st leg
1 March 1966

HONVED 0
Crowd 25,000

LIVERPOOL 0

Round 2 - 2nd leg
8 March 1966

LIVERPOOL 2
Lawler 28; St John 47
H-T 1-0. Crowd 54,631

HONVED 0

LAWRENCE	
LAWLER	
BYRNE	
MILNE	
YEATS	
STEVENSON	
CALLAGHAN	
HUNT	
ST JOHN	
SMITH	
THOMPSON	

After appearing to play well within themselves, Liverpool came away from the People's Stadium in Budapest extremely satisfied with their night's work. The famous

Hungarian Army side passed the ball smoothly but lacked penetration and troubled the Reds' rearguard only rarely. Whenever Tichy and company did fashion a shooting opportunity, the reliable Lawrence dealt capably with the danger. Once he launched himself prodigiously to save a thunderous 30-yarder, then threw himself at the feet of another marauder, though luck was on his side when he deflected a goal-bound effort from Komora on to his crossbar. Liverpool's best opportunity fell to Thompson, who pulled the ball wide after a mazy run.

LAWRENCE	
LAWLER	
BYRNE	
MILNE	
YEATS	
STEVENSON	
CALLAGHAN	
HUNT	
ST JOHN	
SMITH	
THOMPSON	

Rarely has a final score been more inadequate in reflecting the emphatic nature of a Liverpool triumph. After a jittery, frenetic start, during which too many passes went astray, the Reds

settled to humble their Hungarian opponents. Star of the show was full-back Lawler, who saw two efforts hit the woodwork, narrowly missed with two more, and soothed the nerves of a restless Kop by netting with his head after Thompson had struck the post. That was the turning point, after which Liverpool served up a feast of flowing football. However, they managed only one more goal, when St John nodded a deep cross from Thompson inside the far post. Countless chances were created, but Hunt was particularly wasteful and Honved were allowed to escape with their dignity intact.
Liverpool won 2-0 on aggregate

Semi-final - 1st leg
14 April 1966

CELTIC 1
Lennox 52

LIVERPOOL 0

H-T 0-0. Crowd 80,000

LAWRENCE
LAWLER
BYRNE
MILNE
YEATS
STEVENSON
CALLAGHAN
CHISNALL
ST JOHN
SMITH
THOMPSON

Liverpool could count themselves lucky to emerge from this scrappy clash with a deficit of merely one goal. On a windy Parkhead night, they were uncharacteristically hesitant in defence while their attempts to go forward lacked the usual control and creativity. Celtic, as tigerish as expected but showing little composure, squandered numerous scoring opportunities, Chalmers being the prime culprit. Invariably, the chances came when Jock Stein's nippy raiders raced beyond a rather static Reds back four, and it was one such foray that led to the goal. Murdoch found himself free on the flank, Yeats raced out of position to intercept, and from the resultant cross Lennox tucked the ball past Lawrence. But was that slim advantage enough to take to Anfield?

Above right: **Phil Chisnall, deputising for the injured Roger Hunt at Parkhead, battles for possession with John Clark (6) and Bobby Murdoch. The former Manchester United forward made no more impact in this clash with Celtic than he did during the rest of a disappointing Liverpool career.**

LIVERPOOL 2

Smith 61; Strong 67

CELTIC 0

H-T 0-0. Crowd 54,208

LAWRENCE
LAWLER
BYRNE
MILNE
YEATS
STEVENSON
CALLAGHAN
STRONG
ST JOHN
SMITH
THOMPSON

What a transformation! The lacklustre display of five days earlier was forgotten forthwith as Shankly's Reds tore into compelling action. Before long Celtic 'keeper Simpson had been forced to make two blinding saves, Smith struck the bar from 25 yards and Lawler shot over a gaping goal; admittedly the Scots were not without threat, Lennox clipping the bar and missing a sitter, but Liverpool appeared ascendant. Even after a knee injury reduced Strong to the status of crippled passenger after 35 minutes, the Merseysiders marched forward, though it was after the hour before they reaped a tangible reward. Then two goals in the space of six minutes decided the tie. First Smith, upended 25 yards from Celtic's posts, got up to deceive Simpson with a low free-kick that seemed to take a deflection; then Strong secured an eternal niche in the annals of Anfield by springing from his good leg to nod a Callaghan cross past the diving 'keeper. The Celts fought back, but a late Lennox strike was ruled out for offside, and Liverpool were in the final.

Liverpool won 2-1 on aggregate.

Below left: **Turning the tables: Ian St John shoots for goal as a vibrant Liverpool seize the initiative against Celtic at Anfield, making nonsense of their pallid performance at Parkhead. This effort did not produce a goal, but strikes by Tommy Smith and Geoff Strong saw the Reds reach the final.**

Above: **The end of a long and emotional day: Celtic supporters at the Anfield Road end disperse after watching their side lose to two second-half goals.**

The Saint surrenders? Never, but on this occasion Ian St John, his arms raised in a gesture of disappointment, is bested by Borussia Dortmund goalkeeper Hans Tilkowski. Neither team struck top form in a disappointing final, which proved a numbing anti-climax for the newly-crowned English champions.

Sigi's salute: Held (9) turns away joyfully after scoring the first goal at Hampden Park with a scorching volley from the edge of the penalty area. His spectacular strike, which gave Tommy Lawrence no chance, climaxed a precise interchange of passes with fellow German international Lothar Emmerich.

Final at Hampden Park, Glasgow
May 5, 1966

BORUSSIA DORTMUND 2

Held 51; Libuda 107

LIVERPOOL 1
Hunt 68
H-T 0-0. Extra time played.
Crowd 41,657

LAWRENCE
LAWLER
BYRNE
MILNE
YEATS
STEVENSON
CALLAGHAN
HUNT
ST JOHN
SMITH
THOMPSON

For Bill Shankly's newly-crowned League champions, this was an occasion to expunge from the memory. Hard though they battled, little went right in a match that never lived up to its billing. Yet after an eminently forgettable first half, in which two potentially thrilling sides negated each other, Liverpool showed signs of getting on top. Ironically, it was not long before Borussia went ahead following the night's sweetest move. Held fed Emmerich on the left, then dashed to receive the chipped return some 18 yards from goal, whence he gave Lawrence no chance with a destructive volley. The Reds hit back with a controversial equaliser, Thompson reaching the byline - a linesman appeared to signal that the ball was out but the referee ignored him - before crossing for Hunt to find the roof of the net. Now it was all Liverpool and they might have won on 89 minutes when Hunt, struggling with injury, shot weakly when clean through. Extra time brought ultimate frustration when Lawrence blocked a shot on the edge of his box and the ball rebounded to Libuda, 35 yards out. The winger responded with a first-time lob that sailed over the 'keeper, hit the inside of a post and bounced into the net off the stretching Yeats. The fates had spoken and the Cup was lost.

Roger Hunt advances on Hans Tilkowski *(above)* **as Liverpool exert pressure on Borussia at Hampden Park. Come the end of the evening, the 'keeper was the one with a winner's medal, but the situation was soon to be reversed on an even more momentous occasion. That summer at Wembley, Roger helped England lift the World Cup against Tilkowski's West Germany.**

Chapter Three

EXECUTION IN THE FOG

HOW perverse that arguably the most inspirational achievement of Bill Shankly's monumental career should be linked with the heaviest defeat Liverpool were to suffer in more than two decades of European competition. Yet the way he breathed life and hope into his team after their 5-1 first-leg annihilation by Ajax of Amsterdam in the Champions' Cup amounted to an unparalleled act of footballing evangelism. His feat in attracting more than 53,000 fans to Anfield for the second leg on a dank December night, and convincing 11 seasoned professionals that they could do what was apparently impossible, demonstrated the passion, the strength of character, and yes, the genius of this remarkable man in a manner more intense than any of his triumphs.

Before that, though, he had to find a way past Petrolul Ploesti, and that was not as straightforward as might have been imagined. Based deep in the heartlands of Romania's oilfields, Petrolul were very much an unknown quantity, a fact which they sought to turn to their own advantage. Every attempt by the Reds to secure their opponents' domestic fixture list was frustrated, so they could not be watched beforehand. The aura of mystery increased when the visitors ran out at Anfield and the crowd was informed that their names were unpronounceable. Some players were wearing numbers different to those printed in the programme, but the announcer could not say who was who. 'Anyhow, there are only 11 of them,' he added drily.

Soon it became apparent that, though obscure, they were a well-drilled, capable outfit, and Liverpool laboured arduously before late strikes by the two Ians, St John and Callaghan, secured a lead. The Kop was happy enough with that, and making the most of the Romanians' oilfield origins, proclaimed: 'The Esso sign means happy footballing' to the tune of a then-current TV advertising jingle.

But if the Reds thought they had done the hard part, they had another think coming; indeed, their trip to Romania was aggravating from start to finish. After flying in to Bucharest, they were subjected to a tedious 40-mile coach journey along bumpy roads in more than 80 degrees of heat. Tommy Smith recalls: 'It was crude over there, and I don't just mean the oil. The landscape as seen from the coach seemed to consist of semi-detached oilwells. There would be six dowdy-looking houses and then another well. It was depressing.' The hotel was poor, too, and Shanks was appalled by the 'jobsworth' attitude adopted by the staff, every request resulting in delay. Eventually they goaded him too far; after ordering soft drinks for the team, only to be told by a waiter that they were not available, he marched into the kitchen and saw crates of Coke. He rounded on the wretched fellow and said: 'Give those to my lads or I'll report you to the Kremlin.' But if the hotel was hardly five-star, it was a palace compared with the dressing room at the Ploesti stadium. Tommy again: 'There were about eight chairs for all of us to share, and the toilets stank. Shanks threatened to call the game off if they weren't cleaned up, and what seemed like an army of women were called in. It was a terrible place.'

Events on the pitch served only to deepen the gloom. In oppressive heat, the Romanians adopted tough tactics and some of the Liverpool players responded in kind, causing the referee to call the captains together to demand better behaviour. Football-wise, Petrolul displayed alarming enterprise, their big attacker Mircea Dridea proving a free-kick artist of consummate skill. Having been warned of his prowess, Ron Yeats and Tommy Lawrence were stationed at either end of the goal-line for one set piece, but the Romanian curled the ball viciously around the defensive wall, over the centre-half's head and into the net. To be honest, Petrolul probably deserved their 3-1 victory which, with no away-goals rule at the time, earned them a replay in Brussels. First, though, Liverpool were subjected to an incident that was hilarious in retrospect but not so funny at the time. Ten minutes after the final whistle, with many of the players naked and ready for the bath, the power was switched off, apparently as an economy measure, and they were left fumbling around in the blackness. Only when Liverpool officials protested firmly, shall we say, was light restored.

In view of the assorted problems they had caused to date, Petrolul capitulated with unexpected meekness in Belgium, leaving the Reds to make their ill-fated trip to the Dutch capital. At that time Ajax, though seen as a promising team, were not yet a major force in

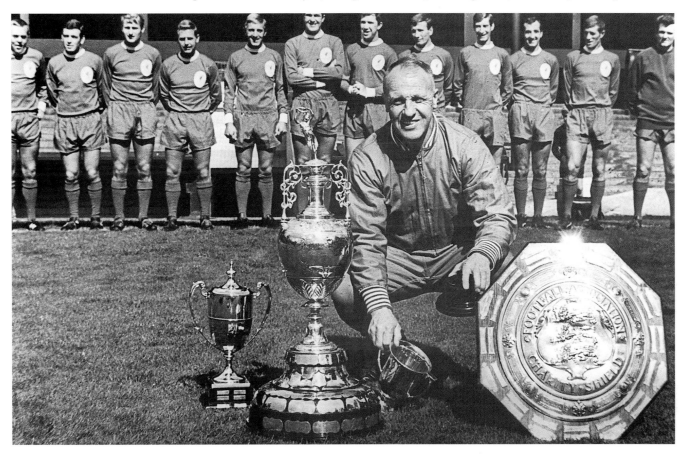

Bill Shankly and his men with the spoils of domestic triumph at the outset of 1966/67. Pride of place goes to the League Championship trophy (second left), but Shanks's burning ambition was to add the European Cup to his collection. Sadly, he never did.

Europe, and Liverpool were caught fairly and squarely unawares. In fact, there had been a measure of relief that the likes of Real Madrid and Inter Milan had been avoided, a state of mind that might have introduced a rare touch of complacency at Anfield.

On the night of the match, Amsterdam was under a blanket of fog and many travelling fans failed to reach the Olympic stadium, being used because the Ajax ground had no floodlights. As kick-off time approached, the shroud grew more impenetrable, the gloom so deep that the linesmen needed torches to inspect the nets, though at that stage neither club favoured a 24-hour postponement. Soon, however, Shanks was cursing the decision to play as his team was overwhelmed, falling four goals behind by the interval. It was almost farcical at times, with players barely able to see from wing to wing, let alone end to end, but as the home side's lead increased, the more difficult it would have been for the referee to abandon the action. Come the second half, the murk was so dense that the Liverpool boss walked on to talk to Willie

Stevenson and the officials didn't see him. Ron Yeats thought the decision to play on was unfathomable: 'It was so bad we had to keeping asking Tommy Lawrence the score! Seriously though, it would have been hard enough against such a fine team in any conditions, but not being able to see them made life impossible. It WAS possible, though, to see that Johann Cruyff was special. I just couldn't get near him. His first touch and running off the ball were magnificent, it was like chasing a shadow. He was a player who had everything.'

The shattered Reds were forced to spend the night in fogbound Amsterdam, returning home the next day to read in a national newspaper that a gleeful Evertonian had phoned the newsdesk to declare: 'So it's true; Ajax does kill 99 per cent of all known germs!' Shanks, however, was in abrasively defiant mood: 'We've got their measure now. They're not THAT good and we can still beat them if we play to our full potential,' he declared to sceptical pressmen. In anyone else his reaction might have been denounced as a blend of arrogance and pique, a mere exercise in face-saving rhetoric, but Bill's irascible railing against the inevitability of elimination came into a different category. Those closest to him sensed that he believed his ostensibly outrageous analysis of Liverpool's prospects and was truly hopeful of beating the Dutchmen by five or six at Anfield. Such was his compelling fervour that the ground was packed and his team went straight for the visitors' throats in a ferocious early assault that was twice denied only by the woodwork. What might have ensued if Geoff Strong's header and Peter Thompson's shot had gone in makes the imagination reel; a soccer miracle might have been on the cards.

A quarter of a century later, such level-headed individuals as Roger Hunt, Tommy Smith and Ian Callaghan - certainly not men prone to self-indulgent flights of fancy - will testify that the great motivator really had communicated his conviction that all was not lost. They are unanimous that it was no act for the media, pointing out that a couple of early goals could have turned the tie on its head. However, Cruyff had other ideas, scoring twice in a masterful display of counter-punching and revealing the all-round talent that would later earn him the

Disappointment is etched on the face of Ian St John as he is thwarted by Ajax goalkeeper Bals at Anfield. Though the Reds struggled bravely, managing a 2-2 draw on the night, they were outclassed by a masterful Dutch side in which Johann Cruyff was outstanding.

Snow ballet at Anfield: airborne Ferencvaros goalkeeper Takacs blocks Geoff Strong's shot as the Reds strive in vain to recover from their first-leg reverse. In the event, the Hungarians adapted more readily to the slippery surface and Liverpool lost again.

title of the world's finest footballer. This time there was no fog, just a light mist, certainly nothing to excuse the obvious gulf in class and technique between two teams who finished all square on the night thanks to the opportunism of two-goal Roger Hunt. Some had believed that the Dutchmen would falter before the Anfield roar and non-stop pressure. But they withstood it calmly, their half-time thumbs-up signals to their bench an apt illustration of their ascendancy. Away from the football, more than 200 people were injured during a first-half surge on the Kop. The little first-aid centre was not large enough to cope and stretcher cases were laid out in the drizzly rain, waiting for ambulances. With about 50 victims of the crush lined up on the grass behind the goal-line, there were fears that the match might be delayed or even abandoned, but by the break the wounded had disappeared in a non-stop procession around the edge of the pitch.

Perhaps the most serious casualty at Anfield that night, however, was Liverpool's credibility on the Continent, which they sought to regain the following season, their first in the European Fairs Cup. Having qualified merely by finishing fifth in the First Division - Shankly's Mk 1 team was showing signs of wear - success was perhaps more urgently needed than usual. The campaign started encouragingly enough, with newly-signed marksman Tony Hateley's aerial power proving too much for Malmo in Sweden, his brace of headers making the return a virtual formality.

On paper at least, Liverpool's next opponents were a far more formidable proposition. After all, only three seasons earlier TSV Munich had stretched West Ham in the final of the Cup Winners' Cup; they were a typically efficient Teutonic outfit, blessed with an exceptional if eccentric goalkeeper in Radi Radenkovic. Yet in the opening encounter at Anfield, the Reds racked up their heaviest victory - excluding wartime matches - for 40 years, putting eight past the woefully out-of-touch Yugoslavian. Naturally, the Kop was ecstatic; too often they saw their team fail to win games by margins commensurate with the enormous pressure they exerted, and this was sheer delight. Understandably but unwisely, they taunted their forth-coming League visitors, singing 'Lord help United'. Three days later they were to pay dearly for their bravado, George Best scoring twice as Matt Busby's men took the points. Inevitably, the TSV second leg was a non-event, with only 10,000 people scattered around the vast Munich stadium. Nothing but pride was at stake this time, and the Germans soothed theirs by winning 2-1. So anti-climactic was the occasion that Ian Callaghan, reminiscing years later, couldn't even remember scoring what was his third goal of the tie.

Next on Liverpool's agenda was a return to Hungary, where they had acquitted themselves so capably against Honved in 1966. This time, though, they encountered sterner opposition in Ferencvaros, as well as receiving an inhospitable blast of seasonal Eastern bloc weather. It was the Hungarians' last match before their three-month winter break, perhaps the only reason the referee did not abandon the game as the snow piled up on the pitch in the second half. To have called it off and waited so long for a replay would have severely disrupted the competition, so the players struggled on and, in the circumstances, the Merseysiders were content to return to Anfield with only a single-goal deficit. In fact, the impending deep freeze jeopardised the journey home. After a two-hour wait at Budapest airport, snowploughs cleared the runway while stewardesses helped de-ice the wings to enable the Reds' plane to fly out. Then the same girls handed round the Scotch, and Tommy Smith recalls that their hands were shaking: 'Just one hour later and take-off would have been impossible. If we hadn't got up when we did we might have missed the kick-off against Fulham that Saturday.'

Hungary was not alone in suffering a bleak winter, and six weeks later the second leg was almost frozen off. A mixture of paid contractors and enthusiastic volunteers cleared most of the snow from the pitch, but that left a treacherously icy surface to which Ferencvaros more readily adapted. Their star was blond international forward Zoltan Varga, whose balance and ball control proved a decisive factor as the visitors won 1-0, thus inflicting the Reds' first home European defeat in their 13th tie. Ron Yeats reckons the match should not have gone on: 'It was a lottery. I know both sides had to cope with the same conditions, but it was harder for us because we were chasing the game.' For Tommy Smith, it had been a fraught midweek. His wife, Sue, went into labour the night before the game, and as he moved off hurriedly in his car to take her to hospital, a manhole cover gave way and a wheel was momentarily trapped. There was a happy ending, though, as Tommy cradled his new daughter, Janette, in his arms.

The two campaigns that followed, in which Shankly was gradually reshaping his ageing side, brought precious little European joy to Anfield. In 1968/69 they found out how Cologne must have felt four seasons earlier, bowing out of the Fairs Cup to Atletico Bilbao on the toss of a disc. Never before had they fallen at the first hurdle, and it was a particularly bitter experience in view of a pulsating, late second-leg comeback in front of the Kop. The spirit that inspired the strikes by Chris Lawler and Emlyn Hughes, and the extra-time pounding of the Spanish goal, deserved better reward, but Ron Yeats was philosophical: 'The disc came down the wrong way and that was that.' When the verdict was announced the crowd was stunned, seemingly unwilling to disperse after such an unworthy end to a splendid match. Eventually, UEFA were to realise the folly of their ways; a penalty shoot-out might not be ideal, but at least it has SOME footballing basis.

Liverpool embarked on their sixth quest for European glory in an unequal contest with Dundalk of the Irish Republic, who narrowly failed to restrict their rampant hosts to single figures in the first leg at Anfield. Afterwards their manager, former Newcastle United winger Liam Tuohy, stated his pleasure that the final score had been ten rather than a mere five or six. His reasoning - which some might see as being typically Irish - was that the fans over the water would surely flock to see any side who could score so many goals, whereas a slightly less emphatic scoreline would merely have ruined the gate.

In the event, the Reds enjoyed their visit to Oriel Park, where they scored four more goals on the bumpy pitch, but also made many new friends. Bill Shankly was especially impressed with the Irish steaks, which he described as the best he had ever tasted, although Ron Yeats pointed out irreverently: 'If we'd been clobbered his description of the food wouldn't have been so glowing!' Bill was a great believer in the virtues of steak, maintaining that his boxing heroes such as Joe Louis and Jack Dempsey had thrived on them, and doing his utmost to ensure that his players were always well fed with prime meat. He insisted that their meals consist of tomato soup, then steak, chips and peas, followed by fresh fruit and cream.

What a way to lose a cup tie! Ron Yeats feels the tension as referee Kurt Tschenscher tosses the disc to separate Liverpool and Atletico Bilbao after extra time at Anfield. Agonisingly, the wretched piece of plastic landed the wrong way for Ron, and the Reds were out.

Anything else was dismissed on sight - particularly more exotic Continental fare, of which he was unashamedly suspicious - and he was once outraged when newcomer Steve Heighway unknowingly stepped out of line by ordering chicken sandwiches. Ron now grins affectionately at the boss's dogmatic approach and makes the point: 'Steak is actually not great before a match because it's slow to digest. Players tend to eat much lighter foods now, but we didn't do badly on it, did we? There's no doubt, though, Bill Shankly would have derided the modern methods.'

After such a pleasant excursion, it was down to earth with a bump when Liverpool were paired with Vitoria Setubal, a richly talented, much underrated side. After losing to the only goal of the game in Portugal, the Reds were entitled to be confident, but - through a penalty and a Geoff Strong own-goal - found themselves three down only half an hour from the end of the Anfield return. Then Tommy Smith netted from the spot and back roared the Reds, with substitutes Alun Evans and Roger Hunt each striking in the final two minutes to level the aggregate score. Then came the cruellest blow of all: as Liverpool stood around waiting for extra time to begin, the referee informed them that their stirring recovery had been in vain and Vitoria had won on the away-goals rule. The players, who had been convinced that the regulation counted only after extra time, were nonplussed, and a public announcement had to be made before the fans would leave the ground. After losing on a toss-up the preceding season, it was hard to take and Shanks grated: 'We were beaten by a penalty, an own-goal and the rules of the competition' - as if, in such circumstances, it didn't really count.

Sadly, Roger Hunt's 90th-minute thunderbolt was to be his last goal for Liverpool in Europe. The following month, the 31-year-old England World Cup hero was allowed to join Bolton Wanderers, whom he had supported as a boy. In his decade as the Reds' premier marksman he had broken the club's scoring record and shared in a succession of memorable triumphs. More than that, he had remained the same unspoilt, self-effacing character who had made his Anfield debut in the pre-Shankly era. The Kop called him 'Sir Roger', a sobriquet that summed up perfectly both his gracious approach and his importance to the Liverpool cause. What a shame that his final effort had been to no avail.

Cally provides a cushion: the workaholic winger volleys Liverpool's second goal in the first leg against Petrolul Ploesti and most observers felt it would be enough to see the Reds safely into the next round. But the Romanians rallied on their home soil and Shankly's men went through only after a replay.

Right: Johann Cruyff, later to become known as the world's finest footballer, looks on as his team-mate Hulshoff (2) contests an aerial duel with Ron Yeats at Anfield.

Preliminary round - 1st leg
28 September 1966

LIVERPOOL 2
St John 71; Callaghan 80

PETROLUL PLOESTI 0

H-T 0-0. Crowd 44,364

| LAWRENCE |
| LAWLER |
| GRAHAM |
| SMITH |
| YEATS |
| STEVENSON |
| CALLAGHAN |
| HUNT |
| ST JOHN |
| STRONG |
| THOMPSON |

Petrolul Ploesti turned out to be a tougher proposition than most pundits had imagined. Employing a back line of five, they were difficult to break down yet could spring from defence with alarming speed. Indeed, the home rearguard almost came unstuck in the 14th minute, when only a saving tackle by Thompson, of all people, prevented an early shock. Liverpool pounded away for most of the game, however,

exhibiting more determination than style, and the Kop had become frustrated when the breakthrough finally came in the form of a St John header from a Stevenson cross. Soon afterwards, Callaghan volleyed home a loose clearance, and Liverpool had an acceptable cushion for the away leg.

Preliminary round - 2nd leg
12 October 1966

PETROLUL PLOESTI 3
Stevenson (og) 36; Moldoveanu 59; Dridea (M) 65

LIVERPOOL 1
Hunt 50
H-T 1-0. Crowd 20,000

| LAWRENCE |
| LAWLER |
| MILNE |
| SMITH |
| YEATS |
| STEVENSON |
| CALLAGHAN |
| HUNT |
| ST JOHN |
| STRONG |
| THOMPSON |

If Petrolul had surprised Liverpool at Anfield, they positively dumbfounded them in Romania. In an unpleasant, bruising encounter which saw the sending-off of home defender Florea near the end, the oil-town side attacked so vigorously that eventually the Reds, having seen their two-goal first-leg lead eaten away, were happy to hang on for a replay. Their first setback was an unlucky one, Stevenson slicing a cross into his own net, and when Thompson set up Hunt's equaliser shortly after the break there seemed little to fear. But two goals in six minutes - Moldoveanu's prod in a goalmouth scramble, and Dridea's free-kick from the edge of the area - changed the complexion of the tie.

Aggregate score 3-3.

Preliminary round - replay in Brussels
19 October 1966

LIVERPOOL 2
St John 13; Thompson 43

PETROLUL PLOESTI 0

H-T 2-0. Crowd 10,000

| LAWRENCE |
| LAWLER |
| MILNE |
| SMITH |
| YEATS |
| STEVENSON |
| CALLAGHAN |
| HUNT |
| ST JOHN |
| STRONG |
| THOMPSON |

In view of the two previous encounters, Liverpool's triumph was gained with astonishing ease. Petrolul, shorn of four key players through injury and suspension, were a different proposition from the abrasive unit that had confronted the Reds in Romania, giving a limp performance that never threatened the progress of Shankly's side into the next round. Hunt created the first goal for St John, battling for possession on the right flank before freeing the Scot six yards out; the second, a low 20-yarder from Thompson that goalkeeper Ionescu could only help into the net, was a piece of pure opportunism. Liverpool's one anxious moment came when Yeats appeared to have handled on the line, but no penalty was given.

AJAX 5

Wolff 3; Cruyff 17; Nuninga 39, 43;
Groot 70

LIVERPOOL 1

Lawler 90
H-T 4-0. Crowd 65,000

LAWRENCE
LAWLER
GRAHAM
SMITH
YEATS
STEVENSON
CALLAGHAN
HUNT
ST JOHN
STRONG
THOMPSON

It was not often that Shankly's Liverpool were outclassed, but the young Johann Cruyff and his Ajax team-mates achieved more than that; on a foggy night in Amsterdam, the Reds received the most comprehensive mauling of their footballing lives. The Dutchmen, who were yet to emerge as the great team they later became, carved gaping holes in the astonished visitors' defence with slick passing interchanges that took the breath away. Wolff's header and emphatic shots from Cruyff and Nuninga, who also tapped in from a Swart cross, left Liverpool four down at half-time. After the break, the mist thickening by the minute, they attempted to salvage the situation by hurling themselves into attack. Ajax sat back, let them come, then counter-punched with a powerful strike by Groot. Lawler clawed one back with the last kick of the match, but that did nothing to disguise the enormity of the defeat.

LIVERPOOL 2

Hunt 54, 88

AJAX 2

Cruyff 49, 70
H-T 0-0. Crowd 53,846

LAWRENCE
LAWLER
MILNE
SMITH
YEATS
STEVENSON
CALLAGHAN
HUNT
ST JOHN
STRONG
THOMPSON

The extent to which Ajax had been underrated became evident when Cruyff and company paraded their talents at Anfield. Their technique, fluency and composure were a joy to behold as they set about absorbing the inevitable pressure from a Liverpool side smarting from their earlier reverse. Admittedly the Reds enjoyed little luck, both Thompson and Strong striking the woodwork in the first half, but in the end only a late strike by Hunt, his second of the match, prevented their first European defeat on their own soil. Though the Merseysiders mounted wave after wave of assaults in the second half, the sturdy Dutch defence remained calm, and two exquisite breakaway goals - each set up for Cruyff by Keizer and Nuninga - emphasised the difference between the two teams. It was a lesson from which Liverpool, to their credit, learnt much that was to stand them in splendid stead during future campaigns.

Ajax won 7-3 on aggregate.

Round 1 - 1st leg
19 September 1967

MALMO 0

LIVERPOOL 2

Hateley 9, 80
H-T 0-1. Crowd 14,314

LAWRENCE
LAWLER
BYRNE
SMITH
YEATS
HUGHES
CALLAGHAN
HUNT
HATELEY
ST JOHN
THOMPSON

Liverpool were never stretched by a run-of-the-mill Malmo side who were efficient enough at the back but lacklustre in most other departments. The Reds' match-winner was big centre-forward Hateley, whose two headers - one at either end of the action - looked certain to have put the tie beyond the Swedes' reach. Ironically, Malmo's most impressive performer was centre-half Elmstedt, but there was nothing he could do to prevent his adversary from converting either Hughes' speculative lob or Thompson's tantalising cross.
The Liverpool goal came under threat but rarely, and the visitors would have won far more convincingly if an out-of-touch Hunt had not spurned several clear-cut chances.

Round 1 - 2nd leg
4 October 1967

LIVERPOOL 2

Yeats 28; Hunt 36

MALMO 1

Szepanski 83
H-T 2-0. Crowd 39,795

LAWRENCE
LAWLER
BYRNE
SMITH
YEATS
HUGHES
CALLAGHAN
HUNT
HATELEY
STEVENSON
THOMPSON

Perhaps Liverpool were a trifle complacent after their comfortable first-leg victory, but Malmo were quick to demonstrate that they were not to be underestimated. Two minutes into the game, only Lawrence's heroic dive at the feet of the bespectacled Tapper prevented a shock goal, and a further two minutes later Yeats was forced to clear the ball off his line. Suitably stirred, the Reds responded by picking up the tempo and netting twice to clinch the spoils. First Yeats rose above Swedish 'keeper Hult to head in a Callaghan centre, then Hunt scored at the second attempt after receiving the ball from Hateley. Few begrudged Malmo their late consolation goal, chipped over Lawrence by Szepanski.

Liverpool won 4-1 on aggregate.

Round 2 - 1st leg
7 November 1967

LIVERPOOL 8

St John 6; Hateley 9; Smith (pen) 43; Hunt 52, 54; Thompson 53;Callaghan 63, 70

TSV MUNICH 0

H-T 3-0. Crowd 44,812

LAWRENCE
LAWLER
BYRNE
SMITH
YEATS
HUGHES
CALLAGHAN
HUNT
HATELEY
ST JOHN
THOMPSON

This was the night when everything went right for the Reds, who smashed their European scoring record against a team riding high in the German Super League. How sweet it was for the Kop to see their heroes reaping numerical reward for their dominance, instead of squandering scoring opportunities as they had done so often of late. Three down at the break - courtesy of Messrs St John, Hateley and Smith (penalty) - TSV looked a dispirited outfit when they emerged for the second half; soon they were to be demoralised completely by three more goals in three minutes, Hunt taking two of them with impudent panache and Thompson striking savagely from the edge of the area. It was left to Callaghan to wrap up proceedings, first emulating his fellow wingman with a scorcher, and then running half the length of the pitch before gulling 'keeper Radenkovic. What a show!

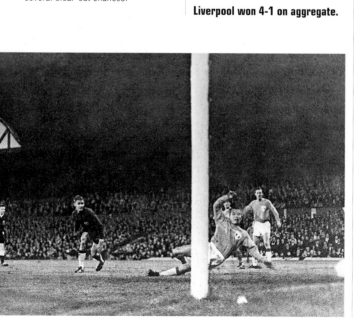

Round 2 - 2nd leg
14 November 1967

TSV MUNICH 2

Mohlars 35; Kohlars 87

LIVERPOOL 1

Callaghan 5
H-T 1-1. Crowd 10,000

LAWRENCE	
LAWLER	
BYRNE	
SMITH	
YEATS	
HUGHES	
CALLAGHAN	
HUNT	
HATELEY (STEVENSON)	
ST JOHN	
THOMPSON	

After the Anfield blitz of the previous week came inevitable anti-climax. Indeed, with the result of the tie a pure formality, nothing else could be expected. Nevertheless the Reds started as they had left off, increasing their lead still further when Callaghan rounded off a sweeping five-man move with a smart finish. Liverpool then selected a cruising gear, leaving TSV to come at them in a bid to repair their battered pride. The patching-up operation began ten minutes before half-time when Mohlars rose to head a superb equaliser, and was completed three minutes from the final whistle when Kohlars netted after picking up a loose ball in the penalty box. After that Smith hit the Germans' bar, but it hardly mattered. The real business was long over.

Liverpool won 9-2 on aggregate

Horizontal H-Bomber: Tony Hateley dives bravely and spectacularly to head Liverpool's second goal in the 8-0 Anfield demolition of TSV Munich.

Round 3 - 1st leg
28 November 1967

FERENCVAROS 1

Katona 44

LIVERPOOL 0

H-T 1-0. Crowd 30,000

LAWRENCE	
LAWLER	
BYRNE	
SMITH	
YEATS	
HUGHES	
CALLAGHAN	
HUNT	
HATELEY	
THOMPSON	
STEVENSON	

Liverpool set out to do a containing job in the huge, snowbound Nep Stadium and the Hungarians, who seemed short of ideas in the absence of star centre-forward Florian Albert, posed few problems to a calm, efficient defence in which Smith was outstanding. Despite the slippery surface, neither side created many chances, and the tie might have remained goalless but for a questionable decision by a linesman and a wicked deflection that gave Ferencvaros their slender advantage. The ball looked to have crossed the byline when Szoke hooked it into the goalmouth; Yeats cleared but only to Katona, whose shot struck the giant centre-half, thus wrong-footing Lawrence and finding the net.

Far left: 'Sir Roger' at work: Hunt drills home for Liverpool against Malmo in the second leg at Anfield.

Round 3 - 2nd leg
9 January 1968

LIVERPOOL 0

FERENCVAROS 1

Branikovits 19
H-T 0-1. Crowd 46,892

LAWRENCE	
LAWLER	
BYRNE	
SMITH	
YEATS	
HUGHES	
CALLAGHAN	
HUNT	
STRONG	
ST JOHN	
THOMPSON	

Ferencvaros, more used to wintry conditions than their hosts, excelled at a snowy Anfield and fully deserved to inflict Liverpool's first home defeat in their 13th European tie. However, the Reds had their chances - Strong going agonisingly close to scoring on two occasions - and the visitors owed much to their 'keeper, Takacs, who put a hesitant start behind him to make several outstanding saves. The Hungarians played a precise passing game, unsettling Yeats and his fellow defenders by turning them quickly on the treacherous surface. Once Branikovits had doubled the first-leg lead, ramming the ball past Lawrence to cap a sparkling five-man move, the outcome was in little doubt.

Ferencvaros won 2-0 on aggregate.

Out of control? Ferencvaros winger Szoke is in danger of crashing into photographers and Liverpool goalkeeper Tommy Lawrence seems unlikely to gather a high cross during the first leg in Hungary.

Round 1 - 1st leg
18 September 1968

ATLETICO BILBAO 2
Estefano 15; Ornaza 38

LIVERPOOL 1
Hunt 67
H-T 2-0. Crowd 35,000

LAWRENCE
LAWLER
WALL
SMITH
YEATS
HUGHES
CALLAGHAN
HUNT
GRAHAM (STRONG)
ST JOHN (ROSS)
THOMPSON

Liverpool recovered spiritedly from a frustrating first half during which they were punished mercilessly for two uncharacteristic errors. First, Smith was caught dithering deep inside his own territory and Estefano netted, via Lawrence's hand and the post, from the resultant attack; then, the 'keeper allowed an innocuous cross to bounce off his chest and into the path of Ornaza, who accepted the gift with glee. Yet although the Spaniards had been enterprising in attack, the Reds - those lapses apart - had been sprightly, too. Hunt had come close to scoring with three efforts, and it was fitting that he should be rewarded for his persistence, rounding Iribar to net after being freed by Hughes. A minute later, Strong nearly equalised with an outrageous backheel, and come the end, it was Liverpool who looked the more confident side.

Round 1 - 2nd leg
2 October 1968

LIVERPOOL 2
Lawler 78; Hughes 87

ATLETICO BILBAO 1
Argoitia 32
H-T 0-1. Crowd 49,567

LAWRENCE
LAWLER
WALL
SMITH
YEATS
HUGHES
CALLAGHAN
HUNT
EVANS
ST JOHN
THOMPSON

Splitting these two valiant teams by the toss of a coin was nothing short of a travesty. Liverpool had surged forward skilfully and relentlessly, while Atletico had resisted with astute defensive tactics and considerable fortitude, and an outcome based on football rather than fortune was the least they deserved. In fact, the necessity of a contrived decision seemed unlikely after the Spaniards had stretched their overall lead to two goals, Argoitia robbing Smith and waltzing past Lawrence to shoot into an empty net. But the Reds refused to capitulate, eventually piercing Atletico's armour twice in the last 12 minutes of normal time, through a Lawler header and a powerful close-range drive from Hughes. On 110 minutes, Evans had the chance to snatch victory when put through with only the brilliant Iribar to beat. He failed, time ran out and the referee reached for that fateful disc.

**Aggregate 3-3 after extra time.
Atletico Bilbao won on toss.**

Above right: **Never say die: only 12 minutes are left and Liverpool are two down when Chris Lawler revives their hopes with a close-range header against Atletico Bilbao at Anfield. Soon Emlyn Hughes snatched an equaliser and the Reds were favourites to win in extra time; cruelly, the toss of a disc decided otherwise.**

Round 1 - 1st leg
16 September 1969

LIVERPOOL 10
Evans 1, 38; Lawler 10; Smith 24, 67; Graham 36, 82; Lindsay 56; Thompson 69; Callaghan 76

DUNDALK 0
H-T 5-0. Crowd 32,656

CLEMENCE
LAWLER
STRONG
SMITH
YEATS
HUGHES
CALLAGHAN
GRAHAM
LINDSAY
EVANS
THOMPSON

This embarrassing mismatch gave Liverpool little more than a gentle practice run-out, rendering meaningless a number of tactical experiments tried by Bill Shankly. In such an atmosphere it was impossible to judge the merits of Graham in the deep-lying role of the rested St John, or of newcomer Lindsay, wearing the number-nine shirt but playing in midfield. Of course, any attempt to assess rookie 'keeper Clemence was even more laughable. Evans commenced the massacre of the outclassed Irish in the first minute, and it continued unabated until the 80th, at which point, having reached double figures, the Reds appeared to relax. By that time, a little restraint was well in order.

Round 1 - 2nd leg
30 September 1969

DUNDALK 0

LIVERPOOL 4
Thompson 13, 31; Graham 48;
Callaghan 81
H-T 0-2. Crowd 6,000

CLEMENCE
LAWLER
STRONG
SMITH
LLOYD
HUGHES
THOMPSON (CALLAGHAN)
EVANS
GRAHAM (HUNT)
ST JOHN
BOERSMA

The main interest in this unequal struggle was the further opportunities afforded to Liverpool youngsters such as Clemence, Lloyd and Boersma. With Dundalk not as overawed before their own fans as they had been in front of the Kop, the contest was slightly more meaningful, although hardly a true test. Clemence, however, did enough to hint that Lawrence may have to look to his laurels sooner rather than later, and Lloyd showed that he may indeed be an embryo Yeats. Boersma, while displaying eagerness and verve, was understandably over-anxious and missed several scoring chances. Most animated of the regular players was Thompson, who seemed intent on the hat-trick he must have gained had he not been substituted.

Liverpool won 14-0 on aggregate.

Round 2 - 1st leg
12 November 1969

VITORIA SETUBAL 1
Tome 40

LIVERPOOL 0

H-T 1-0. Crowd 16,000

LAWRENCE
LAWLER
WALL
SMITH
YEATS
HUGHES
CALLAGHAN
ROSS
GRAHAM (ST JOHN)
STRONG
THOMPSON

Liverpool took the attacking sting from their gifted opponents to place themselves in a strong position for the home leg. Shankly's selection of Ross, a marker, in place of the goal-scoring Hunt betrayed the visitors' intentions, and for most of the match the Reds successfully nullified the quicksilver creativity of the Portuguese. They slowed the game down, using strength and technique to retain possession, and occasionally threatened to snatch a vital goal on the break. The only chink in this wall appeared when Cardoso tried a speculative shot from 40 yards; the ball took a deflection past Lawrence, struck the bar, and Tome knocked in the rebound. Come the last 15 minutes, with Vitoria becoming frustrated, Liverpool began to emerge from their shell, and Yeats almost equalised.

Round 2 - 2nd leg
26 November 1969

LIVERPOOL 3
Smith (pen) 60; Evans 88; Hunt 90

VITORIA SETUBAL 2
Wagner (pen) 23; Strong (og) 56
H-T 0-1. Crowd 41,633

LAWRENCE
LAWLER
STRONG
SMITH
YEATS
HUGHES
CALLAGHAN
PEPLOW (HUNT)
GRAHAM (EVANS)
ST JOHN
THOMPSON

Liverpool bowed out of the competition despite the most rousing comeback of their European history to date. One down at the start, they fell further behind when Lawrence brought down Guerreiro and Wagner netted from the spot. Then, when Strong deflected a Tome shot past his own 'keeper, the Reds - with away goals counting double in the event of a draw - needed to score four times in 37 minutes to go through. Refusing to buckle, they swept forward, but even when Smith converted a penalty, given after a goal-bound shot from Hunt had been handballed, there were few who believed they could seriously trouble the accomplished Portuguese, for whom diminutive custodian Vital was in inspired form. But two goals in the last two minutes - a close-range stab from Evans and Hunt's glorious 20-yarder - claimed victory on the night, leaving overall triumph agonisingly beyond their reach.

Aggregate 3-3. Vitoria Setubal won on away goals.

Left: **Two-goal Peter Thompson, who tantalised the Dundalk defence at Oriel Park and looked set for a hat-trick until he was replaced by Ian Callaghan.**

Chapter Four

LESSONS THAT LED TO GREATNESS

A canny old warrior: in his thirties and plagued by knee injuries, Ian St John could still make a telling contribution to the Liverpool cause. He proved it against Dinamo Bucharest at Anfield, setting up a crucial late goal for Emlyn Hughes with a defence-splitting pass of subtle precision.

THE first two seasons of the new decade constituted a period of brisk transition at Anfield; nothing was won but firm foundations were laid for the years of hitherto unimaginable glory that lay ahead. Old, much-loved faces departed and new ones arrived, the operation carried out with a lack of sentimentality that is a Liverpool hallmark. Bill Shankly had begun ringing the changes in the late 1960s with the introduction of dread-nought wing-half Emlyn Hughes and Alun Evans, a livewire marksman; come 1970/71, the likes of goalkeeper Ray Clemence, defenders Alec Lindsay and Larry Lloyd, midfielder Brian Hall, and Steve Heighway, an exciting, sometimes breathtaking attacker, were consolidating their positions. Welsh international target-man John Toshack had arrived and others such as schemer John McLaughlin, striker Jack Whitham and utility attacker Phil Boersma were all striving to make an impact. Tommy Smith and Chris Lawler at the back and flankman Ian Callaghan remained as long-term links with the glorious past, but names such as Ron Yeats and Ian St John, Tommy Lawrence and Peter Thompson would be out of the reckoning sooner rather than later. In such circumstances it would have been astonishing if the Reds had claimed European silverware for the first time, and they didn't; but they came closer than anyone had a right to expect.

The first round of the Fairs Cup offered the opportunity of revenge on Ferencvaros, their conquerors of three seasons before. But for three-quarters of the tie, this was a different, duller Hungarian combination who dropped their excessively cautious approach only in the final 45 minutes of the second leg in their own Nep Stadium. It wasn't enough, and the Reds managed to ease through by a single-goal margin, courtesy of a powerful strike from Hughes. For many of the Merseyside party, the highlight of an otherwise unmemorable trip came not on the field but in a Budapest restaurant. Upset by what he considered to be unreasonably slow service, and further exasperated by his inability to communicate with the Hungarian waiter, Shanks demanded: 'Can't you understand? Are you all foreigners?'

In their next encounter, the Reds overcame Dinamo Bucharest with relative comfort, thanks partly to the European swansong of that canny old warrior Ian St John. By then 32 and cursed with injury problems, he was no longer a viable proposition over 90 minutes, but demonstrated the value of guile and experience when he came on for the closing quarter of an hour of the first leg at Anfield. Lying deep, as he had during many of Liverpool's finest hours, he inspired the third and killer goal with a pass of visionary perception, his last significant contribution before departing to Coventry in September 1971. Many believed he was ideal management material, but after trying his luck with Motherwell and Portsmouth he found a more secure niche in television, the chemistry of his double act with Jimmy Greaves - the Saint plays the role of knowing, slightly mischievous straight-man offsetting Greavsie's verbal slapstick - striking a popular chord.

All that was a world away, of course, as Liverpool prepared to meet their next opponents, Hibernian, a club in the throes of domestic upheaval. Just hours before entertaining the Reds in the first leg at Easter Road, Hibs had sacked their manager Willie MacFarlane, replacing him with former Manchester City centre-half Dave Ewing, who had been recruited as a coach from Sheffield Wednesday the week before. The new man marshalled his forces well enough to stretch Liverpool at times, but in the end the Scots succumbed to a developing side lifted by the exhilarating talent of Steve Heighway. The unorthodox recruit from non-League Skelmersdale flew thrillingly at defences, lacerating them with an innocent, refreshing verve that might have withered in the tough, sometimes cynical environment of top-class football, but for a combination of his own determination and the sure-handed nurturing of Bill Shankly.

The manager's touch was not infallible, though, as was evident from the experience of John McLaughlin, another promising talent who shone brightly against Hibs. Shanks believed the young play-maker to be a star in embryo, but he failed to maintain his progress and faded from contention before a knee injury ended his career prematurely. Was John a victim of bad luck? Was the manager's judgement at fault? Or did the player's desire simply not burn fiercely enough? Regularly, at clubs up and down the country, such painful questions torment the minds of countless youthful rejects who must jettison their dreams to seek a new future outside the game. An example to them all is Roy Evans, whose sole European outing was against Hibs at Anfield. The Bootle-born left-back, who made only 11 senior appearances over five seasons, was realistic enough to know that he was not making the grade and accepted Bob Paisley's invitation to prove himself as a coach. That was in 1974, since when he has carved himself an influential long-term niche at Anfield.

A further illustration of soccer's eternal uncertainty is afforded by the hero of Liverpool's quarter-final clash with the crack West German outfit Bayern Munich. Alun Evans became British football's first £100,000 teenager when Shankly signed him from Wolves in September 1968; everything was in place for a fabulous future. But after a sparkling start, he suffered some sickening setbacks - including a nightclub attack that left him with a scarred face, and a cartilage operation - and his career lost impetus. Now, surely, he was back on the road to glory thanks to a brilliant first-leg hat-trick against Messrs Beckenbauer, Muller and company to provide Liverpool with a decisive lead. Yet STILL he didn't make it in the long run, failing to overcome further niggling fitness doubts and white-hot competition for places.

For the moment, though, Shankly was well satisfied, saying: 'We've been outplaying teams all season without scoring. Tonight Alun Evans changed all that.' Bayern coach Udo Lattek pointed out that bad weather in Germany had prevented his men taking the pitch in earnest for three weeks, but admitted they had lost to the better side. However, they remained one of the few teams in Europe with the talent to claw back a three-goal lead, and Shankly made an inspired change for the second leg, giving utility player Ian Ross the task of shadowing Beckenbauer's every move. Ian was a willing, averagely skilful performer who found himself in his element, forcing 'Kaiser Franz' to languish in front of his own back four instead of deploying his huge creative powers in more dangerous areas. So complete was the tenacious Glaswegian's hold over his illustrious opponent that he took time off to put Liverpool in front on the night. Afterwards Bill had extravagant praise for his man-marker, who had once carried out a similarly effective job on Alan Ball, but Ian was never to claim a permanent place, lacking the class for the very top level.

Beating Bayern was a tremendous achievement by a side in flux, but no soft touch awaited as a semi-final reward. Instead the Reds were thrown into confrontation with Don Revie's Leeds United, at that time perhaps as formidable a proposition over two legs as could be found anywhere in Europe. Desperate to wring an advantage from their arch-rivals in the first leg at Anfield, Liverpool were committed to all-out assault, though Tommy Smith remembers the management's warning not to allow free headers to players arriving late in their penalty box. Ironically, just such a scenario was to be their undoing. Chris Lawler was in no-man's land as Johnny Giles floated in a free-kick from the left flank, and Billy Bremner found himself with yards of space to score without hindrance. For two months the Leeds captain had been sidelined with a broken leg, and ever since the semi-final draw had made Anfield his comeback target. Though clearly not match fit, his predatory instincts were not impaired, and later he spoke of the need for unremitting concentration on such occasions, stressing: 'Nobody can look away for a moment.' Chris Lawler could offer rueful testimony to that.

Of course, there was still hope of turning the tie round at Elland Road, and the Reds made

'The Kaiser's' shadow: Ian Ross, who showed his mettle as a man-marker by neutralising the efforts of the great Franz Beckenbauer in Munich. So complete was the young Scot's mastery over his illustrious opponent that he even found time to score Liverpool's goal in a 1-1 draw.

a valiant effort before the game ended goalless. Says Tommy Smith: 'I thought we were unlucky. I am convinced that we were the better side over the two games, but the ball just would not go in. Certainly, it was a gigantic disappointment. It was always excruciating to lose to Leeds.' A clue to Don Revie's tactics lay in his half-time substitution of striker Allan Clarke by full-back Paul Reaney; having once nosed in front, no team of 'The Don's' was wont to surrender through over-exuberant commitment to attack. They would never give an inch, a spirit much in evidence as they triumphed over Juventus in the final on the away-goals rule.

Having acquired valuable knowhow from the campaign - and from their progress that term to Wembley, where they were unable to prevent Bertie Mee's much-maligned Arsenal from clinching the League/FA Cup double - this improving, but still rather raw Liverpool combination could approach their next Continental venture with increased confidence. In view of the Gunners' qualification for the European Cup, the Merseysiders were 'promoted' to the Cup Winners' Cup, even though they had been losers. In theory this was senior to the Fairs competition, but in fact - with fewer games and, often, less daunting opposition - it was easier to win. However, neither then nor since has it brought joy to the men of Anfield. Despite the presence of bargain signing Kevin Keegan, whose galvanising vitality would prove as crucial to the club's future as his all-round skills, they got off to a potentially humiliating start. Indeed, the shock 2-1 away defeat against the mundane Servette Geneva might have been even more damaging, a measure of dignity being scraped only through Chris Lawler's late strike. As it turned out, that goal was needed for more than purposes of pride, Liverpool managing no more than a 2-0 home victory against a Swiss team whose resolution appeared to grow as the tie wore on. To make matters worse, Tommy Smith's shin was cut to the bone in his first match after missing five with a calf injury.

Next up were Bayern Munich, but this time there was to be no repeat of the preceding

Hat-trick: Alun Evans collects his third goal in the 3-0 home drubbing of mighty Bayern Munich. Britain's first £100,000 teenager, Alun made an encouraging start at Anfield and seemed set fair to become a long-term Liverpool favourite. But his star fell following a depressing sequence of injuries and he slipped away, potential sadly unfulfilled.

term's success against the classy Germans, a goalless draw at Anfield leaving too much to do in the return. In front of the Kop, Bayern were ultra-defensive, relying on some of the tightest man-to-man marking ever seen on English soil - Breitner on Heighway, Hoeness on Keegan, Schwarzenbeck on Evans. They were so negative that even Gerd Muller, arguably the sharpest marksman in the world, spent much of his time standing shoulder to shoulder with sweeper Beckenbauer. When they gained possession, they barely bothered to cross the half-way line, playing keep-ball till they lost it, then re-forming their nigh-impenetrable rearguard. Predictably, in Munich they looked a different team; two-goal Muller was majestic and Bayern went through 3-1. Even so, they didn't have it all their own way, and Alun Evans contributed a strike of such stunning brilliance that it won a goal of the season award from a leading German television network.

Tommy Smith believes the reverse was due, in part, to over-confidence born out of the earlier conquest. Of course, he is well placed to know, but if true, it was an extremely rare - if not unique - instance of such an attitude during the Shankly reign. What IS certain is that it formed a crucial part of Liverpool's footballing education, and accelerated their growth into the Continental superpower they became. Shanks, Bob Paisley and the rest of the coaching staff looked at Bayern's phenomenal first-leg organisation at Anfield and learned from it, and the club reaped the benefit for many years to come. Indeed the whole European experience was to be a cornerstone of the Reds' future domination of the domestic scene.

Ian Callaghan has no doubts: 'We were exposed to all manner of different overseas methods for season after season and benefited enormously. We were the first British team to pass the ball around like the Continentals, playing from the back in the way they always have. As time went by the players noticed more and more emphasis on ball-work in training, while pounding the track decreased. It was all about touch football; always, always, the ball was the creed. This was unheard of in Britain at the time. At some top clubs

A Red takes on the white wall: Tommy Smith clashes with Allan Clarke of Leeds United as Don Revie's men mount an unremitting rearguard action in the first leg of the UEFA Cup semi-final at Anfield. Liverpool lost by the only goal at home, then drew 0-0 at Elland Road, but Tommy maintained: 'We were the better side over the two games.'

players went all day in training without seeing the ball, the theory being that they would be all the more hungry for it when the match started. Meanwhile, of course, they were not developing their technique.'

Thus Shanks and his team - Bob Paisley, Reuben Bennett and Tom Saunders - went about gathering knowledge, watching teams for weeks before they were due to be faced. Yet never were they slavish copycats of all things Continental; the idea was to take a little bit of knowhow from the Germans, maybe a certain technique from the Dutch, perhaps a tactical hint from the Italians, and so on, then mould it to what was already special about the British game. It was important to know when to build from the back and when to employ the long ball which, when used in moderation, will always have its place. Gradually the bricks were placed, discriminately and with infinite care, in the impressive edifice that was to become the Liverpool way of playing. As Tommy Smith puts it: 'In a manner of speaking, we brought British football into the twentieth century.'

In the early days, no one relished the challenge of playing abroad more than Ron Yeats: 'We loved everything about it. The whole era was so exciting, not just in football but in life generally. There was the Mersey Sound, everything was changing, the old order was going. It was tremendous to be a part of it, there was so much innocence and freshness. Our European expeditions seemed so adventurous. Of course, in terms of football we were guinea pigs. We were a good, well-balanced side, but tended to be naive away from home, attacking when we would have been better advised to hang back and take the sting out of our opponents. We learnt the lesson gradually, and the Liverpool sides who followed picked up the rewards of our experience.'

Keeping pace with the Reds' tactical transformation down the years, huge strides were made in reducing the wear and tear of travelling. In the mid 1960s the players might have met on a Monday, spent Tuesday on plane, train and bus, played the game on Wednesday, then got home late on Thursday, before hitting the road again on Friday for a match in, say, London on Saturday. Scheduled flights were the rule, making them dependent on outsiders for their arrangements. Likewise, there might be problems with foreign food, sometimes leaving players and officials both exhausted and inadequately victualled. Within a decade all that had changed, thanks in huge measure to club secretary Peter Robinson, a supreme administrator and certainly, in his own quiet way, one of the most powerful influences the club has ever known. Now Liverpool began chartering their own flights, often enabling them to depart on a Tuesday afternoon and be home by the Wednesday night. Ian Callaghan recalls: 'The idea was to be in and out as quickly as possible: sometimes it was just a question of meal, bed, practice, game and home. That way, if anyone had a knock they could be on the treatment table at Anfield on Thursday morning, with a much better chance of being fit in time for the weekend. Also we began taking our own food, and sometimes even our own chef, to minimise the change in routine. Shanks was a great one for routine, and sight-seeing was strictly limited. The most we could expect would be a very brief walk around the local town.'

Tommy Smith amplifies: 'We were always hearing about how playing in Europe must be so glamorous. But really it was no fairytale. We were not on holiday, just a bunch of blokes doing their job. The travelling could be a real pain, utterly draining. Hanging around airports and hotels can be very boring; reading and playing cards are all very well, but after a while your mind just goes whacko, and then you have to be lifted for the match. The difference between the reality of playing football in Europe and the public's perception of it came home to me when I went to Rome to watch the 1984 final. I saw more then in two days as an independent traveller than I did in 15 years in Europe as a player. Making the trip is more of a thrill for the fans, who have the freedom to do what they want. For the players, the only thrill comes from the football, certainly not the lifestyle.'

Ron Yeats, too, recalls moments of homesickness and boredom, isolated in the woods in some Eastern bloc hotel, unable to go anywhere. But for all that, he maintains it was refreshing: 'In general, it took our minds off the domestic scene. After playing the best that Europe had to offer, we could feel that nothing we might face at home need cause us any problems.' And, looking at Liverpool's record over a quarter of a century, who could argue with that?

Swiss rolled over: Steve Heighway (far left) is exultant after scoring the winner against Servette Geneva at Anfield, while Kevin Keegan looks merely relieved. In the first leg, the Swiss had beaten the Merseysiders 2-1, one of the most unexpected upsets in the Reds' European history.

Round 1 - 1st leg
15 September 1970

LIVERPOOL 1
Graham 17

FERENCVAROS 0

H-T 1-0. Crowd 37,531

CLEMENCE
LAWLER
LINDSAY
SMITH
LLOYD
HUGHES
CALLAGHAN
EVANS, A
GRAHAM
McLAUGHLIN
THOMPSON

For lovers of good football who recalled the fluent Ferencvaros side that had dumped Liverpool out of Europe three seasons earlier, this 1970 Hungarian vintage was a sore disappointment. Drab and unenterprising, the Magyars were punchless in attack and shaky in defence, and it was to the Reds' discredit that they failed to make the tie safe at the first attempt. Chance after chance was spurned as international 'keeper Geczi escaped unpunished for continuous faulty handling, although the one precious goal was constructed and executed with precision. Evans outwitted a defender before chipping the ball across the penalty box, where Lawler nodded it down and Graham turned it into the net.

Round 1 - 2nd leg
29 September 1970

FERENCVAROS 1
Mucha 47

LIVERPOOL 1
Hughes 65
H-T 0-0. Crowd 25,000

CLEMENCE
LAWLER
LINDSAY
SMITH
LLOYD
HUGHES
HALL
EVANS, A
GRAHAM
McLAUGHLIN
THOMPSON

After the dullness of the Anfield encounter, the tie came to life in the Nep Stadium, with Ferencvaros hunting for goals. In the first half the Reds held them comfortably, with Lloyd marking Albert effectively, although the famous centre-forward did miss several chances. Two minutes after the break, however, the Hungarians struck when Smith's headed clearance dropped at the feet of Mucha, who beat Clemence from 12 yards. Now the rhythm of the game changed, with Ferencvaros flowing forward. Liverpool resisted stoutly, though, and relieved the pressure when Hughes won the ball on half-way and switched it to Graham on the left, before receiving the return and powering it past Geczi from 25 yards. It was the decisive strike, the only subsequent threat to the Reds' goal coming from a Novak 30-yarder that clipped the bar.

Liverpool won 2-1 on aggregate

Left: Revenge is sweet: Bobby Graham hooks in the first-leg winner against Ferencvaros, who had dumped Liverpool out of Europe three seasons earlier. Thus a draw in Hungary was enough to earn the Reds a meeting with Dinamo Bucharest in the next round of the Fairs Cup.

Round 2 - 1st leg
21 October 1970

LIVERPOOL 3
Lindsay 60; Lawler 76; Hughes 82

DINAMO BUCHAREST 0

H-T 0-0. Crowd 36,525

CLEMENCE
LAWLER
YEATS
SMITH
LLOYD
HUGHES
HALL
LINDSAY
HEIGHWAY (ST JOHN)
McLAUGHLIN
THOMPSON

Liverpool demoralised the Romanians with a second-half onslaught after a first 45 minutes of mounting frustration in which they had failed to turn almost constant pressure into goals. Yet the after-break transformation was by no means instant; indeed, when Thompson hit the bar on 48 minutes, Kopites must have wondered if their team would ever score. Eventually the deadlock was broken when Hall, the Reds' most influential creator on the night, crossed for Lindsay to glance in a header from ten yards. Then McLaughlin rattled the bar from 25 yards before Lawler made it 2-0, volleying home from near the penalty spot after Hughes had helped on a Smith cross. Finally that old warhorse St John, on as a substitute for Heighway, split the Dinamo defence with a through-ball for Hughes to complete the scoring.

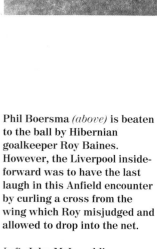

Phil Boersma *(above)* is beaten to the ball by Hibernian goalkeeper Roy Baines. However, the Liverpool inside-forward was to have the last laugh in this Anfield encounter by curling a cross from the wing which Roy misjudged and allowed to drop into the net.

Left: John McLaughlin, a youngster of whom Bill Shankly had great hopes, was given an extended run in the side during the 1970/71 season, but faded thereafter.

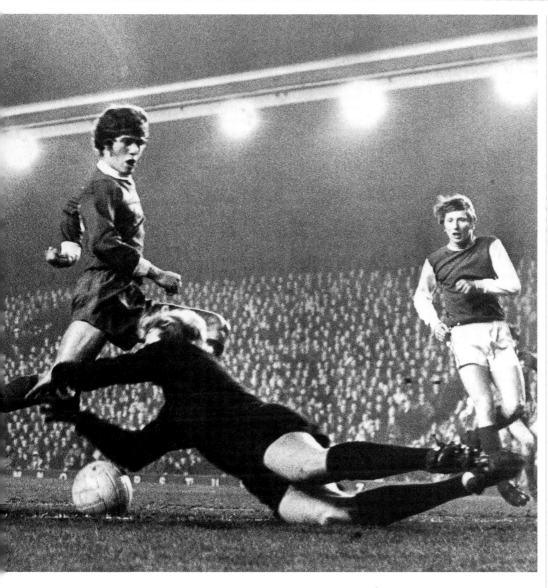

challenge with calm expertise, drawing deeply on their superior European experience, yet there were moments when Hibs had their visitors rattled. After just three minutes, Lloyd appeared to foul Davidson well inside the box but the referee refused a penalty, instead awarding a free-kick on the 18-yard line; and on the hour McBride netted with a header, only for his celebrations to be stilled by an offside flag. The Reds were always the more measured side, however, and with McLaughlin in fine creative form, they fashioned several openings. The crucial strike came after a period of frantic Hibs assault, Toshack poking the ball forward to Heighway, then racing on to lose his marker and meet the Irishman's inch-perfect cross with his trusty forehead.

Round 3 - 2nd leg
22 December 1970

LIVERPOOL 2
Heighway 23; Boersma 50

HIBERNIAN 0
H-T 1-0. Crowd 37,815

CLEMENCE
LAWLER
EVANS R
SMITH
LLOYD
HUGHES
HALL
McLAUGHLIN
HEIGHWAY
BOERSMA
CALLAGHAN

A Steve Heighway goal of the highest quality quelled any flickering hopes of a Hibs recovery. One down from the first leg, the men from Easter Road pushed forward boldly during the early stages, but then the Irishman pounced. After winning possession near half-way, he sped towards goal, nipping between two converging defenders before steering the ball past the advancing Baines. The Reds rubbed in their supe-riority with a fortunate goal on the hour, Boersma dispatching a deep cross from the right that eluded the Scottish 'keeper and dropped into the net. Thereafter Stanton, Hibs' inspirational skipper, refused to let his side capitulate but could do nothing to prevent Liverpool cruising into the quarter-finals.

Liverpool won 3-0 on aggregate.

Round 2 - 2nd leg
4 November 1970

DINAMO BUCHAREST 1
Salceanu 31

LIVERPOOL 1
Boersma 47
H-T 1-0. Crowd 45,000

CLEMENCE
LAWLER
SMITH
LLOYD
LINDSAY
HUGHES
McLAUGHLIN
HALL
EVANS, A (BOERSMA)
HEIGHWAY
THOMPSON

Liverpool moved confidently into the third round, the Romanians never really threatening to loosen the Reds' stranglehold on the tie, despite taking a second-leg lead. Dinamo went ahead when Salceanu drifted beyond the visitors' square back line, tempted Clemence to commit himself and slipped the ball past him. Shankly's men responded soon after the interval when a Lindsay centre from the left flank bounced free for Boersma, who had been brought on as a substitute for the injured Evans, to net with ease. Liverpool's delight at their triumph was tempered by the news that top-scorer Evans, whose knee had been jolted on the rock-hard surface, would need a cartilage operation.

Liverpool won 4-1 on aggregate.

Round 3 - 1st leg
9 December 1970

HIBERNIAN 0

LIVERPOOL 1
Toshack 75
H-T 0-0. Crowd 30,296

CLEMENCE
LAWLER
LINDSAY (ROSS)
SMITH
LLOYD
HUGHES
HALL
McLAUGHLIN
HEIGHWAY
TOSHACK
THOMPSON

Liverpool met a determined Scottish

Round 4 - 1st leg
10 March 1971

LIVERPOOL 3

Evans, A 30, 49, 73

BAYERN MUNICH 0

H-T 1-0. Crowd 45,616

| CLEMENCE |
| LAWLER |
| LINDSAY |
| SMITH |
| LLOYD |
| HUGHES |
| BOERSMA |
| EVANS, A |
| HEIGHWAY |
| TOSHACK |
| HALL |

Liverpool annihilated a star-packed German side, who were subjected to constant pressure on one of Anfield's most memorable nights. Certainly, it will never be forgotten by young marksman Evans, who plundered a hat-trick in his first full match after a cartilage operation. Most spectacular of his strikes was the first, which came as just reward for the Reds' early dominance. Heighway outpaced two defenders on the left, then crossed to Evans, who made time and space with a deft first touch before picking his spot from just inside the area. For his second, he hooked a Lawler header past the plunging Maier from five yards, then earned custody of the match ball by slotting home after the 'keeper had parried a low shot from Hughes. There were many more near misses and Lawler had a 'goal' disallowed before the final whistle put Bayern out of their misery.

Alun Evans beats Bayern 'keeper Sepp Maier for the second of his three strikes in the first leg at Anfield.

Round 4 - 2nd leg
24 March 1971

BAYERN MUNICH 1

Schneider 76

LIVERPOOL 1

Ross 74

H-T 0-0. Crowd 23,000

| CLEMENCE |
| LAWLER |
| LINDSAY |
| SMITH |
| LLOYD |
| HUGHES |
| CALLAGHAN |
| EVANS, A |
| ROSS |
| TOSHACK (THOMPSON) |
| McLAUGHLIN |

Liverpool were never in danger of surrendering their overwhelming first-leg advantage, although seeds of doubt might have been sown if Muller had not been guilty of a glaring miss after 15 minutes. He created the opportunity for himself, nipping between Lloyd and Smith, but then, with only Clemence to beat, scooped the ball over the bar from six yards. Realising the importance of denying Beckenbauer space, Shankly deployed Ross to mark the great man, and only once did he escape his 'jailer', forcing a fine save from Clemence. As the game wore on, with Bayern unable to make an impact, Ross found time to press forward himself and was on hand to round off a smart move, involving Hughes and Evans, by driving home from 20 yards. Two minutes later, Clemence tried to punch away a shot from Schneider, but the ball squirmed past him and over the line. By this stage, however, Bayern's cause was irrevocably lost.

Liverpool won 4-1 on aggregate.

What a sickener: after putting Leeds United under relentless pressure, Liverpool's guard dropped for a moment and Billy Bremner capitalised on a free header to score the decisive goal.

Semi-final - 1st leg
April 14, 1971

LIVERPOOL 0

LEEDS UNITED 1

Bremner 67

H-T 0-0. Crowd 52,577

| CLEMENCE |
| LAWLER |
| LINDSAY |
| SMITH |
| LLOYD |
| HUGHES |
| CALLAGHAN |
| EVANS, A |
| HEIGHWAY |
| TOSHACK |
| HALL |

One moment of slack marking cost Liverpool a crucial advantage in this most closely fought of contests. There was no shortage of red shirts in the penalty area when Giles curled in a free-kick from the left flank, but somehow Bremner found himself free near the angle of the six-yard box. Arching his back, the diminutive Scot made perfect contact to nod the ball out of Clemence's reach into the far corner of the net. It was a devastating blow to the Reds, who enjoyed territorial advantage throughout the match. Indeed, Leeds' only other worthwhile goal attempt had been a Madeley shot which Clemence pushed over the bar, while Liverpool saw several opportunities go begging. The most notable came shortly before the visitors' strike, when Sprake dropped a Toshack shot and Evans drove against the post from four yards. As time ticked by, there were chances for Hughes and Heighway, but Revie's men held firm.

Semi-final - 2nd leg
28 April 1971

LEEDS UNITED 0

LIVERPOOL 0

Crowd 40,462

| CLEMENCE |
| LAWLER |
| YEATS |
| SMITH |
| LLOYD |
| HUGHES |
| CALLAGHAN |
| THOMPSON |
| HEIGHWAY |
| TOSHACK |
| HALL |

If football matches were decided on points rather than goals then, once again, Liverpool might have shaded the verdict over the Yorkshiremen. Despite two remarkable saves by Clemence - from a Jones header in the first half and a Jordan flick near the end - the Reds created the most chances but were unable to convert them. Two efforts from Heighway brought the best out of Sprake, and another beat the Welsh custodian's dive only to fizz narrowly wide of the post. During the final quarter of an hour, so intense were Liverpool's efforts to equalise that the home team were camped in their own half. But despite the intelligent promptings of Hall, the incisiveness of Heighway and the more fitful but potentially lethal probings of Thompson, the white barrier held, and Shankly's side had lost to their deadly rivals.

Leeds United won 1-0 on aggregate.

European Cup Winners' Cup 1971/72

Round 1 - 1st leg
15 September 1971

SERVETTE GENEVA 2
Dorfel 25; Barriquand 47

LIVERPOOL 1
Lawler 81
H-T 1-0. Crowd 16,000

CLEMENCE
LAWLER
LINDSAY
ROSS
LLOYD
HUGHES
GRAHAM
HALL (THOMPSON)
HEIGHWAY
TOSHACK (EVANS, A)
CALLAGHAN

Appalling inaccuracy in front of goal condemned Liverpool to a stunning defeat in Geneva. The Reds had enough chances in the first 15 minutes alone to have secured a place in the next round, but the scoresheet remained blank and slowly the Swiss began to make their presence felt. Even so, it came as a shock when the home side took the lead, Marchi's shrewd pass setting up Dorfel. Heighway hit the bar from an acute angle, but still Liverpool could not reply, and early in the second half Servette doubled their lead when Barriquand converted a corner with a downward header. The visitors continued to struggle until Lawler restored a degree of respectability near the end, also from a corner.

Round 1 - 2nd leg
29 September 1971

LIVERPOOL 2
Hughes 27; Heighway 60

SERVETTE GENEVA 0
H-T 1-0. Crowd 38,591

CLEMENCE
LAWLER
LINDSAY
SMITH (ROSS)
LLOYD
HUGHES
KEEGAN (TOSHACK)
HALL
HEIGHWAY
GRAHAM
CALLAGHAN

Liverpool atoned for their aberration in Switzerland, but without a lot to spare. Servette had gained confidence from their unexpected first-leg victory and offered stolid resistance, although with the Reds swarming around their goal for almost the entire 90 minutes it seemed inconceivable that they could survive. Sadly for 'keeper Barlie, who had performed nobly to frustrate the home side's early attacks, it was his error that gave Liverpool their first and crucial goal, a shot from Hughes escaping his grasp and finding the net. Thus encouraged, the Reds pressed continuously, and it was fitting that the winner should fall to Heighway, who had tortured his opponents all evening. In the end his team were in command, but how the plucky Swiss had made them fight.
Liverpool won 3-2 on aggregate.

Round 2 - 1st leg
20 October 1971

LIVERPOOL 0

BAYERN MUNICH 0
Crowd 42,949

CLEMENCE
LAWLER
ROSS
SMITH
LLOYD
HUGHES
KEEGAN
EVANS, A
HEIGHWAY
HALL (THOMPSON)
CALLAGHAN

On their previous visit to Anfield, Bayern had been whipped soundly; this time they gave Liverpool no chance to repeat the treatment. From first whistle to last, the Germans packed their defence, often drawing all 11 players back to their 18-yard line. Even Europe's most feared striker, Muller, was employed as an extra midfield man, and a good job he made of it, too. However, it was incongruous to see a side boasting the likes of 'Der Bomber' and Beckenbauer so intimidated by the opposition as to be wholly negative, rarely pursuing the ball into the Reds' half. Heighway, Keegan and Evans - of whom Bayern were particularly wary - strove manfully but could not penetrate the wall. Even if they glimpsed a gap, 'keeper Maier was ever capable of plugging it. Rarely can the Kop have endured such total frustration.

Uli Hoeness shoots past the despairing Ian Ross and Larry Lloyd to net Bayern's third goal in Munich.

Round 2 - 2nd leg
3 November 1971

BAYERN MUNICH 3
Muller 25, 27; Hoeness 58

LIVERPOOL 1
Evans, A 37
H-T 2-1. Crowd 40,000.

CLEMENCE
LAWLER
ROSS
SMITH
LLOYD
HUGHES
CALLAGHAN
EVANS, A
HEIGHWAY
KEEGAN
GRAHAM

Make no bones about it, Liverpool were on the wrong end of a hiding, torn apart by the attacking play of a side whose tactics were unrecognisable from those of the first leg. The Germans scored three, but deserved to double their tally. Muller began the demolition job with two goals in two minutes. First he headed a cross from the elusive Hoeness against the bar and rammed the rebound into the net; then, presented with a lucky chance when a clearance was deflected into his path, he smashed the ball home from 15 yards. Bayern continued to find holes in the Reds' defence and seven minutes later Muller hit the post, but soon the best goal of the night was scored by the visitors. After Keegan tried an overhead kick, the ball reached Evans on the edge of the area; facing away from goal, he controlled it on his body, spun like a top and bulged the top corner of the net with a fierce shot. Hoeness completed Liverpool's misery with a rising drive after outpacing Ross.

Bayern Munich won 3-1 on aggregate.

59

Chapter Five

SAVOURING THE MOMENT

T HE sight of Bill Shankly, pacing the touchline in agitation and willing the referee to blow the final whistle some ten minutes early, said it all. After nine years of trying, Liverpool - a goal up on aggregate against Borussia Moenchengladbach in the second leg of the 1973 UEFA Cup Final - were on the verge of their first European triumph. Normally, no matter how high the stakes, Bill could contain himself, more or less. He might be bubbling with excitement and elation, the staccato one-liners perhaps laced more liberally than ever with mischief or venom, but he remained, in essence, a canny, self-possessed general surveying the battlefield. But that night in the compact German stadium, with Borussia having reduced the Reds' three-goal first-leg lead to a mere one, the defences were down and the apprehension was palpable as he took to his feet.

The seconds dragged as he coaxed his weary players, lifting them at the last, then turned to talk abstractedly to supporters behind the wire fence that ringed the pitch. Maybe, in that nerve-shredding hiatus between hope and fulfilment, Shanks thought fleetingly of the long and tortuous road that had brought him to the threshold of glory; of the depressed Second Division outfit he had inherited in 1959, of the subsequent domestic triumphs, and of the moments of glee and frustration that had dotted earlier Continental campaigns. Or perhaps he thought no more than 'Why doesn't that man blow his bloody whistle?'

Either way, when the moment of release duly came, he gave an unrestrained show of emotion that was as moving as it was unusual. Certainly, he was invariably vociferous, yet there remained an impression that his deepest feelings were not for public consumption. But now he was utterly, openly ecstatic, hugging his players and leading them towards their joyful fans. Photographer Steve Hale recalls: 'He went bananas. He had hold of the Cup and he took it to the travelling supporters. It was important to him that the players appreciated what the night had meant to all those who had made the journey to Germany. Bill was savouring the moment, he didn't want to leave.'

The great man's odyssey had reached its memorable climax after a hard-fought campaign which had begun at Anfield against one of the most evocative names in European football. Eintracht Frankfurt owed their eminence not so much to weight of achievement as to their supporting role in one match of such magnificence that more than three decades later it is hailed still, in many quarters, as the finest exhibition of football ever staged. The game in question, of course, was the 1960 European Cup Final at Hampden Park, in which the Germans were eclipsed 7-3 by Real Madrid at their sublime, irresistible peak. Despite the margin of defeat, Eintracht had proved they were a fine team in their own right, and if the side that faced Liverpool 12 years later were not quite of equal calibre, they were no pushover either. Perhaps a little rusty, as it was their first game that term - the start of their domestic season having been delayed by the Munich Olympics - the Germans attempted to emulate the defensive tactics that had borne fruit for Bayern in 1971, but could not prevent the Reds seizing a two-goal home advantage. Then, on one of Europe's truest playing surfaces, Tommy Smith and his fellow defenders weathered a furious onslaught in a goalless second leg.

Next came AEK Athens, whom Liverpool had no intention of underestimating. Clearly, in the light of Everton's elimination from the European Cup by Panathinaikos in 1971, Greek football was a growing force. As it turned out there was little to fear, a 6-1 aggregate victory

Between hope and fulfilment: Bill Shankly on the way to his dugout seat at half-time in the second leg of the UEFA Cup Final against Borussia Moenchengladbach. With ten minutes of the game left and the Reds' three-goal lead having been cut to one, he paced the touchline in agitation. Soon would come blessed release and that longed-for first European triumph.

Peter Cormack appears in danger of decapitation as an Eintracht Frankfurt defender lunges for the ball at Anfield. The constructive Scot supplied the cross for Emlyn Hughes to head the Reds' second goal.

being attained through three goals in either leg, but it was never a doddle. Particularly in Athens - on a bumpy pitch, in searing heat, in front of a vehemently partisan home crowd - the Reds were forced to work their passage. In the intriguingly named North Philadelphia Stadium, they were on the receiving end of constant dirty tricks - sly elbow-digs, hair-pulling and the like - but in the victorious circumstances were content to put it all down to experience. To give the enthusiastic Athenian fans their due, by the end they were won over by Liverpool's excellence and lined the streets to clap the visitors' coach on its way. Emlyn Hughes had particular reason for satisfaction, his dynamic all-round display and two cracking goals underlining the reasons for his recent England recall.

The Reds' next two destinations could hardly have offered greater atmospheric contrast to the bright Mediterranean world inhabited by AEK. First came Dynamo Berlin, whose headquarters were in the east of that tragically divided city. Ian Callaghan remembers: 'Going through the Berlin Wall made a huge impression on me. The passport checks always seemed to take an eternity, and soldiers would come on to the coach to look around. The hotels were grey and so were the cities. We didn't walk out very much, there was no incentive. The sooner we were on our way home, the better we liked it.' Football-wise, however, the Berlin expedition served its purpose, the 0-0 draw setting up a comfortable Anfield win in which a skinny - some said scrawny - youngster named Phil Thompson made his senior debut in midfield. He would have a telling part to play in the club's European story, though sadly the same was not to be true of another blond hopeful, striker Jack Whitham, who made his comeback as substitute after a series of injuries. The £57,000 recruit from Sheffield Wednesday, once seen as a long-term successor to Roger Hunt, was never to regain optimum fitness and drifted out of the League via Cardiff City and Reading.

After Berlin came another Dynamo, this time the Dresden variety, who played well enough in both matches to justify their quarter-final place. An enduring memory of the 2-0 first-leg victory on Merseyside was provided by Brian Hall's opener, which was as comical as it was crucial, at least according to his irreverent team-mates. They were tickled that the tiny Glaswegian's first European goal should come via his head, and congratulations for his expert near-poster were diluted in a gale of merriment. Back behind the Iron Curtain, Liverpool were awesomely efficient, inflicting Dresden's first home defeat for several years as they stretched the aggregate triumph to three goals.

This time the drabness of Eastern bloc life made an indelible impression on Tommy Smith: 'It was so grim. There were women brushing the streets, and they looked so miserable. We went round several department stores but there was nothing to buy, so our £2 a day spending money was of little use for anything except playing cards. Actually we did find one other use for it. We were walking round the shops with one of our directors and he went to the loo; there was no toilet paper so we gave him some of our money to use instead. That's how much good it was to us over there!'

The defeat of Dresden earned Liverpool a last-four clash with Spurs - holders of the trophy, having overcome Wolves in the 1972 final - and a thrilling encounter it turned out to be. In both legs the home side mounted fierce pressure, and four goals were shared over the two matches. The Reds went through, courtesy of Steve Heighway's away strike, a bitterly disappointing way for the North Londoners to surrender their silverware, though they managed to maintain their proud record of never losing a European match at White Hart Lane.

By the time Borussia Moenchengladbach arrived at Anfield for the first chapter of what was to prove an epic final, Liverpool were in the enviable position of being newly-crowned League Champions. Certainly, they were desperate for their first European honour, but the knowledge that they had the top domestic prize safely in the bag meant that the success of their season did not hinge on the UEFA Cup.

It had rained heavily for much of the week before the match, but Austrian referee Erich Linemayr ruled that conditions were playable. However, soon after kick-off the downpour intensified, and with the players unable to pass the ball - the best they could do was scoop it from puddle to puddle - the game was abandoned on 27 minutes. When asked his opinion by the anxious official, Shanks ventured that the pitch was not too bad - he didn't want to convey the impression that he was keen to call it off. In fact, shrewd opportunist that he was, the Liverpool boss was secretly gleeful at the abandonment. Through the wall of water that enveloped the action, he had spotted a weakness in the Germans' defence that he could now exploit. Sure enough, when he announced his side for the next night's restart, the name of midfielder Brian Hall was replaced by that of towering target-man John Toshack, who had been alternately injured and out of favour for the past two months. Gunter Netzer, the gifted Borussia play-maker who now lined up at the back, might be a master with the ball at his size-12 feet, but in the air he was distinctly suspect. In fact, Shanks was rather miffed that his scouts had not identified the flaw during their customary spying missions.

Enter Tosh, to devastating effect. His aerial dominance set up two first-half goals for Kevin Keegan, then Larry Lloyd tied up a swingeing victory with a thumping header which further emphasised the Achilles' heel of Borussia. As if more drama were needed, both sides missed a penalty. Having secured such an emphatic advantage through the inspired application of sheer nous, Bill would not have been human had he not felt that the hardest part of the job was done. But if he did, he was in for a rude awakening. In the second leg the Germans came out fighting, overrunning the Reds with a stunning first-half display that yielded two fine goals to Jupp Heynckes as a thunderstorm raged. This time Netzer, his brilliant footballing brain in overdrive, was inspirational, and with Danner and Wimmer proving able lieutenants, a shock turnaround seemed possible. Yet Liverpool wouldn't capitulate - it just wasn't in their nature - and during the interval Shanks, who

Creative leanings: Steve Heighway strives for a break-through against Dynamo Berlin at Anfield. He was successful, too, paving the way for Phil Boersma to score the first goal, then volleying the second himself.

surely must have been entertaining private doubts, announced blithely that Borussia had shot their bolt. They were, he declared, a spent force. For his players it must have been tempting to put it down as another piece of rhetoric - after all, some of them remembered his summing up of the Ajax débâcle - but, astonishingly, the man was right. Early in the second period it became clear that the hosts' gargantuan initial effort had left them physically and mentally drained. Where they had been vibrant, now they were wan, and Liverpool, looking ever stronger in their 64th game of the season, regained their composure to become the first Englishmen to record a League and European double.

Given the importance of the occasion, the presentation was less than impressive. A small table was carried on to the pitch and the Cup and medals were doled out in a ceremony that was little more than perfunctory. But if the pomp of Wembley was lacking, the elation was as unconfined as anything seen in England's premier stadium. As Tommy Smith recalls: 'It was fantastic. On a personal level, it was a very special feeling to be the first Liverpool captain to pick up a European trophy. I saw it as the crowning achievement of my best season to date. I felt that the older I got, the better player I became; it was a case of my brain taking over from my feet.'

So bulky was the UEFA Cup - which Liverpool had picked up from Tottenham and brought over with them on their plane - that Tommy was hard-pushed to carry it around the pitch for the lap of honour, especially after such a tiring game. 'It had a stone base and it was murder to lift. Nobody wanted to drink out of it. I can remember running along, clutching this huge cup, with a fan hanging round my neck. He was a big, fat lad and the weight of him was dragging me down. I felt like clouting him!'

Yet the night belonged to Bill Shankly, more than anyone else. For the second time since arriving at Liverpool, he had built a side of outstanding quality; now, with the benefit of so much priceless overseas experience, surely there was no limit to what could be achieved.

Now the biggest prize of all, the European Cup, beckoned once again, and the feeling was abroad at Anfield that the time was ripe to claim it. However, the campaign got off to a jittery start in the unlikely surroundings of Luxembourg, hardly a traditional stronghold of football. Jeunesse d'Esch, playing hosts for the first leg, approached their task with cheerful fatalism, clearly expecting a drubbing but oozing determination to die gloriously. In the event, they exceeded their own wildest expectations, pinching a 1-1 home draw thanks to a late goal from their record signing, Dussier, who had cost them all of £600! Sometimes such results are surrounded by extenuating circumstances - poor pitch, extremes of weather, unhelpful natives, or whatever - but this time there was no excuse; the pitch was immaculate, the climate clement, all facilities impeccable and the Luxembourgers could not have been more hospitable. It was simply a bad day at the office, though there was no way Bill Shankly could be philosophical after such a display. As his team readied themselves for the journey home, he stalked around, chuntering ominously, finally venting his spleen on several players who were paying minute attention to their hair in the dressing-room mirror. 'Never mind your bloody hair,' he exploded. 'It's time you got your game together. THEN you can worry about your hair.'

Anfield or paddy field? Liverpool's UEFA Cup Final first-leg clash with Borussia Moenchengladbach is abandoned in a downpour. The action had lasted only 27 minutes, but that was long enough for Bill Shankly to spot the aerial weakness of the German defence. Accordingly, John Toshack was called up for the next night's restart, with devastating results.

The old one-two: John Toshack *(left)* and Kevin Keegan have broken through against Borussia in the Anfield leg of the UEFA Cup Final. The big Welshman nodded the ball across the penalty area and his diminutive partner dived full length to head into the corner of the net from 12 yards.

Amazingly, there was further frustration to come in the second leg, the Jeunesse defence remaining unbreached until after the break, and then it took a freak own-goal to break the deadlock. By the end the Reds had doubled their lead, but the plucky visitors could leave with their heads held high and the Kop, to their credit, gave them an ovation. The only sour note was struck when Jeunesse goalkeeper Rene Hoffman was hit in the neck by a fizzing firework. It was the sort of incident which might have caused the tie to be replayed, but as their man was uninjured the sporting Luxembourgers declined to make an official complaint.

Now Liverpool faced opponents of a far more exalted order. Red Star Belgrade were one of the great Continental clubs, with a glorious European tradition stretching back to the 1950s. Their current coach was the gifted and forthright Miljan Miljanic, later to rebuild Real Madrid and, reportedly, come close to joining Arsenal. He and Bill Shankly exhibited a deep mutual respect based not only on the international language of football but also a shared penchant for verbal sparring. Off the field, the honours were even; on it, unfortunately, the Yugoslavians seized the ascendancy in their home leg and never relinquished it. If anything, the Merseysiders were a trifle lucky to return from Belgrade with no more than a one-goal deficit - they had that extraordinarily prolific full-back, Chris Lawler, to thank for a late strike that kept their hopes alive - and clearly needed a heroic performance at Anfield if they were to progress.

After the first game, Shanks conceded grudgingly: 'Aye, they were not a bad side,' but couldn't resist the rider, 'though the Liverpool fans would never pay to watch that stuff.' He was referring to Red Star's patient method of pushing the ball around with studied delibera-

Bill's bombshell: the Liverpool manager announces his resignation at a hushed press conference in the summer of 1974. His decision shook the soccer world to its foundations, with not even his players or training staff having an inkling of his impending departure. His side had just won the FA Cup but he was, he said, 'tired from all the years'.

tion for long periods before breaking into sudden, incisive action, a mode of play the Kopites were about to witness at its destructive best. Miljanic flew in, pledging to attack, but Shanks surmised that his rival was bluffing and would opt for a rearguard action. In fact, the Yugoslavians were clinically competent at both ends of the pitch to claim a second 2-1 victory, the Reds once again reliant on Lawler to find the net. 'Super Slavs Steal the Show' screamed the headlines, which just about summed up what had happened, but Bill, smarting from the knockout, was less magnanimous: 'We created more chances than in our last four League games put together, and they were all close in,' he said, but could not mask the fact that Belgrade had deserved their victory.

No one knew it at the time, but the sorriest aspect of elimination was that Shanks would never again lead the club into European competition. After a season of gruelling, relentless League combat had ended with Liverpool relinquishing their title to Don Revie's Leeds, a 3-0 Wembley demolition job on Newcastle took the FA Cup to Anfield for the second time. That summer, with the supporters still on a high and speculating eagerly on what they saw as inevitable conquests to come, Bill shocked the soccer world to the core by announcing his retirement. He was 60 and, as he put it so poignantly, tired from all the years. His players and training staff simply could not take it in; they had not had the slightest inkling of their leader's intention when they had parted in May for the close-season break.

When the news had sunk in, the tributes flowed, warm and often emotional, from the hearts of some of the most genuine men in the game. Now, some 27 years later and with Bill in his grave for two decades, recollections of the most influential figure Liverpool FC has ever known are no less vivid or sincere. Ron Moran, not one for flowery phrases but as shrewd and true a football man as ever lived, puts it simply: 'Bill set the base for everything Liverpool have today. I learned more in my first three months under him than in the rest of my career. He was not a great tactician, but a great motivator who made the game simple. He had to have players with the right character, and he got rid of the ones who didn't measure up to his demands. And, of course, Bill Shankly lived for football.'

Few, if any, were closer to Shanks than Ron Yeats, now the club's chief scout, but back in 1961 the rock around whom the Reds' defence was to be remoulded. The manager called Ron his 'colossus', introducing him to the press with a delighted swagger and urging the assembled scribes to 'take a walk around my centre-half.' The two men went through plenty together, and an affectionate grin softens Yeats' rugged features as he remembers. 'He took Liverpool from nothing, and perhaps more difficult, he kept the club on the rails. A lot of clubs come up but they don't manage to keep it going. Bill Shankly laid the foundations right, and he made sure everyone at Anfield knew how to carry it on.'

Ron recalls that 'the boss' had a special regard for Europe. 'He loved it, relished the new test it presented. He always wanted to pit his wits against the great managers and the best coaches in the world. He loved to talk, and many of the European pressmen must have thought he was a head-case. They didn't understand half of what he was saying, but despite that they gave him a great name.'

Despite his enthusiasm for their competition, Bill would never quite trust the Continentals, and Ron describes his attitude, politely, as a bit dogmatic: 'He thought they were always trying to get some advantage over him. Even if they offered us their training ground, he would think there must be an ulterior motive. A lot of it stemmed from the experience with Inter Milan in 1965. He was determined not to be conned again.'

Shanks's phenomenal memory was another characteristic to make a lasting impression on Ron. 'It was photographic. When we were discussing a game we had just played, he would recall exactly what happened in every incident. For example, he would know where I had been standing for every corner, even though I probably wouldn't remember myself! He was a great one for rubbing in our superiority when we got in front, too. He wanted us to get as many fours and fives as possible. He would tell us "The more we score, the more other teams will read about it and worry. Oh yes, they'll fear Liverpool."

'Bill was a great believer in US. He would watch the top players from other teams, then dismiss them in a couple of words, building us up all the time. Because of this, we never knew, really, how good the opposition were until we saw for ourselves what they could do. Even then, according to the boss, all our goals were marvellous, theirs were fluky or offside. Sometimes he urged me to tell the opposing centre-forward that his team was lucky to be on the same pitch as Liverpool. I would reply that I couldn't do it, the man might get a hat-trick. Bill came back with: "Oh well, leave it till the last minute, then."'

To offer a final, telling image, no one is better qualified than Ian Callaghan, who was at Anfield throughout the entire Shankly era: 'He was very much a man of the people, always at home with the fans. I shall never forget him, at some railway station in London, being approached by a Liverpudlian lad who was stranded without cash. Bill reached into his own pocket, gave the boy his fare and told him to be more careful next time. You see, he really did care. What he would have made of the modern football scene, where money and greed seem to count for so much, I just don't know.' As Ian, a down-to-earth soul not prone to displays of sentiment, told the story, there was a faraway look in his eyes. He had captured unerringly the essence of a truly special person, and was moved by his memories. Let no one ever doubt the greatness of Bill Shankly, the man who made Liverpool.

Below: **Not this time: Chris Lawler, who scored in both legs against Red Star Belgrade, is beaten to the ball by Yugoslav goalkeeper Petrovic. Red Star won 4-2 on aggregate and in handsome style, drawing widespread praise from around the world, although eliciting only grudging acknowledgement from a certain Mr Shankly.**

Round 1 - 1st leg
12 September 1972

LIVERPOOL 2
Keegan 12; Hughes 75

EINTRACHT FRANKFURT 0

H-T 1-0. Crowd 33,380

| CLEMENCE |
| LAWLER |
| LINDSAY |
| SMITH |
| LLOYD |
| HUGHES |
| KEEGAN |
| CORMACK |
| HEIGHWAY |
| TOSHACK |
| CALLAGHAN |

The result was satisfactory but Liverpool's performance was disappointing against a workmanlike German side who opted for a policy of containment. The Kop settled back for a feast after the Reds' early goal - disputed by Eintracht who claimed, with apparent justification, that Keegan was yards offside when he was sent clear by Hughes - but their favourites displayed meagre inventiveness throughout the major part of a dull encounter. The pattern did not change until the visitors, who were playing their first competitive match of the season, tired towards the end. Suddenly Liverpool began to create chances, and it was no surprise when Hughes, unchallenged at the far post, headed home a Cormack cross. That was the signal for a frantic attacking burst by the Reds, but a clutch of openings went begging in the final minutes.

Round 1 - 2nd leg
26 September 1972

EINTRACHT FRANKFURT 0

LIVERPOOL 0

Crowd 20,000

| CLEMENCE |
| LAWLER |
| LINDSAY |
| SMITH (STORTON) |
| LLOYD |
| HUGHES |
| KEEGAN (HALL) |
| CORMACK |
| HEIGHWAY |
| BOERSMA |
| CALLAGHAN |

This was one goalless draw that did not lack excitement. After a steady opening, in which Liverpool appeared capable of preserving their two-goal first-leg lead with ease, Eintracht stepped up the pace to rousing effect. In frantic spells on either side of the interval, the Reds found themselves under siege, and they rose to the challenge with insatiable spirit. The whole defence could be proud of its contribution, but two figures stood out; 'keeper Ray Clemence, dealing brilliantly with a bombardment of shots and crosses, underlined his burgeoning claim for full international recognition, and young Trevor Storton, yet to start a League game, gave sterling service at the heart of the rearguard. Towards the end, with the Germans desperate, Cormack and Heighway might have scored on the break, but by then the spoils were safe.

Liverpool won 2-0 on aggregate.

Round 2 - 1st leg
24 October 1972

LIVERPOOL 3
Boersma 9; Cormack 28; Smith (pen) 78

AEK ATHENS 0

H-T 2-0. Crowd 31,906

| CLEMENCE |
| LAWLER |
| LINDSAY |
| SMITH |
| LLOYD |
| HUGHES (THOMPSON, PHIL) |
| KEEGAN |
| CORMACK |
| HEIGHWAY |
| BOERSMA (HALL) |
| CALLAGHAN |

Quite simply, Liverpool were too good for their Greek opponents. From the early moment when Heighway drilled the ball low across the penalty area for Boersma to open the scoring, it was inconceivable that AEK could escape a thrashing. Indeed, if the Reds had not been afflicted by their perennial malaise - missing chances - their victory must have assumed immense proportions. Cormack's strike, a venomous drive that 'keeper Errea reached but could not prevent from crossing the line, threatened to open the floodgates, but the home side did not add to their tally until near the end, Smith converting a penalty after Keegan had been felled. Only twice did the visitors threaten to reply, Dandelis miskicking when well placed, and Papaionannou testing Clemence with a splendid header.

Round 2 - 2nd leg
7 November 1972

AEK ATHENS 1
Nikolaidis (pen) 35

LIVERPOOL 3
Hughes 17, 44; Boersma 87
H-T 1-2. Crowd 25,000

| CLEMENCE |
| LAWLER |
| LINDSAY |
| SMITH |
| LLOYD |
| HUGHES |
| KEEGAN |
| CORMACK |
| HEIGHWAY (BOERSMA) |
| TOSHACK |
| CALLAGHAN |

For ten minutes, AEK set about Liverpool as though they believed that pulling back a three-goal deficit was not beyond them. Indeed, as the Reds struggled to adjust to the uneven pitch and gusting wind, the Greeks might have grabbed the lead, Hughes clearing off the line in the first minute and Clemence being forced to make two fine saves. Soon, though, the visitors settled to their customary impressive rhythm, and underlined their authority when a Hughes 30-yarder cannoned into the net via both crossbar and post. Nikolaidis equalised from the spot after Hughes had handled, but it was not long before the England man (what an eventful match he had) plundered his second, finishing calmly after a surging run and clever one-two with Keegan. Liverpool's third, tucked away by Boersma near the end, was also set up by Keegan.

Liverpool won 6-1 on aggregate.

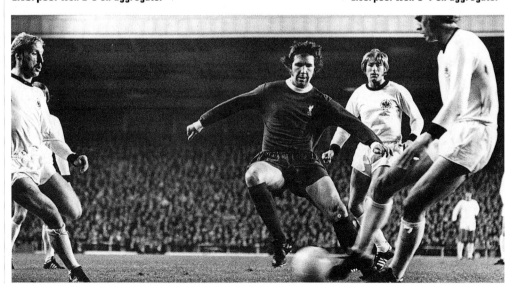

Chris Lawler puts pressure on the Eintracht defence at Anfield. Incredibly, he scored more European goals than either Ian St John or Kenny Dalglish, and only seven Reds have exceeded his total of 11. Five of them - Case, Keegan, McDermott, Neal and Ray Kennedy - pipped him by just one, while Hunt (17) and Rush (19) are out on their own.

Peter Cormack, reckoned by some to be Liverpool's most naturally gifted player of the mid 1970s, scores with a powerful drive against AEK Athens at Anfield. Eventually he lost his place following a bout of cartilage trouble and departed to Bristol City.

Round 3 - 1st leg
29 November 1972

DYNAMO BERLIN 0

LIVERPOOL 0

Crowd 20,000

CLEMENCE
LAWLER
LINDSAY
STORTON
LLOYD
HUGHES
KEEGAN (HALL)
CORMACK
HEIGHWAY
TOSHACK
CALLAGHAN

Throughout a distinctly drab contest, Liverpool yielded territorial advantage to their hosts but never looked likely to concede a goal. The Berliners gave little hint of the imagination necessary to break down the Reds' efficient defence - in which Lindsay and Storton excelled - and with the likes of Keegan and Heighway being shackled effectively, the outcome was stalemate. Indeed, 18 of the game's 50 free-kicks were offside decisions given against the visitors, a reflection of the entertainment level on offer. Dynamo goalkeeper Lihsa was not called upon to make one save, and Liverpool's Clemence was barely more active. For Shankly's men, however, the result offered a stable platform for an all-out assault at Anfield.

Round 3 - 2nd leg
13 December 1972

LIVERPOOL 3
Boersma 1; Heighway 24; Toshack 56

DYNAMO BERLIN 1
Netz 7
H-T 2-1. Crowd 34,140

CLEMENCE
LAWLER
LINDSAY
THOMPSON, PHIL
LLOYD
HUGHES
BOERSMA
CORMACK
HEIGHWAY
TOSHACK (WHITHAM)
CALLAGHAN

It took Liverpool a mere 60 seconds to dim the memory of the arid first leg in East Germany. Heighway hared down the left flank, cut inside past two defenders and shot so powerfully that Lihsa could only push the ball to the feet of Boersma, who netted with alacrity. However, the Reds were to be disabused rapidly of any premature notions that the back of their task was broken. Dynamo broke swiftly from defence, and Schulenberg slipped past Lindsay to gift Netz with a simple equaliser. An away goal to the good, the Germans held the upper hand, but the Kop's dismay was brief. After Heighway restored Liverpool's lead with a sharp volley that took a wicked deflection off the hapless Brillat, the Merseysiders assumed control and their ascendancy was confirmed after the break when Toshack steered the ball home following a Cormack free-kick.

Liverpool won 3-1 On aggregate.

Clemence to the rescue: as Dynamo Berlin press for a second and potentially precious away goal at Anfield, Liverpool's goalkeeper dives to frustrate them. His team-mates - left to right are Lloyd, Cormack, Lawler and Thompson - look on with the utmost confidence.

Round 4 - 1st leg
7 March 1973

LIVERPOOL 2
Hall 25; Boersma 60

DYNAMO DRESDEN 0

H-T 1-0. Crowd 33,270

CLEMENCE
LAWLER
LINDSAY
SMITH
LLOYD
HUGHES
KEEGAN
HALL
BOERSMA
HEIGHWAY (TOSHACK)
CALLAGHAN

Liverpool forced an acceptable, if hardly comfortable lead against opponents who proved far more taxing than their namesakes from Berlin. Indeed, although the Reds were thoroughly worth their win, Dresden's speed on the counter-attack demonstrated that the second leg could not be viewed as a formality. Shankly's side went ahead following a typically incisive build-up, Heighway freeing Boersma on the right and little Hall nodding home the resultant cross at the near post. Provider turned scorer on the hour when Boersma intercepted a team-mate's off-target shot, rounded a defender and slammed the ball high into goal from ten yards. Hall, not a renowned marksman, came closest to increasing the margin of victory, having a shot kicked off the line and a header disallowed controversially for offside.

A rare occurrence: Brian Hall nods Liverpool into the lead at home to Dynamo Dresden.

Round 4 - 2nd leg
21 March 1973

DYNAMO DRESDEN 0

LIVERPOOL 1
Keegan 53
H-T 0-0. Crowd 35,000

CLEMENCE
LAWLER
LINDSAY
SMITH
LLOYD
HUGHES
KEEGAN (TOSHACK)
HALL
HEIGHWAY
CORMACK
CALLAGHAN

Liverpool gave one of the most convincing displays of their European travels to reach the last four, inflicting a second defeat on a talented side that had not lost all season in domestic competition. Forced to attack from the off, the Germans found themselves confronted by a solid Reds rearguard, a workaholic midfield quartet in which first-leg hero Hall was outstanding, and a menacing front pair who combined to devastating effect for the night's only goal. Receiving the ball near the centre spot, Keegan swept a perfect pass to Heighway on the left; the fleet-footed Irishman ran 40 yards along the touchline before crossing low for his sprinting partner to beat the advancing 'keeper with a sharp first-time shot. It was just reward for the effervescent Keegan, who had seen two first-half strikes ruled out. For their part, Dresden threatened only rarely, and by the end Liverpool were coasting.

Liverpool won 3-0 on aggregate.

Semi-final - 1st leg
10 April 1973

LIVERPOOL 1
Lindsay 27

TOTTENHAM HOTSPUR 0

H-T 1-0. Crowd 42,174

CLEMENCE
LAWLER
LINDSAY
SMITH
LLOYD
HUGHES
KEEGAN
CORMACK
HALL
HEIGHWAY (BOERSMA)
CALLAGHAN

Ninety minutes of frenzied attacking earned Liverpool only the most slender of leads against a star-studded Tottenham team capable of significantly more enterprise in the second leg. At Anfield, the North Londoners barely encroached into the Reds' half; they were too busy dealing with a fusillade of shots and headers that seemed certain to pay rich dividends for their hosts but which served only to incite the Kop to new heights of frustration. Even the sole successful strike had a feverish element about it, Smith's free-kick provoking a free-for-all scramble inside Spurs' six-yard box before Lindsay ended the confusion with a firm shot past a prone Jennings. Thereafter Hall hit the bar, several efforts were cleared off the line, and six minutes from time, with Keegan upended in the box, Liverpool's passionate appeals for a penalty were turned down. And so to White Hart Lane . . .

Kevin Keegan lurks as Spurs clear their lines at Anfield in the first leg of the UEFA Cup semi-final.

Double value: Steve Heighway *(bottom)* slips the ball past Pat Jennings to equalise on the night at White Hart Lane, and send Liverpool through on the away-goals rule.

Semi-final - 2nd leg
25 April 1973

TOTTENHAM HOTSPUR 2
Peters 48, 71

LIVERPOOL 1
Heighway 55
H-T 0-0. Crowd 46,919

| CLEMENCE |
| LAWLER |
| THOMPSON, PHIL |
| SMITH |
| LLOYD |
| HUGHES |
| KEEGAN |
| BOERSMA |
| HALL |
| HEIGHWAY |
| CALLAGHAN |

After Liverpool, against most expectations, had dominated a goalless first 45 minutes, Tottenham roused themselves in a pulsating second-half revival that stretched the Reds to the uttermost limit. The North Londoners' first blow fell just after the interval, the old fox Gilzean nodding on a Chivers throw for the unmarked Peters to nudge a simple goal. Yet when the visitors replied seven minutes later - Keegan winning a tussle with England before sliding the ball for Heighway to place his shot into an empty net - it seemed that the tie was dead. With the value of away goals doubled if the scores were level, Spurs needed two, a tall order against Liverpool's formidable defence. Nothing daunted, Bill Nicholson's men picked up the gauntlet; Peters rattled the crossbar, then set the scene for a frenetic finale by netting from a loose clearance. Over the remaining 20 minutes the Reds were subjected to blistering punishment, surviving several moments of panic, but none could deny that, over two legs, they deserved their triumph.

Aggregate 2-2. Liverpool won on away goal.

A majestic header by centre-half Larry Lloyd gives Liverpool a seemingly impregnable three-goal lead in the first leg of the UEFA Cup Final against Borussia Moenchengladbach. The Germans came back strongly on their own soil, however, and the Reds took the trophy by a single goal.

Final - 1st leg
10 May 1973

LIVERPOOL 3
Keegan 21, 33; Lloyd 62

BORUSSIA MOENCHENGLADBACH 0

H-T 2-0. Crowd 41,169

| CLEMENCE |
| LAWLER |
| LINDSAY |
| SMITH |
| LLOYD |
| HUGHES |
| KEEGAN |
| CORMACK |
| TOSHACK |
| HEIGHWAY (HALL) |
| CALLAGHAN |

Liverpool overwhelmed the sophisticated Germans - Gunter Netzer *et al.* - to place themselves convincingly on course to lift their first European trophy. Shankly's Reds displayed skill and passion in equally generous quantities to send the Anfield faithful wild with delight. The man who caught the eye most irresistibly was Keegan, who might have had a hat-trick in an action-packed 12-minute sequence midway through the first half. First, after Toshack had nodded across the goalmouth, he dived forward to head into the far corner of the net from 12 yards; then he saw his penalty kick, awarded for handball, saved by 'keeper Kleff; next he hit the target with a ten-yard volley, courtesy of another Toshack knockdown. Even then, the inspirational imp had not finished, taking the corner that enabled an unchallenged Lloyd to stretch Liverpool's lead to three with a powerful header. In between Borussia's Rupp had rapped the post, but the Germans' best chance fell to Heynckes from the penalty spot in the 65th minute. Crucially, Clemence dived to his right to push the ball clear, and the Reds could face the second leg in a truly commanding position.

Final - 2nd leg
23 May 1973

BORUSSIA MOENCHENGLADBACH 2
Heynckes 30, 39

LIVERPOOL 0

H-T 2-0. Crowd 35,000

| CLEMENCE |
| LAWLER |
| LINDSAY |
| SMITH |
| LLOYD |
| HUGHES |
| KEEGAN |
| CORMACK |
| HEIGHWAY (BOERSMA) |
| TOSHACK |
| CALLAGHAN |

The Reds survived a tumultuous bombardment from one of the world's finest sides to win the UEFA Cup. After such a stirring first-leg performance, it was difficult to imagine any team of Bill Shankly's wilting so close to ultimate victory, yet there were moments when the unthinkable seemed downright probable. Borussia had been expected to attack, but not with the waspish potency that brought two goals in the first half and might have produced more. Both strikes came from the irrepressible Heynckes, the first when he stabbed home from six yards after Rupp had surged to the byline, the second an exquisite curler from the left angle of the penalty box. At the interval, the hearts of Liverpool fans might have fluttered, but they need not have worried. The Germans appeared to have burnt themselves out, and, certainly for the final half-hour, were but a pale shadow of their earlier selves. During that time the Reds, who had never ceased to battle, grew in confidence and might have added to their overall lead. Even so, the final whistle was more than welcome.

Liverpool won 3-2 on aggregate.

Worth the effort: Larry Lloyd *(left)* and Tommy Smith, fresh from their stirring battle against a gallant Borussia Moenchengladbach, brandish the UEFA Cup.

Round 1 - 1st leg
19 September 1973

JEUNESSE D'ESCH 1
Dussier 88

LIVERPOOL 1
Hall 43
H-T 0-1. Crowd 5,000.

CLEMENCE
LAWLER
THOMPSON
SMITH
LLOYD
HUGHES
KEEGAN
HALL
HEIGHWAY
BOERSMA
CALLAGHAN

This was the night the football form-book was turned upside down. The amateurs from Luxembourg were no more accomplished than expected - they displayed plenty of guts but little technique - yet the mighty Reds could not put them to the sword. True, Liverpool dictated the play, but the goals that would have reflected their superiority would not come, even after Hall tucked away a rebound from a Heighway shot to give them the lead shortly before the break. The second half saw plenty of assaults on the Jeunesse goal - Smith, Lloyd and Hughes all brought fine saves from 'keeper Hoffman - but it was the home side who were to break through, Dussier tapping a late equaliser after a misunderstanding between Clemence and Thompson.

Round 1 - 2nd leg
3 October 1973

LIVERPOOL 2
Mond (og) 47; Toshack 56

JEUNESSE D'ESCH 0

H-T 0-0. Crowd 28,714

CLEMENCE
LAWLER (THOMPSON)
LINDSAY
SMITH
LLOYD
HUGHES
KEEGAN
HALL
HEIGHWAY
TOSHACK
CALLAGHAN

Liverpool's frustration at being unable to deal summarily with their humble opponents continued into the second leg. Throughout the first half the Reds piled into attack, yet somehow Jeunesse survived everything thrown at them, and when the inevitable breakthrough came it was down to sheer good fortune. Admittedly, after a series of near misses, it was high time the ball bounced kindly for the English champions; even so, it was difficult not to feel sorry for the Luxembourg defender, Mond, when he deflected a harmless effort from Hughes past his own 'keeper. Ten minutes later, Liverpool's dynamic midfielder shot more accurately, the overworked Hoffman could only parry it and Toshack followed up to put the result beyond doubt.

Liverpool won 3-1 on aggregate.

On the rebound: Jeunesse d'Esch goalkeeper Hoffman has parried a shot from Steve Heighway, only to see Brian Hall *(left)* pounce to squeeze the ball adroitly just inside a post.

Round 2 - 1st leg
24 October 1973

RED STAR BELGRADE 2
Jankovic 40; Bogicevic 47

LIVERPOOL 1
Lawler 72
H-T 1-0. Crowd 40,000

| CLEMENCE |
| LAWLER |
| LINDSAY |
| SMITH |
| LLOYD |
| HUGHES |
| KEEGAN |
| CORMACK |
| HEIGHWAY |
| TOSHACK |
| CALLAGHAN |

Red Star Belgrade presented Liverpool with opposition of the highest class. From the start the Yugoslavians played fast, accurate, attacking football that pinned the Merseysiders inside their own half, and it was entirely on merit that the home side seized the advantage with goals on either side of the break. Jankovic struck first with a devastating drive high into the far corner of the net from just outside the right corner of the penalty area. Then Bogicevic sprang the offside trap to meet a chip from Jovanovic - later to play briefly for Manchester United - with an eight-yard volley that gave Clemence no chance. Thus stung, Liverpool began to assert themselves, and reduced the arrears through a low, bobbling 20-yarder from Lawler. Having tasted blood, the visitors pushed forward, and a Toshack header nearly produced a late equaliser that would, in truth, have flattered the visitors. Now the tie was perfectly balanced for the return at Anfield.

With Chris Lawler's away goal featured on the cover of the programme, hopes were high in the Anfield camp as Liverpool readied themselves for the second leg against Red Star Belgrade. But Miljan Miljanic, the inspiring and forthright Yugoslavian coach, was destined to come out on top in his personal duel with his respected rival, Bill Shankly.

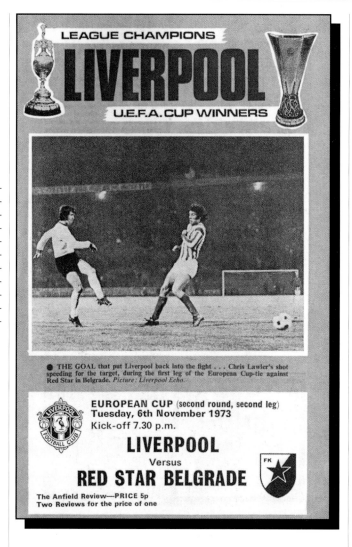

LEAGUE CHAMPIONS
LIVERPOOL
U.E.F.A. CUP WINNERS

● THE GOAL that put Liverpool back into the fight . . . Chris Lawler's shot speeding for the target, during the first leg of the European Cup-tie against Red Star in Belgrade. *Picture: Liverpool Echo.*

EUROPEAN CUP (second round, second leg)
Tuesday, 6th November 1973
Kick-off 7.30 p.m.

LIVERPOOL
Versus
RED STAR BELGRADE

The Anfield Review—PRICE 5p
Two Reviews for the price of one

Round 2 - 2nd leg
6 November 1973

LIVERPOOL 1
Lawler 84

RED STAR BELGRADE 2
Lazarevic 60; Jankovic 90
H-T 0-0. Crowd 41,774

| CLEMENCE |
| LAWLER |
| LINDSAY |
| THOMPSON |
| LLOYD |
| HUGHES |
| KEEGAN |
| McLAUGHLIN (HALL) |
| HEIGHWAY (BOERSMA) |
| TOSHACK |
| CALLAGHAN |

Liverpool's courage and commitment were never in question, they enjoyed the lion's share of possession and exerted most of the pressure, yet for all their huffing and puffing they were outdone by the calm, controlled football of a more sophisticated team. The first half passed with Shankly's men unable to dent the Yugoslavians' composure, and only the most rabid of Reds loyalists could cavil when Lazarevic put the visitors ahead on the night, deceiving Clemence with a dipping shot from 18 yards. Four minutes later, though, Liverpool might have had grounds for complaint when a Keegan effort appeared to cross the line before the 'keeper clawed it to safety, but the referee ruled 'no goal'. Home hopes were revived fleetingly when Lawler netted after controlling a back-headed knock-down from Toshack, but in the final minute Jankovic's fierce 20-yard free-kick gave Red Star the rare distinction of a second win over Liverpool in the space of a fortnight.

Red Star Belgrade won 4-2 on aggregate.

Chapter Six

OUT OF SHANKS'S SHADOW

LIVERPOOL embarked on a new era with an old, if somewhat reluctant hand at the helm. When Bob Paisley was offered the opportunity to step up from coach to manager, his reaction was characteristically modest, and he even attempted to persuade Bill Shankly to continue. But having accepted the job, the quiet, dry north-easterner was to prove in the most emphatic manner that he was no mere cipher. Certainly, he had spent the past decade and a half in the shadow of Shanks, but his contribution during that eventful period had been, perhaps, far more telling than many had realised. Now, in typically downbeat fashion, he would spend a season adapting to his changed role before showing that he could, despite his initial diffidence, make a fair fist of running a football club. The Reds went on to lift at least one major trophy in each of his remaining eight terms in charge as Bob became, indisputably, the most successful English manager of all time.

In fact, on the European front it looked as if a campaign of consolidation might be surplus to requirements, as Liverpool began their tilt at the Cup Winners' Cup with an 11-0 Anfield massacre of Stromsgodset Drammen. Nine Reds got their names on the scoresheet as the hapless, overawed Norwegians were overwhelmed by a withering non-stop onslaught. Goalkeeper Thun - who was to be immortalised in the inevitable, but undeniably apt newspaper headline 'Thun-derstruck' - was at fault with several first-half goals, but he rallied after the interval, making a series of thrilling saves that kept the Liverpool tally out of the teens. The second leg was meaningless, of course, though Kopites expecting a cricket score were disappointed as Stromsgodset cast off their inferiority complex and turned in a creditable performance. Thus the Reds, who could be expected to do no more than go through the motions, settled for a single-goal victory. The one man who did seem anxious to make an impact was Kevin Keegan, back in the side after a six-week suspension following his FA Charity Shield dismissal along with Leeds' Billy Bremner. Try as he might, though, Kevin could not get it right.

After such an undemanding opening, it was back to the real world as Liverpool drew Ferencvaros in the second round, a tie which offered a realistic opportunity to find out just how much they had learned from the sophisticated, restrained tactics of Red Star the previous term. It was the third time the Merseysiders and Magyars had met in European competition, with each having a victory to their credit; sadly for Paisley's Reds, their opponents were to take the lead in this particular private rubber. In retrospect, the tie slipped away in the first leg at Anfield, in which Liverpool outplayed Ferencvaros but were frustrated by a superb display by custodian Istvan Geczi. After Keegan, having rediscovered his touch, had secured a first-half lead, the Hungarian 'keeper - resplendent in a pair of Gordon Banks gloves - kept his team in contention through a combination of brilliant judgement and the sort of luck which saw one goal-bound shot rebound to safety off his back. Then, in the final minute, with the Reds consumed by frustration, Ferencvaros broke away to grab what proved a decisive equaliser.

The second leg was a scrappy, tetchy affair which ended goalless, the unadventurous hosts doing little more than protect the status quo, so the Reds went out on the away-goals rule. At the time, their manager was not amused: 'It was sickening to go out of the competition without losing a game, and to a side like this. We are far more advanced than

Ray Kennedy (left) homes in on the Ferencvaros goal but goalkeeper Istvan Geczi has the ball covered. After a 1-1 draw at Anfield, this tetchy, scrappy second leg finished goalless and the Reds went out on the away-goals rule, leaving a frustrated Bob Paisley to dub his opponents 'the worst Hungarian side we have met'.

Ferencvaros, who are the worst Hungarian side we have met. I thought the referee was atrocious; in fact, I've never seen three worse officials in my life.' Not unnaturally the Magyars' technical director Florian Albert, whose brilliant centre-forward displays had illuminated the 1966 World Cup, saw it differently and made a reasonable point: 'I thought Liverpool had precious few ideas up front,' he said.

The sorriest aspect of an unsatisfactory encounter involved Tommy Smith who, near the end of the match, was hit by a bottle thrown from the crowd. On impulse, he went down, pretending to be hurt, thinking that such an incident might bring about a replay. 'Later I saw the fellow who threw the bottle being beaten up by police. I had thought of having a go at him myself, but when I saw what the police could do, I thought I might be ill-advised to get involved.' Eventually Tommy - by nature an honest man, whose action was entirely out of character - was suspended by UEFA, who decided that he had feigned injury. As he puts it now: 'All in all, the whole thing was very ill-judged.'

Happily, better days were not far away, although Smith's offence meant he was banned from facing Hibernian in the opening UEFA Cup tie of 1975/76. This turned out to be a pulsating meeting between two teams who were both capable of attacking exhilaratingly. At Easter Road, with accomplished midfielder Pat Stanton - coveted by a bevy of English clubs - prompting intelligently, the Scots had the better of exchanges, and but for a Ray Clemence penalty save would have set off for the second leg with a formidable two-goal advantage. At Anfield, John Toshack's all-headed hat-trick proved decisive, though had Hibs managed one more strike they would have gone through on the away-goals rule. It was the first, but not the last time that season that the Reds would teeter on the brink.

Next stop was Spain's beautiful Basque country, where the opponents were the skilful Real Sociedad and football is followed with a fanaticism that rivals that of Merseyside. Indeed, the game is so integral a part of community life that a cannon on a hilltop overlooking Real's stadium is fired every time a goal is scored - one blast for a home success, two if the visitors find the net. It turned out to be a noisy night for the locals, with Liverpool switching on the style in a splendid 3-1 victory which was greeted by generous applause from knowledgeable Sociedad supporters, who knew a good team when they saw one. Two weeks later, the gunsmoke had cleared but the Spaniards remained in a haze as the Reds hit a vein of even more rampant form. Liverpool struck six times without reply as the Kop, perhaps cheekier and more relaxed than for any game since the meeting with Reykjavik 11 years earlier, took to cheering the despondent visitors. Young Brian Kettle, making his senior debut at full-back, caught the eye with a polished contribution, and there was understandable optimism that he had the right stuff for a long-term Anfield career; sadly, though, the competition proved too severe, and after trying his luck in the United States, Brian joined Wigan for a brief farewell to the professional game.

Liverpool's destination for the third round offered chilling contrast to the balminess of the Basque region. They were bound for the heart of Poland to take on Slask Wroclaw, just as winter was tightening its grip on Eastern Europe. On arrival at Poznan airport, the temperature stood at ten degrees below freezing, which was relatively mild, as they were to discover soon enough. There followed a daunting three-hour coach journey along slippery, tortuous country roads to reach the unprepossessing industrial city of Wroclaw. Tommy Smith remembers it as a miserable place: 'People were queueing for soup in the extreme cold, everyone walking the streets looked depressed; it was very harrowing. We felt sorry for those who had to live there.'

By the time of the match there were 15 degrees of frost and the pitch resembled a skating rink, but Liverpool were better equipped for the conditions than their hosts. The Reds had acquired a set of specially designed French boots that enabled them to stand up on the most treacherous of surfaces, a tribute to thorough preparation for all eventualities. In fact, despite the fancy footwear - which players were never allowed to take with them when they left the club; after use it was stashed away carefully in the Anfield bootroom - the ground was barely playable. Joe Fagan offered the eminently sensible advice: 'Just kick the ball the way you're facing, as long as it's not in your own net,' and Liverpool heeded it, notching a

Battering the Basques: Kevin Keegan gets in a cross against Real Sociedad at Anfield during the 6-0 thrashing of the despondent Spaniards. The Kopites were at their cheekiest and most relaxed, eventually cheering the visitors' every move in an echo of the Reykjavik encounter of 11 years earlier.

memorable 2-1 win in the process. A delighted Paisley described it as 'probably the most difficult match we have ever played in Europe.' Accordingly, the home leg was relatively comfortable, and will be remembered as the game in which Jimmy Case came of age. The 21-year-old Liverpudlian cracked a stirring hat-trick, prompting Horace Yates of the *Liverpool Echo* to describe him as potentially the greatest scoring opportunist Liverpool had unearthed since the glory days of Roger Hunt. Although the young man's career was to develop along rather different lines - he was to become an influential figure in midfield - it was difficult to disagree with the veteran sportswriter's summation at the time.

Old rivals awaited the Reds in the quarter-final, Dynamo Dresden, of whom they had disposed with a 3-0 aggregate victory at the same stage of the 1972/73 competition. This time, though, the margin of victory was tight, with the Reds' progress owing much to Ray Clemence's penalty save in the goalless first leg. Since taking over between the posts from Tommy Lawrence, Ray had become the complete all-round goalkeeper, and many would argue that he was superior to Peter Shilton, who denied him so many England caps. Whether in constant action or retaining his concentration during long periods of isolation, Ray was a man to count on, as Dresden discovered to their cost. On this occasion he dived to his right on the advice of scout Tom Saunders - who deserved full marks for doing his homework - but had the ball gone in, it would have represented an outrageous miscarriage of justice. Ray Kennedy was dumbstruck when the referee awarded a spot-kick after the aptly named Schmuck had appeared to take a dive. The Anfield leg was no formality, however, and even though Liverpool were by far the better team on the night, a 2-1 scoreline left no margin for error. Once again, another goal by the visitors would have meant elimination.

And so to one of the most memorable encounters in Liverpool's entire European experience; barring their way in the semi-final was the might of Barcelona, one of the most revered - and feared - names in world football. Of course, by now the Reds could scarcely be classified as bit players on the Continental stage, so the scene was set for a tumultuous confrontation. The match also renewed the Reds' acquaintance with a certain Johann Cruyff, who had never been handed his comeuppance for humbling the Merseysiders as an Ajax player nearly nine years earlier.

Jimmy Case, whose arrival as a substitute for John Toshack in the Anfield leg of the UEFA Cup Final clash with FC Bruges played a major part in transforming a game in which Liverpool had been floundering. Rampaging down the right flank, Jimmy unsettled the Belgian defence repeatedly, and also chipped in with the Reds' second goal.

Arriving for the first leg at the fabulous Nou Camp stadium was an event in itself. Walking out to inspect the pitch in that vast bowl, with tier after tier of roaring, gesticulating fans seeming to disappear into the clouds, might have instilled fear into the stoutest heart. But the Liverpool lads, as ever, had their feet on the ground; they knew that Barcelona consisted of just 11 players - human beings, not supermen - and no mere venue, not even a giant cauldron with seething sides, was going to put them off. Of course, they could not help being impressed, as Ian Callaghan explains: 'Everything at the Nou Camp is so opulent, on the grand scale; from entrance hall to trophy room, the place is magnificent. The fans, too, have to be seen to be believed. Spain is a passionate nation and this is reflected in its football.' Certainly the surroundings and the fervour, the sheer drama of it all, made an indelible impression on Kevin Keegan. It helped to open his eyes to all that was on offer if he took his talents abroad; post Barcelona, some say, he never again felt completely fulfilled in English football, and that night helped to sow the seeds for his eventual departure in 1977.

Before then, though, some stirring adventures were in store, starting with that first clash with the famous Spaniards. Tommy Smith recalls that Bob Paisley, for once, was showing nerves: 'He told us before the match that we had got nothing to worry about, but he was anxious all right. He was so much on edge that he got muddled in his team talk, telling us at one point that "Their left-back is not very fast, but he's quick!"'

When the action got under way, however, there was no doubt that Bob had prepared his side ideally. Kitted out in all white - to Barcelona fans, their appearance was irritatingly reminiscent of deadly domestic rivals, Real Madrid - Liverpool stroked the ball around with composure and took an early lead after Keegan freed John Toshack in the box. Rarely can there have been a more telling illustration of the near-telepathic understanding between the two men, and their hosts never recovered from the shock. Cruyff and his fellow Dutchman, Johann Neeskens, were blotted out as Paisley's men gave one of their most convincing performances. The Merseysiders couldn't manage to build on their lead but the home supporters knew their heroes had been outplayed, and as the second half wore on seat cushions showered on to the pitch in protest at such a woebegone Barcelona display. As the missiles landed around the visitors' bench, Joey Jones, one of the substitutes, took umbrage at what he thought was an unwarranted attack and started hurling them back. The Liverpool contingent explained hurriedly that he was not the intended target, but hustled him away to the safety of the dressing room as a precaution against further trouble. In all fairness, the Spanish fans had no gripe with the Reds - or the Whites as they were that evening - and many applauded them sportingly at the final whistle.

Certainly from the Merseyside viewpoint, the tie was poised appetisingly, and on the night of the second leg Anfield and its environs seemed like the centre of the world. Photographer Steve Hale takes up the story: 'The traffic was jammed for miles around the ground. People were leaving their cars anywhere and everywhere. It was a case of "To hell with the parking regulations, we can't risk missing any of THIS game." The police just couldn't cope, but once everyone was inside the ground the traffic wardens had a field day, dispensing tickets all over the place. There were reporters from all across Europe and the press box was bursting, so some writers had to sit next to the photographers on the touchline. The pressmen formed a solid wall from goalposts to corner flags at both ends of the pitch. Of course, it was a record Anfield attendance for a European match - more than 55,000 - and the atmosphere was incredible. It was such a crush that it must have been difficult to breathe on the terraces.'

Yet despite the inspired showing at the Nou Camp, and the euphoria of the supporters, Bob Paisley knew that a place in the final was far from secure. Indeed, although they spent most of the second leg soaking up pressure, Barcelona carried a far more potent threat this time, and Cruyff responded to Phil Thompson's goal by brilliantly laying on the equaliser a minute later. Thereafter Liverpool resumed the ascendancy, but there was always the nagging knowledge that the two Johanns and their gifted colleagues were capable of cancelling the celebrations with another thrust. To vast communal relief, that latent menace never materialised into a second goal, and Liverpool were through to their third European final.

Compared with that of Barcelona, the name of FC Bruges did not loom large in the annals of Continental soccer, but they were a well-balanced combination who had earned their right to contest the UEFA Cup Final with a series of impressive conquests. Along the way they had defeated Lyon of France, fought back from a three-goal deficit to overcome Ipswich Town, disposed of Italian giants AS Roma and AC Milan, and beaten Hamburg in a tense semi-final. Clearly the Belgians were no easy mark, and when they arrived on Merseyside for the first leg, the Reds had a considerable distraction on their minds; six nights later they were due to face Wolves at Molineux, needing either a victory or a low-scoring draw to clinch the League Championship.

It was a beautiful spring evening at Anfield, dry, warm and with no need for floodlights. There was a festive feeling, but the tension was running high, even among the journalists. Steve Hale recalls that seasoned professionals, who had covered finals all over the world, were affected by the air of expectancy that hung over the ground. Yet Liverpool started the game as if their thoughts were elsewhere. The mobile, skilful Belgian forwards, with the prematurely balding Lambert prominent, had the Reds' rearguard on the run and after only 12 minutes the visitors found themselves with a two-goal lead. Now Hughes, Smith and company fought tooth and nail to repel the tide that was flowing against them. They reached the interval with no further calamities, and then faced another fusillade - verbal this time - from Bob Paisley and coach Ron Moran. Tommy Smith looks back: 'It was quite a shock to go two goals down. No one could believe it. We had a right rollicking from Bob Paisley, and it was a combination of that and the Kop that pulled us back.'

Bringing on Jimmy Case for John Toshack made a difference, too, the youngster rampaging down the right flank and unsettling the hitherto composed Belgian defence. The resulting resurrection justified fully the next day's headlines about a 'miracle' comeback. In one five-minute-spell the Reds wiped out the deficit and took the lead, goals from Ray Kennedy, the ubiquitous Case and Kevin Keegan (penalty) effecting the transformation. In view of Phil Neal's magnificent record with spot-kicks, it was surprising, perhaps, that Kevin was entrusted with the responsibility, but the full-back had not enjoyed one of his better games and his confidence might have been sagging at that point. Now it was Bruges' turn to be stunned. Maybe they had become over-confident; certainly they were taken aback by the second-half passion that flowed from the terraces and galvanised their opponents. As Tommy Smith puts it with a grin: 'They didn't know what they had taken on.'

By the second leg Liverpool had claimed the League title and demonstrated their reserves of character yet again, picking themselves off the floor to beat Wolves with three late goals. Thus boosted, they set off for Belgium, yet still faced a daunting task if they were to repeat their double of 1972/73. In front of an intimidatingly vociferous crowd - although after the Kop's recent performance the Reds could hardly complain about that - they went behind to an early penalty. Later Tommy Smith claimed he had handled the ball accidentally but had not argued with the referee as the Liverpool players were under strict instructions not to do so. Crucially, the visitors were back in front within three minutes, courtesy of a Keegan free-kick, and thereafter put on an immaculate show of defensive covering that frustrated their hosts. As Tommy tells it, Bruges just didn't have the class to grab the game and win it.

Understandably, the Merseyside party was ecstatic not only about the result, but with the courageous manner in which it had been achieved. Kevin Keegan told the press: 'You get only what you earn in this game. We have the sort of side that, if we are knocked down, then we come back twice as strong.' Skipper Emlyn Hughes, who had dropped the heavy trophy in attempting to wave it at the fans, proclaimed: 'We won because we are the best side in England, and probably in Europe,' adding a deeply-felt personal footnote: 'I hope this shows Don Revie something. I think I deserve to be back in the England team.' But no one summed up the overall feeling better than Bob Paisley: 'The second half was the longest 45 minutes of my life. There was an awful lot of pride in this game because we came representing England. We did not let the country down and I am very proud of the lads. Now I just have no voice left.' Thus Bob, ecstatic in his own quiet way, saluted his first European triumph as manager. Even in such glorious circumstances, he never enjoyed facing the Continent's media in the way Shanks had done, though as the seasons went by he grew in confidence. After all, to Bob Paisley, the making of a victory speech was hardly going to be a novelty . . .

Phew, that was close! Having swapped shirts with their opponents, John Toshack *(left)* and Kevin Keegan give vent to their joy and relief at pipping FC Bruges for the UEFA Cup. After going two down in the first leg, then conceding an early goal in the second, the Reds bounced back in magnificent style to take the overall lead and survive a frantic late Belgian bombardment.

Round 1 - 1st leg
17 September 1974

LIVERPOOL 11

Lindsay (pen) 2; Boersma 13, 40;
Thompson 30, 74; Heighway 42; Cormack
65; Hughes 76; Smith 85; Callaghan 87;
Kennedy 88

STROMSGODSET DRAMMEN 0

H-T 5-0. Crowd 24,743

CLEMENCE
SMITH
LINDSAY
THOMPSON
CORMACK
HUGHES
BOERSMA
HALL
HEIGHWAY
KENNEDY
CALLAGHAN

Brian Hall must have wondered where he had gone wrong! The busy midfielder was the only outfield player who failed to find the net as the merciless Reds annihilated Stromsgodset to smash the club scoring record for any competition. It was not a meaningful encounter, of course, the Norwegians being hopelessly out of their depth, and in such circumstances it is difficult to single out individuals for praise. Even so Lindsay, who commenced the massacre with a penalty, deserves an honourable mention for his immaculate left-footed distribution. The carnage reached its height with three goals in three minutes near the end, though there was still time for Olsen to miss the chance of a consolation when he poked wide of an empty net.

Round 1 - 2nd leg
1 October 1974

STROMSGODSET DRAMMEN 0

LIVERPOOL 1

Kennedy 17

H-T 0-1. Crowd 17,000

CLEMENCE
SMITH
LINDSAY
LAWLER
HUGHES
HALL
KEEGAN
BOERSMA
HEIGHWAY
KENNEDY
CALLAGHAN

Playing on their own soil appeared to galvanise the Norwegian amateurs, whose gentle approach at Anfield contributed in no small measure to their humiliating demise. This time they battled gamely and came close to taking an early lead when Amundsen bungled with only Clemence to beat. Liverpool's riposte was predictably swift, Kennedy controlling a lob from Smith before picking his spot and dispatching a low shot past 'keeper Thun from 20 yards. Stromsgodset, playing for their pride, did not give up, and Clemence was forced to make several saves although the Reds missed enough chances to record another heavy victory. Keegan, not at his sharpest after a lengthy suspension, was off target twice when well placed, but this was one occasion when it didn't matter.

Liverpool won 12-0 on aggregate.

Back on form: Kevin Keegan has just given Liverpool a first-leg lead against Ferencvaros at Anfield.

Round 2 - 1st leg
23 October 1974

LIVERPOOL 1

Keegan 36

FERENCVAROS 1

Mate 90
H-T 1-0. Crowd 35,027

CLEMENCE
SMITH
LINDSAY
LAWLER
HALL (TOSHACK)
HUGHES
BOERSMA
KEEGAN
CALLAGHAN
KENNEDY (CORMACK)
HEIGHWAY

Liverpool paid a high price for failing to convert their territorial domination into goals. Having taken a first-half lead - Keegan blasting high into the net after Kennedy touched on a Hall cross - the Reds were stunned by an injury-time equaliser. Ironically, the referee was compensating for time-wasting tactics by the Hungarians when Mate drifted past Lawler, sidestepped Lindsay and ran on to place the ball clinically past Clemence for a magnificent goal. What a different story it might have been if Boersma had not miscued in front of a gaping net when set up by Keegan in the first minute, and then repeated the performance after good work by Heighway in the 24th. Others were guilty of misses, too, and Ferencvaros 'keeper Geczi made some fabulous saves as well as riding his luck. The result left Liverpool facing an ominously difficult task in the second leg.

Of this Reds line-up *(left)* **against Stromsgodset, only Ray Clemence and Brian Hall failed to score.**

Round 2 - 2nd leg
5 November 1974

FERENCVAROS 0

LIVERPOOL 0

Crowd 30,000

CLEMENCE
SMITH
LINDSAY
LAWLER
BOERSMA
HUGHES
KEEGAN
HALL
HEIGHWAY (CORMACK)
KENNEDY (TOSHACK)
CALLAGHAN

For the second time in the tie, Liverpool enjoyed the best of their exchanges with Ferencvaros without having the goals to show for it. Although the Hungarians carried the game to their visitors during the opening 15 minutes, they were content to sit back and soak up pressure for the rest of the match, knowing that a goalless draw would see them through on the away goals rule. Wary of falling prey to the over-anxiety that had plagued them at Anfield, the Reds were more measured this time, and their approach came close to paying off. Twice Kennedy appeared to be fouled inside the box, but the referee was unmoved by concerted penalty appeals. The official incurred Liverpool's displeasure at the end, too, adding only a token few seconds in respect of Ferencvaros's blatant delaying tactics. It all added up to a sour and unsatisfactory exit from a competition the Reds were deemed well capable of winning.

Aggregate 1-1. Ferencvaros won on away goal.

UEFA Cup 1975/76

Round 1 - 1st leg
17 September 1975

HIBERNIAN 1
Harper 22

LIVERPOOL 0

H-T 1-0. Crowd 19,219

CLEMENCE
NEAL
JONES
LAWLER
CORMACK
HUGHES
KEEGAN
HALL
HEIGHWAY (BOERSMA)
KENNEDY (TOSHACK)
CALLAGHAN

Liverpool could consider themselves lucky to escape from Easter Road with a one-goal defeat, Hibernian having dominated most of the match. After two early flurries in which Heighway and Callaghan went close for the Reds, the hosts gained control of midfield, and Harper's goal was well deserved. It came when Neal failed to cut out a through-pass, Duncan wrong-footed the defence with a first-time cross and the former Evertonian met it crisply from ten yards. Liverpool managed a few attacking sorties, and a Neal 'goal' on 57 minutes was disallowed for offside. But the balance of power remained with the Scots, who seemed about to be rewarded when they won a penalty - Lawler having downed Duncan - ten minutes from time. However, Clemence dived athletically to his right to repel Brownlie's kick, making the Reds marginal favourites to reach the next round.

Round 1 - 2nd leg
30 September 1975

LIVERPOOL 3
Toshack 21, 53, 64

HIBERNIAN 1
Edwards 33

H-T 1-1. Crowd 29,963

CLEMENCE
NEAL
LINDSAY
THOMPSON, PHIL
CORMACK
HUGHES
KEEGAN
HALL
HEIGHWAY (CASE)
TOSHACK
CALLAGHAN

Liverpool overcame a splendid, spirited Hibernian challenge in one of Anfield's most thrilling European encounters.

Although Bob Paisley's team earned their victory through steady pressure, the Scots were menacing on the break and were a solitary strike away from triumph through the away-goals rule. Toshack was the hero of the night, his aerial dominance producing a stirring hat-trick of headers. The first, a well-directed far-post effort from a Keegan cross, levelled the scores on aggregate, but the Reds found themselves trailing again 12 minutes later when Bremner set up Edwards for a brilliant first-time strike. The tie swung Liverpool's way in the third quarter when their Welsh marksman converted a centre from Hall, then nodded down a free-kick from Callaghan which bounced awkwardly to elude 'keeper McArthur. Hibs fought on, though, and the outcome was uncertain to the end.

Liverpool won 3-2 on aggregate.

Aerial might: John Toshack completes his hat-trick of headers against Hibernian at Anfield, converting a flighted free-kick from Ian Callaghan. Until the Welshman's third strike, the battling Scots held the balance of power through an away goal and were in with a chance of victory.

Round 2 - 1st leg
22 October 1975

REAL SOCIEDAD 1
Amas 86

LIVERPOOL 3
Heighway 18; Callaghan 61;
Thompson 82
H-T 0-1. Crowd 20,000

CLEMENCE
NEAL
LINDSAY
THOMPSON, PHIL
CORMACK
HUGHES
KEEGAN
HALL
HEIGHWAY
TOSHACK
CALLAGHAN

Liverpool crushed the Basques' resistance with an overwhelmingly convincing performance. The Reds were superior in all departments to a side unbeaten in home League games for more than two years, but the key area was midfield, where Keegan and Callaghan sparkled. Heighway's pace had the Spaniards struggling, too, and he might have scored four times in the opening 25 minutes. In fact, he found the net just once, rounding a defender and placing a firm shot wide of the 'keeper. Liverpool continued to dominate, only the woodwork and inaccurate marksmanship denying them a winning lead before half-time. The second period was more productive, however, Callaghan netting from a narrow angle after Toshack had headed against the angle of bar and post, and Thompson nodding home from a corner. Amas's late strike for Real was mere consolation.

Round 2 - 2nd leg
4 November 1975

LIVERPOOL 6
Toshack 14; Kennedy 30, 75;
Fairclough 72; Heighway 77; Neal 79

REAL SOCIEDAD 0

H-T 2-0. Crowd 23,796

CLEMENCE
NEAL
KETTLE (THOMPSON, MAX)

THOMPSON, PHIL
SMITH
CALLAGHAN (FAIRCLOUGH)
KEEGAN
HALL
HEIGHWAY
TOSHACK
KENNEDY

Anyone hoping to watch a competitive match, with the Spaniards striving to make up for their surrender on home soil, were sorely disappointed. In fact, Liverpool won as they pleased, with Real even more toothless than in the first leg. Toshack put the result beyond doubt when he headed home a cross from Kettle; then, after Keegan had missed a penalty, the promising left-back made a second telling contribution, starting the move that ended with Kennedy increasing the lead with a brisk drive. Thereafter the Reds coasted until a destructive spell of four goals in seven minutes near the end. The rush started with Fairclough intercepting a back-pass and notching his first senior strike; next Kennedy made it four before Heighway, then Neal scored after enterprising dribbles.

Liverpool won 9-1 on aggregate.

Spanish sighs: Steve Heighway scores for Liverpool against Real Sociedad at Anfield, (left) the third of four goals in a late seven-minute spell that demoralised the already well-beaten Basques.

Round 3 - 1st leg
26 November 1975

SLASK WROCLAW 1
Pawlowski 81

LIVERPOOL 2
Kennedy 60; Toshack 75
H-T 0-0. Crowd 40,000

CLEMENCE
NEAL
SMITH
THOMPSON, PHIL
KENNEDY
HUGHES
CASE
HALL
HEIGHWAY
TOSHACK
CALLAGHAN

Liverpool put in a superbly professional performance on an icebound pitch in some 15 degrees of frost, keeping their heads and their feet to outwit and outplay the Poles. The Reds controlled the midfield, with Callaghan at his most industrious and skilful best, and the Wroclaw defence could never come to terms with the aerial threat posed by Toshack. The visitors might have been happy to come away with a goalless draw, but they achieved the breakthrough their display deserved through a piece of good fortune. Kennedy tackled defender Faber, and as the ball rebounded goalwards, 'keeper Kalinowski slipped and failed to prevent it from crossing the line. Smith set up Toshack to slot home the second, before Wroclaw gave themselves a glimmer of hope for the return, Pawlowski hooking the ball past Clemence following a free-kick.

HEIGHWAY
FAIRCLOUGH (HALL)
CALLAGHAN

Liverpool left East Germany with the upper hand after a goalless thriller which brought out the best in two accomplished sides. The most dramatic moment of a fascinating encounter in which the Reds set themselves to resist a barrage of Dynamo attacks came after 50 minutes. Kennedy was penalised for an innocuous challenge on Schmuck, and the referee pointed to the spot; Kotte stepped up to strike the ball crisply towards the corner of the net but Clemence threw himself to his right and pulled off a crucial save. Then, as Dynamo toiled desperately to make home advantage count, Reidel squandered a great chance before forcing Clemence to another brilliant stop. In the last 15 minutes, with the Dresden passion seemingly spent, Liverpool surged forward and Thompson headed against the bar. Finally, after the visitors had forced a succession of corners, Dynamo broke clear and Schade hit the post with Clemence beaten.

Round 4 - 2nd leg
17 March 1976

LIVERPOOL 2
Case 24; Keegan 47

DYNAMO DRESDEN 1
Heidler 63
H-T 1-0. 39,300

| CLEMENCE |
| NEAL |
| SMITH |
| THOMPSON, PHIL |
| KENNEDY |
| HUGHES |
| KEEGAN |
| CASE |
| HEIGHWAY (FAIRCLOUGH) |
| TOSHACK |
| CALLAGHAN |

Liverpool were in irresistible form, pummelling the Dresden defence throughout most of the match, yet the resilient Germans battled back to give their hosts some anxious moments. The Reds started at breakneck pace, launching wave after wave of attacks, with Keegan and Toshack especially prominent. However, the first goal fell to Case, who had already seen one shot rebound from a post. The young striker seized possession from a defender's error, cut in from the right and eluded a

tackle before dispatching a firm left-footer past the 'keeper from 12 yards. Soon after the break, when Keegan hooked into the net from close range after controlling a raking cross from Smith, it seemed that the contest was over. But Heidler had a shock for the exultant Kop, gulling Hughes on the edge of the box, then sprinting forward to drill the ball below Clemence. The Reds dominated the remaining exchanges, though a second Dresden riposte was never out of the question.

Liverpool won 2-1 on aggregate.

Semi-final - 1st leg
30 March 1976

BARCELONA 0

LIVERPOOL 1
Toshack 13
H-T 0-1. Crowd 70,000

| CLEMENCE |
| NEAL |
| SMITH |
| THOMPSON, PHIL |
| KENNEDY |
| HUGHES |
| KEEGAN |
| CASE (HALL) |
| HEIGHWAY |
| TOSHACK |
| CALLAGHAN |

Liverpool's demolition of Barcelona - for such it was, despite the narrow margin of victory - rates as arguably their most stirring achievement on a foreign field. Shrugging off the apparent magnitude of their task, the Merseysiders carried the game to their illustrious opponents, reducing Cruyff and his colleagues to the occasional breakaway; indeed, Bob Paisley's men might have scored four or five times, so complete was their superiority. The goal they did manage was a gem. Toshack glanced a long clearance to Keegan, who controlled it immaculately on his chest before pushing an inch-perfect return pass to his sprinting partner. His markers lagging behind, the Welshman drew back his foot and drove an unerring 12-yard cross-shot beyond the keeper's reach and into the far corner of the net. There followed an exemplary team performance in which Callaghan, who seemed to be improving with age, stood out. The only flaw was the finishing, with Keegan and Case (twice) missing chances that would have booked a final place beyond doubt.

Round 3 - 2nd leg
10 December 1975

LIVERPOOL 3
Case 22, 29, 46

SLASK WROCLAW 0
H-T 2-0. Crowd 17,886

| CLEMENCE |
| NEAL |
| SMITH |
| THOMPSON, PHIL |
| KENNEDY (CORMACK) |
| HUGHES |
| KEEGAN |
| HALL |
| CASE |
| TOSHACK |
| CALLAGHAN |

The match belonged to 21-year-old Jimmy Case, who plundered his first senior hat-trick as the Reds eased into the quarter-finals. The Poles, one down from the first leg, never looked capable of reviving their cause and Clemence was a virtual spectator throughout the proceedings. Toshack, with whom Wroclaw could never cope, created the first goal, touching it to Case, who wrong-footed a defender before shooting firmly just

inside a post from 15 yards. Thereafter the young man was rampant, hitting a post with a tremendous drive before scoring again after Keegan had split the defence with a teasing run. This time the 'keeper reached the ball but the power of the shot defeated him. With the sparse crowd baying for a third, Case obliged early in the second half, knocking home a rebound after Hall's effort had been saved.

Liverpool won 5-1 on aggregate.

Round 4 - 1st leg
3 March 1976

DYNAMO DRESDEN 0

LIVERPOOL 0
Crowd 33,000

| CLEMENCE |
| NEAL |
| SMITH |
| THOMPSON, PHIL |
| KENNEDY |
| HUGHES |
| KEEGAN |
| CASE |

Semi-final - 2nd leg
14 April 1976

LIVERPOOL 1
Thompson, Phil 50

BARCELONA 1
Rexach 51
H-T 0-0. Crowd 55,104

CLEMENCE
NEAL
SMITH
THOMPSON, PHIL
KENNEDY
HUGHES
KEEGAN
CASE (HALL)
HEIGHWAY
TOSHACK
CALLAGHAN

Having grabbed Barcelona, metaphorically, by the scruff of the neck in the first leg, Liverpool went for the jugular at Anfield. For most of the 90 minutes the Spaniards could only fight a frenetic rearguard action as the Reds charged forward with unremitting intensity, but as in the quarter-final clash with Dynamo Dresden, there was always the lurking fear of a sudden deadly thrust from such high-calibre opponents. Liverpool's approach work was magnificent, with every outfield player contributing in full measure, though their finishing let them down. At the other end, Clemence did all that was asked of him, which, in the first half, amounted to no more than saving a free-kick from Rexach. Impossible though it seemed, the game gathered pace after the break. Thompson seemed to have won it for the Reds when he turned a Toshack cross-shot over the line, but straight from the restart, Cruyff surged down the left before clipping a perfect centre to Rexach, who rammed it unstoppably past Clemence. Another goal would have sufficed for Barcelona, but Liverpool resumed control for a well-deserved triumph.

Liverpool won 2-1 on aggregate.

Centre: **Phil Thompson, with Kevin Keegan in close attendance, bundles the ball into the net for the opening goal of the home clash with Barcelona.**

Conquering heroes: Barcelona have been beaten and the Reds, looking drained after an epic struggle, salute the Anfield faithful.

The heat is on: Liverpool pound the Barcelona goal at Anfield, with John Toshack *(left)*, Jimmy Case and Ray Kennedy (5) prominent in this attack. But though the Reds had the best of the game, such high-class opponents were always dangerous on the break.

LIVERPOOL 3

Kennedy 59; Case 61; Keegan (pen) 64

BRUGES 2

Lambert 5; Cools 12
H-T 0-2. Crowd 49,981

CLEMENCE
NEAL
SMITH
THOMPSON, PHIL
KENNEDY
HUGHES
KEEGAN
FAIRCLOUGH
HEIGHWAY
TOSHACK (CASE)
CALLAGHAN

Here was a contest worthy of any cup final, though Liverpool could hardly have started in more disastrous fashion. The game was still settling down when Neal attempted to head the ball back to Clemence, only for the quicksilver Lambert to nip in and lift the ball over the 'keeper's head, a supreme piece of opportunism. Seven minutes later the Reds' crisis deepened when a Belgian passing movement of bewildering accuracy was climaxed by a savage shot from Cools. Liverpool were playing without cohesion, their passes were going astray, but they refused to disintegrate. For the second half the manager brought on Case for Toshack, thus pitching Keegan into attack, and suddenly his side looked more purposeful. But even Bob Paisley could hardly have envisaged what would happen next. First Heighway set up Kennedy to lash home from 20 yards; next Keegan turned adroitly to find Kennedy, who shot against the post and Case tapped in the rebound; then Heighway was felled in the box and Keegan scored from the spot. Three goals in five minutes had transformed the match and set up a cliff-hanging second leg.

Top: **A timely reply: Kevin Keegan, partly hidden behind a Belgian defender, drives in the equaliser just three minutes after Bruges had opened the scoring in the second leg of the UEFA Cup Final.**

BRUGES 1

Lambert (pen) 12

LIVERPOOL 1

Keegan 15
H-T 1-1. Crowd 33,000

CLEMENCE
NEAL
SMITH
THOMPSON, PHIL
KENNEDY
HUGHES
KEEGAN
CASE
HEIGHWAY
TOSHACK (FAIRCLOUGH)
CALLAGHAN

Liverpool clinched their second European trophy with a dour, splendidly disciplined display against one of the Continent's most talented sides. As the first team to score twice against the Reds in the competition, Bruges attacked with confidence, and reaped an early dividend when Smith was judged to have handled in the area, Lambert crashing the resultant penalty high into Clemence's net. Liverpool reacted with stirring vigour, throwing themselves into attack to such effect that within three minutes they were level, Hughes touching an indirect free-kick to Keegan, who breached the defensive wall with a low shot from 18 yards. Then the Merseysiders, with Thompson, Hughes and Smith in majestic form, held their own until the interval. The final period however, proved more insecure as the Belgians launched an all-out offensive. The ubiquitous Lambert beat Clemence on 50 minutes but saw his shot bounce back off a post, and that was the nearest Bruges came to breaking through. As the pressure intensified in the last 15 minutes, the England 'keeper made a cluster of fine saves and the job was done.

Liverpool won 4-3 on aggregate.

The biggest grin in football: Emlyn Hughes holds aloft the UEFA Cup. Lifting silverware was becoming a habit for the Reds' skipper, who had taken custody of the League Championship trophy only two weeks earlier.

Chapter Seven

RAPTURE IN ROME

EVER since Liverpool had stepped into the Continental arena for the first time, back in 1964 against those gentle souls from Reykjavik, there had been an unshakeable conviction at Anfield that one day they would win the European Cup. But for cruel fortune they might have succeeded at the first attempt, and had they done so they would have been hailed, quite rightly, as miracle-workers. Yet perhaps, in some deep and subtle way, the triumph in Rome was all the more meaningful in that it was the culmination of 13 consecutive campaigns of concentrated endeavour, encompassing myriad highs and lows, celebrations and disappointments. Now, after putting Borussia Moenchengladbach to the sword amid scenes of unbelievable emotion on that glorious May evening, there was a sense that the Reds had paid their dues, that success was theirs by unalienable moral right, not merely the result of an isolated clutch of good performances. Here were no upstart crown princes mounting a throne which might have been theirs by right but which they did not really fit. No, Liverpool were the true and worthy Kings of Europe, and no mistake.

Their first opponents on the road to Rome, though hardly threatening to end their progress, proved more difficult to subdue than might have been expected. Indeed, Crusaders of Northern Ireland lived up to their rousing name, limiting the mighty Merseysiders to two goals in the first leg at Anfield, and collapsing only in the last nine minutes of the return. From the moment before the draw in Zurich when Derek Wade, their chairman, had announced his premonition that his club would be paired with Liverpool, the Ulstermen had radiated good cheer and fighting spirit. To them the tie represented both a considerable financial windfall and an unprecedented opportunity to enjoy themselves, and they were going to make the most of it. Before the first match, manager Billy Johnston sought advice from an old friend and countryman, Everton boss Billy Bingham. After taking his consultation, Johnston said: 'We've got to be sponges, soak up what Liverpool throw at us, and hope they have bad luck with their finishing. We can't match them for skill, and I worry about their pace, but I want my players to come off the field, look me in the eye and know they have given 100-per-cent effort. That is one area where we can hope to match Liverpool.'

They did, too, their mixture of dockers, civil servants and suchlike excelling themselves, none more so than insurance salesman Roy McDonald, who was a magnificent last line of defence. It was a courageous display, properly honoured with an ovation from the Kop, but Bob Paisley put it in perspective by remarking: 'I hear one of their players lost a contact lens, but he's got a good chance of finding it. After all, there's only two places it can be - the two penalty areas!' Billy Johnston, though, was not cowed and warned the Reds: 'You're in for a hell of a game across the water.'

And so to Seaview, sounding more like a guesthouse than a soccer ground, where Liverpool arrived direct from England. Wisely, UEFA had waived their rule that a visiting club must be in the host country 24 hours before a game, feeling that an overnight stay in the troubled province might pose needless security problems. On the field, Crusaders rose to the occasion, rattling the woodwork twice before the Reds consolidated their lead, and deserved a better fate than to concede a late deluge of goals. Nevertheless, the Ulstermen had covered themselves in a kind of glory, and Liverpool were over the first hurdle, complete with one overdue bonus. Since his move from Newcastle United nearly two years earlier, skilful midfielder Terry McDermott had not fulfilled his potential. Now, admittedly in circumstances that were not the most exacting, he had come on as substitute and made a good impression. Was he close to that elusive breakthrough?

Having made friends and influenced people in Ireland, the Reds now encountered opposition of a more hostile nature. Their second-round destination was Trabzon, a small town on Turkey's Black Sea coast that might, with reason, have been dubbed the Last Resort. Not since the expedition to Ploesti a decade before had Liverpool been made to feel more unwelcome. To begin with, the trek had caused organisational problems for secretary Peter Robinson, who always tried to ensure that the party spent as little time abroad as possible. For this trek, though, having to go way beyond Istanbul, he could not bypass the necessity of staying two nights in Turkey. Unfortunately, the establishment they had been recommended did not come into the salubrious category. Indeed, an outraged Bob Paisley described it as a dosshouse, and with some justification. In the words of David Johnson, it was dirty and depressing: 'It was very hot in the hotel, and there was no air-conditioning. The manky bunk-beds made matters worse, then after finally getting off to sleep we were awakened at 5 am by wailing chants from a nearby mosque. On top of all that, the people were unfriendly and the food was foul. It was a good job that we had taken some of our own supplies to see us through.' However, both Phil Thompson and Ray Kennedy felt ill enough to need medical treatment.

The nightmare scenario continued when the team arrived for the match, having travelled to the small stadium through grim, grey, barely made-up streets patrolled by beggars. Supporters banged provocatively on the sides of the coach before the players decamped into a primitive dressing room. The match with a niggly Trabzonspor side brought no relief, the Reds losing to a controversial penalty conceded by Emlyn Hughes, who called the referee's decision the most ridiculous he had ever known. The pitch was bumpy, the ball tatty and out of shape - Paisley likened it to a pig's bladder - and in one corner of the ground spectators were throwing rocks. When added to confusion over training and transport arrangements, it was enough to make the Liverpool boss denounce the trip as a disaster from start to finish. Nevertheless Ian Callaghan, who overcame an attack of fibrositis to play his 79th European game - thus breaking Norman Hunter's record for a British player - admired the way Bob coped: 'He didn't think much of it but he took it in his stride, making the best of a bad job. It was the only way to handle it. It was all part of a test of our European expertise and our collective character. I would like to think we passed it.'

Pressmen recall that Emlyn Hughes moaned all the way home on the plane, then kissed the ground in the manner of the Pope on arrival back in England. Forty-eight hours later, he and his colleagues demonstrated their resilience by holding Leeds to a draw at Elland Road, a fabulous result in the circumstances. Even more satisfying, though, was streaking to a three-goal lead over Trabzonspor in the first 18 minutes of the second leg, effectively silencing the 3,000 Turkish fans who had clamoured ceaselessly prior to kick-off. After that the Reds were subjected to a series of outrageous tackles and could be proud of their refusal to be provoked. Kevin Keegan said he felt more in danger of losing his legs than his head, and afterwards the Trabzonspor coach, one Ahmet Suet, had the grace to apologise for his players' conduct.

Awaiting Liverpool in the quarter-finals were St Etienne, and even the pundits who predicted a classic confrontation were to be startled by the drama that unfolded before this most memorable of ties was settled. The Frenchmen had captivated fans all over the Continent with their dazzling flair in the 1976 European Cup Final against Bayern Munich, and it was agreed generally that the methodical Germans had been fortunate to win. Les Verts (the Greens) were seen as THE exciting new power on the Continent and the Reds could not have faced a sterner examination of their own credentials. In fact, the two teams had met once before, Billy Liddell equalising to secure a 1-1 draw in a 1956 friendly; this time, if the French newspapers were to be believed, the decisive contribution was likely to come from a far more flamboyant figure. In the build-up to the clash, much of the publicity centred on Dominique Rocheteau, the so-called golden boy of French football, who wore his hair on his shoulders, had pop-idol status and was touted as the new George Best. Actually Rocheteau was similar to Liddell in that he was essentially a modest man who did not revel

Tormenting the Turks: Kevin Keegan causes mayhem in the Trabzonspor defence as the Reds erase the memory of their unhappy trip to the Black Sea coast. Steve Heighway, David Johnson and Kevin himself all netted in the first 18 minutes to make the remainder of the game a virtual formality.

in adulation, but that did not come across in the media overkill that surrounded him. As a footballer he was undeniably gifted, a quicksilver attacker who could take defenders on, but there was a suggestion that he was not at his most effective when the tide of battle was flowing against his team. Suffice it to say that Liverpool were not overawed by his reputation; their attitude seemed to be: 'Shouting the odds is all very well, but let's see what he can do when he gets his boots on.' In the event, though he looked sharp, Rocheteau could not shake off the attentions of Joey Jones and exerted minimal influence on the first leg, played before an impassioned audience in the Geoffrey Guichard Stadium.

As the players took the field, to a thunderous chorus of 'Allez les Verts', the Reds fans who had made the trip realised to their dismay that Kevin Keegan was missing. He had pulled an ankle ligament shortly before the match and was replaced by Terry McDermott, but on a night when Liverpool were concentrating on taking the sting out of the opposition, it did not prove a significant handicap. St Etienne, unbeaten at home for four years, won with a late, rather fortuitous goal, but it was the admirably composed visitors who had the firmer grounds for optimism at the final whistle.

As the second leg approached, the media hype intensified, and for once, incredibly, a game lived up to the hours of broadcasting time and acres of newspaper coverage devoted to it. The omens were good for Liverpool: Keegan was fit again and the French were deprived of their defensive kingpin, Oswaldo 'The Beast' Piazza, who had been banned after receiving his second caution of the competition for a wild challenge on Ian Callaghan two weeks earlier. In the mammoth crush that enveloped Anfield, a number of French supporters - who had been arriving in their coachloads since the weekend - were locked out despite having tickets; some got in late, others not at all, an unhappy occurrence for which Peter Robinson apologised afterwards. Those who did miss the start also missed a goal, Keegan drifting in a long-range aggregate equaliser from wide on the left. The Kop erupted with a spontaneous rendition of 'Allez les Rouges' and the Anfield Road end, Green for the night, was momentarily subdued. However, with both sides making positive thrusts - the buzzing Rocheteau, in particular, appeared capable of breaking the deadlock - the excitement mounted unbearably until, early in the second half, Bathenay beat Clemence

Speculation pays off: Kevin Keegan's long-range floater from the left flank - it might have been a shot, though it looked like a cross - drops into the net beyond the despairing grasp of St Etienne goalkeeper Jurcovic, while John Toshack and Tommy Smith have yet to register a reaction. Kevin's second-minute breakthrough set up one of the most emotional nights even Anfield has seen.

with a long shot that gave the England 'keeper no hope. Tommy Smith reckons it was as venomous an effort as he has seen, the ball twisting and turning several ways before bulging the net.

Now Liverpool needed two to win and, against such high-class opponents, the odds were not in their favour. When Ray Kennedy struck with just over half an hour left, the match was balanced delicately, but now perhaps, with the fervour inside Anfield swelling to unimaginable heights, the advantage had switched to the Reds. Even so, time was fast running out when David Fairclough, called on as a late substitute for John Toshack, earned what was surely the most tumultuous roar ever to rend the Merseyside skies. After planting the ball calmly past Jurcovic in the St Etienne goal, the 'Bionic Carrot' was buried beneath a writhing mass of ecstatic team-mates. Later he recalled that timeless moment in which he justified his manager's gamble: 'Kevin Keegan leapt on me and said "Supersub, you've done it again." I don't know why I've got this knack of scoring as a substitute. It must be a bit of luck I carry with me. The lads tell me I'm lucky, that things just seem to come off for me both in training and matches, sometimes almost stupid things you would never expect to work.' Though David's fortune would never extend to winning for himself a long-term berth in the Liverpool attack, nothing could ever erase that supremely exhilarating achievement that guaranteed his place in Merseyside folklore. For the fans, too, it was an experience they would never forget. Eddie Marks, a mild-mannered accountant who has been an Anfield regular for more than 40 years, still glows at the memory: 'I have never known such emotion on a football ground. In the stands and on the terraces, people were hugging complete strangers. Some found themselves with their arms round people they couldn't stand the sight of, but for those few moments it didn't matter. It was a scene of utter pandemonium and sheer joy. How David Fairclough kept so cool under such amazing pressure, I'll never know. It was as clinical a piece of finishing as I have ever witnessed.' That calmest of indi-

Immortality beckons for the 'Bionic Carrot': after this ultra-clinical finish against St Etienne, the name of David Fairclough was assured a permanent place in Reds folklore. As the ball hit the net, Anfield erupted in pandemonium. In the stands and on the terraces, complete strangers were embracing each other; some even found themselves hugging people they couldn't stand the sight of!

Cool Phil: Reds full-back Neal slots home an equaliser against FC Zurich in Switzerland with the utmost precision. The hosts had taken a shock lead when a Tommy Smith tackle was judged to be illegal and Risi netted from the penalty spot.

viduals, Ian Callaghan, who had seen most things before, felt it was one of the most special nights even Anfield had known: 'We had played well, coming from behind to win against one of the best sides we had ever faced. Now the fans believed we could go all the way.'

Certainly, the semi-final draw gave Liverpool every chance of doing just that, pitting their strength against the comparatively modest resources of FC Zurich, while Borussia Moenchengladbach met Dynamo Kiev in the other match. Predictably, after the highly-charged emotion of the St Etienne encounter, the two legs against the Swiss proved anti-climactic. But while neutrals may have been disappointed at such a one-sided tie, Liverpool's previous exertions had earned them any luck that came their way. In fact, for a short period of the first leg in Zurich, the home side were riding high, courtesy of a fifth-minute penalty conceded by Tommy Smith. The Reds were soon level, however, going on to a comfortable 3-1 victory with Tommy making amends by marking danger-man Rene Botteron out of the game. At Anfield the Swiss were plainly out of their depth, allowing Liverpool - only three days away from their FA Cup semi-final against Everton - a welcome opportunity to coast. Watching Goodison boss Gordon Lee described the Reds' perfor-mance, accurately enough, as a leisurely stroll, but that shouldn't detract from the fact that their 6-1 winning margin was the most emphatic at that stage of the competition for 13

years. Bob Paisley was in no doubt: 'We have reached a summit we have never reached before, and that is an honour in itself.' Kevin Keegan, who had announced before the season that he would be leaving for the Continent in the summer of 1977, made his feelings clear, too: 'The only reason I have stayed here is to get to the European Cup Final, and now we have done it.'

And so all roads led to Rome for the momentous clash with Borussia Moenchengladbach on 25 May, a game and an occasion that will be remembered as long as there is a Liverpool FC. By then, the Reds were just that one match away from the end of a long and remarkable season, in which they had pipped Manchester City and Ipswich to the League title by a single point, then lost the FA Cup Final to Manchester United through a fluke goal by Jimmy Greenhoff. That Wembley reverse, four days before taking on the Germans, might have deflated a lesser team, but as they approached their greatest test, Emlyn Hughes and his men were quick to rebuild their morale. The healing began, incongruously enough, on Watford station as the players waited for a train to take them back to Merseyside. They were hanging about in groups, chatting desultorily and trying not to look as despondent as they felt, when Ray Clemence - who found defeat harder to take than most - began to dance. It might have looked ridiculous, but as therapy it was ideal. Suddenly, the jokes started, there was a bit of a party on the train and, long before the flight to Rome, the collective mood had been transformed.

The players' wives travelled with the official party, and although they headed for a different hotel on touchdown, their presence nearby was a boost to morale. Spirits had remained buoyant throughout the journey, thanks in no small measure to incessant banter between Bill Shankly, delighted to be travelling with the team, and Denis Law, who was working as a summariser for BBC Radio. Also, there was a comfortable feeling that with so many fans making the trip from Merseyside, there would be no shortage of friendly faces in the Eternal City. The club had opted to spurn the traditional custom of isolating the players in some hotel deep in the countryside, which would have offered privacy and calm in the run-up to the match. Instead they used a hotel in Rome, besieged by fans, friends and press, treating it as an occasion to be enjoyed. After all, they had already won the League, so there was no question of ending the season empty-handed. Bob Paisley, revealing ever more of his dry humour as his self-confidence grew, set the tone by telling pressmen: 'The last time I was in Rome was 33 years ago. I helped to capture it.'

David Johnson, for whom the great day would be blighted by disappointment - after being substituted at Wembley he was omitted from the side to face Borussia - remembers vividly the last hour or so before the game. 'The lads knew that a lot of our fans - between 5,000 and 8,000, according to the media - had made the trip from England, and were anxious to give them something to cheer after the disappointment of losing to United. On arrival for the match, we disappeared into the bowels of the Olympic stadium, and it was some time before we strolled out to look at the pitch. When we did, we were absolutely staggered by the atmosphere that greeted us. The place had been taken over by Liverpool fans - we learnt later that there were 26,000 of them - and all we could take in was this heaving mass of red and white. We all looked at each other and grew about four feet taller. With such support, there was absolutely no way we could possibly lose. Looking back, it seems as if we had won even before the game had started. The Germans are traditionally loud supporters, but they were absolutely overwhelmed. Our sections of the crowd swayed like the Kop, having one hell of a party, while Borussia's contingent stood still. It was no contest.'

In fact, it was estimated that that crazy, loyal, loveable army must have spent in excess of £1 million making their pilgrimage by car and coach, train and boat and plane, some even parting with their life savings rather than miss the trip. A large number had booked holidays from work, others had neither the time nor inclination to bother, just heading for the Continent direct from Wembley. With them went their banners, bearing legends both original and hackneyed, quaint and crass, none capturing the joyous spirit of the day better than 'Joey ate the Frogs' legs, made the Swiss roll, now he's Munching Gladbach'. The affectionate reference to left-back Joey Jones, a footballer of limited natural talent in a team of thoroughbreds, was due partly to his honest, wholehearted approach, but also owed plenty to his own years as a devoted Kopite.

Now the action had to match the build-up, and it did so with something to spare. Liverpool, looking highly motivated but marvellously relaxed, took a deserved first-half lead when Terry McDermott rounded off a sweet move with a precise strike, but Allan Simonsen levelled spectacularly soon after the interval. Now the ultra-efficient Borussia machine clicked up a gear, and threatened to grind out a typically remorseless German victory. But if that was the script, then Tommy Smith - in his 600th, and what was expected to be his last, senior outing for the Reds - had not read it. That earthy, four-square personification of all things Scouse timed his run perfectly to crash home an unstoppable header from a Steve Heighway corner, and the direction of the match altered irrevocably. Thereafter it was left to Kevin Keegan - he WAS playing his final game for Liverpool - to cap a tireless, imaginative display by scampering through the Borussia defence, only to be felled by Bertie Vogts as he was about to apply the final touch. Vogts's desperate lunge had merely delayed the inevitable, however, Phil Neal stepping up to steer the penalty inside a post with his customary aplomb.

Then it was celebration time, the team doing laps of honour in front of the barbed-wire barricade that separated them from their fans. The players greeted triumph in their own individual ways, Joey Jones cavorting with top hat, union jack and umbrella, Ian Callaghan progressing more sedately. There was not the slightest doubt, however, what this win had meant to Cally, who had been on his knees in an attitude of prayer as Neal had netted from the spot. Ian, restored to the side after being omitted from the Wembley starting line-up, knew he was approaching the end of a wonderful career and that this might be his last chance of achieving ultimate European glory. He recalls: 'I had experienced plenty of triumphs down the years, but this was the night of nights, the highlight of my life in football. The game and the atmosphere were magical and I wanted to soak it all up.' For Tommy Smith, the other survivor from the Reds' first season in European competition - who had played only because of injury to Phil Thompson - the experience was even more dramatic. That crucial goal in what was to have been his swansong before retirement made certain of that: 'That ball seemed to take ten minutes to go from my head into the net. Afterwards I thought of having a brass plate put in my nut to mark the spot.' One of the most enduring images of the moments immediately following the final whistle was provided by a *Liverpool Echo* photograph of Tommy engulfed in a Ronnie Moran bearhug. It looks as if the Reds' hero is roaring with glee, but as he loves to recount, that was not quite the case: 'I had a couple of false teeth, which I would keep in for ceremonies before big games, then hand to Ronnie, who would look after them for me. Naturally, he would be the first man I looked for after the match, and what I'm really saying to him in that photo is "Put me down, you soft bugger, and give me my bloody teeth!"' That night of triumph offered a storybook ending to Tommy's career but, no doubt fired with new enthusiasm by the events of Rome, he played an extra term for the Reds, then went on to extend his playing days still further with John Toshack's Swansea.

As deliriously happy fans surged out of the Olympic stadium to continue their revels in the streets, Liverpool skipper Emlyn Hughes - whose vast, unceasing grin threatened to cut his head in half - admitted to reporters that he had feared the worst after the FA Cup Final defeat. 'I thought we might have left our chances behind at Wembley. But when I saw all our fabulous fans I felt confident. I didn't know it was possible to feel as good as I feel now.' For Kevin Keegan, the feelings were more complex. His inspired showing, when it had truly mattered, offered final evidence - if any were needed - that he ranked with Liverpool's all-time greats, but his love affair with the Kopites had become strained during the year since he had announced his intention to depart. The fact that they had chanted his name in Rome could never quite erase the jibes he had suffered in the months before.

But for the supporters it was time to party, and they did so with a vengeance. Later the players were eating in a private room at a big hotel, but it's not possible to keep many secrets from victorious, footloose Scousers on the scent of their heroes. They banged on the doors until it was decided to let them in; then they surged through a massive official buffet

Well done lads, you did us proud! Not a balcony is empty in this Liverpool block of flats as the Reds return to Merseyside with the European Cup. More than half a million people lined the streets as the team's open bus made the ten-mile journey from Speke airport to the city centre.

'King Kevin's' crowning glory: the indefatigable Keegan holds off a challenge from his 'shadow', Bertie Vogts, during the European Cup Final. The little striker, who had been under something of a cloud with Reds fans after announcing his intention to leave at the end of the season, put on a scintillating show in his last match for the club.

like a swarm of locusts, leaving not a crumb in their wake. They were not out for trouble, though, keeping the peace impeccably throughout their Roman holiday, and somehow it was appropriate that they should share intimately in their club's greatest triumph.

After a while the players left them to it, continuing their own celebrations in much-needed privacy. David Johnson explains: 'At such a time, you need to unwind with the people closest to you, sit and relate to the players who have done the job alongside you. We told our own stories and sang our own songs, it went on all night. The next morning we sat by the pool and, one by one, the press were thrown into the water.' Naturally David, a Liverpudlian whose boyhood idols had been St John and Hunt, felt hurt that he had been dropped for the final: 'You always feel you should be in - if you don't you might as well not be there - and I was absolutely gutted to be left out. I'll be honest and say it happened too many times for my liking at Liverpool. But I had played in quite a few of the ties that season, including the semi-final, and felt an integral part of all that was happening.'

Certainly, the unforgettable scenes on returning to Liverpool transcended any sense of personal disappointment. 'It was incredible. We drove the ten miles from Speke airport to the city centre on an open bus, and there were more than half a million people lining the streets, some even perched on lamp-posts just to get a glimpse at the team. Even the tiniest kids were decked out in red and white. I remember vividly one man running backwards alongside the bus, holding up his little boy, and saying: "Look son, that's Liverpool, and they've won the European Cup."'

That simple statement said it all, but let the final word go to Bill Shankly - who else? At the ceremony to install Bob Paisley as manager of the year, his predecessor, asked to contribute a few appropriate words, rasped: 'If you think I'm feeling a wee bit jealous' - he paused significantly - 'then you're bloody right.'

Round 1 - 1st leg
14 September 1976

LIVERPOOL 2

Neal (pen) 18; Toshack 64

CRUSADERS 0

H-T 1-0. Crowd 22,442

CLEMENCE
NEAL
JONES
SMITH
KENNEDY
HUGHES
KEEGAN
JOHNSON
HEIGHWAY
TOSHACK
CALLAGHAN

If the Reds thought life might be easy against a collection of Irish part-timers, the plucky Crusaders made them think again. The Ulstermen barely crossed the half-way line and didn't manage one attempt on Clemence's goal, but they frustrated the English champions with a defiant defensive display that limited their illustrious opponents to only two successful strikes - and the first of those was highly debatable! Liverpool went ahead when the referee awarded a penalty for a nudge in Toshack's back by the visitors' captain, McFarland; the contact was so slight that many officials would have waved play on, but Mr Sorensen was a stickler and up stepped Neal to take advantage. The Reds doubled their lead in the second half when Heighway's cross from the right was met powerfully by the trusty forehead of Toshack.

Round 1 - 2nd leg
28 September 1976

CRUSADERS 0

LIVERPOOL 5

Keegan 34; Johnson 81, 90; McDermott 84; Heighway 87
H-T 0-1. Crowd 10,000

CLEMENCE
NEAL
JONES
SMITH
KENNEDY
HUGHES
KEEGAN
JOHNSON
HEIGHWAY
CASE (McDERMOTT)
CALLAGHAN

Liverpool progressed to the second round with due ease, but even the most committed of Kopites must have felt for gallant Crusaders, who were denied a respectable scoreline by a four-goal blitz in the final nine minutes. In fact, if they had enjoyed even a small measure of the much-vaunted luck of the Irish, the home side might have inflicted severe embarrassment on the mighty Reds. Twice in the first 15 minutes, McAteer came agonisingly close to scoring, first lifting the ball over Clemence only to see it bounce off the crossbar, then watching a shot rebound from the post. Thus warned, Liverpool settled to their task and went ahead when a Johnson pass found Keegan with only the 'keeper to beat. In that moment, Crusaders' dreams died, but they fought on and the four late goals - crackers all - represented harsh reward for their efforts.

Liverpool won 7-0 on aggregate.

Round 2 - 1st leg
20 October 1976

TRABZONSPOR 1

Cemil (pen) 63

LIVERPOOL 0

H-T 0-0. Crowd 25,000

CLEMENCE
SMITH
JONES
THOMPSON
KENNEDY
HUGHES
KEEGAN
McDERMOTT
HEIGHWAY (FAIRCLOUGH)
TOSHACK (JOHNSON)
CALLAGHAN

Liverpool travelled to Trabzon to avoid defeat, and were outraged by the refereeing decision which ruined their plan. The second half of a sterile encounter was well advanced when Hughes tackled Necmi - cleanly and rather expertly, it seemed - inside the box. But the Turk took a tumble, the Romanian official signalled a penalty and the hosts' skipper, Cemil, gave Clemence no hope with his kick, placed perfectly just inside a post. Now the Reds, who until the goal had concentrated on containing tactics, brought on Johnson and Fairclough, but by the end of 90 minutes had not succeeded in getting one shot on target. Indeed, they won only one corner, an accurate reflection of their approach on a bumpy pitch and using a misshapen ball - hardly conducive to high adventure.

Round 2 - 2nd leg
3 November 1976

LIVERPOOL 3

Heighway 8; Johnson 10; Keegan 18

TRABZONSPOR 0

H-T 3-0. Crowd 42,275

CLEMENCE
NEAL
JONES
THOMPSON
KENNEDY
HUGHES
KEEGAN
McDERMOTT
HEIGHWAY
JOHNSON
CALLAGHAN

Liverpool exacted rapid revenge for their travails in Trabzon, sinking the Turks with three goals in the opening 18 minutes. Heighway had the simple job of knocking in the first after Keegan nodded on a McDermott cross. Within two minutes Johnson added a second, nipping in to flick the ball over the line after Cemil had failed to make a clearance, then Keegan wrapped up the result by heading home from a Callaghan cross. Thereafter the Reds might have run riot, but opted for a restrained approach, although Neal, Keegan and Johnson all found the net only for their efforts to be disqualified for offside. In the second half the disappointed visitors became over-physical, and substitute Cemil (M) was sent off for clattering Neal as the game reached an unsavoury close.

Liverpool won 3-1 on aggregate.

Courage of the Crusaders: Emlyn Hughes gets in a shot against the valiant Irish part-timers, whose stubborn resistance at Anfield limited the Reds to a two-goal advantage. At the end of the game the Kop honoured the Ulstermen with a well-earned ovation.

Pop idol: Dominique Rocheteau *(second from right)* was touted in France as the man who could bamboozle the Reds, but though he buzzed threat-eningly when St Etienne came to Anfield, his menace was contained by the close attentions of Joey Jones *(left)* and Tommy Smith.

Round 3 - 1st leg
2 March 1977

ST ETIENNE 1
Bathenay 80

LIVERPOOL 0

H-T 0-0. Crowd 28,000

CLEMENCE
NEAL
JONES
THOMPSON
KENNEDY
HUGHES
McDERMOTT
CASE
HEIGHWAY
TOSHACK (SMITH)
CALLAGHAN

Liverpool played controlled football against the multi-talented French champions, heading back to Merseyside with an acceptable one-goal deficit. In truth, St Etienne never quite lived up to their glittering reputation, having been unable to cope effectively with a Reds side locked firmly into their cautious, away-from-Anfield mode. Although the Greens attacked brightly, especially in the early parts of each half, Liverpool always seemed capable of containing them, and Paisley's men broke so smoothly out of defence that they created more clear-cut goal opportunities than their hosts. In the first half 'keeper Jurcovic was forced to save from Case and Heighway, and Thompson was wide with a free header from a corner. The Reds came even closer to breaking the deadlock when Case freed Heighway after 70 minutes, but the Irishman shot against a post. Ten minutes later, St Etienne took the lead when a corner bounced to Janvion beyond the far post; the full-back miscued but the ball reached Bathenay, who volleyed adroitly past Clemence. Now the tie was perfectly poised for a rousing climax.

Round 3 - 2nd leg
16 March 1977

LIVERPOOL 3
Keegan 2; Kennedy 58; Fairclough 84

ST ETIENNE 1
Bathenay 51
H-T 1-0. Crowd 55,043

CLEMENCE
NEAL
JONES
SMITH
KENNEDY
HUGHES
KEEGAN
CASE
HEIGHWAY
TOSHACK (FAIRCLOUGH)
CALLAGHAN

Liverpool made an ideal start to one of their most memorable European clashes. With battle barely joined, Keegan received a short corner from Heighway, moved ten yards infield and floated a speculative cross cum shot that deceived 'keeper Jurcovic and dropped into the net. Any French thoughts of sitting on their lead were thus scuppered and, while St Etienne relied heavily on offside tactics, both teams put together some enterprising moves. In fact, the visitors looked the more penetrative at times, with Rocheteau forcing Clemence to make two acrobatic stops, but the Reds' 'keeper was helpless when Bathenay struck a viciously swerving shot from 30 yards. Because of the away goals rule, Liverpool now HAD to score twice, a formidable proposition against such accomplished opponents. Cue Kennedy, with two decisive contributions. First he netted with a low shot from the edge of the box after Toshack had knocked back a Callaghan cross, then he lifted the ball over the Greens' defence for the substitute, Fairclough, to shrug off a challenge and run on to slide the ball home with nerveless precision from eight yards. Thereafter bedlam reigned on a great, great night.

Liverpool won 3-2 on aggregate.

Semi-final - 1st leg
6 April 1977

FC ZURICH 1
Risi (pen) 5

LIVERPOOL 3
Neal 14, (pen) 67; Heighway 47
H-T 1-1. Crowd 30,500

CLEMENCE
NEAL
JONES
SMITH
KENNEDY
HUGHES
KEEGAN
CASE
HEIGHWAY
FAIRCLOUGH
McDERMOTT

After surviving an early setback, Liverpool cruised towards their first European Cup Final. The reverse came when Smith's sliding tackle on Schweiler was deemed illegal by the Turkish referee and Risi netted from the spot, via a post. As if outraged by such temerity, the Reds swarmed into attack and soon they were level, Kennedy driving a long free-kick beyond the Swiss defence for Neal to steal in and poke the ball home from the angle of the six-yard box. Retaining the initiative, the visitors continued to press and went ahead when McDermott passed cleverly to Heighway, who evaded three defenders before slipping the ball into the net from a narrow angle. Botteron then missed a rare opening for Zurich, but Liverpool scored the third goal their dominance merited when Heighway - clean through with only the 'keeper to beat - was downed and Neal struck a copybook penalty.

Semi-final - 2nd leg
20 April 1977

LIVERPOOL 3
Case 33, 79; Keegan 83

FC ZURICH 0

H-T 1-0. Crowd 50,611

CLEMENCE
NEAL
JONES
SMITH
KENNEDY
HUGHES
KEEGAN
CASE
HEIGHWAY (WADDLE)
McDERMOTT
JOHNSON

As semi-finals go, Liverpool's return encounter with Zurich was a flaccid affair. Barring miracles, the Reds' ticket to Rome had been booked by their first-leg performance, and the Swiss were not of sufficient calibre to mount a recovery. Accordingly, and with an FA Cup semi-final against Everton only three days away, Bob Paisley's side took the game at a leisurely pace, doing just enough to win by respectable proportions. Apparently fearful of stirring their hosts to greater efforts, Zurich packed their defence, and the outcome was stultifying. Two of Liverpool's goals came from Case, the first a simple drive after a defender had slipped, and the second a powerful 25-yard free-kick. Keegan completed the scoring, nodding home the rebound after Waddle had headed Kennedy's centre against the bar. Rarely can 50,000 fans have been offered such desultory entertainment.

Liverpool won 6-1 on aggregate.

Final in Rome
25 May 1977

LIVERPOOL 3
McDermott 28; Smith 64;
Neal (pen) 82

BORUSSIA MOENCHENGLADBACH 1
Simonsen 52
H-T 1-0.
Crowd 57,000

CLEMENCE
NEAL
JONES
SMITH
KENNEDY
HUGHES
KEEGAN
CASE
HEIGHWAY
CALLAGHAN
McDERMOTT

Goal of the game: Steve Heighway climaxes a characteristic dash past three defenders before scoring from an acute angle in Zurich. The Irishman's enterprise put Liverpool in front for the first time, and the Merseysiders grew increasingly dominant as the semi-final progressed.

Liverpool became champions of Europe with a polished and spirited display against opposition of the highest quality. The Reds were quickly into their stride, moving the ball around with confidence, but received a jolt after 22 minutes when Bonhof flexed his muscles and rattled Clemence's post with a low 20-yarder. The Merseysiders continued to enjoy the bulk of the possession, however, and made it tell six minutes later. Callaghan won the ball in midfield and fed Heighway on the right; cutting inside, the winger moved menacingly goalwards before splitting the German defence with a perfectly weighted pass to McDermott, who swept the ball unerringly inside the far post from 12 yards. Borussia kept their heads, still content to play the Continental waiting game, and they capitalised on a mistake soon after half-

time. It came from Case in the form of a wayward back-pass which Simonsen seized, ran into the box and lashed a magnificent rising cross-shot into the far top corner of the net. Ten minutes later, as the Germans showed signs of assuming control, Clemence made the save of the night, diving at the feet of the onrushing Stielike. Arguably it was the turning point, for Liverpool were soon on the victory path as Heighway drove a corner from the left and Smith rose majestically to head high into the net. Even then it might have slipped away but for a brave double save by Clemence on the edge of the area. The spoils were secured, finally, when the tireless Keegan surged into the area and was on the point of shooting when he was upended by his 'shadow', Vogts. Neal made no mistake from the spot and the Reds were left to revel in their finest hour.

Top: **Terry McDermott strikes crisply and accurately to open the scoring in the European Cup Final.**

Two faces of victory: Ecstatic Emlyn Hughes with the Cup, and a thoughtful David Johnson, who was left out of the team in Rome.

Plain Tommy Smith or Roy of the Rovers? Liverpool's iron man, in what was to have been his farewell appearance, heads powerfully into the net to restore the Reds' lead against Borussia in Rome. It was better than Boys' Own fiction, and he said later: 'I thought of having a brass plate put in my nut to mark the spot.'

Phil Neal, perhaps the most reliable British penalty-taker of his generation, does the honours to clinch the European Cup. Here was no chancy blast, but a perfect example of the spot-kicker's art, the goalkeeper going one way and the ball, hit firmly and low, going the other.

The Gaffer: Bob Paisley emerges from the tunnel at Anfield. No extrovert in the mould of Bill Shankly, nevertheless he possessed a droll sense of humour that he aired with increasing confidence as the trophies rolled in.

Chapter Eight

KENNY'S FROM HEAVEN

HAVING reached the pinnacle of achievement in Rome, the Reds moved on rapidly to a critical crossroads. The travails of Manchester United in the years following their European Cup triumph of 1968 illustrated graphically the perils of complacency; could Liverpool - having lost their most influential player, Kevin Keegan, to Hamburg in the summer - now fall prey to the same creeping malaise? The answer, emphatically and triumphantly, was in the negative. To have done so would have denied the Anfield ethos created by Bill Shankly, then carried on and amplified by Bob Paisley and his able lieutenants. It boiled down to the deceptively simple creed of keeping the feet of everyone at the club, from star performers down to the humblest apprentices, solidly in touch with terra firma. If there has been a secret for Liverpool's phenomenal success down the decades, some magic ingredient which others have sought in vain to copy, it is no more than that. Anyone who doubts that unadorned truth, believing that there MUST be some complicated formula for 30 years of almost uninterrupted excellence, would do well to talk to Ronnie Moran. Now Paisley and Joe Fagan have gone, no one is better qualified to deliver a verdict; Ronnie served the Anfield cause as a loyal full-back through the lean seasons of the 1950s, sampled glory in the early years of Shanks's reign, became a coach and key motivator to the Liverpool sides that swept all before them in the 1970s and 1980s, and even stepped in as caretaker manager in the troubled springs of 1991 and 1992. Indeed, it is hard to believe there is anyone in the land who knows more about the game. Ronnie tells it straight: 'First of all you need people who can play the game, and who have the right character. After that, you have to make sure that those people remain level-headed. It's no good getting too high when you win, because then you'll get too low when you lose.' He shakes his head in disbelief when telling of opponents' disproportionate joy in defeating Liverpool: 'I have watched players from other clubs go absolutely berserk after winning a League match against us. I have even seen a chairman break out the champagne for nothing more than a routine victory. I asked him "What's the point of celebrating like that over one result? The end of the season is a long way off." He replied "Ah, but we've beaten Liverpool" as if they deserved a trophy for that alone. Of course, they lost their next match, and that chairman's reaction after the game with us might be part of the reason why. Any team, whoever they are, are only as good as their last result. If we win a championship or cup, we don't spend time talking about it. We don't even dwell on the last match, let alone the last season. Keeping on an even keel and looking ahead, that's all that matters.'

Thus from such a stable base did the Reds approach 1977/78 and the campaign to retain the European Cup. In the close season Paisley had filled the void left by Keegan's departure, paying Celtic a British record fee of £440,000 for Kenny Dalglish. The newcomer was no Kevin clone, of course, his silkier skills opening new avenues of team play. Another significant arrival at this time was Alan Hansen, a slim young central defender from Partick Thistle, then unknown south of the border but who was destined to become, quite simply, the best in the business.

As European champions the Reds were exempt from the preliminaries, not being required to begin their defence until October, when they were paired with Dynamo Dresden.

The East Germans were well-known opponents, having been beaten on the road to the UEFA Cup triumphs of 1973 and 1976, but were a well-equipped side unbeaten so far that season. Unfortunately for Dynamo, when they watched Liverpool prior to the tie, John Toshack was sidelined by injury. Unwisely, as it turned out, they assumed he would not be back in time for the Anfield first leg, and did not prepare to meet an aerial threat. Hence the Welshman destroyed them, creating a succession of chances, three of which were converted as the Reds romped to a 5-1 advantage. Now, surely, the tie was safe; any other outcome would have represented the upset of the decade in European competition. Yet with Toshack not there to plague them, the East Germans gave a far better account of themselves on their own soil and a double strike after the interval brought a meaningful Dresden comeback distinctly within the bounds of possibility. However, when the hitherto negative Merseysiders decided finally that attack was the best form of defence, they killed off the contest with a goal from Steve Heighway.

Liverpool's next overseas opponents were Cup Winners' Cup holders Hamburg - Keegan *et al.* - in the so-called European Super Cup. German fans could not get excited about the prospect, only 16,000 turning up for the first leg, which ended 1-1. Anfield regulars were more enthusiastic, however, nearly 35,000 paying to watch Kevin's new team crushed 6-0 by his old one. Few neutrals cared either way, but there was no denying the mouth-watering prospect thrown up by the Champions' Cup quarter-final draw: Liverpool, currently the dominant power in Europe, against Benfica, who had usurped Real Madrid's mantle as the Continent's premier side in the early 1960s. Admittedly, though their very name continued to carry an undeniable resonance, this current Portuguese vintage did not compare favourably with that of Eusebio and company. Even so, the Eagles remained a considerable force, going into the first leg at the Stadium of Light with a 46-match unbeaten record in all competitions, and clearly, those who seek to write off their subsequent mauling do less than justice to a sizeable Liverpool achievement.

The back of the Merseysiders' task was broken in Portugal when they fashioned a 2-1 victory after falling behind in a veritable mudbath. Tommy Smith remarked, with commendable charity, that the conditions might have favoured his team but that should not take away one shred of credit. The winning of trophies demands as much character as ability, and anyone who witnessed Liverpool toiling valiantly on that Portuguese paddyfield, while the bedraggled Eagles looked as if they wished they were somewhere else, could be in no doubt who deserved to win. After that it was inconceivable that the Reds should surrender their lead, and they didn't, hammering a timorous Benfica 4-1 at Anfield without ever needing to stretch themselves. No doubt Liverpool were sparing a thought to their League Cup Final meeting with Nottingham Forest the following Saturday. That ended in a draw, though Brian Clough's side won the replay before adding insult to injury by stripping the Merseysiders of their League title.

Back in Europe, Liverpool found themselves matched once more with a fiercely determined Borussia Moenchengladbach, hell-bent on revenge for their defeat in Rome the preceding year. At the time, the Reds were only fifth in the First Division table and there was the unthinkable prospect that the door to the Continent might be closed in 1978/79 unless they qualified as holders of the European Cup. With so much at stake, Bob Paisley opted to play it safe in Germany in the first leg and was not displeased with a 2-1 reverse, despite conceding an 89th-minute winner just 60 seconds after David Johnson had equalised. Before the return, the Anfield boss indulged in some Shankly-style psychology designed to make his men feel like world-beaters. He ran through the Borussia squad, dismissing Vogts as over the hill at 32 and speculating that 29-year-old Bonhof had seen his best days. All the while Ian Callaghan, who had just celebrated his 36th birthday, and Tommy Smith, a comparatively youthful 33, were wondering where that left them! As Joe Fagan pointed out, though, footballers are as young as they feel, and Tommy looked as frisky as a teenager as the visitors were pulverised 3-0.

Chief architect of a glorious win was a recent signing from Middlesbrough, one Graeme Souness, whose potent blend of delicate skill and naked aggression was unmatched by any British play-maker of his era. 'Suey' took the anchor role while the underrated Ray

Undone by a pick-axe: Tommy Smith, here thundering a shot goalwards against Borussia Moenchengladbach at Anfield, was set for his second successive European Cup Final appearance until he broke a toe in an accident at his home.

Kennedy lurked menacingly on the left, pugnacious Jimmy Case patrolled the right, and Terry McDermott, that creative workhorse, roamed at will. Together this majestic quartet formed as effective a midfield combination as could be found in club football anywhere in the world, as the devastated Germans were ready to acknowledge. Indeed, at the end of the game the Moenchengladbach players were sportsmen enough to remain on the pitch and join in the applause as their conquerors completed a lap of honour.

The only sad sight on an exhilarating evening was that of poor David Johnson hobbling on the touchline, and hugging each of his team-mates as they ran off the pitch. David - who had been dropped from the 1977 final, then fought back to play a major part in the current campaign - had strained knee ligaments in the League clash with Leicester four days before the Borussia return, and would now be out for the rest of the season. He recalls: 'It came as a terrible blow. There I was, full of the joys of spring after battling to regain my place, then suddenly it was all over. I went straight into hospital for an operation and was still on crutches by the time of the final. Consequently I couldn't even be a substitute and missed out on a medal.' That particular hard-luck story was to have a happy sequel, but more of that later.

In view of the marvellous showing against the Germans, and with the final being played at Wembley, Liverpool were red-hot favourites to brush aside FC Bruges and retain their most prized trophy. So they did, but not before a TV audience of millions endured perhaps the drabbest final in memory. The blame for that sorry circumstance rested entirely with the Belgians, who opted for a spoiling game from the first whistle, frustrating the Reds with passive resistance while presumably hoping to grab a goal on the break. Admittedly, injury had deprived them of several influential players - the lively Lambert was a notable absentee - but that hardly excused such fear-ridden tactics. Liverpool - themselves minus Johnson and Tommy Smith, who missed out after dropping a pick-axe on his foot - attacked unremittingly but with precious little penetration until the 65th minute. Then Souness and Dalglish each produced superb examples of their characteristic talents - Souness an inch-perfect pass, Dalglish a subtle touch that was more caress than shot - and Liverpool had taken a decisive lead. Only once did their unenterprising opponents threaten to equalise, but the danger was cleared and a continent of football-lovers was spared the mind-numbing experience of an extra 30 minutes. The Reds had beaten Bruges in a European final for the second time, and despite the dreariness of the action, the victors were entitled to their glee. An understandably proud Emlyn Hughes declared, not for the first time, that Liverpool were the greatest club in the world and added: 'The Cup felt as though it had never been out of my hands.' And Scouser Phil Thompson, who had suffered the mortification of missing the Roman conquest through injury, was beside himself with joy, explaining: 'It was so hard for me last time. I was involved to an extent, but the big thing is to be out there on the pitch.' In the opposite camp, Bruges' coach Ernst Happel summoned the audacity to say he was disappointed with the Merseysiders' performance, claiming that Bob Paisley's side were not a patch on previous Anfield teams. That was rich, coming from the man responsible for arguably the most negative display ever seen in a Wembley showpiece.

Tommy Smith, viewing from the stands, reckoned the Belgians were terrified, both of Liverpool and of losing. As he said: 'It was a pathetic attitude. You never win anything like that.' Unfortunately, such a hidebound approach was to become relatively common in future European finals, reaching an appalling nadir in 1991 when Red Star Belgrade admitted playing for a penalty shoot-out from the off. Unbelievably they achieved their objective, then converted more spot-kicks than Marseilles to claim European football's top club prize. Somehow the tawdriness of such strategy was emphasised by the fact that it was employed by one of the pioneers of the very competition they now debased. After the 1978 final the pundits panned the match unmercifully - and with total justification - but they riled Paisley by suggesting that his side had triumphed in a poor season. Indeed, one of the manager's persistent gripes in the years ahead was that the Reds rarely got the credit they deserved.

One man who did get his just deserts, eventually, was David Johnson, thanks to the initiative of Steve Heighway. Saddened by his team-mate's excruciating luck, the Eire international wrote to FIFA, outlining the important part David had played in reaching the final and asking if he could have a medal in recognition of his efforts. The rest of the players signed the letter and the club weighed in with their backing, but as the months went by nothing more was heard. David takes up the story: 'I had given up hope and forgotten all about it, concentrating on regaining my place in the side. At last things were going pretty well for me. I was scoring goals and was rewarded with an international recall by Ron Greenwood. On the England trip, I bumped into FA Secretary Ted Croker, who said 'Ah David, I've got something for you.' I wondered what on earth it might be, and was absolutely made up when he gave me a European Cup medal sent to him by FIFA. I'd got one already for being a non-playing substitute in Rome, and now had two without kicking a ball. That might make a quiz question one day!'

Another footnote to the 1978 European Cup Final was the departure from Anfield, on the day after the match, of Ian Callaghan, who had given 18 years of sterling senior service, first as a traditional winger, then as a workaholic midfielder. In 1977 he had been offered the chance to follow Johnny Giles as player-boss of West Bromwich Albion, but decided that the management rat-race was not for him. Now he crossed the Atlantic to join Fort Lauderdale Strikers - rooming with George Best, of whom he speaks nothing but good as both player and man - before joining John Toshack's ever-growing contingent of former Reds at Swansea. During his tenure with Liverpool, Ian had seen football transformed from an essentially working-class occupation to a money-dominated business far removed from

Double disappointment: David Johnson, who had been dropped for the 1977 European Cup Final, missed the Wembley date with FC Bruges after straining knee ligaments in a League clash with Leicester City. Team-mates ensured he didn't miss out on a medal, but that was no substitute for playing. However, David's day would come.

Finding the gap: Jimmy Case is airborne after blasting a free-kick through Dynamo Tbilisi's defensive wall to put Liverpool in front at Anfield. Graeme Souness is the picture of nonchalance, while the Soviet defenders appear to be consoling each other in advance. It would be Dynamo, though, who would have the last laugh.

everyday life. His reminiscences are not sentimental, and he would be the first to admit that he has enjoyed the material benefits he has earned from the game, but there is a certain wistfulness when he thinks back to 1960. 'I used to queue for a bus to get to the match, along with those fans who liked to get there early. Sometimes I would be recognised and they would let me go ahead of them so I would be there on time. There would always be plenty of good-natured banter, and there was definitely a close relationship with the supporters.' Three decades later, the rising star is much farther removed from the people who pay his wages. While they are still lining up for the bus, he has the use of a plush sponsored car, provided for him by sponsors with pound signs in their eyes. Meanwhile TV cash rules football with ever-increasing rigidity, ticket prices soar as top clubs invest fortunes in new seating, and the poor old fan likes it or lumps it. What price 'the people's game' in the twenty-first century?

But we digress. After winning the European Cup two seasons in succession, the Reds' new objective was to complete a coveted hat-trick, a feat performed previously by only Real Madrid, Ajax and Bayern Munich. Standing in their way in the first round was the familiar but ever-more-formidable obstacle of Nottingham Forest; the draw could hardly have been less kind. Against the Midlanders, Liverpool's European expertise counted for nothing, both legs being played in the same manner as typical English League games, and as was proved by the outcome of the two clubs' six meetings between December 1977 and September 1978 - two Forest victories, four draws and just one goal scored by Paisley's team - the Clough camp had a clear edge. In the first game, at the City Ground, Liverpool went behind early on, but as the final whistle neared they seemed content and the travelling Kopites sang that one goal would never be enough. As if in answer to the taunt, Forest grabbed a second two minutes from time, and suddenly the task facing the Merseysiders assumed daunting proportions. Sure enough, at Anfield they strove without inspiration to wipe out the deficit, the visitors' assured defensive display giving rise to their fans' chanted assertion that 'Shilton is better than Clemence.' When the referee ended proceedings, a desolate Phil Thompson sank to his knees and lowered his head to the turf. It had been that kind of night. It was Liverpool's first European elimination since November 1974, the first time in a decade that they had fallen at the first hurdle and the end of their hat-trick dream. No wonder Bob Paisley described it as the saddest event of his managerial career.

For full-back Alan Kennedy, who had been signed from Newcastle United at the start of the season, it had been an anti-climactic introduction to Continental competition. He recalls: 'It didn't seem like Europe at all. We seemed to approach it just like any domestic game and maybe that was a mistake. But let's be fair, Forest were a marvellous side at the time and, over the two matches, they deserved to win. In those days they were THE English opposition to Liverpool and it was a shame we met in the first round. I'm sure both clubs were keen to avoid each other.' In fact, the sides were well matched, and while Forest went on to win the Cup that had spent two years in the Anfield trophy room, the Reds reclaimed the League title that had gone to Nottingham the season before.

That meant an instant return to Europe - their Super Cup defeat against Anderlecht of Belgium in December 1978 did not really count - and the chance to tilt once for for the premier prize. What awaited, however, was chastening disappointment as Liverpool were subjected to their second successive first-round knockout, this time at the hands of Dynamo Tbilisi. The warnings were there for all to see in the first leg at Anfield, despite the Merseysiders managing a 2-1 triumph. The Soviets, who spent 15 minutes parading their slick skills to the Kop before kick-off, continued their exhibition when the game began and, in all honesty, only abysmal finishing prevented them inflicting a home defeat on the English champions. The expedition to Georgia, two weeks later, was ill starred from the start, the Liverpool party flying into Moscow only to be denied permission to cross interior air-space to reach Tbilisi. Their chartered plane was parked in a hangar as they waited some five hours for a scheduled domestic flight. Come the match, the Merseysiders defended resolutely in a downpour to achieve a blank scoresheet at the interval, but were engulfed in the second period, conceding three goals as Dynamo turned on the style. An enraptured crowd in the Lenin Stadium lit thousands of torches and chanted their heroes' names in Western style as the end drew near. Significantly, there were no excuses from Liverpool; there was no argument, the best team won. Indeed, men such as play-maker Kipiani, midfielder and captain Machaidze and striker Schengeliya, the USSR player of the year, would have graced any English First Division side. At that time, no Eastern European club had lifted the Cup, but Dynamo looked more than capable of making the breakthrough. Alas for the accomplished and deserving Soviets, they bowed out in the next round to a Hamburg side inspired by Kevin Keegan. And the European Cup? That remained in Nottingham, for the time being . . .

Round 2 - 1st leg
19 October 1977

LIVERPOOL 5
Hansen 14; Case 21, 57; Neal (pen) 44;
Kennedy 66

DYNAMO DRESDEN 1
Hafner 76
H-T 3-0. Crowd 39,835

CLEMENCE
NEAL
JONES
HANSEN
KENNEDY
HUGHES
DALGLISH
CASE
HEIGHWAY
TOSHACK
CALLAGHAN

Liverpool played exceedingly well and took their chances with aplomb, yet the feeling persisted that Dresden were a better team than the scoreline indicated. The principal difference between the two protagonists was Toshack, who failed to find the net himself but had a hand - or rather a head - in three goals. His first significant contribution was a delicate glance across goal from a corner that Hansen headed powerfully home for the opener. Next, the Welshman flicked the ball to Case, who nodded in the second, then he headed down for Kennedy to knock in the fifth. In between, Neal scored a penalty after Dalglish had been fouled and Case thrashed in a 30-yarder. Dynamo's late reply, dispatched neatly by Hafner, inspired further German raids, leaving Liverpool distinctly thankful for their comfortable lead.

Though suffering fitness problems in his final campaign at Anfield, John Toshack remained a formidable opponent as Dynamo Dresden discovered to their cost. The Welshman didn't score himself but his aerial might and often-underrated subtlety made goals for Alan Hansen, Jimmy Case and Ray Kennedy.

Round 2 - 2nd leg
2 November 1977

DYNAMO DRESDEN 2
Kotte 46; Sachse 52

LIVERPOOL 1
Heighway 67
H-T 0-0. Crowd 33,000

CLEMENCE
NEAL
JONES
HANSEN
KENNEDY
HUGHES
DALGLISH
CASE
HEIGHWAY
McDERMOTT (FAIRCLOUGH)
CALLAGHAN

The suspicion that Dynamo might be wolves in lambs' clothing was borne out by a spirited display. From the off, the Reds sought to preserve their hefty first-leg advantage, and Clemence found himself in frequent action. With the scoresheet blank at the break, it seemed that Liverpool were safe, but a swift double-strike changed all that. First Dorner's free-kick was deflected to Kotte, who scored from close range; then Sachse headed in a Hafner cross. Now Liverpool were wobbling, and had the home side accepted either of two further presentable chances, then a sensation was clearly possible. In their moment of greatest danger, however, the Reds responded like true champions. Substitute Fairclough broke free on the left, his centre caused confusion in the Dresden ranks and Heighway stabbed the ball home. Suddenly, it was all over.

Liverpool won 6-3 on aggregate.

Round 3 - 1st leg
1 March 1978

BENFICA 1
Nene 18

LIVERPOOL 2
Case 37; Hughes 72
H-T 1-1. Crowd 70,000

CLEMENCE
NEAL
SMITH
THOMPSON (HANSEN)
KENNEDY
HUGHES
DALGLISH
CASE
HEIGHWAY
McDERMOTT
CALLAGHAN

Liverpool revealed all their ruthless efficiency and strength of character to overturn a Benfica side that had not been beaten for 46 games. On a filthy night when torrential rain turned the pitch into a swamp, the Reds showed the greater appetite for the fray and their comeback from a goal down must rank as one of their most valiant European achievements. The slick Portuguese went ahead when Nene sprinted on to a long clearance, outstripped the chasing defenders and beat the advancing Clemence with a precise shot. Liverpool refused to buckle, however, and equalised when Case netted with a free-kick from the edge of the box. Benfica poured into attack as the second half commenced, but Smith and company held firm and the Eagles became flustered. Then it was Liverpool's turn to advance, and Hughes secured a precious lead with a speculative floater from the left flank.

The mark of class: despite the close attentions of two defenders, Kenny Dalglish sends the ball humming goalwards against Benfica at Anfield.

Semi-final - 2nd leg
12 April 1978

LIVERPOOL 3
Kennedy 6; Dalglish 35; Case 56

BORUSSIA MOENCHENGLADBACH 0

H-T 2-0. Crowd 51,500

CLEMENCE
NEAL
SMITH
THOMPSON
KENNEDY
HUGHES
DALGLISH
CASE
HEIGHWAY
McDERMOTT
SOUNESS

Arguably it was Liverpool's performance of the season; certainly it was one of their most convincing in 14 European campaigns. They brushed aside the powerful Germans, who appeared awestruck at the volume attained by the Kop choir, to reach the final with something to spare. The Reds wasted little time in wiping out the one-goal first-leg deficit. The increasingly influential Souness freed Dalglish on the right, the striker delivered a delightful curling cross and Kennedy planted a firm header beyond the reach of 'keeper Kleff. Thus encouraged, Liverpool refused to relax their grip and scored again before the break, Kennedy heading a Heighway cross to Dalglish, who squeezed his volley just inside a post. Borussia regrouped at half-time and menaced briefly, but their resistance was crushed finally when Kennedy found Case, who cut past a defender before thrashing the ball high into goal. Thereafter the visitors had little relish for their work, and seemed relieved when the final whistle ended their ordeal.

Liverpool won 4-2 on aggregate.

Why me? Ray Clemence registers remorse after being beaten by Bonhof's ferocious free-kick in the dying minutes of the semi-final first leg.

Round 3 - 2nd leg
15 March 1978

LIVERPOOL 4
Callaghan 6; Dalglish 17; McDermott 78; Neal 88

BENFICA 1
Nene 25
H-T 2-1. Crowd 48,364

CLEMENCE
NEAL
SMITH
THOMPSON
KENNEDY
HUGHES
DALGLISH
CASE
HEIGHWAY
McDERMOTT
CALLAGHAN

It was a scrappy, unsatisfying game, but that hardly mattered to the Reds as they eclipsed the famous Benfica to reach the semi-finals. The outcome was beyond reasonable doubt early in the first half, after a Callaghan cross was deflected into the net, and Dalglish had seized on Toni's sloppy back-pass to score with a perfectly placed shot from just inside the area. Soon afterwards, however, the Portuguese were given the merest glimmer of hope when Case emulated Toni's carelessness and Nene reacted instantly to give Clemence no chance. Liverpool found better form in the second half but could not pierce the visitors' rearguard until near the end. Then they scored twice, 'keeper Bento failing to stop a McDermott drive from crossing the line, then watching bemused as Neal netted with a fierce cross-shot after McDermott had miskicked.

Liverpool won 6-2 on aggregate

Semi-final - 1st leg
29 March 1978

BORUSSIA MOENCHENGLADBACH 2
Hannes 28; Bonhof 89

LIVERPOOL 1
Johnson 88
H-T 1-0. Crowd 66,000

CLEMENCE
NEAL
SMITH
THOMPSON
KENNEDY
HUGHES
DALGLISH
CASE
HEIGHWAY (SOUNESS)
McDERMOTT (JOHNSON)
CALLAGHAN

A cautious encounter, which for most of its duration would have satisfied connoisseurs of tactics but frustrated seekers after thrills, erupted into stunning action in the closing minutes. Until then, as the two sides probed each other for weaknesses without committing themselves to all-out attack, defences had reigned largely supreme. As expected of the hosts, Borussia enjoyed the better of the first half, but all they had to show for it was one strike from Hannes, who swept home a crashing ten-yarder following a corner. Liverpool began to assert themselves after the interval, and both McDermott and Case went close, although Heynckes hit the post for the Germans. With two minutes left, the Reds grabbed a precious away goal when Johnson dived ahead of Vogts to nod into the net. However, retaliation was instant. Bonhof pierced the Reds' defensive wall with a 22-yard free-kick of fearsome force, the ball grazing the shoulder of the startled Clemence on its way into the net. Even so, Liverpool were not unhappy with their night's work.

Final at Wembley
10 May 1978

LIVERPOOL 1
Dalglish 65

FC BRUGES 0
H-T 0-0. Crowd 92,000

CLEMENCE
NEAL
THOMPSON
HANSEN
KENNEDY
HUGHES
DALGLISH
CASE (HEIGHWAY)
FAIRCLOUGH
McDERMOTT
SOUNESS

Through no fault of Liverpool, this was a nonentity of a cup final. Bruges were utterly negative, content to soak up wave after wave of pressure while waiting, presumably, for a chance on one of their rare breakaways. The first half was an interlude of uninterrupted frustration for the Reds and their legions of fans. Fairclough, Case, Dalglish and McDermott all came excruciatingly close to ending the stalemate, but all were denied by 'keeper Jensen, whose mixture of excellence and good fortune kept the Belgian goal intact. But when Liverpool did manage, finally, to breach that white wall, it was a moment worth waiting for, a simple but devastatingly

effective combination between two master footballers. Souness wrong-footed the Bruges defence with an immaculately weighted through-ball, for Dalglish to dink over the diving Jensen with a sureness and delicacy reminiscent of Jimmy Greaves. Astoundingly, the Belgians almost found a way back ten minutes from time when Sorensen seized on a casual back-pass from Hansen; Clemence blocked the shot but it took a goal-line clearance from Thompson to save the day.
For Liverpool to concede would have been a travesty of justice, but the Cup was theirs and how richly they deserved it.

Jimmy Greaves couldn't have done it any better, and in terms of strikers, that's the ultimate compliment. Having been freed by Graeme Souness's incisive pass, Kenny Dalgish clips the ball over Bruges goalkeeper Jensen to land Liverpool's second successive European Cup.

Round 1 - 1st leg
13 September 1978

NOTTINGHAM FOREST 2

Birtles 26; Barrett 88

LIVERPOOL 0

H-T 1-0. Crowd 38,316

CLEMENCE
NEAL
KENNEDY, ALAN
THOMPSON
KENNEDY, RAY
HUGHES
DALGLISH
CASE
HEIGHWAY
McDERMOTT (JOHNSON)
SOUNESS

Liverpool were distinctly second best to the new force in English soccer. Nottingham Forest appeared hungrier for success and quicker to the ball, their forwards - especially Robertson, the wily left-winger - frequently stretching a visiting defence that in recent seasons had stood firm against some of the finest sides in the world. Brian Clough's men went ahead when Bowyer passed penetratingly to Woodcock, who ran on to set up the simplest of chances for Birtles. The Merseysiders were more positive in the second half, bringing on Johnson for McDermott, but couldn't find a chink in the home rearguard, although Heighway reckoned he should have had a penalty when tackled by Anderson. The real hammer-blow fell two minutes from time, when Woodcock nudged a Birtles cross to Barrett, who cracked the ball home with gleeful finality.

Above right: **Ray Kennedy, master of the ball as usual, is tracked by Viv Anderson and John McGovern at the City Ground. However, the Merseysiders were well-beaten by a Nottingham Forest side that was destined to win the European Cup and retain it the following year.**

Mutual respect from two outstanding performers: Peter Shilton and Kenny Dalglish find time for a quiet word during the heat of battle at the City Ground. In both legs of a tight contest, the Forest 'keeper proved equal to everything the Reds could throw at him.

Round 1 - 2nd leg
27 September 1978

LIVERPOOL 0

NOTTINGHAM FOREST 0

Crowd 51,679

| CLEMENCE |
| NEAL |
| KENNEDY, ALAN |
| THOMPSON |
| KENNEDY, RAY |
| HUGHES |
| DALGLISH |
| CASE (FAIRCLOUGH) |
| HEIGHWAY |
| McDERMOTT (JOHNSON) |
| SOUNESS |

Liverpool set off frantically in an attempt to wipe out the two-goal deficit conceded at the City Ground, but a formidable Forest defence - in which Lloyd, a former Red, and the combative Burns were outstanding - held them at bay. McDermott threatened with an early lob, then Kennedy poked over from a Neal cross but, in all honesty, a breakthrough never appeared to be imminent. In a second half of increasing desperation, manager Bob Paisley pitched marksmen Johnson and Fairclough into the fray but they made no more impact than the men they replaced. Still the predatory instincts of Dalglish held out a measure of hope, but when Shilton saved brilliantly from two 15-yarders - one a cunning, low drive on the turn, the other a fierce snap-shot - it was clearly not going to be Liverpool's night.

Nottingham Forest won 2-0 on aggregate.

European Cup 1979/80

Round 1 - 1st leg.
1 September 1979

LIVERPOOL 2
Johnson 19; Case 44

DYNAMO TBILISI 1
Chivadze 33
H-T 1-1. Crowd 35,270

| CLEMENCE |
| NEAL |
| KENNEDY, ALAN |
| IRWIN |
| THOMPSON |
| FAIRCLOUGH (HEIGHWAY) |
| DALGLISH |
| CASE |
| JOHNSON |
| McDERMOTT |
| SOUNESS |

In Dynamo Tbilisi, Liverpool were confronted by opponents of unalloyed class. Inspired by midfielder Kipiani, the Soviets displayed superb all-round technique, fashioning at least half a dozen clear-cut scoring opportunities. The Reds could be thankful that all but one of the openings were squandered, though the warning for the second leg was menacingly clear. Two of the chances had gone begging already when the Merseysiders went ahead, Johnson leaping between two defenders to propel McDermott's deep cross into the net with a magnificent header. Tbilisi levelled, deservedly, when Chivadze played the ball out of defence before charging down the pitch to slot a perfect pass from Kipiani under the diving Clemence. Undeterred, Liverpool hit back enthusiastically and regained the advantage when Case smashed a low 20-yard free kick through a narrow gap in the Soviets' defensive barrier. Paisley's men attacked briskly after the interval, but were contained with ominous comfort.

Round 1 - 2nd leg
3 October 1979

DYNAMO TBILISI 3
Gustaev 55; Schengeliya 75; Chivadze (pen) 85

LIVERPOOL 0
H-T 0-0. Dynamo Crowd 80,000

| CLEMENCE |
| NEAL |
| IRWIN |
| THOMPSON |
| KENNEDY, RAY |
| HANSEN |
| DALGLISH |
| CASE (FAIRCLOUGH) |
| JOHNSON |
| McDERMOTT |
| SOUNESS |

Throughout a rain-soaked first half in which Liverpool held out resolutely against repeated Soviet thrusts, there was hope that a second successive first-round exit from the European Cup could be avoided. Clemence made a series of fine saves, and there were even occasions - notably when Case broke away - when the Reds caused their accomplished hosts to man their own ramparts. But it was asking too much of Thompson and his fellow defenders to survive a second 45 minutes. The first and most telling setback occurred when Kipiani outwitted Irwin on the right and crossed low and hard for Gustaev to slide the ball home. Twenty minutes later Gustaev beat two defenders as he tore down the left flank, then fed Schengeliya, who chipped neatly into the net from a narrow angle. Now the game was dead, but a final blow was struck when Thompson fouled Gustaev in the box and Chivadze stroked in the penalty.

Dynamo Tbilisi won 4-2 on aggregate.

No excuses: Liverpool were outplayed in Georgia by Dynamo Tbilisi, who condemned the Reds to their second successive first-round European Cup exit.

Collectors' item: the programme for Liverpool's opening European tie, a one-sided contest against the gentlemanly amateurs of Reykjavik in Iceland.

Shankly's pioneers, the men who put Liverpool on the European trail by lifting the League Championship in 1964. Back row *(left to right)*; Gerry Byrne, Gordon Milne, Tommy Lawrence, Ronnie Moran, Willie Stevenson. *Front row:* Ian Callaghan, Roger Hunt, Ian St John, Ron Yeats, Alf Arrowsmith, Peter Thompson.

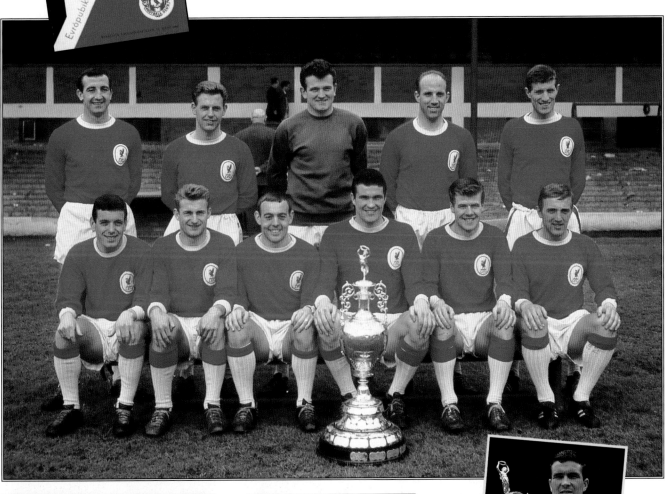

Roger Hunt, whose club record of 17 European goals remained intact for more than two decades, before being overhauled by Ian Rush.

Folk heroes: Ian St John *(left)*, the fiery Scottish centre-forward whose spirit and guile were crucial to Liverpool's early Continental campaigns, and his colossal countryman Ron Yeats *(above)*, the Reds' skipper and defensive cornerstone.

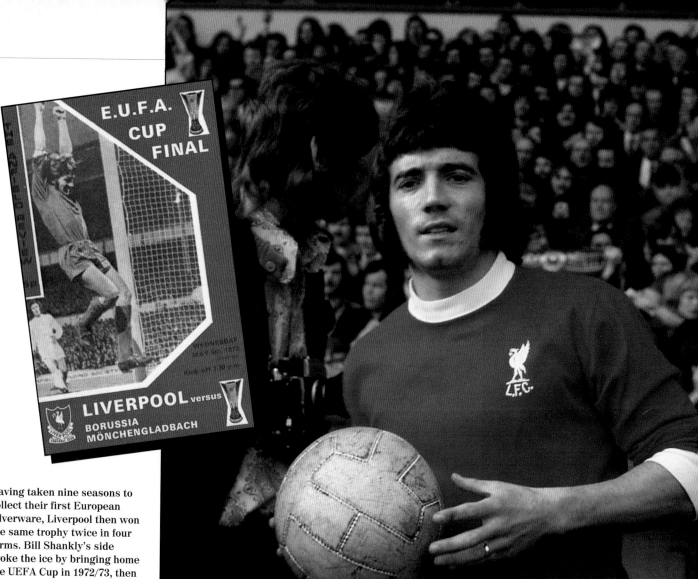

Having taken nine seasons to collect their first European silverware, Liverpool then won the same trophy twice in four terms. Bill Shankly's side broke the ice by bringing home the UEFA Cup in 1972/73, then Bob Paisley's men consolidated the Reds' burgeoning reputation by repeating the triumph in 1975/76. The two-legged finals, against Borussia Moenchengladbach and FC Bruges, were both dramatic affairs that rank among the Merseysiders' most exciting encounters.

Mine at last! After an evening of unbearable tension, Bill Shankly holds court in the Borussia dressing room, the UEFA Cup safely ensconced on his knee.

Kevin Keegan, who was at his irresistible sharpest against Borussia in 1973, poaching two splendid first-leg goals that paved the way for victory. Three years later he netted in both legs of the final against FC Bruges.

Ray Clemence, whose penalty saves against Borussia at Anfield in the 1972/73 final, and against both Hibernian and Dynamo Dresden in 1975/76, proved to be turning points.

COPPA-
EUROPEA EUROPEAN
CUP

final

BORUSSIA MOENCHENGLADBACH
v
LIVERPOOL

WEDNESDAY 25th MAY, 1977 SOUVENIR PROGRAMMA PREZZO 1000 LIRE

The ultimate triumph: Liverpool finally lifted the European Cup in 1977, eclipsing Borussia Moenchengladbach on a night of high emotion in Rome. The Reds' stirring victory was all the more remarkable for coming just four days after their morale-sapping FA Cup Final defeat by Manchester United.

Home are the heroes: skipper Emlyn Hughes, proudly grasping the spoils of victory, leads out Liverpool at Anfield in August 1977. A rapturous reception from the 'Red Army' lasted for several minutes.

Celebration time: old warhorses Tommy Smith *(left)* and Ian Callaghan *(centre)* with Phil Neal shortly after the presentation ceremony. Each man had contributed royally to one of the Merseysiders' finest hours: Tommy's majestic header had turned the tide against the Germans, Ian had been tirelessly inspirational in midfield and Phil's penalty had put the result beyond doubt.

Same again! In 1978 the Reds retained the European Cup on home soil, beating FC Bruges in a Wembley final marred by the Belgians' negative tactics.

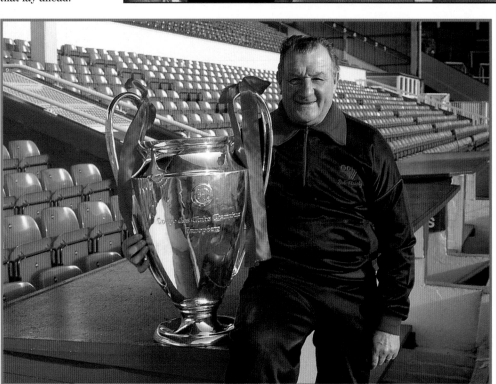

New faces: Graeme Souness *(centre)* and Kenny Dalglish *(right)*, the Wembley match-winners, savour the moment with Ray Kennedy. The two superbly talented Scots were to figure hugely in the avalanche of triumphs that lay ahead.

Bob Paisley, back at Anfield, exudes the satisfaction of a job well done. He had become the first British manager to lift the European Cup for a second time, and he had not finished yet...

Mr Dependable: Phil Neal *(opposite)*, who was to play in all five of Liverpool's European Cup Finals, scoring in two and barely putting a foot wrong.

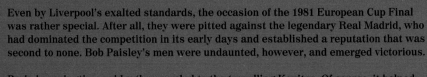

Even by Liverpool's exalted standards, the occasion of the 1981 European Cup Final was rather special. After all, they were pitted against the legendary Real Madrid, who had dominated the competition in its early days and established a reputation that was second to none. Bob Paisley's men were undaunted, however, and emerged victorious.

Paris in springtime evidently appealed to the travelling Kopites. Of course, it helped that the Reds had just won the European Cup for the third time!

Alan Kennedy - 'Barney Rubble' to his fans - with the trophy secured by his dramatic late strike. In fact Alan had been in danger of missing the match, his broken wrist knitting together just in time for him to play and enjoy the experience of a lifetime.

Overjoyed: Liverpool captain Phil Thompson *(opposite),* a Scouser to the depths of his soul, realises a passionately held ambition. The spindly youth once described by Bill Shankly as 'the matchstick man with a sparrow's legs' had come a long way indeed.

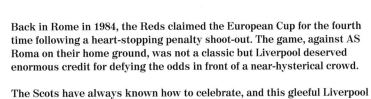

Back in Rome in 1984, the Reds claimed the European Cup for the fourth time following a heart-stopping penalty shoot-out. The game, against AS Roma on their home ground, was not a classic but Liverpool deserved enormous credit for defying the odds in front of a near-hysterical crowd.

The Scots have always known how to celebrate, and this gleeful Liverpool quintet proved no exception. Left to right are Steve Nicol, whose penalty miss proved to be irrelevant, Kenny Dalglish, Alan Hansen, Gary Gillespie and Graeme Souness.

No trace of a wobble now! Bruce Grobbelaar, whose jelly-legs routine had enlivened the penalty shoot-out, in more tranquil surroundings.

Left: Ian Rush, whose ice-cool appearance when slotting home his penalty had belied his inner turmoil, with Continental club football's most coveted trophy.

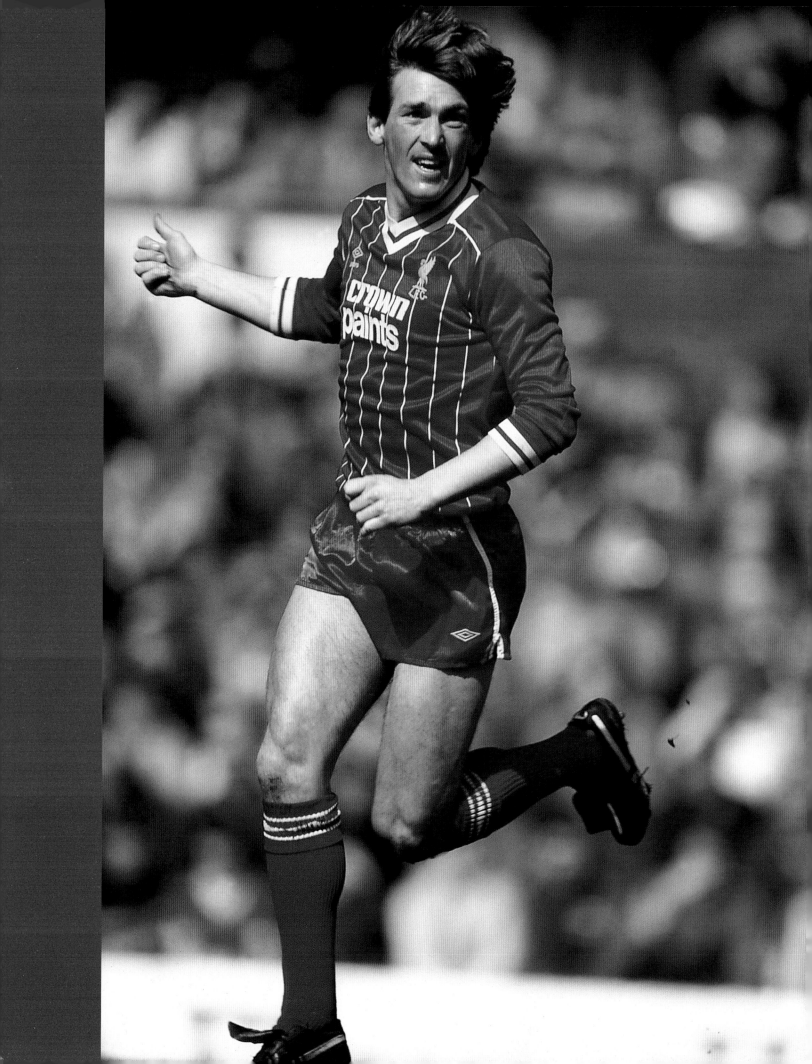

The 1985 European Cup Final, Liverpool v Juventus in Brussels, will be remembered forever, but not for the football played on that black evening at the Heysel stadium. Dozens lost their lives in a terrace riot and a pall of gloom settled over soccer as a result.

Left: Kenny Dalglish, who became the Reds' player-manager in the summer of 1985, assumed control at a difficult time. But he proved equal to the task, leading his side to the League/FA Cup double in his first season in charge and going on to encounter further glory, as well as the stark tragedy of Hillsborough, before succumbing to the pressure and resigning.

Going through the motions: Gary Gillespie heads clear from Paolo Rossi in a match that was rendered meaningless by the events before the kick-off. For the record, Juventus won 1-0.

Coupe des Clubs Champions Européens 1984/85

Europese Beker der Landskampioenen 1984/85

FINALE
LIVERPOOL F.C.
JUVENTUS F.C.

29.5.1985 - 20.15
Stade du Heysel - Bruxelles
Heizelstadion - Brussel

Programme officiel
Officieel programma · 40 BF

Liverpool are back: their six seasons of European exile at an end, the Reds line up with Finnish champions Kuusysi Lahti for the first round of the 1991/92 UEFA Cup. Most of the faces are different, the shirts have changed and the Kemlyn Road stand in the background is about to be converted into a double-decker, but the supporters' fervour for Continental competition remains happily intact.

The new order: Steve McManaman, perhaps the brightest of Liverpool's young stars, shoots for goal against Kuusysi Lahti.

Ian Rush *(left)* just fails to connect with a cross in the 1992/93 home tie with Spartak Moscow. The Welshman has scored more goals for Liverpool in Europe than any other player.

Graeme Souness, who masterminded the Reds' UEFA Cup effort before suffering the trauma of a heart by-pass operation. He would make a full recovery in time to lead Liverpool's 1992/93 quest for the one European trophy that had thus far eluded them, the Cup Winners' Cup.

Chapter Nine

BARNEY GOES TO PARIS

THE subtle thrusts of Dalglish, the vision of Souness and the shrewd planning of Paisley had all failed to end the stalemate as Liverpool and Real Madrid scrapped with apparent weariness late in the second half of an undistinguished European Cup Final. Enter Alan Kennedy, in footballing terms a trusty yeoman among aristocrats, to complete a mission that had proved beyond his more sophisticated comrades. The crash of broadsword was not difficult to imagine as the combative Wearsider latched on to a throw from Ray Kennedy, burst unstoppably past a startled Spanish defender and bludgeoned the ball into the net from a narrow angle. The man the Kop called Barney Rubble - a tough but sensitive character who at times had felt vulnerable in a team of stars - had won the Cup for the Reds and, in doing so, somehow grew in stature. After a brief absence following the arrival of Mark Lawrenson at the start of the next season, Alan went more than three years without missing a senior game, making the left-back berth his own beyond question and earning a belated England call-up.

It was a rousing, heart-warming end to a campaign that had begun in decidedly prosaic surroundings, on the rough-and-ready pitch of Finnish amateurs Oulu Palloseura. Such was the state of the turf that the game was reduced to a lottery, and after the Reds had been held to a 1-1 draw, a distinctly peeved Bob Paisley ventured the suggestion that his hosts should invest in a new groundsman. In fact, it was a shame to detract from Oulu's greatest day, a rare taste of glory on their first foray into Europe. Their little stadium was overflowing, fans even crowded on to the roof of the stand, and such was local enthusiasm that the game was played to the accompaniment of a full running commentary on the public-address system, allowing supporters without tickets to keep in touch with the action from the street outside. Their reward was an 82nd-minute goal from Puotiniemi that left Oulu coach Taisto Horneman more than satisfied: 'It was a very fine result against world-class opponents. We started nervously but once we found they could make mistakes, that they were human too, then our confidence increased,' he beamed. Two of the Finnish heroes were Englishmen, midfielder Hugh Smith and former Newcastle forward Keith Armstrong, who had failed to make the grade on Tyneside but had excelled in less demanding surroundings.

However, if Oulu had their heads in the clouds after the first leg, they returned to the real world with a resounding thud at Anfield. Liverpool, perhaps feeling a measure of pique after being held so unexpectedly two weeks earlier, were at their most merciless, putting on a ten-goal show as they showed the visitors just what could be achieved on a true surface. Merseyside fans had not expected a meaningful contest so the gate was modest, allowing photographers to move into empty sections of the stands in search of different picture angles.

The cameramen enjoyed no such luxury at Pittodrie, where there wasn't an inch of spare space as Alex Ferguson's resurgent Aberdeen faced the Reds in the second round. Whenever English and Scottish clubs meet in Europe, the encounter is hyped inevitably into the 'Championship of Britain', and this time the Dons' boss was a godsend to the media men, his brash confidence serving their purpose ideally. However, although Fergie was destined to lift European trophies eventually, with both Aberdeen and Manchester United, this time he was in line for a short, sharp lesson. But for their vast experience of playing on the Continent, the Liverpool players might have been intimidated by the partisan home support. Alan Kennedy remembers: 'When we got there the fans were going mad, doing their best to put us under pressure, and Bob Paisley said it must be our priority to quieten them down.' The visitors accomplished that task in the most effective way possible, Terry McDermott scoring a goal of sheer quality after only five minutes. Aberdeen reacted predictably by going for Liverpool's jugular, but although they huffed and puffed with commendable energy, and their players showed plenty of individual skill, they lacked the necessary knowhow. Such a situation brought the best out of the Reds, who played some lovely measured football, absorbing pressure before breaking upfield with immense menace.

Undismayed by their favourites' single-goal disadvantage, a legion of Dons supporters descended on Anfield in noisily optimistic mood, brandishing a colourful and imaginative range of banners. On the field their side fought well but were not clever enough to redress the balance, and one of their slogans, 'Willie Miller eats soft centres', was to prove distressingly ambiguous. The embarrassment followed a cross from Avi Cohen that was nodded on by Alan Hansen only for Miller, an international stopper, to deflect past Jim Leighton for the first of Liverpool's four goals; a case of not so much a soft centre as a soft centre-half! That was the signal for the hosts to relax; a sparkling display ensued and the Kop responded impudently by chanting 'Oh why are we so GUID?' with a most creditable attempt at a Scottish accent.

The Reds' quarter-final mission was welcomed by fans as an opportunity to cock a snook at Nottingham Forest, whose recent domination of the Merseysiders had left its mark. CSKA Sofia had conquered Clough and company in the first round; thus Liverpool had the chance to show their upstart domestic rivals, who by now had won two consecutive European Cups, just who were the premier English power on the Continent. They did, too, thrashing the Bulgarians 5-1 at Anfield, though the margin didn't do justice to a skilful Sofia side who happened to meet Graeme Souness on a night when everything he touched turned to gold. Indeed, the masterful midfielder's scorching hat-trick is still referred to with reverence by everyone privileged to witness it.

The result proved a timely tonic for Liverpool, who had just been dumped out of the FA Cup by Everton and had fallen behind in the title race. Of course, the second leg was now a formality, and although the Bulgarians competed stoutly, they could not prevent David Johnson snatching the only goal of the game. Despite that, the trip holds few happy memories for the striker, who pulled his hamstring and was unimpressed by Sofia, which he describes as yet another grey, dreary Eastern European city. Alan Kennedy echoes David's feelings, adding that such expeditions invariably provoked Bob Paisley into criticism of the local food and drink. 'We'd all be dying for a drink, and but if anyone went to the dressing-room tea urn, Bob would shout something like "Hey, leave that alone, you never know what's in there!" He just didn't trust foreign fare. That used to be particularly hard on Joe Fagan and Ronnie Moran, as well as the players. They loved their tea, and sometimes they'd taste it when Bob was out of the room. If they said it was okay, we'd have some; then when Bob came back, he'd see the level in the urn had dropped and make a face. He knew what was going on.' On their longer trips, Liverpool took to including their own chef in the party, an example of the minute attention to detail which extended to all aspects of their European campaigns.

For Alan, though, culinary considerations when travelling abroad paled before a more pressing personal problem. Particularly in his early Anfield days, he was afflicted with a chronic fear of flying. He recalls: 'At take-off and landing, I would be terrified, gripping the armrests for all I was worth. Then there would be a sudden bang behind me as one of my thoughtful team-mates - probably Steve Nicol or Kenny Dalglish - burst a paper bag. Everyone in the team was a joker in those days, it helped to pass the time on long trips. After showing my nervousness on two or three flights, I was allowed into the cockpit as the plane left the ground and as it came down. The pilots were very understanding. It helped enormously to see just what was involved.' At less tense moments on his journeys, he was

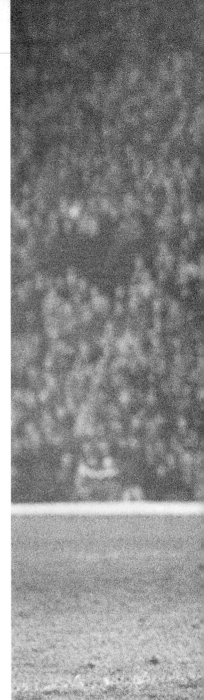

part of a card school which tended to include Ian Rush, Ronnie Whelan and Alan Hansen, whom Alan recalls was as cool at the gambling table as he was on the pitch: 'I don't think Alan has lost a game of cards in his life. He had a memory like Leslie Welch, and always seemed to know what people had in their hand. He's a smart lad, it's easy to imagine him making a living on a Mississippi riverboat.'

Such an intriguing possibility, however, would have to wait; for now Hansen and his colleagues were concentrating on the challenge provided by the semi-final, in which they could expect a titanic clash with mighty Bayern Munich. With David Johnson injured and out of the first leg at Anfield, Bob Paisley called up a young fellow named Ian Rush to make his European debut. Although the callow Welshman had done well at Wembley in the victorious League Cup Final replay against West Ham the week before, most of his football had been of the Central League variety, and Bob's decision to pitch him into action against

Same nationality, same job, but wildly differing emotions. Alan Hansen, Liverpool's Scottish central defender, is overjoyed as the Reds take the lead against Aberdeen at Anfield - thus going two up on aggregate - while Willie Miller, his Dons counterpart, is understandably miffed. Willie has just deflected Alan's header into his own net.

one of the world's best teams was seen as a huge risk. Ian remembers: 'The Boss kept the pressure off me by not announcing his side until the last moment, so I had no time to worry.' In the event, the youngster had little chance to shine as the Germans stifled the Reds' attack and went away with a goalless draw.

The match remains a painful memory for Alan Kennedy, who fractured his wrist in a first-half collision with Paul Breitner. 'We both got up afterwards and it didn't seem too bad, so I had it bandaged at the interval and went back out for the second half. The doctor was more concerned with Terry McDermott, who had dislocated his thumb. It was assumed I had suffered only a sprain and after the game he had a sling while I didn't. That evening we went out for a few drinks, and I found I couldn't sign autographs because of the pain. It kept me awake all night and the next day an X-ray revealed the fracture. I was told I'd be out of action for six or seven weeks, which was worrying with competition for my place coming from Avi Cohen, Richard Money and Colin Irwin. At that time, playing in the back four alongside established internationals Phil Neal, Phil Thompson and Alan Hansen, it was difficult to feel secure.' Breitner, also, was to look back on the first leg with mixed feelings. Not that the Bayern star did not play well - he hardly put a foot wrong on the pitch - but after the game he committed a grave error. Journalists reported him as writing off the Liverpool display as unintelligent, which achieved nothing bar winding up the Reds for the second leg. Paul claimed he had been misquoted, alleging that he had been referring uncritically to the simplicity of his opponents' style, but the damage was done.

Though the Merseysiders' preparations for Munich were hampered by an injury which ruled out skipper Thompson, they relished the unaccustomed role of underdogs; even so, they could have done without the stunning setback that descended on them early in one of the most tense and closely fought battles in their European history. The opening exchanges had barely been made when Kenny Dalglish limped out of the fray with ligament damage and was replaced by the inexperienced Howard Gayle, a gifted but mercurial attacker. Yet the 22-year-old Liverpudlian was to play an integral part in his side's ultimate triumph. Betraying not a tremor of the nervousness to which he admitted later, Howard ran the Germans ragged, dribbling, sprinting and tackling with a combination of fervour and naivety that severely unsettled his cultured opponents. So rattled were they that he was fouled repeatedly, and eventually, when his spirited reprisals began attracting the referee's attention, he was taken off and replaced by Jimmy Case. Thus Bob Paisley had used his second substitute, a decision he regretted at once, as David Johnson pulled up with a hamstring strain. With Dalglish already gone, David was the only recognised striker left on parade, and he recalls that the manager was not overjoyed at this latest development: 'I heard later that after I signalled to the bench, Bob turned to one of the armed guards patrolling the touchline and said "Give us your gun and I'll shoot the bastard."' In the end it wasn't to matter, as David laid on the vital goal for Ray Kennedy, who was deputising as skipper. Ray, of the celebrated left foot, demonstrated his versatility by knocking this one home with his right, cool as you please, from just inside the box.

With only seven minutes left and away goals counting double if the scores were level, Liverpool were surely safe. But suddenly a Rummenigge strike revived Bayern hopes, and the Reds were besieged, prompting Alan Kennedy to liken the visitors' penalty box in the last three minutes to a scene from the Alamo. Happily, the difference was that the Alamo fell, whereas the Merseysiders held firm, moving Paisley to declare: 'That was the greatest performance we have given in Europe. Everything was going wrong for us but the players did everything right and showed real character. Mind you, I didn't have to motivate the lads after Breitner called us unintelligent.' And he grinned: 'I think we were intelligent tonight.' Phil Thompson thought so too, and was magnanimous enough to nominate his understudy, Colin Irwin, as man of the match, adding: 'He's the fellow I must now try and displace and it won't be easy.' It would be pleasing to report that Howard Gayle's highly-charged performance proved the first step towards the glittering top-level future that some pundits predicted for him, but sadly it wasn't to be. Thereafter, with such a wealth of midfield and forward talent on the Anfield payroll, senior opportunities failed to present themselves and he departed to pursue a worthy career elsewhere, notably with Blackburn Rovers.

Meanwhile Liverpool marched on to Paris and a final showdown with Real Madrid at the Parc des Princes. The Spaniards possessed a matchless European Cup pedigree - having lifted the trophy six times, including for the first five years of its existence between 1956 and 1960 - and if they were no longer invincible, they remained a formidable proposition. Certainly their coach, the Yugoslavian Boskov, talked a good game, electing not to learn from Breitner's clanger and describing the Reds as having too many 'old men' in their team. With only Clemence, Neal and Dalglish the wrong side of 30, and the last-named two only just, his assessment was barely accurate and, it need hardly be added, decidedly rash. In fact, Bob Paisley's main anxieties in the run-up to the match concerned not age but fitness, with Dalglish in plaster and Alan Kennedy, Johnson, Fairclough and Thompson all struggling with injuries. Come the day, all except Fairclough were available, even though Dalglish had not trained for several weeks.

For the Reds' army of fans, it had been a difficult period. Some 26,000 of them had travelled to Rome in 1977, yet now there were only 12,000 tickets available. In the event, many arrived without tickets, hoping to pick them up in France, though a lot were unlucky, being reduced to hanging around outside the stadium and gauging the progress of the game by crowd reaction. For photographer Steve Hale, pursuing his dream of encountering Real Madrid in the European Cup Final and shooting the winner, it was a hectic time: 'I convinced various newspapers that it was worth sending me over early and I spent a week foraging around for stories. Paris was crawling with Liverpool fans looking for cheap hotels but they were to be disappointed, most establishments having doubled their prices for the occasion. I took a group of Scousers along to the Arc de Triomphe, which made a nice picture for the *Echo*. Everyone was revelling in this unique atmosphere, a combination of Paris in the spring and the excitement of pre-match preparation. Despite the injury problems, Bob Paisley was in fine form, and I remember him giving myself and other pressmen a lift back to our hotel on the team coach after we'd got stranded on the wrong side of town.'

Unfortunately, the game itself was a letdown, over-cautious and utterly unmemorable apart from the goal. The ingredients had been perfect - two great clubs with outstanding players on both sides - but the fear factor dominated. One of the major disappointments, at least from a neutral point of view, was the contribution of Laurie Cunningham, Real's England winger, who had been sidelined and now returned for his first senior match since November. Clearly not fully fit, he was marked tightly and made little impact in what frequently descended into a fearsomely bruising contest. Though Liverpool were not blameless in this respect, Camacho was the worst offender, first ripping Neal's sock with a wild tackle, then almost tearing Johnson's shirt from his back. It seemed that nothing was going to give on either side, until Alan Kennedy's thrilling intervention decided a match which he had come so close to missing: 'I had learned only the week before that I would be playing. My wrist was better but Colin Irwin had played so well in my absence that I could take nothing for granted.' Alan admits that, because of his lay-off, he wasn't super-fit and nor was Dalglish, who nevertheless did a magnificent if unobtrusive job, dropping back into midfield to draw his markers out of position. The Reds were further handicapped when Graeme Souness took a heavy knock soon after the start, yet were still managing to hold their own as extra-time approached.

And so to Alan's moment of inspiration, one which he remembers with complete clarity: 'I don't know why I should have been so far forward. I was tired and my thoughts were turning towards an extra 30 minutes. When I made the run I didn't really expect to be given the ball; I suppose it was in my head that I might make space for someone else, but Ray threw it to me. Now usually, if the ball is in front of me and there is something in my way, then I move it. I saw their player coming at me. He took a wild kick, missed the ball and caught me, but I wasn't going to stop for that. I was running into the left side of the penalty area near the touchline, wondering whether to cross or shoot. It flashed across my mind that the 'keeper had come out for several other crosses and would be expecting another; anyway, when you're only eight or ten yards out there's only one real option. So I hit the ball hard and it went beyond him into the far corner.' On seeing the ball hit the net, Alan ran on towards the Liverpool fans massed at that end of the ground: 'I didn't hear the referee whistle for a goal and didn't look round. Deep inside I feared there had been an offside or a foul or whatever. It must have been ten seconds before I knew for sure that he'd given it.' Still there were nine minutes to play, but Alan was confident the Cup wouldn't slip away now, and when the final whistle blew, Bob Paisley cast his customary restraint to the winds, hugging the scorer within an inch of his life. As Alan says: 'Bob was beside himself with joy, on cloud nine. It meant so much to him to beat the great Real Madrid.' Again though, Paisley was to be miffed at the grudging praise that came the way of his team, especially in view of the trying circumstances surrounding this latest victory. He said: 'We've won the European Cup three times for Liverpool and England. Sometimes you have to win these games the best way you can, not the way you'd like to in an ideal world. If any other team had done it I'm sure the press would have made allowances.'

But nothing could sour the celebrations. Certainly for captain Phil Thompson, who had been dismayed at his recent omission from the England squad for World Cup games against Hungary and Switzerland, there could have been no headier consolation. At the presentation ceremony, his elation and pride were all-consuming; from the moment he mounted the steps to collect the spoils of victory, his eyes barely left that huge, shining trophy, even as he shook hands and received congratulations. Afterwards he revealed that excitement had deprived him of sleep the night before: 'I tried counting sheep but ended up counting Spaniards instead,' he laughed.

It was a special night, too, for Ray Clemence, winning his 12th major honour with Liverpool before leaving Anfield that summer to seek a fresh challenge with Tottenham Hotspur, though it is doubtful whether anyone felt more supreme fulfilment than David Johnson, who had suffered frustration at two previous finals. He sums up his feelings: 'It was the most satisfying European night of my career. It meant so much to me after being on the bench in 1977 and on crutches in 1978. This time I had actually played, and for the whole 90 minutes, too!' So often had David been substituted in the past that whenever he saw the number 12 warming up, he feared the worst. 'I looked up, saw Jimmy Case preparing to come on and thought "Oh no, here we go again." But they took off Kenny Dalglish this time, leaving me to continue chasing all across the Real Madrid back four, a specific job that Joe Fagan and Ronnie Moran had identified as being vitally important.' After the presentation the players headed back to their hotel to start the celebrations minus two of their number. Phil Neal and Graeme Souness had been selected to give urine samples for a random drugs check, and both had sweated so much during the match that they were drained of excess moisture, taking two hours to produce the requisite amount. Later, having failed to find a taxi and hitched a lift with some gendarmes, they reached the official reception three hours late. David recalls that later, when the party was invaded by fans, Souness led a contingent of players to the famous Paris Lido nightspot, taking the European Cup with them: 'When we walked in the Bluebells were performing, but the spotlight was switched on to us. We were given the best tables, close to the stage, and enjoyed a brilliant end to a perfect day.'

It had been a red-letter day, too, for British football. Liverpool's fifth European trophy had been the 20th lifted by teams from these islands since international club competition had been launched in 1955/56. The first final, too, had been in Paris, and also featured Real Madrid, who defeated Reims of France 4-3. That match had been one of those famous, romantic confrontations that had captured the imagination of Merseyside schoolboy Steve Hale and given birth to his fantasy of shooting the winner against the great Spaniards. Now, a quarter of a century later, Steve left the French capital for home, his shot of Alan Kennedy's goal tucked away in his safest pocket.

Looking tolerably pleased with life, Alan Kennedy - Barney Rubble to his fans - cuddles the European Cup. No one could be more deserving of the privilege; Liverpool had just lifted the famous trophy for the third time, courtesy of the amiable Wearsider's inspired late run and shot against Real Madrid.

Round 1 - 1st leg
17 September 1980

OULU PALLOSEURA 1
Puotiniemi 82

LIVERPOOL 1
McDermott 15
H-T 0-1. Crowd 14,000

CLEMENCE
NEAL
COHEN
THOMPSON
KENNEDY, RAY
HANSEN
DALGLISH
LEE
FAIRCLOUGH
McDERMOTT
SOUNESS

The mighty Reds suffered rare embarrassment at the hands of the industrious Finnish amateurs. True, Bob Paisley's men dominated proceedings in terms of possession, but they failed to convert their superiority into goals and paid the price by conceding a late equaliser. McDermott climaxed early Liverpool pressure by nodding his side ahead from a Lee corner, but thereafter it was Oulu who appeared to grow in confidence, continually catching their visitors in an efficient offside trap. An uneven pitch played its part in the Reds' discomfiture, disrupting the customary smooth flow of their football, and only Souness - whose passing was delightful - coped effectively with the surface. The Oulu goal came when the Liverpool defence dithered over clearing a long throw and Puotiniemi drove into the roof of the net.

Above right: **Overworked: an Oulo Palloseura defender bids to clear from Sammy Lee at Anfield on a night when little went right for the visitors. Having somehow squeezed out a draw in Finland, Oulu were faced by the Reds at their most rampant and left for home contemplating a 10-1 defeat.**

Round 1 - 2nd leg
1 October 1980

LIVERPOOL 10
Souness 5, 24, (pen) 52; McDermott 29, 41, 83; Lee 53; Kennedy 66; Fairclough 68, 81

OULU PALLOSEURA 1
Armstrong 47
H-T 4-0. Crowd 21,013

CLEMENCE
NEAL
COHEN
THOMPSON
KENNEDY, RAY
HANSEN
DALGLISH
LEE
FAIRCLOUGH
McDERMOTT
SOUNESS

The Finnish fairytale ended in slaughter at Anfield as the ruthless Reds ran up double figures. The most eager executioner was Souness, who grabbed an early goal and went on to complete his first hat-trick for the club. McDermott plundered three, too, as Liverpool's attack clicked into top gear. Four to the good at half-time, they might have relaxed; instead they carried out to the letter manager Paisley's instruction to avoid complacency, thus providing a light-hearted treat for the fans. Pick of the goals were the seventh, a brilliant header by Lee from Fairclough's centre, and the tenth, a McDermott volley from 20 yards. Oulu's solitary reply had the stamp of quality, too, the Englishman Armstrong outwitting Hansen before tucking a neat shot past Clemence.

Liverpool won 11-2 on aggregate

Round 2 - 1st leg
22 October 1980

ABERDEEN 0

LIVERPOOL 1
McDermott 5
H-T 0-1. Crowd 24,000

CLEMENCE
NEAL
KENNEDY, ALAN
THOMPSON
KENNEDY, RAY
HANSEN
DALGLISH
LEE (CASE)
JOHNSON
McDERMOTT
SOUNESS

The Scottish champions blustered straight on to the offensive, but it was Liverpool who administered an early blow. Ray Kennedy found Dalglish in the inside-left channel, and he switched the ball inside to Johnson, who played an immaculate first-time pass to McDermott, sprinting through the Dons' defence. The midfielder ran wide before beating 'keeper Leighton with a sweet, acute-angled chip from 12 yards. It was a beautiful goal, notable for both precision and composure, and it illustrated aptly the difference between the teams; both worked hard, both were skilful, but Liverpool had the knowhow gained from a decade and a half in Europe. Aberdeen continued to press forward, yet although Clemence saved well from Rougvie and McGhee, the counter-punching visitors looked the more dangerous. Leighton saved superbly from Souness near the end, but the Scots knew they faced an uphill struggle at Anfield.

Round 2 - 2nd leg
5 November 1980

LIVERPOOL 4
Miller (og) 38; Neal 43; Dalglish 57; Hansen 71

ABERDEEN 0

H-T 2-0. Crowd 36,182

CLEMENCE
NEAL
KENNEDY, ALAN (COHEN)
THOMPSON
KENNEDY, RAY
HANSEN
DALGLISH
LEE
JOHNSON
McDERMOTT
SOUNESS

Liverpool won in glorious style, although not before Aberdeen had offered noble resistance and, just once, threatened to wipe out the first-leg deficit. The Dons' moment of hope came after 23 minutes when McGhee escaped the close attentions of Thompson and bore down on Clemence, but the 'keeper clung expertly to the subsequent shot and the danger was gone. Thereafter it was all Liverpool, although it took a lucky break to give them the lead on the night, Miller diverting a Hansen header into his own net. Suddenly, the tension was lifted and the Reds served up a feast of flowing football, going further ahead when Neal ran on to an impudent Dalglish backheel to shoot past Leighton. The gulf in class between the two sides grew ever more apparent as Dalglish headed home Lee's cross for the third and Hansen rounded off a breathtaking seven-man move for the fourth.

Liverpool won 5-0 on aggregate.

LIVERPOOL 5

Souness 16, 51, 80; Lee 45;
McDermott 62

CSKA SOFIA 1

Yonchev 58
H-T 2-0. Crowd 37,255

CLEMENCE
NEAL
KENNEDY, ALAN
THOMPSON (IRWIN)
KENNEDY, RAY
HANSEN
DALGLISH
LEE
HEIGHWAY
McDERMOTT
SOUNESS

Judged by the number of goal-scoring chances they created, Liverpool and CSKA were reasonably well matched; but measured by their ability to *take* them, the two teams were on opposite sides of a yawning divide. The Bulgarians had been wasteful already when Souness, who contributed one of the most spectacular hat-tricks ever seen at Anfield, opened the Reds' account with a low, firm shot from 14 yards after shrugging off an opponent. Then Clemence saved Liverpool twice as defensive slips let in CSKA, before Lee doubled the lead, drilling in a venomous half-volley from just inside the box. Soon after the restart, Souness made it three when he met a square pass from Heighway with immense, exhilarating power from 25 yards. Deservedly, Yonchev pulled one back after the Liverpool back four were caught square, but the Bulgarians enjoyed only momentary relief. Ray Kennedy laid on two more, McDermott cleverly converting a short cross and Souness meeting a glancing header to bludgeon home from 18 yards.

CSKA SOFIA 0

LIVERPOOL 1

Johnson 10
H-T 0-1. Crowd 65,000

CLEMENCE
NEAL
KENNEDY, ALAN
IRWIN
KENNEDY, RAY
HANSEN
DALGLISH
LEE
JOHNSON (HEIGHWAY)
CASE
SOUNESS

After the sensational sharp-shooting of the first leg, this was always likely to prove an anti-climax, yet there was no shortage of action at the Levski Stadium. Despite the dampener of Johnson's early goal - a close-range formality after Lee had capped a strong run by hitting the post - the Bulgarians were determined to salvage some pride. They were a good side, too, their skill and pace opening the Liverpool defence on a number of occasions. Clemence had to be at his best to deny them, and Hansen, Neal and Thompson all had to clear off the line. Liverpool created chances, too, with Souness, Heighway and Lee going close. It seemed that CSKA would at least manage a goal when, in the 80th minute, they won a penalty after a foul by Case. Clemence had other ideas, though, diving to his left to parry the shot from Markov.

Liverpool won 6-1 on aggregate.

Sammy Lee's fierce half-volley puts the Reds two up against CSKA Sofia at Anfield.

Semi-final - 1st leg
8 April 1981

LIVERPOOL 0

BAYERN MUNICH 0

Crowd 44,543

CLEMENCE
NEAL
KENNEDY, ALAN
THOMPSON
KENNEDY, RAY
HANSEN
DALGLISH
LEE
RUSH
McDERMOTT
HEIGHWAY (CASE)

Bayern Munich gave an away performance of which Liverpool themselves would have been justly proud, and could leave Anfield quietly confident of their ultimate passage into the European Cup Final. Alternately, they had frustrated the Reds with the efficiency and organisation of their rearguard, and threatened them with the speed and penetration of their counter-attacks. Though there were no goals, it was a fascinating encounter with plenty of penalty-area incident. Dalglish, inevitably, was in the van of the Liverpool offensive and twice, early on, he tested reserve 'keeper Junghans, first with a stinging 25-yarder, then with a close-range volley. But the home side missed the absent Souness and the most impressive midfield work came from the Germans, for whom Niedermayer clattered the bar from 25 yards, then Rummenigge and Breitner might have scored. The Reds had a late penalty appeal rejected after Dalglish went down, emphasising that it was just not their night.

Semi-final - 2nd leg
22 April 1981

BAYERN MUNICH 1
Rummenigge 87

LIVERPOOL 1
Kennedy, Ray 83
H-T 0-0. Crowd 77,600

CLEMENCE
NEAL
MONEY
IRWIN
KENNEDY, RAY
HANSEN
DALGLISH (GAYLE, CASE)
LEE
JOHNSON
McDERMOTT
SOUNESS

Liverpool's achievement on a dramatic night in Munich ranks with the most remarkable of their European adventures. Their chances, thought to be remote after the first leg, took a further knock after seven minutes when injury removed Dalglish from the action. Yet in a first half in which the Reds' more experienced campaigners were content to absorb German pressure, Gayle, the Scot's rookie replacement, unsettled Bayern by running at their defence with innocent abandon. Indeed, so enthusiastically and effectively did he throw himself into the fray that he became a target for the home side's hard men, and after showing signs of retaliating, he was substituted by Case. By then the game had drifted into a stalemate that was to be shattered by Ray Kennedy seven minutes from the end. Johnson, hobbling with a hamstring strain, hooked the ball to the predatory midfielder, who turned and scooped it into the corner of the net with apparent nonchalance from 16 yards. Four minutes later Bayern equalised when Irwin's attempted clearance was volleyed in by Rummenigge, but Liverpool's away goal had booked their Paris passage.

Aggregate 1-1. Liverpool won on away goal.

Left: **Man of the match: Colin Irwin, (centre) who did a magnificent job standing in for Phil Thompson in the semi-final second leg against Bayern Munich.**

The man who fell to earth: Kenny Dalglish takes a tumble against Bayern Munich at Anfield, foiled by a vigorous but apparently fair sliding tackle. The tie was not one of Kenny's happiest; he could not break through in the first leg, then went off injured early in the second.

Performance of a lifetime: after coming on as a seventh-minute substitute for Kenny Dalglish, Howard Gayle *(centre)* ran the Bayern defence ragged in Munich. So effective was the young Merseysider that the Germans goaded him into re-taliation following several scything tackles, and he in turn was replaced by Jimmy Case.

Final in Paris
27 May 1981

LIVERPOOL 1
Kennedy, Alan 81

REAL MADRID 0
H-T 0-0. Crowd 48,360

CLEMENCE
NEAL
KENNEDY, ALAN
THOMPSON
KENNEDY, RAY
HANSEN
DALGLISH (CASE)
LEE
JOHNSON
McDERMOTT
SOUNESS

It was by no means a classic final - and that's being charitable - but Liverpool could hardly be expected to care about that after lifting the Cup, courtesy of an inspired sortie by Alan Kennedy nine minutes from the end. The buccaneering full-back received a throw-in from his namesake, Ray, then galloped past a wild but ineffectual challenge from Cortes; the angle was acute, but Alan drove an ambitious eight-yard cross-shot over the 'keeper's shoulder and into the far side of the net. Such an enterprising strike belied most of the drab fare that had gone before, as two cautious teams had fallen prey to the big-match fear factor. The Reds had started brightly, with Alan Kennedy and Dalglish both bringing saves from Agustin, but slowly Real Madrid began to emerge from their shell and as the match wore on they got marginally the better of the midfield exchanges. Both sides indulged in some fearsome tackling, with Dalglish and Cunningham, Real's England international, among the principal targets. The prospect of extra-time and a penalty shoot-out was looming when Alan Kennedy rewrote the script.

A moment fit to crown any career: Alan Kennedy drives the ball beyond Real Madrid 'keeper Agustin for the only goal of the European Cup Final. The next second he was sprinting towards the Liverpool fans, fearing all the while that the referee would blow for some infringement.

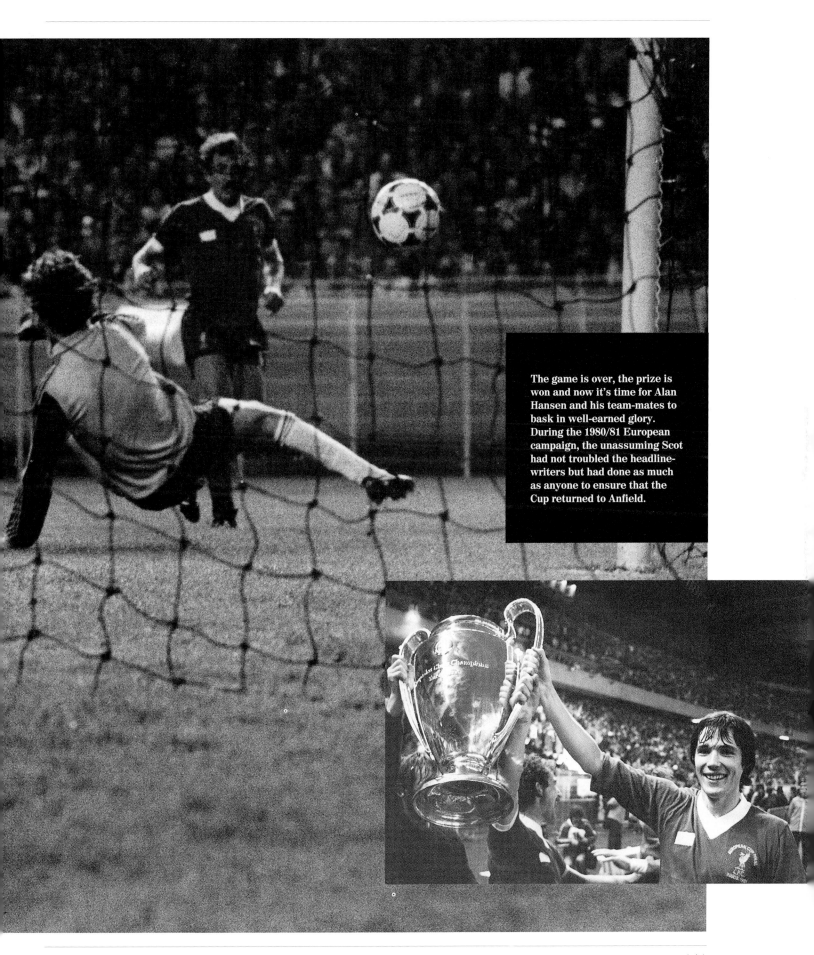

The game is over, the prize is won and now it's time for Alan Hansen and his team-mates to bask in well-earned glory. During the 1980/81 European campaign, the unassuming Scot had not troubled the headline-writers but had done as much as anyone to ensure that the Cup returned to Anfield.

Chapter Ten

A TEST OF NERVE

BY the early 1980s, Liverpool were dominating the domestic scene to an unprecedented and - certainly to their competitors - an embarrassing extent. They were in the process of winning seven League Championships in nine seasons - only Nottingham Forest and Aston Villa managed to secure the coveted trophy on temporary loan - and as success bred more success, there wasn't the slightest sign of an end to their supremacy. On the Continent, however, the Reds did not have it all their own way.

They began their defence of the European Cup in the autumn of 1981 against familiar and modest opposition, little Oulu Palloseura of Finland. The first leg was on the pitch Bob Paisley had criticised so roundly a year earlier, and this time it was even worse, bearing deep scars from a recent athletics meeting. Nevertheless, Liverpool improved on their 1980 result, winning through a late strike from Kenny Dalglish after laying siege to Oulu's goal. Alan Kennedy remembers it as a wholly one-sided encounter, totting up a dozen personal attempts on goal from left-back! The return was unremarkable for the football - the Reds ran in seven at their leisure - but remains etched in the memories of Anfield loyalists for the pre-match tribute to Bill Shankly, who had died two days earlier. There was the expected minute's silence, but, of course, the real emotion poured down from the Kop, as supporters who understood their club's debt to that great man raised their voices and sang: 'We all agree, name the stand after Shankly.' Bill would have appreciated that.

He would have approved, too, of Liverpool's masterful display in taking a two-goal lead in the first leg of the second round, against AZ67 Alkmaar. Indeed, when Sammy Lee scored the second just after half-time in Amsterdam's Olympic stadium - the game had been switched from the Dutchmen's own cramped quarters to cope with the demand for tickets - there was every prospect of a rout. Alan Kennedy, temporarily supplanted by Mark Lawrenson at left-back, was doing radio commentary and ventured the not unreasonable opinion that the Reds were not in the remotest danger. Soon, however, the rookie broadcaster was to learn the pitfalls of making rash predictions: 'Not long after I had made the remark, Alkmaar scored. Then they got an equaliser and might even have snatched a late winner. What could I say?

Who changed the script? The Liverpool camp register anxiety as Dutch champions Alkmaar push the Reds all the way, losing eventually only by the odd goal in nine over the two legs. Left to right are substitute David Fairclough, scout Tom Saunders *(behind),* **coaches Ronnie Moran and Ray Evans, assistant manager Joe Fagan and trainer Reuben Bennett.**

Dutch defiance: Alkmaar goalkeeper Treytel dives at the feet of Ray Kennedy at Anfield, with Ian Rush lurking in case of a rebound. The visitors pushed their hosts to the limit before capitulating near the end.

The best I managed was "Anyone can make a mistake." Some tipster I turned out to be!' In fact, the Merseysiders need not have been surprised by the resilience of a talented and disciplined side who had shown their mettle in the previous term's UEFA Cup Final, losing to Ipswich Town over two legs but only by the odd goal in nine. Certainly they had deserved better than to be jeered by their own fans as Liverpool seized the initiative. Afterwards, Bob Paisley was galled at the concession of 'two silly goals', while the Alkmaar coach, George Kessler, admitted: 'We were very lucky. The door had closed, but now it is open, just a little bit.' Those expecting a thriller at Anfield were not disappointed, with the Dutchmen equalising twice before Alan Hansen put the Reds in the quarter-final with a dramatic 85th-minute winner. The visitors' outstanding player was schemer Johnny Metgod - later to play for Nottingham Forest and Spurs - whose 25-yard effort led to the bizarre Phil Thompson own goal that made the score 2-2. Alan Kennedy recalls: 'I shall never forget that goal. The ball hit the crossbar, bounced down on to Phil's foot and went over the line. He just looked up at that bar and shook his head; he couldn't believe it. It wasn't his fault, though; it was just one of those things.'

After falling 3-0 in Tokyo to the Brazilian club, Flamengo, in the less than momentous World Club Championship, Liverpool turned their attention to less flamboyant but formidably workmanlike opposition in the form of CSKA Sofia. The Bulgarians, chastened by their 5-1 reverse at Anfield in 1980/81, returned to Merseyside committed to defence in depth. Graeme Souness, who had plundered a wonderful hat-trick a year earlier, was tightly marked and the hosts had to be content with a sole strike by Ronnie Whelan. Bob Paisley was not impressed, though, estimating that his men had got in 20 more shots than last time: 'Our finishing was the difference on that occasion,' he added. Perceiving an opportunity for revenge, the Bulgarian crowd was in fearsome voice for the second leg, maintaining an intimidatory barrage of sound throughout the game. Thus was set a most hostile scene for one of Liverpool's sourest European experiences, and out they went, 2-0 after extra time. They were left to reflect on the Ian Rush header that was disallowed despite appearing to cross the line by a clear 12 inches, the horrendous Grobbelaar clanger when they were just a few minutes from securing a semi-final place, the chronic luck to hit the woodwork twice near the end, and the sending-off of Mark Lawrenson - all set against a background of repeatedly over-physical Bulgarian tactics.

The following campaign, Bob Paisley's last before retirement, began undemandingly against Dundalk in the Republic of Ireland. It was a trip relished particularly by Ronnie Whelan, who was revisiting his native region, where he had starred for Home Farm before being recommended to Liverpool by Jim McLaughlin. Now Jim managed Dundalk, and before the game was half an hour old might have been regretting his tip-off as Ronnie scored twice to set the Reds on the way to a comfortable 4-1 victory. Giving his verdict on the action, the home boss said: 'They never gave us a chance. They played as though they were fighting for their lives and there was nothing a team like ours could do about it. I've never seen any side exert such intense pressure.' Despite the disparity in class, the visitors endeared themselves to their hosts with their friendly, down-to-earth attitude. Apparently the Merseysiders' approach contrasted favourably with that of Spurs, who had played Dundalk a season earlier and raised Irish hackles by criticising the small ground and rather dim floodlights. Goodwill notwithstanding, the League of Ireland players were intent on selling their lives dearly in the second leg and were determined to prevent a repetition of the 10-0 defeat suffered when the two clubs had met at Anfield in 1969. In front of 12,000 or so spectators - Liverpool's lowest home gate in European competition - Dundalk battled valiantly, losing only to a late goal scored, inevitably enough, by Ronnie Whelan.

Perhaps understandably, the Reds were a little less than whole-hearted about the affair and, for once, their professionalism might be called into question. One man whose commitment could not be queried, however, was Terry McDermott, who was making his farewell appearance for the Merseysiders before rejoining Newcastle. In the circumstances, he was desperate to do well and hoped to sign off with a goal. However, he had few chances, and a poignant *Liverpool Echo* photograph of Terry lofting a pass in front of an empty stand described a disappointing occasion more eloquently than a thousand words. As his former St James's Park team-mate Alan Kennedy says, he had been a vital component of Bob Paisley's team: 'Terry was a smashing footballer, whose mere presence was great for morale. Even when his form declined towards the end, he was still worth his place for his bubbly attitude.' The last word that night, though, went to Jim McLaughlin, who said: 'We may have lost the game, but we won back our respect.'

Complacency apart, however, the lesson from Dundalk was that even clubs from hitherto unfashionable footballing countries could no longer be taken for granted, and if further evidence was needed it was offered in even more compelling fashion by the Reds' next opponents, JK Helsinki. Boasting only two full-time players, they inflicted a 1-0 first-leg defeat on a dumbfounded Liverpool, a result that was greeted as arguably the most monumental sporting upset ever witnessed on Finnish soil. Indeed, so confidently predicted was a Reds cakewalk that fewer than 6,000 fans bothered to turn up at the 60,000-capacity Helsinki stadium, and before the match JK's English goalkeeper, Jeff Wood, had said that only a miracle could save his side. Previously Finnish teams had managed to defeat opponents from Malta and Cyprus only; now they bested the mighty Merseysiders, who had failed to convert considerable pressure into goals.

Alan Kennedy recalls the remarkable defeat with a wry smile: 'We were so much on top that I felt like I was playing outside-left and I might have scored three in the first ten minutes. But they took their chance just before half-time, and we just couldn't find a way through. Although the result did not seriously threaten our progress in the Cup, it was seen as a major catastrophe in Liverpool. The players felt terrible, and on the way home it was awful to think of the pressmen, in the seats behind us, preparing their critical reports. That sort of thing always hurts, although in my experience, English journalists are usually fair. Of course, JK reacted as if they had won the European Cup, and who could blame them?' The Finnish fantasy could not stand the test of Anfield, of course, as the Reds restored their pride to the tune of 5-1. Every Liverpool man except goalkeeper Grobbelaar took a shot, and it wouldn't have been too

A scramble in the Helsinki
goalmouth at Anfield and Ian
Rush *(partly hidden)* is foiled.

difficult to imagine Bruce storming forward to try his luck. It is a night that stands out in the memory of Alan Kennedy, as he scored twice in a match for the first and only time: 'One of them was a real cracker; I played a quick one-two, then hit it from 25 yards. After that I wondered if I should go looking for my hat-trick, but despite our 5-2 aggregate lead, I could imagine Bob Paisley accusing me of being unprofessional, so I didn't risk it. I think it would have been wrong to break with our traditional approach. But it felt so good to be given time on the ball to show what you could do. Certainly, that was a pleasant change.' Maintaining his sense of humour, Jeff Wood, when asked afterwards about the pressure of playing Liverpool at their most rampant, said: 'We were under no pressure - until they kicked off.'

Having been shaken twice by lower-class opposition, then recovering their poise, the Reds might have felt their name was on the 1983 European Cup, but they were destined for unexpected elimination at the hands of Widzew Lodz. For Alan Kennedy, though, the 2-0 first-leg defeat in Poland represented only part of the trauma. As has already been mentioned, flying was not the Wearsider's favoured mode of transport, and on the outgoing descent he suffered his most terrifying airborne experience. He looks back with a shudder: 'As we were coming down, suddenly we heard the pilot say something like "Ooooohhhhh" and we went back up. He had come through the clouds and discovered that he was too far along the runway to land safely. He announced that he had miscalculated and was sorry, which I thought was brave of him, and would circle round for another attempt. I was so frightened I dived under my seat. It's terrible when you can't see anything and you suddenly feel the plane getting this tremendous power boost.

'Anyway, I think it's fair to say I felt the omens were not on our side when we touched down on a wet afternoon. Then we had a two-hour coach journey through a succession of drab villages to reach Lodz, which is a miserable-looking mining town surrounded by slag-heaps. There was snow on the ground, the people were all huddled up against the cold, and suddenly I thought how lucky we were, being well paid for playing a game we enjoyed.' The match was lost 2-0, due partly to another Grobbelaar blunder, and Ian Rush recalls that the manager seemed more disappointed than ever before. At Anfield, though deprived of stomach-bug victim Kenny Dalglish, the Reds poured forward like men possessed, but though a late onslaught secured victory on the night, it was not enough. For Bob Paisley it was an anti-climactic finale to a glorious European career, but at the end of the season he was able to step down with a smile on his face. After all, he could console himself with his sixth League title in nine seasons as manager.

The fresh hand on the helm was that of Joe Fagan, another graduate from the Liverpool bootroom, and, although in his sixties, he had about him a lively, mischievous air. For sure, there would be no chance of stagnation under Joe, as he was to prove with a vengeance. His first European examination was set by part-timers BK Odense, whose performance over two legs underlined the fact that Danish international strength was not matched at club level. Their players were highly skilled but lacked sufficient organisation to trouble the Reds, who won 1-0 away and 5-1 at home. Kenny Dalglish netted three times in the tie to eclipse a record held by one of his childhood heroes, Denis Law; the former Celt's second strike at Anfield was his 15th in the European Cup, now more than any other British player. But perhaps the most relieved man that night was fellow marksman Michael Robinson, whose two goals were his first in nine games since signing for the Reds. The Republic of Ireland international, an archetypal workhorse, had enjoyed an unusual career to date. He had first entered the public consciousness when Manchester City's Malcolm Allison outraged soccer opinion by paying Preston £756,000 for the untried youngster during one of the most inflationary transfer sprees ever mounted. Amid the inevitable hype that ensued, Michael struggled to make an impact and was shuttled off to Brighton where he performed creditably if not spectacularly before Joe stepped in. At Anfield, while lacking the class to carve out a long-term future, he laboured honestly alongside Messrs Dalglish and Rush, and was to play an honourable part in the lifting of two trophies before moving on.

A sterner test awaited Liverpool in the second round where they faced Atletico Bilbao, and after a goalless first leg at Anfield - in which Andoni Goicoechea, the so-called 'Butcher of Bilbao', kept tabs on Rush and Robinson in a hard but not excessive manner - the Spaniards were confident. They had achieved a clean sheet by relinquishing the traditional Continental man-to-man marking technique in favour of the British zonal system - manager Javier Clemente had picked up priceless hints during a six-week fact-finding mission at Ipswich in 1980 - and although they upset the crowd with their theatrical time-wasting, there was no denying that they had played well. Ian Rush recalls: 'After holding us, Atletico thought they were all but through. But Joe Fagan told us we had played well, too, and that we could win if we kept our heads. Away from home, it is always important to quieten the crowd because when you achieve that, it often takes the fizz out of their players as well. We managed that for long periods in the first half, then got the goal I felt we deserved in the second. I shall always remember that one: first came a right-foot cross from Alan Kennedy, which was rare, and then a header from me, which was rarer!'

That goal is stamped vividly on Alan's memory, too: 'I chased a ball hopefully towards their corner flag, the full-back committed himself to a rash tackle, and unexpectedly I found the ball on my right foot. Seeing Rushie on his own in the middle, I didn't stop to think, just swung and hoped. The ball reached him perfectly and he scored, even though he misheaded it slightly.' As the ball hit the net for what was to be the only goal of the game, thousands of hitherto buoyant Basques fell silent, and afterwards were sporting enough to clap their conquerors from the field. In some ways Bilbao is the Spanish Liverpool - both are traditional-ly seafaring cities in which football fervour is immense - and even when vying for a place in the European Cup quarter-finals, that rapport shone through. Alan Kennedy says: 'The fans were really brilliant and so were the Atletico players, wishing us all the best for the rest of the competition. Sometimes, after a defeat, professional footballers don't want to speak to anyone, but those lads were wonderful.' The fabulous contribution of Graeme Souness remains clear in Alan's mind, too: 'He was so confident and powerful, it must have been one of his finest performances. He was a marvellous skipper whom I respected, but we didn't always see eye to eye. He imposed himself on people, stood for no nonsense, and always

The grin that says Kenny Dalglish has just equalled Denis Law's British record of 14 European goals, five of which were scored as a Celtic player. Later in the same match, at home to BK Odense, he made the record his sole property with his third strike of the tie.

wanted to win, on the training ground as much as in the match. I'm like that, too, and we had our fiercer moments.'

In the last eight the Reds were paired with Benfica, against whom they always seem to find something special. This time a single-goal victory at Anfield was followed by a majestic 4-1 triumph in Portugal, an achievement that must have left the rest of Europe quaking. Alan remembers running out at the Stadium of Light - something of a misnomer, for the floodlights are on the dim side - to be greeted by a deafening roar: 'There seemed to be tier after tier of spectators, sensing that our one-goal lead would not be enough and baying for our blood. There were thousands of flags and crackers were going off all over the place; it was an amazing spectacle.' Joe Fagan had known what to expect, though, and he confused the Eagles by withdrawing Dalglish into midfield, thus leaving Rush to forage on his own at the front. His strategy was perfect as the Reds, after weathering a storm of early Benfica attacks, settled to give one of their most spellbinding European displays to run out 4-1 winners. Ian was particularly delighted to score with a header in each leg: 'Continental 'keepers tend to stay on their line more than the British, which gives you a better chance in the air. Heading had never been my strongest suit, but I reckoned it was improving; after all, I knocked home 14 with my head that season and won a bet with a journalist who reckoned I wouldn't get anywhere near that many.'

Ronnie Whelan (below), who made an often unobtrusive, but invariably crucial contribution to Liverpool's Continental campaigns in the first half of the 1980s.

In terms of tradition, Liverpool's semi-final opponents could hardly compare with the famous Portuguese, but Dinamo Bucharest were by no means in the lightweight category of, say, FC Zurich seven years earlier. The Romanian champions had already seen off Hamburg and Dynamo Minsk and had built a reputation for ruggedness and negativity that did less than justice to their considerable technique. At Anfield, however, they lived up to their name, committing a foul at the slightest hint of danger, a cynical but effective tactic. Accordingly, Swiss referee André Daina showed his yellow card to four Romanians, though he might have been more justified in reaching for the red. Graeme Souness, never a shrinking violet in the face of physical aggression, clashed with fellow midfielder Movila, who walked away from the confrontation with a suspected broken jaw. At the final whistle Dinamo left the pitch with the jeers of the Kop ringing in their ears, but satisfied with a single-goal deficit. Now Liverpool would need to draw on every ounce of experience, commitment and skill, qualities which they possessed in abundance.

The welcome in a packed Bucharest stadium was predictably hostile, with Souness singled out for the bulk of the vitriol. The local press had carried lurid accounts of the Movila incident, and there was a chorus of catcalls every time the Scot touched the ball, even during the pre-match kick-in. But even in such a tense situation, there was humour to be found, as Alan Kennedy remembers: 'As the fans booed, we tried to give Graeme the ball as much as possible, and once he wound them up by pretending to go for it, then letting it go. If they could have got at him, I'm sure he would have been crucified. It was

all very intimidating, but Joe Fagan had anticipated this and had warned us not to dwell on the ball. Stupidly, I didn't heed him and was nearly cut in half by an early tackle, ending up on the cinder track around the ground. I'd learned my lesson after that.'

As the match progressed, however, it became clear that far from putting Souness off, the tirade of abuse was bringing the best out of him. Like everyone else, Ian Rush was mightily impressed: 'Graeme just loved that type of pressure. Other players might have hidden, but he was everywhere, wanting the ball all the time. He seemed to grow in stature all the time.' Indeed, it was a masterful touch from the Reds' schemer early in a game played in torrential rain that set up one of Ian's most brilliant and valuable goals, a precise dink from an acute angle that was reminiscent of Kenny Dalglish's winner against Bruges in the 1978 final. After Dinamo had equalised, the Welshman struck again to secure a magnificent 3-1 aggregate victory. At the end, Souness left the pitch with his socks shredded by a succession of scything tackles, but an expression of gleeful satisfaction on his face, while Joe Fagan had rarely been more ebullient: 'I'm proud of the way my players helped and sustained each other when things might have gone wrong. They didn't seem to have any nerves - I had them all for us!'

By the time of the final, Liverpool had added the League Championship to a Milk Cup triumph over Everton, and now sought an unheard-of treble. The odds, however, were stacked monumentally against them, for they were to play Roma on their OWN ground. In a staggering display of inflexibility, UEFA refused to change the nominated venue even when the Romans reached the final. Happily Europe's premier club competition will never again be decided in such unequal circumstances, thanks to an overdue alteration to the rules, but that offered little consolation to the Reds at the time. The task facing them was awesome, as Alan Kennedy recalls: 'We travelled to the ground by coach, and I can remember catching sight of the Olympic stadium from a hilltop some ten or fifteen minutes before we reached it. Then we went down and down, it was as though we were heading for the bowels of the earth. There was this feeling that everything was against us, with our 10,000 fans having to shout against

Carefree pair: how far removed from the worries of management were Graeme Souness and Kenny Dalglish as they settled back for a European flight in the early 1980s. A few years later they were each in charge of one of Britain's major clubs. Immediately behind them is David Hodgson, whose Liverpool career never quite took off.

Take heed, oh ye of little faith! Alan Kennedy sends goalkeeper Franco Tancredi the wrong way to climax the penalty shoot-out in Rome, thus becoming the only Briton to score the winning goal in two European Cup Finals. Yet the Wearsider's team-mates had been less than confident about his ability from the spot.

their 60,000. Even so, Joe Fagan always believed we could win.' The world had moved on since Liverpool's previous Roman final, to which most of their fans had travelled overland. This time the exodus had been largely aerial and more dispersed, so there was less of a feeling of mass migration. Even so, before the game there were the usual happy scenes of Englishmen on holiday, though photographer Steve Hale detected also an air of brooding menace, with gangs of Italian youths apparently bent on finding trouble.

The match - scrappy and unsatisfying, the life throttled out of it by the fear of defeat - was played in a colourful haze caused by smoke-bombs and flares, creating a scene reminiscent of Milan nearly 20 years before. Phil Neal capitalised on a defensive mistake to give Liverpool an early lead, then Roma achieved parity shortly before the break; for the rest of the match, two sides packed with wonderful players failed to live up to their potential, though for Liverpool there were massively extenuating circumstances. In such a one-sided atmosphere, had they not kept the game tight, had they allowed their hosts to seize the initiative, they would have sunk without trace. Instead they called on every shred of experience and dredged up the last grain of determination to remain in contention, and in that context, every man was a star. Especially outstanding were that quick and cultured centre-back Mark Lawrenson, whose

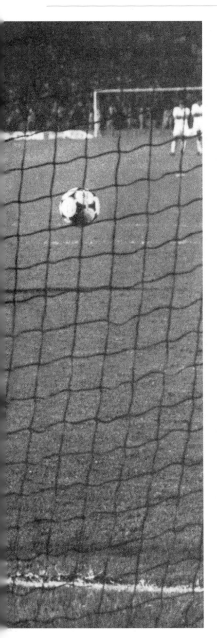

nigh-infallible ball-winning technique owed more to timing than ferocity, much-maligned custodian Bruce Grobbelaar, and industrious midfield man Sammy Lee, who harassed his illustrious opponents constantly. Indeed, the likes of Brazilian World Cup giants Falcao and Cerezo, and Italian idols Graziani and Conti, were unable to run the game as pundits had predicted, even though Roma enjoyed by far the biggest percentage of possession while the Reds worked and worked.

Eventually, agonisingly, when extra time failed to produce a winner, the players shaped up for the refined torture of a penalty shoot-out. People faced the pressure in different ways, none more flamboyantly than Bruce Grobbelaar, who defused some of the tension by his immortal wobbly-legs routine between kicks. Some said it was gamesmanship aimed at unsettling Roma, but Bruce was entitled to settle his own nerves in his own way and the touch of humour was undeniably welcome, somehow putting what seemed a life-or-death show in perspective. Others argued, with good reason, that the Italians were the masters of every psychological trick in the book and it did them no harm to taste their own medicine. For young Steve Nicol, who had been called into the action as a substitute for Craig Johnston, the only way was to volunteer for the first kick, a philosophy of 'Let's get it over as quickly as possible.' The fact that he missed, and had to be consoled by Graeme Souness, must have seemed like the end of the world at the time; as it turned out, it didn't matter at all. Ian Rush describes the shoot-out as one of the most nerve-wracking times of his life, though he managed to appear perfectly cool: 'As I walked up to take the kick, it seemed like everyone in the stadium was whistling at once. My legs felt like jelly, tired from all the effort, not only from that match but from a long season. But I never thought about missing; I just picked out the corner and put it in for 3-3. The 'keeper went the wrong way and I was so relieved. We had practiced a lot and I had missed too many times for comfort. The funny thing was that in training the worst of the lot was Alan Kennedy; we didn't fancy him doing it at all!'

Neither, of course, did Alan, though he was shortly to become the biggest hero of the lot, the man who scored the winning goal in TWO European Cup Finals. The memory of those moments will remain with him forever: 'None of us wanted it to go to penalties, and certainly didn't play for that, as Red Star did in 1991. We had only three reliable takers - Neal, Souness, Rush - and after that we were in the lap of the gods. Ian is right, I did badly in practice, and during a pre-season game in Rotterdam I had missed twice from the spot. I don't know why Joe Fagan picked on me, but he had to provide five names after extra time and mine was among them. I'm nervous at the best of times, and when Steve Nicol missed I thought "That's it, it won't get to me after all." But as the kicks were taken we got right back into it, and when my turn came I had to score for Liverpool to win the Cup. I could hear Alan Hansen, Mark Lawrenson and others talking behind me, and it was obvious they weren't too happy about my chances because they were wondering who would take the sixth, seventh and eighth penalties. But something extra seemed to be spurring me on; my record was not good but I was determined, and uncharacteristically confident. I didn't look at the 'keeper, I didn't want him to put me off. I didn't look at the ranks of photographers, or pay attention to the crowd either. In such intense moments, I tend to think of my family; I think that somebody out there is proud of me. This time I thought of Joe Fagan, too, and it flashed across my mind that if Joe had such faith in me I'd repay him with a goal. Then I managed to tuck it away, and it was all over.'

It was a supremely emotional moment for everyone in the Liverpool camp, who felt they had pulled off the impossible. There were even tears from hard-man skipper Graeme Souness as the enormity of the achievement sank in. They had played a European Cup Final in their opponents' backyard, taken everything some of the greatest players and most passionate supporters in the world could throw at them, survived the torment of penalties, and now they were walking off with the trophy. Afterwards they celebrated at a villa in the hills, drinking and dancing the night away. It was hardly the time to consider the rights and wrongs of deciding so important a match in such an artificial manner. The Reds had played by the rules and they had won, and that was enough. Those who draw up those regulations, however, would do well to ponder on the morals of rejecting replays on commercial and logistical grounds. What about such little matters as sporting ethics, and yes, justice?

Round 1 - 1st leg
16 September 1981

OULU PALLOSEURA 0

LIVERPOOL 1

Dalglish 84
H-T 0-0. Crowd 8,400

GROBBELAAR
NEAL
KENNEDY, ALAN
THOMPSON
HANSEN
LAWRENSON
DALGLISH
KENNEDY, RAY
JOHNSON
LEE
SOUNESS

Liverpool dominated their Finnish hosts but let themselves down with a display of finishing that verged on the inept. Eventually it took a late goal by Dalglish - his first since April - to win the match. Until then, the Reds had done everything but score, missing the target with a series of clear-cut openings that their midfield superiority had fashioned. When they did manage an accurate strike, the likes of Ray Kennedy and Dalglish were frustrated by the acrobatics of Oulu's stocky, balding 'keeper Rantanen, an unlikely figure for a hero but, unquestionably, the star of the night. In the end it took a slice of luck to beat him, when he appeared to make a fine save from Dalglish, only for the ball to squirm against a post and over the line.

Round 1 - 2nd leg
30 September 1981

LIVERPOOL 7

Dalglish 26; McDermott 40, 75;
Kennedy, Ray 46; Johnson 60; Rush 67;
Lawrenson 72

OULU PALLOSEURA 0

H-T 2-0. Crowd 20,789

GROBBELAAR
NEAL
KENNEDY, ALAN
THOMPSON
KENNEDY, RAY (LAWRENSON)
HANSEN
DALGLISH
LEE

JOHNSON (RUSH)
McDERMOTT
SOUNESS

The spectre of another night of shoddy marksmanship was raised when Dalglish and Neal missed early opportunities, but in the end the Kop's appetite for goals was satiated to the full. Dalglish commenced the festivities with a diving header - Liverpool's 100th strike in the European Cup - and then set up McDermott for the midfielder to make immediate inroads on a second century. The Finns offered nothing but dogged defence - they managed just one breakaway, on which Jalasvaara shot over Grobbelaar's bar - and the Reds racked up the goals with consummate comfort. Best of the night was the last, a sweet left-foot curler by McDermott from the right corner of the penalty box.

Liverpool won 8-0 on aggregate.

Round 2 - 1st leg
21 October 1981

AZ67 ALKMAAR 2

Kist 60, Tol 86

LIVERPOOL 2

Johnson 21; Lee 48
H-T 0-1. Crowd 15,000

GROBBELAAR
NEAL
THOMPSON
LAWRENSON
KENNEDY, RAY
HANSEN
DALGLISH (WHELAN)
LEE
JOHNSON
McDERMOTT
SOUNESS

Liverpool outclassed Alkmaar for most of the match, then paid dearly for uncharacteristically lax defensive work. With Souness and Lee dictating the pattern of play from midfield, the Reds created ample opportunities to put the result beyond doubt, though in fairness to the attackers, the two they did manage to convert should have been enough. The first was scored by Johnson, who received a pass from Dalglish before wrong-footing 'keeper Treytel with a low, slow shot from 15 yards, then Souness and Ray Kennedy combined to set up Lee for an opportunist's 20-yard chip. Alkmaar hit back on the hour when Neal and Hansen dallied over clearing a Van der Meer cross and Kist whacked the ball into the net from 12 yards, but worse was to come. With four minutes left, a perceptive through-ball from Peters caught the Liverpool defence square and Tol swooped to beat Clemence with emphatic expertise.

Alan Hansen, whose name appeared infrequently on the scoresheet, sinks Alkmaar with an 85th-minute winner in the second leg at Anfield.

LIVERPOOL 3

McDermott (pen) 42; Rush 68; Hansen 85

AZ67 ALKMAAR 2

Kist 53; Thompson (og) 72
H-T 1-0. Crowd 29,703

GROBBELAAR
NEAL
LAWRENSON
THOMPSON
KENNEDY, RAY
HANSEN
DALGLISH
WHELAN
RUSH
McDERMOTT
SOUNESS

The spirited Dutchmen deserved enormous credit for their part in a night of thrilling theatre at Anfield. After the Reds had commanded first-half proceedings and taken the lead through a McDermott penalty - awarded for a foul on Dalglish - shortly before the break, the second period seemed likely to be one-sided. That proved far from the truth, although there was a suspicion of offside about Alkmaar's equaliser, tucked away firmly by Kist. Now the visitors swarmed forward and Grobbelaar saved well from the Dutch striker before Rush converted a low Dalglish cross to restore Liverpool's lead. Alkmaar's reaction was not long in coming; a 25-yard lob from Metgod caught the Reds' 'keeper out of position, hit the underside of the bar and bounced over the line off Thompson. Such a scenario demanded a dramatic climax, and it was provided by Hansen, who stormed forward to poke home a late winner from close range.

Liverpool won 5-4 on aggregate.

LIVERPOOL 1

Whelan 65

CSKA SOFIA 0

H-T 0-0. Crowd 27,388

GROBBELAAR
NEAL
KENNEDY, ALAN
WHELAN
LAWRENSON
HANSEN
DALGLISH
LEE
RUSH
McDERMOTT
SOUNESS

The Bulgarians came to Anfield to defend and did so to telling effect, frustrating a Liverpool attack that, yet again, was short on accuracy. The Reds opened with a whirlwind offensive, winning eight corners in one frenetic spell, and 'keeper Velinov saved ably from Lee (twice), Dalglish and Hansen. Plenty of other efforts were off target and the game continued on its one-sided course until 40 minutes, when Grobbelaar made his first save, diving smartly to his left to repel a 25-yarder from Kerimov. CSKA started the second half brightly, Mladenov shooting wide from a useful position, but it was not long before Paisley's side resumed its siege on the visitors' goal. Eventually the pressure paid off when Lee found Whelan to the left of the box and the young Irishman squeezed a low shot through the legs of a defender and inside the far post. But it was not a satisfying result for the Reds, who now faced a testing task in Sofia.

Top: **No way through: Ian Rush thumps the ball goalwards against CSKA Sofia at Anfield, only to be thwarted by 'keeper Velinov.**

CSKA SOFIA 2

Mladenov 78, 101

LIVERPOOL 0

H-T 0-0. Crowd 60,000

GROBBELAAR
NEAL
LAWRENSON
KENNEDY, ALAN
THOMPSON
WHELAN
DALGLISH
LEE
RUSH (JOHNSTON)
McDERMOTT (JOHNSON)
SOUNESS

From first to final whistle, nothing went right for Liverpool. Their initial setback was an outrageous one, suffered after only two minutes, when a Rush header appeared to have crossed the goal-line but the referee waved play on. Two minutes later, Whelan was through with only Velinov to beat, but the 'keeper blocked his shot. Still the Reds played with composure and appeared in little danger of surrendering their advantage, though CSKA mounted steady pressure after the interval. Just when it seemed that Liverpool would survive, Grobbelaar dashed out for a cross, changed his mind too late, and Mladenov nodded into a vacant net. Another sickening blow was to fall in extra time, when Mladenov's deflected shot eluded a posse of defenders on the line. Even then the Reds came close to recovery, both Whelan and Lawrenson hitting the woodwork, before the visitors' woes were completed by the sending off of Lawrenson for retaliation.

CSKA Sofia won 2-1 on aggregate after extra time.

Round 1 - 1st leg
14 September 1982

DUNDALK 1

Flanagan 89

LIVERPOOL 4

Whelan 7, 26; Rush 31; Hodgson 75
H-T 0-3. Crowd 16,500

GROBBELAAR
NEAL
KENNEDY
THOMPSON
WHELAN
HANSEN
DALGLISH
LEE
RUSH
HODGSON
SOUNESS

Liverpool steamrollered their plucky but unsophisticated opponents, who never appeared capable of causing an upset. The Reds were just too slick and composed, effectively winning the match with three goals before half-time. The first two fell to Whelan on his return to his homeland, the opener coming when the perky, promising midfielder dribbled past two defenders and shot clinically past 'keeper Blackmore, the second following a deft set-up by Hodgson 20 minutes later. The visitors went on to double their lead through Rush and Hodgson as they put on a stirring exhibition of football for the appreciative Irish fans. The biggest cheer of the night, however, went to Flanagan, who scored a consolation goal for Dundalk following a free-kick near the end.

Round 1 - 2nd leg
28 September 1982

LIVERPOOL 1

Whelan 81

DUNDALK 0

H-T 0-0. Crowd 12,021

GROBBELAAR
NEAL
KENNEDY
THOMPSON
WHELAN
HANSEN
DALGLISH
LEE
McDERMOTT
JOHNSTON
SOUNESS

In front of the smallest Anfield crowd in their European history, Liverpool failed to find inspiration against the well-organised Irish part-timers. Sitting on a three-goal lead from the first leg, the Reds could afford to be complacent, but it produced precious little entertainment for the faithful fans who did make the effort to turn out on a rainy night. Most of the interest concerned McDermott, making his farewell appearance before rejoining Newcastle, but despite his considerable efforts to sign off with a goal, the ball would not run for him. In the end, though, he was instrumental in creating the winner, his shot bouncing off the back of Dalglish's head and falling to Whelan, who volleyed into the net. At that stage, however, even the Kop would not have begrudged brave Dundalk parity on the night.

Liverpool won 5-1 on aggregate.

Round 2 - 1st leg
19 October 1982

JK HELSINKI 1

Ismail 43

LIVERPOOL 0

H-T 1-0. Crowd 5,722

GROBBELAAR
NEAL
KENNEDY
THOMPSON
WHELAN
HANSEN
DALGLISH
LEE
RUSH
HODGSON
SOUNESS

Liverpool slumped to their most surprising and ignominious European defeat at the hands of the inexperienced Finns, few of whom relied on football for a living. As expected, the Reds enjoyed almost complete territorial advantage, creating at least a dozen clear-cut chances, but were denied by their own poor marksmanship and the excellence of Helsinki's English goalkeeper, Wood. After a nervous start, the former Charlton Athletic custodian made a series of brilliant saves, and when he was beaten, defender Soini headed a Hansen effort off the line. Early 'goals' by both Dalglish and Rush were ruled out for offside, and the Welshman was guilty of the night's most glaring miss, heading wide from five yards when unmarked. So the scoring honours went to JK's Ismail, who broke free to beat Grobbelaar after a rare mistake by Souness.

Round 2 - 2nd leg
2 November 1982

LIVERPOOL 5

Dalglish 26; Johnston 30; Neal 44;
Kennedy 61, 69

JK HELSINKI 0

H-T 3-0. Crowd 16,434

GROBBELAAR
NEAL
KENNEDY
THOMPSON
JOHNSTON
HANSEN
DALGLISH (HODGSON)
LEE
RUSH
LAWRENSON
SOUNESS

After two below-par European performances, Liverpool needed to reassert their authority, and they did so to demoralising effect. The Reds controlled the match throughout, the only surprise being that the first goal was delayed for so long. It was worth the wait, though, Dalglish demonstrating sheer quality as he controlled the ball on his chest and sidestepped a defender before beating 'keeper Wood from a narrow angle. Soon afterwards Johnston scored with a skidding 25-yarder and then Neal played a smart one-two passing interchange with Dalglish before netting from 12 yards. Now the fate of the tie was decided, but Liverpool - and Kennedy in particular - did not let up. First the marauding left-back powered past two defenders before deceiving Wood with a low shot, then he appeared in the box to shoot home the fifth.

Liverpool won 5-1 on aggregate.

Right: **Bees round a honeypot: Liverpool swarmed all over JK Helsinki at Anfield, thrashing them 5-0 in a venomous backlash for the shock reverse in Finland two weeks earlier.**

Top right: **David Hodgson, whose 89th-minute goal against Widzew Lodz at Anfield was enough to win the match but not the tie, is policed by a Polish defender.**

Round 3 - 1st leg
2 March 1983

WIDZEW LODZ 2
Tlokinski 48; Wraga 80

LIVERPOOL 0

H-T 0-0. Crowd 45,531

GROBBELAAR
NEAL
KENNEDY
LAWRENSON
WHELAN
HANSEN
DALGLISH
LEE
RUSH
JOHNSTON (HODGSON)
SOUNESS

Grobbelaar's uncertainty at dealing with crosses was highlighted again as Liverpool conceded a two-goal deficit. Ironically, before his costly blunder

early in the second half, he had saved the Reds by diving bravely at the feet of Grebosz when the overlapping defender had seemed odds-on to score. Shortly after that incident, Rush broke clear at the other end, only to be hauled back by Wojcicki, who escaped without a caution. For the remainder of the first period, a fast, skilful Lodz side carried the game to Liverpool without causing notable alarm. Then Surlit delivered a deep centre, Grobbelaar dropped the ball and Tlokinski accepted the gift. The Reds responded by attacking vigorously and a Kennedy 30-yarder brought a flying save from Mlynarczyk. But the pressurised Poles broke clear, Grebosz crossed and Wraga netted with a superbly judged diving header from 15 yards. For Liverpool, now, the way back would be difficult.

Round 3 - 2nd leg
16 March 1983

LIVERPOOL 3
Neal (pen) 15; Rush 80; Hodgson 89

WIDZEW LODZ 2
Tlokinski (pen) 33; Smolarek 53
H-T 1-1. Crowd 44,494

GROBBELAAR
NEAL
KENNEDY (FAIRCLOUGH)
LAWRENSON
WHELAN (THOMPSON)
HANSEN
HODGSON
LEE
RUSH
JOHNSTON
SOUNESS

Liverpool needed a vintage performance to survive in the competition; quite simply, it wasn't forthcoming. Even after the boost of an early penalty by Neal -

awarded for handball - the Reds never clicked into top gear, and the Poles' equaliser 12 minutes before half-time was a shattering blow. It was presented to them when Souness, dithering on the edge of the penalty area, was robbed by Smolarek, who advanced on Grobbelaar only to be brought down. Tlokinski tucked home the spot-kick, and the Poles settled back to let Liverpool resume their fruitless offensive. Now the Reds were vulnerable to the counter-punch, and it came when Filipzcak stretched their defence with an enterprising run, before slipping the ball to Smolarek, who netted a simple goal. To their credit the Merseysiders battled on, and won the game when Rush converted Fairclough's cross and Hodgson volleyed home from close range. By then, sadly, the tie was beyond redemption.

Widzew Lodz won 4-3 on aggregate.

European Cup 1983/84

Round 1 - 1st leg
14 September 1983

BK ODENSE 0

LIVERPOOL 1
Dalglish 15
H-T 0-1. Crowd 30,000

GROBBELAAR
NEAL
KENNEDY
LAWRENSON
JOHNSTON
HANSEN
DALGLISH
LEE
RUSH
ROBINSON
SOUNESS

Joe Fagan's Reds flowed stylishly against the Danish amateurs, but without converting their massive superiority into goals. At times, the passing movements of the visitors took the breath away and Odense 'keeper Hogh was in frequent action, making one magnificent early save from Dalglish. The Scot was not to be denied for long, however, and after quarter of an hour he gave Liverpool the lead, crashing the ball home from five yards after Robinson had miscued from a Johnston cross. Thereafter the chances came regularly; Kennedy went close, Rush missed a sitter and Dalglish might have had a hat-trick, but Hogh was not beaten again. To their credit, the skilful Danes kept the game open and played some positive football, although Grobbelaar was stretched only rarely.

Round 1 - 2nd leg
28 September 1983

LIVERPOOL 5
Robinson 14, 72; Dalglish 32, 40;
Clausen (og) 65

BK ODENSE 0

H-T 3-0. Crowd 14,985

GROBBELAAR
NICOL
KENNEDY
LAWRENSON
JOHNSTON
HANSEN
DALGLISH
LEE
RUSH
ROBINSON
SOUNESS (HODGSON)

It was a tale of two strikers as Liverpool put the Danish champions to the sword at Anfield. Dalglish, in prime form, scored the two goals he needed to beat Denis Law's British record in the European Cup, and Robinson hit the target for the first time since joining the Reds. Robinson swept home the opener from eight yards after Rush had laid back a wayward Kennedy shot. Next it was the turn of Dalglish, who tapped the ball into an empty net after a lightning break from Rush, then steered the ball past 'keeper Hogh from 12 yards after latching on to a through-pass from Souness. A disastrous back-pass from Clausen gave Liverpool their fourth, and it was left to Robinson to complete the scoring, waltzing round the hapless custodian after a smooth one-two with Rush. It was a fitting way to cap a night of exhilarating entertainment.

Liverpool won 6-0 on aggregate.

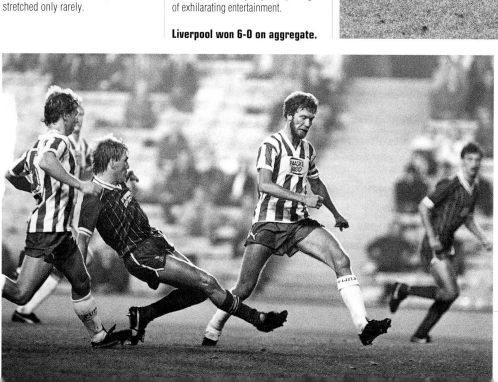

Kenny Dalglish nets against BK Odense to succeed his boyhood idol, Denis Law, as the top-scoring Briton in the European Cup.

One for the archives.
As Ian Rush describes this
goal against Atletico in Bilbao:
'First came a right-foot cross
from Alan Kennedy, which
was rare, and then a header
from me, which was rarer!'

Round 2 - 2nd leg
2 November 1983

ATLETICO BILBAO 0

LIVERPOOL 1
Rush 66
H-T 0-0. Crowd 47,500

GROBBELAAR
NEAL
KENNEDY
LAWRENSON
NICOL
HANSEN
DALGLISH
LEE
RUSH
ROBINSON (HODGSON)
SOUNESS

Liverpool produced one of their
most mature, patient European
displays to silence a roaring crowd
of partisan Basques. Ecstatic over
the goalless draw at Anfield, the
Bilbao fans appeared to view the
Reds as so much cannon fodder.
Initially Atletico fuelled the optimism
by attacking and both Noriega and
Gallego shot marginally wide.
But the Merseysiders remained
calm, slowly drew the Spanish
sting, and then proceeded to
dominate the match. With Souness
in commanding form, Liverpool
launched a series of measured
assaults before half-time, one of
which saw Nicol bring a splendid
diving save from Zubizarreta.
After the restart, the Reds probed
relentlessly until their enterprise
paid off. Hansen found Kennedy
on the left, the full-back crossed to
Rush, whose downward header
bounced beyond the 'keeper's
despairing clutch. Then Liverpool,
whose goal was never seriously
threatened, might have increased
their lead, but could be content with
a famous victory.

Liverpool won 1-0 on aggregate.

Round 2 - 1st leg
19 October 1983

LIVERPOOL 0

ATLETICO BILBAO 0

Crowd 33,063

GROBBELAAR
NEAL
KENNEDY
LAWRENSON
JOHNSTON
HANSEN
DALGLISH
LEE
RUSH
ROBINSON
SOUNESS

Atletico ran out at Anfield with one
apparent ambition - to keep their
scoresheet blank - and they achieved it
with a tightly disciplined, if occasionally cynical display of defence in depth.
Though the Spaniards didn't resort to
the intimidatory tactics that had been
predicted, there was no shortage of
niggly, so-called professional fouls and
they wasted time shamelessly. But they
deserved their draw because Liverpool
never revealed the powers of invention
necessary to breach the barrier. The
Reds, accustomed to running matches
through the midfield domination of
Souness and company, found little
space in the central areas, and their
most telling threats came from
overlaps by full-backs Neal and
Kennedy. Indeed, the closest Fagan's
side came to squeezing a lead came
when Neal let fly from 30 yards, but
Zubizarreta tipped the shot over the
bar. The second leg loomed as a
formidable proposition.

Round 3 - 1st leg
7 March 1984

LIVERPOOL 1
Rush 67

BENFICA 0

H-T 0-0. Crowd 39,09

GROBBELAAR
NEAL
KENNEDY
LAWRENSON
WHELAN
HANSEN
ROBINSON (DALGLISH)
LEE
RUSH
JOHNSTON
SOUNESS

The introduction of Dalglish for the second half lifted Liverpool and inspired a narrow victory. During the first 45 minutes, Benfica's composed rearguard had coped capably with the Reds' insistent but rather unimaginative attacks, but it was a different story after the Scot, returning from a long injury lay-off, replaced Robinson. Suddenly there was subtlety and penetration to the Merseysiders' forward movements, and the chinks in the Portuguese armour began to appear. The decisive strike was delightful in its simplicity: Whelan freed Kennedy on the left, the defender delivered a deep, tantalising cross and Rush, drifting beyond the far post, rose high to net with a crisp header. Then Souness tested 'keeper Bento with a 20-yard scorcher, and Liverpool stepped up the pressure. In the final 15 minutes three good openings were spurned, and a loud penalty appeal (for handball) was turned down, leaving plenty for the Reds to do in the Stadium of Light.

Above: **Springs in his heels: Michael Robinson takes flight to head for goal against the Eagles of Benfica at Anfield.**

Round 3 - 2nd leg
21 March 1984

BENFICA 1
Nene 74

LIVERPOOL 4
Whelan 9, 87; Johnston 33; Rush 79
H-T 0-2. Crowd 70,000

GROBBELAAR
NEAL
KENNEDY
LAWRENSON
WHELAN
HANSEN
DALGLISH
LEE
RUSH
JOHNSTON
SOUNESS

Liverpool turned on a demoralising show, outclassing and eventually embarrassing the much-vaunted Eagles. The Portuguese champions started buoyantly enough, and the Merseysiders were forced to repel several spirited early raids. But the complexion of the game changed radically when Benfica 'keeper Bento fumbled a routine header from Whelan, the ball slipping between his legs and over the line, and from that moment there was only one team in it. Dalglish, in particular, was a constant torment to his hosts' rearguard and he had a decisive hand in his side's three subsequent goals. He exchanged passes with Rush before setting up Johnston's emphatic 20-yarder with an incisive diagonal pass, he crossed for Rush's precise header, and he freed Whelan to outwit Bento from a tight angle. In between Nene had beaten Grobbelaar with a looping header from 15 yards, but that was scarcely relevant on a night of sheer despair for one of Europe's footballing institutions.

Liverpool won 5-1 on aggregate.

Semi-final - 1st leg
11 April 1984

LIVERPOOL 1

Lee 25

DINAMO BUCHAREST 0

H-T 1-0. Crowd 36,941

GROBBELAAR
NEAL
KENNEDY
LAWRENSON
WHELAN
HANSEN
DALGLISH
LEE
RUSH
JOHNSTON
SOUNESS

Liverpool emerged from a sour, joyless encounter with a hard-earned advantage, courtesy of a rare headed goal from little Lee. It came after 25 scrappy minutes in which the rugged Romanians disrupted the Reds' rhythm with a succession of calculated fouls. Inevitably the goal emanated from a free-kick, a clear case of poetic justice: Johnston was grounded by a scything tackle, Kennedy lifted the ball into the box and Lee lost his marker to glance home. Thereafter Liverpool attacked incessantly, but Dinamo packed their penalty area and the Merseyside forwards became lost in the crowd. Although Souness bridled menacingly, the home side showed admirable restraint, and the visitors were lucky to escape with just four bookings. Ironically, they could play good football, as they showed in the first half when Augustin outpaced the Reds' defence and shot past Grobbelaar, only to see his shot bounce back off a post. In the circumstances, it was difficult to feel sympathy.

Semi-final; - 2nd leg
25 April 1984

DINAMO BUCHAREST 1

Orac 38

LIVERPOOL 2

Rush 11, 84
H-T 1-1. Crowd 60,000

GROBBELAAR
NEAL
KENNEDY
LAWRENSON
WHELAN
HANSEN
DALGLISH (NICOL)
LEE
RUSH
JOHNSTON
SOUNESS

The Reds took their revenge on the savagely physical Romanians in the best possible way: by brushing them aside to reach the European Cup Final. From the early moment when they stretched their overall lead to two, Liverpool's progress seemed in little doubt, though they endured long periods of pressure. That vital strike oozed class, and it was fitting that Souness - playing superbly despite being the prime target for Dinamo's spite - should be instrumental in its creation. When a Lee corner was headed out of the box, the skipper volleyed instantly to Rush, who ran past a defender before lifting the most delicate of narrow-angled chips over the 'keeper. The Romanians' equaliser was also of the highest order, Orac curling a 20-yard free-kick over the defensive wall and just inside a post. After that, the Reds defended stoutly and broke away to underline their superiority when Rush netted from eight yards. Justice had been done and in glorious fashion, too.

Liverpool won 3-1 on aggregate.

Bucharest's public enemy number one: Graeme Souness *(Top left),* **seen here in the Anfield tussle with Dinamo, was vilified by the Romanian crowd for his physical approach, but spited them by helping Liverpool claim a place in the final.**

Left: **Pure class: Mark Lawrenson, whose speed, intelligence and perfect timing in the tackle were seen to best advantage in the 1984 European Cup triumph over Roma.**

It wasn't a classic goal, but Liverpool fans were not complaining as Phil Neal put the Reds ahead in the European Cup Final against Roma. The full-back poked the ball past Tancredi after the 'keeper had allowed it to squirm from his grasp.

Sheer euphoria: after defying the odds to beat Roma on their own ground, Liverpool line up for the traditional team picture with the European Cup. It was the fourth time the Reds had lifted the trophy, a record that no British team seems likely to challenge in the foreseeable future.

Final in Rome
30 May 1984

LIVERPOOL 1
Neal 15

AS ROMA 1
Pruzzo 43
H-T 1-1. Crowd 69,693

GROBBELAAR
NEAL
KENNEDY
LAWRENSON
WHELAN
HANSEN
DALGLISH (ROBINSON)
LEE
RUSH
JOHNSTON (NICOL)
SOUNESS

After a threadbare spectacle in which neither side lived up to their potential, Liverpool won the European Cup amid the climactic drama of a penalty shoot-out. The evening started well for the Reds, who dampened the enthusiasm of a passionate Italian audience with their controlled passing before going ahead with a scrappy goal. Johnston crossed from the right, 'keeper Tancredi dropped the ball, and after a hectic skirmish Neal stabbed into the net from seven yards. Now, though much of the play was mediocre, Roma attacked purposefully and their equaliser, which came through Pruzzo's flicked header from Conti's hanging cross, was well merited. In the second half the Italians were marginally the better side, although Souness, Grobbelaar and, in particular, Lawrenson were in outstanding form for the Reds. Extra time came and went with scant incident; now coolness from the penalty spot would decide the outcome. First the rookie, Nicol, blazed over for Liverpool, then Di Bartolomei netted; Neal equalised calmly, Conti missed and Souness nudged Liverpool in front; Righetti levelled, but the Romans fell behind again when Rush scored; then, crucially, Graziani shot over, and it was left to Kennedy to send the 'keeper the wrong way for the winner.

Liverpool won 4-2 on penalties after extra-time (scorers: Neal, Souness, Rush, Kennedy).

Above: **Just deserts: no one earned the right to lift the European Cup more surely than manager Joe Fagan** *(left)* **and coach Ronnie Moran. Both are wise, down-to-earth characters, who relished success without letting it go to their heads. How football needs more men like them!**

Chapter Eleven

TRAGEDY

GLORY and romance, beauty and excitement, they are all to be found in the story of Liverpool's European crusades. But in the spring of 1985 came a tragic event which sickened football fans worldwide and scarred Liverpool FC's European involvement. This is a book about football, but it is impossible - and would be wrong - not to mention the disaster that claimed 39 lives in the Heysel Stadium, Brussels, on the sunny evening of 29 May as supporters gathered to watch Liverpool meet Juventus in the European Cup Final. Millions of words have been committed to print in analysis of the tragedy, and this is not the place to do more than restate that this awful event was a truly dark moment for Liverpool FC. The club will always remember those who lost their lives in terrible circumstances. It is this writer's duty in the context of the book to review the season chronologically, and though it was to lose all relevance in the light of subsequent happenings, there was some fascinating football played on the way to Heysel.

The road began in Poland, whose teams are never a soft touch; indeed, the Reds' previous Polish opponents, Widzew Lodz, had dumped them out of Europe. This time, though, Joe Fagan's men, who had been suffering from poor League form, snatched a crucial away victory against Lech Poznan, thanks to a solitary goal by John Wark. The swashbuckling Scot, who seemed to reserve his most eye-catching performances for Continental opposition, made an even greater impact in the Anfield return, his hat-trick forming the centrepiece of a comfortable victory. It took his total of European goals - for Liverpool and his former club, Ipswich - to 22 in 27 games, a sensational return for a midfielder.

Next, for the second successive season, the Reds were drawn against Benfica, a side showing signs of emerging from years in the shadow of an illustrious past. Certainly the Eagles were thirsting for revenge, having never beaten Liverpool in four European games, but in an Anfield downpour (why does it always rain when these two clubs meet?) they slithered to another defeat. The principal executioner was Ian Rush, who scored three times and remembers the occasion with relish: 'It was my first European hat-trick, which came at a good time for me because it was only my second match after a cartilage operation and I wasn't feeling as sharp as usual. The pitch was slippery and everyone was making mistakes, which meant that chances were always likely to come.' Invariably, Ian's memory of his goals is near-photographic, and this occasion was no exception: 'For the first one, the ball skidded to me across a crowded area and I put it in a corner; next, after they had equalised, I slid in and touched home a rebound; then they stopped for a supposed infringement when they should have carried on, I swung my foot from near the penalty spot and the ball nipped low inside the post.' In the context of the game, the second strike was the most crucial because the Kop had become subdued. Says Ian: 'We are always very conscious of the fans becoming quiet. Then we know we have got to work just that little harder to pick ourselves up and give them something to shout about. That's when the value of teamwork is most noticeable. If a particular player is having a bad time, then the others rally round to help him. It's always been that way at Liverpool.' The Welshman's assessment is endorsed by Alan Kennedy, who adds his own tribute to Ian's contribution: 'Rushie destroyed Benfica that night, and without doubt he's the most natural finisher I have ever seen. He must rank with Jimmy Greaves and the other all-time greats. I don't think he knows himself how he gets into some of his positions; it must be down to instinct. I just know that when we took the field without him, it was a bad feeling.' For Joe Fagan, who had added bite to midfield by moving Mark Lawrenson forward and bringing in Gary Gillespie as a replacement at the back, the result was a relief. He told reporters: 'Thank God for that. It's been doom and gloom for a few weeks and this win will do the lads good.

When Mark won his first tackle, you could see the team grow a little taller. We have been missing too many tackles lately.' Of his match-winner, he added: 'I have told Ian Rush he's a lucky devil, but what a difference the man makes. He gave us a hell of a psychological boost tonight, and in two weeks' time he will be fitter!'

Another man who looks back warmly on the visit of the Eagles was photographer Steve Hale, who bagged one of the finest pictures of his career, which can be seen on pages 166 and 167 of this book. He calls it 'Storm over Anfield'. 'I was drenched to the skin when I took it, but I felt at the time that it was a bit special. I used a wide-angle lens to catch the waves of rain sweeping over the ground as the game went on. People think that being a sports photographer is a glamorous job, but they might have changed their minds that night if they had been sitting beside me, sharing my puddle.' It poured, too, for the second leg, in which Benfica finally managed to beat the Reds, but 1-0 on the night was not enough to turn the tie. Bruce Grobbelaar was handicapped, perhaps, by the slippery surface when he made the error that led to the early Portuguese goal, and thereafter he made up for the lapse with some blinding saves as Liverpool came under relentless pressure. As Alan Kennedy says: 'Benfica had their chances, and probably felt hard-done-by on the run of play, but we fought well with our backs to the wall.'

Before the quarter-final in March, the Merseysiders faced two 'showpiece' games, both of which ended in defeat. In Tokyo they went down 1-0 to Independiente of Argentina in the World Club Championship, while Juventus finished 2-0 winners of the European Super Cup in Turin, a couple of encounters that swelled the club coffers considerably but had little further relevance. It was back to business in earnest, though, when the European Cup campaign resumed with a trip to face Austria Vienna. Steve Nicol emerged as the hero by grabbing a late equaliser, but the plaudits should really go to the manager, whose half-time talk probably prevented the tie from slipping away. Trailing by one goal, the Reds had been scurrying frenet-

Poles under pressure: two Lech Poznan defenders are unable to prevent Michael Robinson from unleashing a shot in the second leg at Anfield. The Eire international gave valuable short-term service to the Reds without quite having the class to become fully established.

ically to all corners of the pitch, allowing their more composed opponents to dictate play. Joe calmed his men down, told them that if they were patient and did the simple things well, then they would gain the upper hand. So it proved and their 1-1 draw was the least they deserved.

At Anfield it was a different story, with Liverpool in steady command, which was reflected by the 4-1 scoreline. It should have been five but for a penalty miss by two-goal Paul Walsh, who was press-ganged into taking the kick by team-mates anxious for him to complete his hat-trick. Ian Rush recalls: 'Paul didn't want to take it but he was playing so well that everyone urged him to have a go. He was a tremendous player who was terribly unfortunate with injuries during his time at Anfield. The problem is that competition for places is always so hot here, and even if you drop out through no fault of your own it can be hard to get back.' However, an insight into the single-mindedness that has served Liverpool so well is given by Fagan's reportedly caustic reaction to his players' well-intentioned act of comradeship towards Walsh, who was in the side only because Kenny Dalglish was suspended. Though progress into the last four was already assured, it seems Joe saw the change of penalty-taker as unprofessional and voiced his opinion in no uncertain terms.

The draw for the semi-final paired the Reds with Panathinaikos, certainly no giants on the Continental stage, but any club once good enough to reach a European Cup Final (against Ajax in 1971) merited considerable respect. For once Liverpool could afford no mistakes, having been eliminated from both domestic cups and being on the verge of seeing their League title cross Stanley Park to Everton. In the event they were never in danger, crushing the Greeks 4-0 at Anfield with the final goal coming from rookie left-back Jim Beglin, who had been drafted in for his European debut in place of the injured Alan Kennedy. Quick, skilful and intelligent, the young Irishman looked set for a glittering future; heart-rendingly, that was to go by the board as a shattered leg, suffered against Everton in January 1987, effectively ended his top-class career. For now, though, he continued to develop promisingly alongside that most accomplished trio of defensive partners, Phil Neal, Mark Lawrenson and Alan Hansen. It is difficult to imagine a more effective central pair than 'Lawro' and Alan, though sifting through old cuttings it is fascinating to note that while the Eire international was deservedly lauded for his talents, the immaculate Scot - while hardly devoid of honourable mentions - tended to be undervalued until late in his career. Indeed, a succession of Scottish managers saw fit to omit him from sides which cried out for his coolness under pressure and cultured distribution, and it must remain one of British soccer's unfathomable mysteries that the most complete centre-back of his era retired with a mere 26 caps to his name.

However, to return to that semi-final against Panathinaikos, it seemed that the Greek manager might have taken lessons at the knee of Bill Shankly following Liverpool's 1966 drubbing by Johann Cruyff's Ajax. Before the second leg he proclaimed that his side could win 5-0, an outrageous proposition that was shown up for the hot air it was when the Reds took a second victory, this time by a single goal from Mark Lawrenson. So understandably confident had Joe Fagan been that he had omitted Ian Rush, already booked during the competition and therefore out of the final if he received another yellow card.

And so to the Heysel Stadium, Brussels, and utter catastrophe, a human disaster on a scale that shook the world of football to its very core. In cold, basic terms, what happened was this: as supporters from both teams gathered on the terraces, a group of fans flattened a fence and invaded the Juventus section; the Italians fled, a wall collapsed in the ensuing scrum, and people were crushed to death.

Alan Kennedy, not playing this game through injury but present at the ground says, 'The scene in the stadium was hellish; it will always stay with me. Some of our players knew what was going on, some were not sure. It was impossible for them to concentrate on the job in hand.' Ian Rush testifies to an atmosphere of utter confusion: 'We had been told the start of the game was delayed, though at one time it seemed certain we were not going to play. There were all sorts of rumours about casualties, and no one knew what to believe. When we did get out on the pitch we tried to play as normal, but there was something missing deep down. At the end the Juventus players were pleased to have won the European Cup but there could be no celebrations, and everyone just walked off. Though we didn't know the full extent of the tragedy at that time, clearly it was not a night to be worried about football.'

Right: **Ian Rush holds off a Panathinaikos defender at Anfield in the first leg of the European Cup semi-final. The Welshman virtually booked Liverpool's passage to Brussels by scoring two goals in a minute shortly after the interval.**

The game had gone ahead in a bizarre atmosphere, as though in some vacuum beyond reality. Juventus won through a controversial penalty - converted by the great Michel Platini - and in normal circumstances the Reds might have claimed they were robbed. They had the better of the exchanges, intelligently neutralising the efforts of the French play-maker by back-pedalling whenever he got the ball, but the refereeing decisions all went against them. When Bonini brought down Ronnie Whelan, it seemed that a penalty must be awarded, but it wasn't and no one questioned the verdict.

Lifelong Liverpool follower Eddie Marks, watching at home on television, felt sickened at the scenes. 'As well as grieving for the dead, I felt so sorry for the club. This was our 140th game in Europe, and there had been very little trouble connected with the previous 139. I am not making excuses, but I believe strongly that this tragedy could have befallen any British club abroad.'

As a result of Heysel, English clubs were banned indefinitely from European competition, with the Reds being condemned to an extra three seasons' absence when the sentence was lifted. Later that further exile was commuted to a single year, and they returned to the Continental arena in 1991.

Comprehensive media coverage had ensured that countless images had been beamed around the world, yet one unsensational picture told the story more poignantly than any of them. It was of Joe Fagan, due to retire as manager after the match, his homely features contorted with grief. That such an honourable, inspiring character should be reduced to bitter tears on his last day in the game summed up the sadness that engulfed the sporting world. For many, many people, football would never be the same again.

Overleaf: **Storm over Anfield. This atmospheric study, taken by Steve Hale during the Reds' clash with Benfica, is understandably dear to the photographer's heart. 'I was drenched to the skin when I took it, but I felt at the time that it was a bit special,' he recalls.**

Top left: Heysel Stadium just a few weeks before the disaster. Built in 1930, the stadium was finally pulled down in 1989 and rebuilt as the King Badouin Stadium

Top Right: Phil Neal and Schirea exchange Club pennants before the match. Since the disaster Juventus and Liverpool have made great strides in improving the relationship between their fans.

Bottom left: Joe Fagan as Liverpool fans will want to remember him, brightly animated and totally absorbed in the game. He was to bow out of football with those homely features contorted by grief following the disaster in Brussels.

Bottom right: Schirea and Craig Johnston jump to head the ball.

Round 1 - 1st leg
19 September 1984

LECH POZNAN 0

LIVERPOOL 1

Wark 63
H-T 0-0. Crowd 35,000

GROBBELAAR
NEAL
KENNEDY
LAWRENSON
WHELAN
HANSEN
DALGLISH
LEE
WALSH
WARK
NICOL

Liverpool put indifferent League form behind them to prove that their traditional European efficiency had not deserted them. Faced with energetic opponents who, perhaps, were a little in awe of them, the champions enjoyed the better of the first-half exchanges. Wark had the chances to score a hat-trick, while Dalglish and Neal both went close, but Piesniercwicz managed to keep his goal intact. After the restart the Poles grew in confidence. Indeed, they almost went ahead after Lawrenson committed a foul on the edge of his own box and, from the free-kick, Adamiec headed firmly against Grobbelaar's bar. However, the Reds retaliated in their time-honoured fashion by mounting an instant counter-attack, during which Dalglish crossed for Wark to volley in at the far post. Now Poznan streamed forward, Niewiadomski hit the bar and the Liverpool goal had several narrow escapes before the end.

Round 1 - 2nd leg
3 October 1984

LIVERPOOL 4

Wark 13, 19, 89; Walsh 38

LECH POZNAN 0

H-T 3-0. Crowd 22,143

GROBBELAAR
NEAL
KENNEDY
LAWRENSON
WHELAN
HANSEN
DALGLISH
LEE
WALSH
WARK
ROBINSON

The Poles, desperate to make up for their disappointment at home, attacked from the off, and Okonski almost scored in the first minute. But it was not long before Liverpool asserted their authority with a goal which left the Poznan defence bewildered and helpless. Lawrenson chipped the ball forward to Dalglish, the Scot executed a sublime first-time lay-off to Wark and the midfielder strolled into the box, side-stepping a defender before slotting the ball into the far corner of the net from 12 yards. Stunned but not yet beaten, the visitors hit back by creating a glorious opening which Araszkiewicz spurned - and what a costly miss that turned out to be. Wark put the Reds further ahead with a close-range header, then Walsh side-footed home from six yards after a penetrating run by Neal. Wark administered the final rites, completing his hat-trick with a downward header from a Walsh cross.

Liverpool won 5-0 on aggregate.

John Wark scores the second goal of his hat-trick at home to Lech Poznan with a powerful close-range header. Was there ever such a prolific midfielder in European competition? In 27 outings for Ipswich Town and Liverpool, the swarthy Scot hit the target 22 times.

170

The day that the rains came down: hat-trick man Ian Rush salutes the crowd, Ronnie Whelan goes for a cuddle and John Wark looks fed up with the weather as Benfica buckle at Anfield.

Round 2 - 1st leg
24 October 1984

LIVERPOOL 3
Rush 44, 71, 76

BENFICA 1
Diamantino 51
H-T 1-0. Crowd 27,733

GROBBELAAR
NEAL
KENNEDY
LAWRENSON
WHELAN
HANSEN
DALGLISH
LEE
RUSH
WARK (JOHNSTON)
GILLESPIE

In torrential rain, Rush notched a true opportunist's hat-trick that made Liverpool favourites for a place in the last eight. First-half exchanges between the Reds and a confident Portuguese side were inconclusive until the Welshman struck for the first time, shortly before the break. The goal was made by Lawrenson, relishing his new midfield role, who surged past two defenders and pulled the ball across the box; Wark's shot was off target but Rush was on hand to turn it home from two yards. Benfica equalised early in the second period when Gillespie was robbed on the edge of his area and Diamantino ran on to deceive Grobbelaar at his near post from the narrowest of angles. Liverpool regained the lead when a low Whelan 18-yarder was redirected by an instinctive Rush side-foot, and increased it when the striker prodded home a rebound from another Whelan shot.

Round 2 - 2nd leg
7 November 1984

BENFICA 1
Manniche (pen) 5

LIVERPOOL 0

H-T 1-0. Crowd 50,000

GROBBELAAR
NEAL
KENNEDY
LAWRENSON
WHELAN
HANSEN
DALGLISH
NICOL
RUSH
JOHNSTON
WARK

An early blunder by Grobbelaar condemned Liverpool to a lengthy battle for survival in the rain-soaked Stadium of Light. Perhaps undone by the slippery surface, the colourful 'keeper failed to gather the ball near the byline and, although his goal was in no immediate danger, brought down Silva, who had seized possession. Having been sent the wrong way by Manniche's penalty, Grobbelaar went on to make amends with two blinding saves - one when Wando thrashed the ball towards the roof of the net, the other from a point-blank Silva header - though his judgement on crosses was erratic throughout. Liverpool's problems increased on 45 minutes when Dalglish, their most inventive player, was sent off along with Pietra following a silly scuffle, and there were times when it seemed the Eagles' pressure must bring the overall equaliser that would put them through on the away-goals rule. But Hansen, Lawrenson and company stood firm and the Reds came close to sneaking a draw on the night when Rush hit a post.

Liverpool won 3-2 on aggregate.

Round 3 - 1st leg
6 March 1985

AUSTRIA VIENNA 1
Polster 23

LIVERPOOL 1
Nicol 86
H-T 1-0. Crowd 21,000

GROBBELAAR
NEAL
KENNEDY
LAWRENSON
NICOL
HANSEN
WALSH
WHELAN
RUSH
MacDONALD
WARK

Liverpool fought back to achieve parity against a patient and resourceful Austrian side, who troubled the Reds with some fluent first-half raids. The Viennese broke through just once, when Polster gave Lawrenson the slip and beat Grobbelaar with a difficult, bouncing 25-yard shot. At that point the Merseysiders were looking shaky but their hosts made the mistake of sitting back, as though admiring their lead. Liverpool regrouped during the interval and looked a different team in the second period, although the Austrians should have scored again when a delightful move produced a clear opening for Steinkogler, who shot wide. Thereafter the resurgent Reds took the initiative, and Rush, Walsh and Neal all went close to scoring. Eventually the honour went to Nicol, who shot against 'keeper Koncilia, ballooned the rebound against the bar, then dived forward to nod home. With two minutes left, Rush was through on Koncilia, who dived bravely to save at the Welshman's feet.

Round 3 - 2nd leg
20 March 1985

LIVERPOOL 4
Walsh 16, 55; Nicol 39;
Obermayer (og) 46

AUSTRIA VIENNA 1
Prohaska 63
H-T 2-0. Crowd 32,761

GROBBELAAR
NEAL
KENNEDY
LAWRENSON
NICOL
HANSEN
WALSH
WHELAN
RUSH
MacDONALD
WARK

Liverpool swept the Austrian champions out of the European Cup on a wave of dazzling attacking football. Determined not to fall victim to Vienna's speciality of counter-punching, the Reds engulfed their opponents from the start. Hansen had a decisive hand in the two opening goals. First he found Kennedy on the left with a perceptive, perfectly measured pass, the full-back crossed and Walsh dived horizontally to head home; then the unflappable centre-back freed Whelan, again on the left, and Nicol drove the resultant centre into the net off a post from close range. Obermayer added to Austrian woes when he deflected a Rush pass, intended for Walsh, over the head of his stranded 'keeper. Walsh himself made it four, leaning back to deliver a spectacular 12-yard volley from a skied clearance, before missing a penalty that would have completed his hat-trick. The visitors' only consolation came when a Prohaska free-kick scraped Liverpool's defensive wall and crept inside a post. By then, though, the Reds' semi-final place was assured.

Liverpool won 5-2 on aggregate.

Below: **Paul Walsh dives spectacularly to head Liverpool in front against Austria Vienna at Anfield. In one of his finest performances for the club, the waspish raider notched his second with a superb volley before missing a penalty. At the latter occurrence, Joe Fagan was not amused.**

Kenny Dalglish didn't score in the home leg against Panathinaikos, but it wasn't for the want of trying. Here he hurdles Greek goalkeeper Laftsis, who has plunged at the Scot's feet to pull off a courageous save.

Semi-final - 1st leg
10 April 1985

LIVERPOOL 4
Wark 35; Rush 48, 49; Beglin 85

PANATHINAIKOS 0

H-T 1-0. Crowd 39,488

GROBBELAAR
NEAL
BEGLIN
LAWRENSON
LEE
HANSEN
DALGLISH
WHELAN
RUSH
MacDONALD
WARK

The Greeks, though a tough and skilful side who were not to be underrated, were no match for the rampant Reds.

Fagan's men started the match briskly with MacDonald, who tested Panathinaikos 'keeper Laftsis with two powerful long-range efforts, taking the eye. Sure enough, it was the gangly midfielder who was instrumental in the first goal, his 25-yard drive rebounding from the post and into the path of Wark, who slid the ball into the net. The outcome of the match - and, surely, the tie - was decided when Rush scored twice in a minute early in the second half, heading in a centre from Whelan, then side-footing home a bouncing cross from Lee. To their credit the Greeks battled on, and they gave the Liverpool defence cause for alarm, notably when Rocha's inswinging corner bounced back off Grobbelaar's near post. But it was the Reds who were to score again, Beglin meeting Dalglish's floated free-kick with a bullet header five minutes from time.

Semi-final - 2nd leg
24 April 1985

PANATHINAIKOS 0

LIVERPOOL 1
Lawrenson 61
H-T 0-0. Crowd 60,000

GROBBELAAR
NEAL
BEGLIN
LAWRENSON
NICOL
HANSEN
DALGLISH
WHELAN
WALSH (JOHNSTON)
GILLESPIE
WARK

Calmly, professionally and with a minimum of fuss, Liverpool eased into yet another European Cup Final. In truth, the game was something of an anti-climax for the excitable home supporters, who bayed for their heroes to attack. That was easier said than done against a Reds defence in which Hansen was at his impeccable best, and only once, when Rocha brought a brilliant save from Grobbelaar, was there the remotest prospect of a home goal. Not that there was any more action at the other end, one Whelan power-drive being the sole test of Greek 'keeper Laftsis in the first hour. Then he had no chance as the visitors notched the only goal of the night, Lawrenson exchanging passes with Whelan before cracking the ball into the net. It was an invigorating strike that belied most of what had gone before and all that followed. Thereafter the Greeks launched a handful of assaults but never stretched Liverpool and the contest petered out in inevitably limp fashion.

Liverpool won 5-0 on aggregate.

Final in Brussels
29 May 1985

JUVENTUS 1
Platini (pen) 57

LIVERPOOL 0

H-T 0-0. Crowd 60,000

GROBBELAAR
NEAL
BEGLIN
LAWRENSON (GILLESPIE)
NICOL
HANSEN
DALGLISH
WHELAN
RUSH
WALSH (JOHNSTON)
WARK

On any night other than the blackest in European football history, the contrast between the deliberate style of the much-lauded Italians and Liverpool's more zestful approach would have been fascinating. As it was, the game was played in an unreal atmosphere, and performances could not be judged meaningfully. Even so, there was a trophy to be won, and the soccer fates appeared to conspire against it going to the Reds. They lost Lawrenson through injury after two minutes and Walsh just before half-time, saw Juventus 'keeper Tacconi make magnificent saves from Wark and Whelan, and conceded the only goal of the match through a controversial penalty. That decisive moment came when arch-schemer Platini released a penetrating long-distance through-ball for Boniek, who - chased by Hansen and Gillespie - was brought down on the edge of the box. Liverpool thought the offence took place outside the area, the referee ruled otherwise, and Platini sent Grobbelaar the wrong way from the spot. A quarter of an hour later, Whelan appeared to be fouled in the Italians' area but no penalty was forthcoming. The Reds launched a furious late assault, but it was all to no avail.

Michel Platini raps in the penalty that won the 1985 European Cup for Juventus, while Gary Gillespie *(left),* **whose tackle on Boniek was judged controversially to be inside the penalty area, looks on helplessly. However, in the context of earlier events, it really didn't matter.**

Chapter Twelve

OUT OF EXILE

WHEN the Reds returned to the European fold after their enforced absence of six seasons, they presented a radically changed face to Continental opponents. Though the name of Liverpool would always be respected in Europe - indeed, throughout the football-playing world - the club could hardly hope to resume business on the same lofty level to which they had been accustomed in the late 1970s and early 1980s. At the time of Heysel they were THE team to beat. Only Real Madrid had won more European Cups and, but for the tragedy, the Spaniards' proud record of six premier trophies may well have been broken by the dawn of the 1990s. But now the 'old masters' had given way to a side made up of comparative rookies led by a new manager, Graeme Souness, whose European experience with his previous club, Glasgow Rangers, had been notable only for its lack of success. In addition, English clubs were now handicapped by a rule which allowed them to play only four so-called foreigners, a category which included Scots, Welshmen and Irishmen. Thus the Reds would have to perm only four from the likes of Bruce Grobbelaar, Steve Nicol, Ray Houghton, Jan Molby, Ian Rush, Ronnie Whelan, Dean Saunders, Ronny Rosenthal, Glenn Hysen and, later, Istvan Kozma. For managers of all top clubs, it presented a Catch-22 situation: if they concentrated on acquiring mainly English players because of their eligibility for Europe, they might overlook outstanding performers who could help to win the League. No one placed the task facing Liverpool into perspective more realistically than Ron Moran: 'We would have found it difficult even if we had been out for only a couple of years. To be out for six made it very, very hard. Some people thought we'd just slip back in as though we'd never been away, but I knew that could never be. European football is so different to the First Division, and there is a learning process which has to be gone through.'

Of course, a return to Continental competition involved issues more delicate and complex than those concerning merely football. The people of Liverpool - even those with no interest in the game - had suffered as a result of the Reds' exile. Liverpudlians told tales of European holidays ruined by a post-Heysel stigma. To a disconcertingly significant number of Continentals, Scousers were branded as hooligans, and no matter how ludicrous or unfair such a tag might have been, it was deeply hurtful. Liverpool is a proud city, and many of its native sons and daughters were already resentful of its image as portrayed in other parts of the country. This latest insult was seen by many as the final straw. Also there was the fear of what might happen to the Reds' travelling fans on re-entry. Would old scores demand settlement? Acutely mindful of the problems, the club left no avenue unexplored in ensuring that the minefield of potential pitfalls was negotiated as safely as possible. In the event the operation proved an organisational triumph, thanks in no small measure to the efforts of Liverpool chief executive Peter Robinson. The newly-formed Football Supporters Association was consulted, and tickets were made available only as part of an approved travel package. Streetwise and sympathetic Merseyside policemen were recruited to accompany the supporters, thus being on hand to help avoid confusion with overseas police. There was a nagging fear that some small incident, the type that bedevils every club, might be blown up out of all proportion by the world's media with dire consequences. True, the European press were happy enough to run modest stories about the genuine efforts being made in Liverpool to repair relations with Italians - for example, youngsters from Turin, the home of Juventus, enjoyed a visit to Merseyside in the summer of 1991 - but how much more avidly might they have fallen on the slightest misdeed by travelling English supporters?

It was against such a background that the Reds prepared for their opening UEFA Cup

Men with a mission: Ronnie Moran *(left)* and Graeme Souness on the day the Scot returned to Anfield as boss.

encounter, at home to Kuusysi Lahti of Finland. There was no formal recognition of Heysel at Anfield that night, though the Juventus flag took its place at the Shankly Gates alongside flowers commemorating those who died at Hillsborough. The match itself was a pleasant enough reintroduction to Europe, but although the final score of 6-1 was overwhelming, it flattered Liverpool and the relatively even balance of play served to underline the strides made by hitherto unconsidered footballing nations. The wider spread of refined coaching techniques and increased television exposure of the top teams have accelerated the levelling-out process which, in the early 1990s, was evident not only on the Continent but also between the First and Second Divisions in England. The Finnish part-timers - their shirts bearing the legend 'Kop', an appropriate choice of sponsor if ever there was one - gave a splendid account of themselves until weariness overtook them in the final quarter-hour. Nevertheless, it should be remembered that only three Liverpool players - Nicol, Rush and Steve McMahon (with Everton) - had previous European experience and nothing should detract from the achievement of Dean Saunders in netting four times, which went some way towards making up for the expensive striker's disappointing start in the League. For their four 'foreigners' Liverpool had chosen Nicol, Saunders, Houghton and Rush, thus including Mike Hooper in place of Grobbelaar. The extrovert Zimbabwean was recalled for the return, though his only memorable contribution was the blunder which gifted Kuusysi's Englishman, Mike Belfield, with the only goal of the match. It was fitting reward for a skilful, energetic footballer who had failed to make the grade at Wimbledon and was now settled happily in Finland. On his showings against Liverpool it was fair to assume he had improved radically since his Plough Lane days, and he looked capable of doing well in English football, should he desire a second chance.

It would be wrong to be over-critical of the Reds for their unexpected reverse. Already severely weakened by an injury crisis that was to last the whole season - any side would be affected by the loss of John Barnes, Mark Wright, Ronnie Whelan etc - they started with an unassailable lead, and were facing a buoyant team then topping the Finnish League and through to their cup final. So strained were the Merseysiders' resources that they could name only four substitutes instead of the permitted five, and young defender Barry Jones was called on to make his senior debut when David Burrows was injured. The game went ahead in a festive atmosphere, a band playing throughout, and if the defeat was disappointing, the off-the-field aspects of the trip were not. Though Finnish police turned back seven English fans at the ferry terminal, there wasn't a hint of trouble, and Liverpool deserve credit for their attention to detail. Kuusysi, too, played their part, drafting in 70 policemen rather than rely on the two who patrol their trim stadium for domestic matches.

A more searching test awaited the Reds in Burgundy, headquarters of second-round opponents Auxerre. The Frenchmen, little known outside their own league, turned out to be a slick-passing outfit oozing with flair and but for an inspired display by Bruce Grobbelaar, Liverpool would have been sunk without trace in the first leg at Stade Abbé Deschamps. Before the game one French newspaper had written of 'Le Retour du Clown', but the locals were not laughing at the controversial 'keeper for long. On a bracing night, Graeme Souness gave the gifted Jamie Redknapp his first senior start in midfield, but then watched his side surrender possession with appalling profligacy. Prospects of survival grew even bleaker when the excellent Steve Nicol suffered a hamstring strain and failed to reappear for the second half, and the Reds must have been relieved to escape with a two-goal deficit. Once again, there was consolation for an away defeat in the impeccable behaviour of Liverpool's travelling fans, although the French police took no chances, turning out in force.

Back at Anfield there was finally a night worthy of the Reds' rich European tradition. Not even the great sides led by Shankly, Paisley and Fagan had bounced back from a two-goal first-leg reverse in Continental competition - admittedly they had rarely found themselves in such dire straits - but now Souness's men showed their mettle. In response to an emotional appeal from Graeme, the Kop was in magnificent voice, and the players responded with every ounce of fervour, skill and pride they could summon. Boosted immeasurably by an early penalty, earned by the enterprise of the precocious Steve McManaman, they overran an Auxerre side that appeared as timorous and pallid on English soil as they had been bold and brilliant at home. One Liverpool player reckoned the Frenchmen had fear in their eyes from the moment they stepped on to the pitch, and that they blanched visibly as a crescendo of sound rolled down from the Kop. Though live television coverage limited the gate to some 23,000, it might have been a full house as the chanting continued throughout a thrilling contest. 'We love you Liverpool, we do' might have lacked the wit and originality of former offerings - there isn't a crowd in the country who can match their 1960s counterparts - but at least the spirit was willing. Indeed, when Mike Marsh scored his first senior goal to level the scores, and even more markedly when Mark Walters settled the tie seven minutes from time, there was a delicious whiff of that old St Etienne atmosphere in the Anfield air.

No one was more wound up than Souness, who was spoken to by the Portuguese referee after trainer Phil Boersma had protested vehemently following a particularly gross French foul. Indeed, it was difficult to be sure, but as Senor da Silva Valente returned to the action at the end of their chat, Graeme appeared to salute the departing official in a manner that was vaguely Churchillian; on the other hand, of course, it might have been a placatory gesture acknowledging the referee's words of wisdom. Either way, there was striking contrast with the manager's after-match mien in a TV interview. Then, all tautness gone, Graeme gave Mark Walters a hug and a kiss - hardly the Dalglish approach! - and positively exuded bonhomie as he paid tribute to the supporters, ending up with an invitation for the cameras to come again. Before the game Alan Hansen, increasingly adept as a media pundit, had said it was time for the Liverpool players to stand up and be counted. They had done so to stirring effect.

Now the Reds were getting a taste for this European business, and demonstrated growing confidence at the expense of their next opponents, Swarovski Tirol. After a two-and-a-half-hour delay due to a punctured tyre on their plane, the Liverpool party settled into a delightfully situated hotel in a mountainside village near Innsbruck. With Austrian football at a low ebb

To Mark Walters, here racing for the ball with a Genoa defender, fell the honour of scoring the most dramatic and satisfying goal of Liverpool's Continental comeback campaign. Indeed, his late winner against Auxerre at Anfield produced just the faintest whiff of that old St Etienne-style euphoria.

The best possible start: Jan Molby strolls up to convert the fourth-minute penalty that threw the Anfield return against Auxerre wide open. Few would dispute that, in his prime, the beefy Dane was the most artistic playmaker in British football, though he didn't quite fulfil that vast potential.

- the national team had lost recently to the Faroe Islands and had failed to qualify for the European Championship finals - such beautiful surroundings might have engendered a feeling of complacency, but none was evident as the Merseysiders went to work with supreme professionalism. An afternoon start had been agreed because the intense cold would have affected playing conditions by the evening, though the temperature did nothing to cool the ardour of a highly vocal, drum-beating, sparkler-waving crowd, who were warmed up prior to kick-off by an enthusiastic rock'n'roll band. When the game began, Swarovski looked both eager and skilful, most of their ideas coming from play-maker Gorasito. But like most of his colleagues, the long-haired Argentinian - who, with Grobbelaar out of his goal, brought Liverpool hearts into mouths with a Pele-type shot from near the half-way line - did not back his undoubted technique with sufficient commitment, and the visitors gradually assumed the ascendancy.

Dean Saunders won the match with two clinically taken goals, a feat which said as much about the Welshman's character as his ability. He had not been scoring in domestic football and had been subjected to cruel criticism, some observers decrying his first touch on the ball, others saying he would never blend with Ian Rush. In addition, there had been widespread speculation that the Reds were ready to part with him in exchange for Nottingham Forest's Roy Keane, and though the claim had been denied by the club, it must have been unsettling for a young man struggling to justify a transfer fee of £2 million-plus. At the Tivoli Stadium he linked impressively with Steve McManaman and appeared to thrive on the service of Jan Molby, demonstrating that he was at his best running on to the ball rather than having it played to his feet. Afterwards he admitted: 'The pressure's been on me a bit, but I'm looking forward to see what the critics have got to say now.' Another happy and relieved man was centre-half Mark Wright, who performed superbly in his first outing after a lengthy lay-off through injury. Together with Nicky Tanner - who had stagnated under Dalglish but was prospering under Souness - he had formed an impregnable barrier at the heart of the Reds' defence.

The weather was equally icy on the night of the return at Anfield, but under-soil heating defeated the frost and the fans - many of whom sported jaunty Santa Claus headgear - were treated to an enjoyable if unequal contest. The Austrians, whose gesture in laying flowers on the Hillsborough memorial on their way to training had been much appreciated, seemed to have little stomach for what was admittedly a mammoth task. Several of the visitors wore gloves, though on such a chill evening they could hardly be blamed for that, and one terrace wag cracked that if John Barnes had been playing, he'd have needed a fur coat! The game will be best remembered for a high-quality hat-trick from the resurgent Saunders - the chants of 'Deano, Deano' must have been sweet music to ears that had grown more accustomed to abuse - who took his total of European goals to nine, thus beating Roger Hunt's 1964/65 Reds record for a single campaign. Kopites were also delighted by a comeback goal from Barry Venison, who came on as substitute for Mike Marsh and who had last played ten months earlier, towards the twilight days of the Dalglish regime. David Burrows played in midfield - where his strength and single-mindedness as a man-to-man marker could be mightily effective - and young full-back Steve Harkness was, for a spell, employed as an emergency central striker. Indeed, such was the strain on his playing resources that Graeme Souness faced a perplexing exercise in selecting his side. He said: 'As a Liverpool player, I always felt threatened, that someone else was trying to take my place. This season, for various reasons, we haven't been able to put people under any pressure - and at a big club, they need that kind of motivation.' In recent days he had been attempting to enlarge his squad by signing Michael Thomas from Arsenal, but the England midfielder was vacillating, wondering whether to try his luck abroad. Gunners boss George Graham, standing to receive a much-reduced fee if Thomas headed for the Continent when his contract expired at the end of the season, did his best to persuade the Londoner to go north, and in the end he did. The last time the two clubs had struck a deal, it had been in respect of Ray Kennedy, so there could scarcely be a more favourable precedent from the Anfield viewpoint.

For the present, however, Liverpool had done well to reach the UEFA Cup quarter-finals on their return to Europe, though clearly, much more was expected. However, they were about to step up a league, facing opposition of an infinitely superior standard to anything encountered thus far. At 99 years old, Genoa were Italy's oldest club, and although they had never qualified for Europe before - it was 68 years since 'Il Rossoblu' had won their domestic championship - their side was packed with thoroughbred performers. In attack they were particularly potent, boasting the complementary talents of towering, glowering Czech Tomas Skuhravy, top scorer in the 1990 World Cup, and dapper little Carlos Aguilera, a quicksilver Uruguayan who could fashion a goal out of nothing. But the first leg, in Genoa, was more than just a football match; it was the Reds' first competitive game against Italian opponents since the Heysel disaster, and it was crucial that there were no clashes between rival supporters. The city of Genoa did much to ease any possible tension, staging an open-air concert of Beatles' songs to welcome the Merseysiders, and generally extending the hand of friendship. As insurance, there was a policeman for each of the 1,600 visiting fans at the beautiful terracotta-coloured Luigi Ferraris Stadium, located conveniently close to the city centre. For Graeme Souness it was an occasion of vast and varied significance. In the early 1980s, he had spent two highly successful years with Sampdoria, Genoa's ground-share partners, and was now revisiting what had been a happy haunt. Then there was the immense intrinsic importance of the tie to the Reds; if they reached the last four of the UEFA Cup, their presence would sound a clear warning to all Europe that Liverpool were back as a major power. Finally, triumph over Genoa would do much to distract from what had been a sadly disappointing term in the First Division.

As he prepared for what was sure to be a searching test, Graeme was handicapped still by injuries to many key players, with Barnes and Rush among notable absentees. The situation was no less galling for the stricken men, especially the Welshman whose image in Italy had taken a battering during his difficult year with Juventus, a sojourn marred by illness and misfortune. How he would have relished the opportunity to redress the balance in front of the very critics who had written him off; but it was to be denied him. The thinness of Souness's resources was highlighted by the situation of Steve McManaman, who had earned widespread plaudits for his exhilarating form during his first full season. In ideal circumstances the manager would almost certainly have rested the young Merseysider at intervals, allowing him to recuperate between big occasions instead of keeping his nose to the grindstone. As it was,

Steve was the only player to start all Liverpool's European games, and as Graeme observed drily before sending him out to face Genoa: 'He's English, he's a forward and he's available - so he's a key man.'

One fit man forced to sit out the action was Grobbelaar, presumably to facilitate the inclusion of Saunders as the fourth 'foreigner', and Bruce was remarkably understanding about his fate. His replacement, Mike Hooper, had been performing well in the reserves but represented something of a risk as he hadn't made a senior appearance since October; in the event he was to let no one down, playing solidly yet with a dash of enterprise that would have done credit to Grobbelaar himself. One surprise inclusion in the party was Ronnie Whelan, who had played only an hour of Central League football after a long absence with an injured knee, but he did not make the side.

In the dressing room before the match, Graeme Souness, Ron Moran and company were striving to calm their men, urging them not to be intimidated by the atmosphere. That was easier said than done: shortly before kick-off the pitch was engulfed in clouds of red and blue smoke, and stretched down one side of the ground, the height and length of the grandstand, was a gigantic banner proclaiming 'We are Genoa', lest there be the slightest confusion! The fans were close to the touchlines, every man, woman and child seeming to howl like a banshee. Liverpool's initial task was to keep the game tight for the first 20 minutes and quieten the racket; that much they did, but it was not to be enough. They began admirably, containing the Italians and finding time to menace Braglia's goal, but they were undone by a sensational strike towards the end of either half. First Fiorin lashed home the most vicious of volleys; then, with only two minutes remaining before the final whistle, Brazilian full-back Branco propelled an unstoppable free-kick past the helpless Hooper from 35 yards. Until that moment the Reds must have felt optimistic about seizing the upper hand in front of the Kop, but the second goal was a hammer-blow indeed. In fact, although never overwhelmed by Genoa, Liverpool surrendered possession far too easily during a second half in which the pressure mounted inexorably. Amid such tension, it was hardly reasonable to expect such an inexperienced side to hold out, and that they so very nearly did may be seen as a cause for congratulation rather than condemnation.

A fearsome finish by Aguilera leaves Rob Jones and Mike Hooper helpless as Genoa take a first-half lead, and score a precious away goal into the bargain, at Anfield.

Left: A frustrating moment during his sole UEFA Cup outing - against Genoa at Anfield - sums up 1991/92 for John Barnes. A crippling series of injuries confined him to a watching brief for most of the season.

Graeme Souness - never one to shrink from a challenge, nor to hide the reality of a grim situation - prefaced the second leg by declaring: 'This is the biggest game in my year as manager. We'll be attacking them with all guns blazing.' At least he was closer to fielding a full-strength side than at any juncture of the season to date, with Saunders, Barnes and Rush set to start a game in harness for the first time. Though woefully short of match practice, Ian had a notion to emulate a feat he had achieved against Genoa for Juventus, that of scoring 52 seconds after the kick-off; sadly there was to be no such derring-do on this occasion. Nevertheless the Reds kept their manager's promise, roaring into instant attack backed by a formidable barrage of noise - the Kop's uplifting response to Graeme's pre-match appeal for even more inspirational support than usual. As well as gambling on quality, the Anfield boss had demonstrated boldness in switching David Burrows to central defence, thus freeing the more penetrative Nicol to maraud down the left flank. Early on, Steve troubled the Italians sorely, and John Barnes did his self-confessed ambition of a lucrative overseas move no harm at all with one scintillating run, but though half-chances were created, each one was spurned.

Unfortunately the momentum was interrupted by the enforced withdrawal of Mark Wright, victim of a hamstring strain, then halted unceremoniously on 27 minutes when the waspish Aguilera capped a flowing move with the sharpest of finishes. Suddenly it was the turn of the 3,000 travelling Genoese supporters - far more than follow the club to its away league games - to rend the air with their anthems. Soon after the break, an Ian Rush header produced a pinprick of light in the gloom and restored a sense of urgency to the proceedings. Now the beefy Molby scurried with uncharacteristic haste to place the ball for a corner, and Barnes and McManaman switched wings as the Reds gathered themselves for a final assault. Clear openings had been fashioned, and gone begging, when - with the prodigiously pacy and promising Rob Jones having joined the casualty list - Liverpool suffered the sucker punch, a second Aguilera goal with just 18 minutes left. Now it remained only for Molby and company to fire long shots towards the Italian net, efforts that were spectacularly entertaining but not particularly dangerous. On the night, arguably, Liverpool were unlucky to lose, but over the two legs they had been second best. Without being world-beaters, Genoa had exhibited greater incisiveness on the break, surer control and superior passing ability - with the honourable exception of Molby - and fully deserved their victory.

So Liverpool were out of Europe, but could hold their heads high after a campaign which offered invaluable experience to a new generation of Reds. They had played eight games, winning and losing four each, and used 22 players, a figure which offered ample proof of the difficulties under which Graeme Souness was compelled to operate. Lying ahead was consolation in the form of FA Cup triumph over Sunderland and a consequent place in the 1992/93

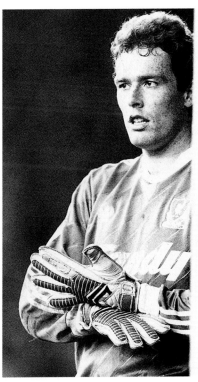

Mike Hooper, an able replacement for Bruce Grobbelaar, was blameless for the Reds' elimination by Genoa. However, following the arrival of David James from Watford, it seemed unlikely that Mike would become the long-term replacement for the extrovert Zimbabwean.

European Cup Winners' Cup. So with the Continent beckoning alluringly once more, at that time just how important was it to Liverpool, the players and supporters? Eyeing the prospect avidly in the close season, Ian Rush was in no doubt: 'I love playing in Europe, it's so completely different to our League. Everything happens at 100 mph in the First Division, while against the Continentals there might be little going on for a quarter of an hour, then there is a mad five minutes. Foreigners like to draw you in slowly, then hit you with a lightning break, and if you are not expecting it you get caught out. Personally, I have to work much harder because the Europeans employ rigid man-to-man marking, but I relish the challenge. When I first got in the team I was interested only in scoring goals, but now I have learnt so much more, and a lot of it is due to experience against the Italians, the Germans and the like. Certainly my year with Juventus improved my game, showed me how to give more to the team, and I'm in no doubt that Liverpool's seasons in Europe have benefited the players enormously.'

Ian conceded that English teams had lost ground during their absence from European competition – he reckoned that the home international sides had suffered, too – but cited Manchester United's 1991 Cup Winners' Cup victory as evidence that the gulf was not unbridgeable: 'No top Continental team relishes playing the English. Of course, we still have a lot to learn, but I am convinced we can come back strongly. For example, we were terrible in Auxerre, but then the team spirit and tradition we have at Liverpool helped us turn the tie around. There is every reason to be optimistic about the future.' In fact, Rush's up-tempo assessment was to be misplaced, at least in the short term, as Liverpool were about to spend the next two seasons far from the lofty perch they had once inhabited so proudly.

The Cup Winners' Cup represented a meaningful challenge, not least because it was the only major European competition which the club had never won. In fairness, they had taken part on only two previous occasions and had reached the final in 1966, losing to Borussia Dortmund. Graeme Souness spent the summer of 1992 recovering from heart surgery and continuing his reconstruction of Dalglish's fading champions. In came Watford's immensely promising England under-21 goalkeeper David James – the fee of £1.3 million was set by a transfer tribunal – and midfielder cum marksman Paul Stewart was recruited from Tottenham Hotspur for £2.3 million. On his way out of Anfield was Ray Houghton, who failed to see eye-to-eye with the manager in contract talks and was sold to Aston Villa for around £825,000. Many fans were dismayed by his exit and, in the event, his skill and industry would prove to be sorely missed as the Reds began to struggle. Also surplus to requirements was Barry Venison, who was to give sterling service to Newcastle United after being released for the paltry sum of £250,000.

Such was the gathering force of the wind of change blowing through Anfield that, with the season barely started, Dean Saunders was offloaded, too. He had failed wholly to convince after being recruited from under the nose of Everton only a year earlier, and following a lethargic start to the newly launched FA Premier League, a fretful interlude during which the Reds garnered only two wins in their first eight matches, the energetic Welsh striker joined Houghton at Villa Park.

That was shortly before the opening of the European campaign, an encounter with Apollon Limassol, and it was against the backdrop of that ominously unsatisfactory start to the season that only 12,769 spectators filed into Anfield to watch the 6-1 rout of the Cypriots. Stewart, who preferred the midfield role in which he had thrived latterly at White Hart Lane, was pressed unwillingly into attack in the wake of Saunders' surprise departure and he helped himself to a brace. He was overshadowed, though, by the evergreen Ian Rush, the prolific Welshman plundering four goals to break the long-standing European club record of 17 set by Roger Hunt.

The match was hardly a meaningful contest and afterwards Souness preferred to concentrate on Rush's fabulous achievement in accumulating 19 goals against Continental opposition. 'Ian deserves the record,' said the Liverpool manager. 'He's the best goal-getter I've seen, and there's a lot of life in him yet!' Sadly for Souness, the opposite was true of Paul Stewart. In the return match in Limassol, the burly England international fell victim to his own petulance and was dismissed for lashing out at Apollon 'keeper Christophi. 'It was foolish of him. If you raise your hand in any game you will go off,' shrugged the regretful boss, but he added: 'Paul didn't strike out; it was more of a brush and the goalkeeper threw himself down for two or three seconds after the incident. Hopefully, Paul will have learned from it.' In fact, Stewart was to make little long-term impression on Merseyside, eventually leaving on a free transfer after three miserable, injury-ridden seasons.

Liverpool ventured to Moscow for the next round and, in a match played in driving snow, the Reds' world collapsed around them. Before a ball was kicked against Spartak, Steve Nicol suffered a recurrence of a thigh strain and David Burrows was pushed into the centre of defence, with Rob Jones shifting to an unfamiliar left-back slot. The game itself could have been saved but for a calamitous final five minutes during which Bruce Grobbelaar was sent off after bringing down an opponent and conceding a penalty.

The Reds had done superbly well to reach such an advanced stage of the match still level at 2-2 and even though Burrows, who took over between the posts following Grobbelaar's unscheduled departure, failed to save the spot kick, even a 3-2 reverse would have been creditable in the circumstances. However, a last-minute goal from Karpin piled on the agony, leaving Liverpool with the massive task of overturning a two-goal deficit at Anfield. Graeme Souness had done himself no favours with his post-match criticism of the officials and he was handed a five-match touchline ban for his abusive words in the wake of the 4-2 defeat.

Thus he was restricted to the directors' box during the second leg as his largely makeshift, injury-ravaged side, spurred on by an amazing barrage of noise from their loyal, ever-hopeful supporters, gave their all. They spent much of the evening laying siege to the Spartak goal and were unlucky not to fashion a breakthrough in the first half. Then, in the quest for more firepower, the dangerous but unpredictable raider Ronny Rosenthal was brought on for Rob Jones; sadly, this enterprising if rather desperate ploy proved to be the Reds' undoing. The Russians exploited the space vacated down the right flank for Radchenko to score and the tie was as good as over. When Marsh became the third Liverpool player to be dismissed in successive matches, the game ended in acrimonious manner. Piatnitski delivered the last rites to Liverpool's Cup Winners' Cup aspirations with a goal a minute later, leaving Souness with 'no complaints', although he could not resist calling the Spanish referee, Diaz Vega, 'very disappointing.' The same words would have offered an apt summation of his team's performance.

For Liverpool and Souness much more pain was to follow. With the old enemy, Manchester United, rising to ascendancy under Alex Ferguson, the increasingly beleaguered Anfield boss mixed and matched a frankly bizarre collection of players in his attempt to revive the club's flagging fortunes. Signings such as Stig Inge Bjornebye, Mark Wright and Rob Jones were to make positive contributions to the Reds' cause in seasons to come, but the likes of Paul Stewart, Julian Dicks, Torben Piechnik and Nigel Clough all failed to make a telling impact.

Off the field, other changes were made, including the demolition of the famous Boot Room and some of the timeless philosophy that went with it. Stalwart aides Ronnie Moran and Roy Evans were gradually marginalised as the manager invested power and trust in another former Red, Phil Boersma. Complaints circulated that five-a-side games, the staple diet of Liverpool's training regime during the glory years, had become less central under the new leadership, while laborious set-piece routines tried the patience of many of Souness' charges. It was hardly surprising, then, that some of the senior professionals experienced differences of opinion with the manager, and rumours of internal strife became common currency.

Eventually his failure to guide the club to a meaningful title challenge and embarrassing domestic cup exits at the hands of Bolton, Peterborough and, finally, Bristol City left the hapless Souness with no option but to offer his resignation on 29 January 1994. 'Liverpool Football Club is all about winning things and being a source of pride to our fans. It has no other purpose,' said chairman David Moores after negotiating the manager's departure. Within three days he had turned from one great friend to another, looking to Roy Evans to bring sorely needed stability to a club in turmoil.

Round 1 - 1st leg
18 September 1991

LIVERPOOL 6
Saunders 11, 77, 85, 86;
Houghton 32, 89

KUUSYSI LAHTI 1
Lehtinen 34
H-T 2-1. Crowd 17,131

HOOPER
ABLETT
BURROWS
NICOL
MARSH (WALTERS)
TANNER
SAUNDERS
HOUGHTON
RUSH
McMANAMAN
McMAHON

The final score was satisfactory enough, but the Reds displayed ample signs of European rustiness against modest opponents. For long periods the Finnish part-timers matched them, pass for pass and tackle for tackle, and it was not until Kuusysi tired towards the end that the home side cashed in. Saunders got Liverpool off to the ideal start, pouncing on a loose ball and finishing accurately from 18 yards. When Houghton made it two with a perfect looping header, a goal deluge seemed likely, but the Finns hit back at once, albeit with an element of good fortune, Lehtinen's 20-yarder taking a deflection off Tanner. Yet, incredibly, the visitors fashioned further openings, and with a little more coolness in front of goal might have embarrassed the Reds. They could not last the pace, however, and four goals in the final 13 minutes saw Liverpool safe. Saunders grabbed three - two marvellous headers and a close-range blast - and Houghton nodded home the sixth.

Round 1 - 2nd leg
2 October 1991

KUUSYSI LAHTI 1
Belfield 66

LIVERPOOL 0
H-T 0-0. Crowd 8,800

GROBBELAAR
ABLETT
BURROWS (JONES, BARRY)
NICOL
MARSH
HARKNESS
ROSENTHAL (CARTER)
McMANAMAN
RUSH
WALTERS
McMAHON

With neither need nor intention to extend themselves, Liverpool suffered the first defeat of their European return. Their lack of enterprise was understandable in view of an injury-stricken squad, though such a reverse is never welcome. In fact, Kuusysi had the chances to win by more, former Wimbledon striker Belfield and Anfield scorer Lehtinen spurning acceptable chances. For the Reds, Rush went close on two occasions but the Welshman was not at his sharpest after a recent lay-off. The solitary goal came half-way through the second half, courtesy of a mistake by Grobbelaar who advanced from his line but failed to take Jarvinen's cross, leaving Belfield to head into the unguarded net.

Liverpool won 6-2 on aggregate.

The old magic: Ian Rush rediscovers his taste for European competition against Kuusysi Lahti at Anfield.

Round 2 - 1st leg
23 October 1991

AUXERRE 2
Ferreri 43; Kovacs 60

LIVERPOOL 0
H-T 1-0. Crowd 16,500

GROBBELAAR
ABLETT
BURROWS
NICOL (HARKNESS)
McMANAMAN
TANNER
REDKNAPP (MARSH)
HOUGHTON
RUSH
WALTERS
McMAHON

An outplayed Liverpool had Grobbelaar to thank for preserving their interest in the UEFA Cup. It was bad enough to be returning to Anfield with a two-goal deficit; had it not been for a sterling display by the 'keeper the arrears must have been doubled. The fluently passing Frenchmen attacked from the start and, in the first 25 minutes alone, Grobbelaar saved brilliantly from Ferreri, plucked the ball from the feet of Kovacs, and blocked Dutuel's goal-bound effort with his legs. Walters threatened sporadically for the Reds, but Auxerre remained dominant and deserved their lead shortly before the break, Ferreri shooting through Nicol's legs after a crisp interchange with Kovacs. The second strike came on the hour, the Liverpool defence failing to clear a Cocard cross and allowing Kovacs to net in the ensuing confusion. Thereafter, Harkness cleared off the line and Grobbelaar continued to restrict the score to manageable proportions.

Round 2 - 2nd leg
6 November 1991

LIVERPOOL 3
Molby (pen) 4; Marsh 30; Walters 83

AUXERRE 0
H-T 2-0. Crowd 23,094

GROBBELAAR
ABLETT
BURROWS
MARSH
MOLBY
TANNER
McMANAMAN
HOUGHTON
RUSH
WALTERS
McMAHON

Here at last was a night of glory in the old Anfield tradition. Liverpool showed all the passion and belief that had been missing in France to overturn a two-goal deficit for the first time in their European history. Molby set them on their way with an early penalty won by young McManaman, who was felled by Mahe as he worked his way along the byline towards goal. Auxerre did not capitulate immediately, however, and four minutes later Grobbelaar was called on to repeat his first-leg heroics by blocking a Kovacs shot from point-blank range. Yet the Reds had the initiative, and made it tell by equalising on the half-hour, the splendid Marsh arriving with perfect timing at the far post to head his first goal for the club. In the second half there were odd flashes of danger from the visitors, who had Darras dismissed for fouling Walters, but Liverpool mounted inexorable pressure which told when the winger was fed by Molby and placed his shot past the advancing Martini to cap a rousing recovery.

Liverpool won 3-2 on aggregate.

Round 3 - 1st leg
27 November 1991

SWAROVSKI TIROL 0

LIVERPOOL 2
Saunders 57, 78
H-T 0-0. Crowd 12,500

GROBBELAAR
HARKNESS
ABLETT
NICOL
WRIGHT
TANNER
SAUNDERS
MARSH
McMANAMAN
MOLBY
McMAHON

Liverpool displayed impressive authority in overcoming the challenge of an Austrian side whose undeniable technique was not equalled by their self-belief. Saunders was the hero, with two goals to help him forget his travails in domestic football, but there were other significant contributors. Grobbelaar was at his most alert, offering no encouragement to Swarovski as they attacked briskly early in each half, and Wright was in commanding form on his return from a 21-match absence. For all the Austrians' skill, they rarely looked likely to score, and the closest they came was when Nicol tested Grobbelaar with a mishit chipped back-pass. Liverpool secured their lead with two expertly taken goals by Saunders. First he accepted a throw-in from Ablett on the left, and brushed past a defender before shooting under 'keeper Oraze from a tight angle; then he took an incisive Molby through-ball in his stride before steering a shot into the corner of the net from 15 yards.

Round 3 - 2nd leg
11 December 1991

LIVERPOOL 4

Saunders 39, 57, 68; Venison 84

SWAROVSKI TIROL 0

H-T 1-0. Crowd 16,077

GROBBELAAR
HARKNESS (REDKNAPP)
BURROWS
NICOL
WRIGHT
TANNER
SAUNDERS
ABLETT
McMANAMAN
MOLBY
MARSH (VENISON)

Liverpool eclipsed a sluggish Swarovski side on a frosty night at Anfield. Although most of the first half had gone before the first goal materialised, it was difficult to envisage any outcome but an emphatic home win. Yet again the honours fell to Saunders, who scored his second hat-trick of the European campaign. The opener was the product of McManaman's vision, the teenager sending Molby charging through the centre with a perfectly weighted pass; the Dane turned the ball to his right, and the Welshman cut in to score with a neat cross-shot. Saunders cracked in his second when the ball ran free following a corner, then delivered the best goal of the night. Receiving a pass from Marsh,

he turned a defender and bamboozled Oraze with a drop of his shoulder before chipping sweetly over the prone custodian. It was left to the substitute, Venison, to complete the scoring with a 20-yard scorcher that the 'keeper reached but could not keep out.

Liverpool won 6-1 on aggregate.

Round 4 - 1st leg
4 March 1992

GENOA 2

Fiorin 39; Branco 88

LIVERPOOL 0

H-T 1-0. Crowd 40,000

HOOPER
JONES, ROB
BURROWS
NICOL
WRIGHT
MARSH

SAUNDERS
HOUGHTON
WALTERS (VENISON)
MOLBY
McMANAMAN

Liverpool battled gamely against the most formidable opponents they had yet faced on their European return, but could do nothing to prevent a brace of truly sensational strikes. Hooper had already saved well from an Aguilera drive and deflected a close-range Skuhravy toe-poke when he was passed by a shot he could scarcely have seen. Skuhravy beat Wright in the air and Aguilera touched the ball back to Fiorin whose ferocious first-time volley tore into the net from 12 yards. Until then Liverpool had contained the Italians coolly enough, and Houghton had come close to giving them a lead after bursting through from the left flank. After the break Genoa probed patiently but Ruotolo did nothing to help their cause with a ludicrous dive, for which he was rightly booked. On 57 minutes Skuhravy headed against the bar with the goal gaping, then Walters miskicked

when an equaliser beckoned. The final act came when Liverpool were infuriatingly close to a satisfactory result, Branco finding the top corner of the goal with a wickedly swerving free-kick from 35 yards. Poor Hooper was blameless; he never had a chance.

Round 4 - 2nd leg
18 March 1992

LIVERPOOL 1

Rush 49

GENOA 2

Aguilera 27, 72
H-T 0-1. Crowd 38,840

HOOPER
JONES, ROB (VENISON)
BURROWS
NICOL
MOLBY
WRIGHT (TANNER)
SAUNDERS
MARSH
RUSH
BARNES
McMANAMAN

Liverpool attacked from the off and created several half-chances before their momentum was interrupted by the withdrawal of Wright with a torn hamstring. Still they poured forward, and Saunders might have done better with his header from a Rush cross, but three minutes later the tie died as a meaningful contest when Genoa scored. It was a goal of delightful simplicity: Onorati's exquisite first-time pass found Ruotolo on the right, Burrows could only touch the winger's cross into the path of Aguilera, and the Uruguayan controlled immaculately before drilling in from ten yards. Now the Reds needed four, and they bagged one soon after the break, Rush wrong-footing 'keeper Braglia with a downward header from Barnes' centre. With 20 minutes left the Welshman spurned a golden opportunity to reduce the arrears further, side-footing a McManaman cross wide with the net at his mercy, but Liverpool's last remaining hopes were dashed soon afterwards when Eranio set up Aguilera for a neat tap-in. For the rest of the game Molby and company rained shots on the Genoa goal, but Braglia proved equal to all demands.

Genoa won 4-1 on aggregate

185

Right: **Paul Stewart takes control against Apollon at Anfield. The burly Mancunian scored two goals that night but proved unable to make a telling long-term impact as a Red.**

Round 1 - 1st leg
16 September 1992

LIVERPOOL 6

Stewart 4, 38; Rush 40, 50, 55, 74

APOLLON LIMASSOL 1

Spoljaric (pen) 83
H-T 3-0. Crowd 12,769

JAMES
HARKNESS (CHARNOCK)
BURROWS
NICOL
REDKNAPP
WRIGHT
MARSH
STEWART (ROSENTHAL)
RUSH
MOLBY
WALTERS

The second-smallest crowd in Anfield's 73-match European history saw the Reds comfortably dispatch the Cypriots in a contest most notable for a four-goal salvo by Ian Rush. This took the Welsh marksman's European tally for the club to 19, thus eclipsing the 17 notched by Roger Hunt in the 1960s. Stewart gave the Reds an early lead with a strong drive and added a second with a header after 38 minutes. When Rush turned sharply to convert a Marsh pass two minutes later, the game was effectively over, and any hopes of a respectable scoreline for Apollon were extinguished when Charalambous was dismissed just before half-time for a second bookable offence. Walters supplied a low cross for Rush to fire in his second, and soon the Welshman completed his hat-trick with a header after the 'keeper had parried a Walters shot. The hapless Christophi then spilled a drive from Redknapp and Rush, inevitably, prodded home his fourth. A late penalty conceded by Marsh gave Spoljaric the chance to register a consolation for the visiting side, but the night belonged to Ian Rush.

Round 1 - 2nd leg
29 September 1992

APOLLON LIMASSOL 1

Spoljaric 60

LIVERPOOL 2

Rush 62; Hutchison 68
H-T 0-0. Crowd 12,000

GROBBELAAR
MARSH
BURROWS
TANNER
REDKNAPP
HUTCHISON
McMANAMAN
STEWART
RUSH
MOLBY
WALTERS (HARKNESS)

With the tie effectively decided after the first leg, Liverpool found it hard to motivate themselves during a lacklustre first-half and it took a splendid left-foot strike from Spoljaric on the hour to rouse the Reds. Soon a typically opportunistic effort from Rush levelled the score on the night, and Don Hutchison contributed the winner on 68 minutes. The tie ended on a sour note with Stewart being dismissed after a tangle with the Apollon 'keeper Christophi. The England striker appeared to raise his hand in the incident, and was left to reflect on an indiscretion which saw him suspended for the formidable challenge of Spartak Moscow in round two.

Liverpool won 8-2 on aggregate.

Round 2 - 1st leg
22 October 1992

SPARTAK MOSCOW 4

Pisarev 10; Karpin 68, 82 (pen);
Lediakhov 89

LIVERPOOL 2

Wright 67; McManaman 78
H-T 1-0. Crowd 55,000

GROBBELAAR
MARSH
BURROWS
JONES (TANNER)
WRIGHT
HUTCHISON
McMANAMAN
WALTERS
RUSH (ROSENTHAL)
REDKNAPP
THOMAS

Liverpool were within five minutes of gaining a meritorious 2-2 draw in the Central Stadium, having come from behind twice against Spartak in a match played in a swirling snowstorm. The visitors were under severe pressure after Pisarev gave the Russians an early lead, then a blanket of green shirts worked overtime to ensure that no more goals were added in the first half. Wright levelled with a deflected header, but soon Liverpool were in arrears again after Grobbelaar miskicked a back-pass to the dangerous Karpin, who dispatched with aplomb. Stung into retaliation, Graeme Souness' men pushed forward enterprisingly, only to see Walters hit a post before McManaman scored his first European

goal, beating the 'keeper from close range after nimbly turning a defender. Sadly, all the fine work was undone when Grobbelaar received his marching orders for bringing down Radchenko. Burrows took over in goal as Karpin put away the spot-kick and the blond defender was helpless to prevent Lediakhov scoring a killer fourth goal two minutes from time, when he latched on to a Karpin cross which had deflected off Wright.

Right: **The effervescent Ronny Rosenthal heads for goal against Spartak Moscow at Anfield, but to no avail.**

Round 2 - 2nd leg
4 November 1992

LIVERPOOL 0

SPARTAK MOSCOW 2
Radchenko 63; Piatnitski 89
H-T 0-0. Crowd 37,993

HOOPER
JONES (ROSENTHAL)
BURROWS
NICOL
WRIGHT
HUTCHISON
McMANAMAN
MARSH
RUSH
REDKNAPP
THOMAS

The Anfield faithful did their best to spur Liverpool in their bid to overturn a two-goal deficit during a frenzied first half which saw the Spartak goal under siege for lengthy spells. Hopes remained high as the second period opened with a Thomas shot being cleared off the line, but then the Russians' clinical counter-attacking football came into play and Hooper was tested on three occasions before Radchenko coolly finished off a cross from Beschastnykh. Soon the scorer was the centre of attention again when he was the victim of a rash challenge by Marsh, whose dismissal meant that a Liverpool man had been red-carded in three successive European matches. A late second goal for the visitors after more intricate build-up play confirmed a deserved victory, while for Liverpool the challenge of European competition would be out of reach for another two seasons.

Spartak Moscow won 6-2 on aggregate.

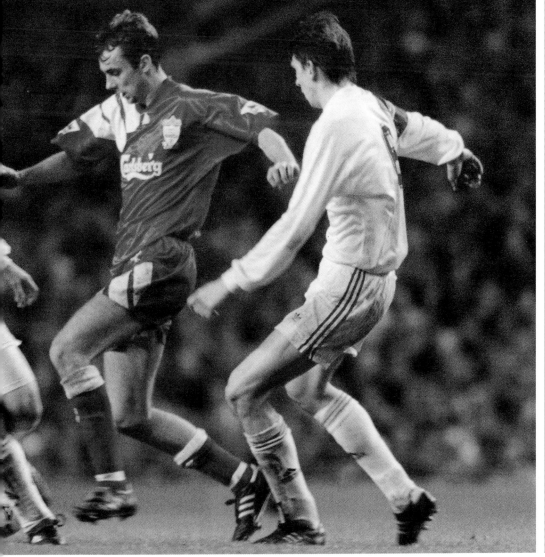

Left: **Don Hutchison, an immense talent who never quite blossomed as a Red, wrong-foots the Spartak Moscow defence.**

Chapter Thirteen

THE MEN IN WHITE SUITS

Below: **Familiar face, new responsibility. After taking charge of the team, Roy Evans is greeted by the players at Melwood, with Steve Harkness leading the congratulations. Other members of the welcoming committee are, left to right, Ronnie Moran, Ian Rush, Dominic Matteo, Steve Nicol, Mark Wright, Mark Walters, Nicky Tanner, Nigel Clough, Bruce Grobbelaar and Steve McManaman.**

WHEN Roy Evans was offered the manager's role on 31 January 1994, it was an appointment that had been widely expected since his installation as assistant to the under-fire Graeme Souness in the summer of 1993. Indeed, his name had been thrust forward as a candidate for the Anfield hot-seat in both 1985 and 1991. Now, finally, Roy's hour had come and he took 'all of two seconds' to ponder before accepting the mammoth task of rebuilding the sagging morale of his beloved Reds.

Realising that the club needed to be put back on an even keel, Roy set about eradicating disharmony among factions of the playing staff and improving the stuttering performances on the pitch. The closing months of the 1993/94 season were spent in assessing the situation, and in the summer Evans splashed out on John Scales and Phil Babb to shore up the centre of the defence alongside Neil Ruddock. Roy's first full season in charge was one of great optimism for the club. He presided over a seemingly contented and committed group of players who, on their day, could produce football as attractive and cultured as any of their Premiership rivals. Duly his side attained fourth place in the title race, reached the quarter-finals of the FA Cup and won the Coca-Cola Cup by beating Bolton Wanderers

2-1 at Wembley.

The lifting of silverware so early in his reign was an enormous source of satisfaction to Evans, who summed up his team's efforts thus: 'If somebody had said to me at the start of the season that we'd qualify for Europe, which was always our main objective, and win a competition, then we'd have taken it. We've made progress, which is pleasing, and I have been delighted with the style of our play which, I believe, has been entertaining. The important thing to remember, though, is that there is still plenty of room for improvement.'

Delighted to be back on the European stage, Roy could hardly wait for his developing side to be tested on foreign soil. Before taking a well-earned summer break Evans mused on the forthcoming 1995/96 season: 'Europe is such a nice distraction from the domestic competitions. The biggest hope is that we get a good run in the UEFA Cup and collect some experience along the way. Obviously we'd love to win it, but perhaps it's a bit early for us yet. There's a different mentality in European games and the tactics have to be different. You have to learn to be patient because Continental sides are never easy to break down as they defend so well.'

With the record-breaking £8.5 million transfer of Stan Collymore from Nottingham Forest, Liverpool seemed to have added the firepower needed to lift the club out of the ranks of mere pretenders, and after a positive beginning to their League campaign they ventured east for a tough UEFA Cup opener against Russian League leaders Spartak Vladikavkaz. Evans opted for Collymore as the lone striker, leaving the prodigious talents of Fowler on the bench until the latter stages of the game. Despite going behind early on, Liverpool rallied impressively as goals from Steve McManaman and then Jamie Redknapp – whose 30-yarder was truly spectacular – turned the contest around. Thereafter Spartak were urged on by a vociferously partisan crowd of 40,000, equivalent to a tenth of the population of Vladikavkaz, but the Merseysiders stood firm to maintain their advantage.

Record signing Stan Collymore, who might have achieved so much for Liverpool but who departed after a brief and turbulent sojourn.

Afterwards Evans was particularly proud of his charges: 'It was a famous victory. There have been a few of those for this club, but it was a bit special for me as it was my first European game in charge. The effort from the team was magnificent. I couldn't be more delighted with them. As it turned out, the hard work had been done and in a game of little excitement, Liverpool played out a goalless draw in the Anfield return. Next, for only the second time in their long European history, Liverpool were paired with opponents from Denmark. Odense had been swept away with lordly disdain a dozen years earlier, but Brondby were to provide far more formidable opposition. For the first leg in Copenhagen, around 35,000 pumped-up home fans raised the roof of their compact stadium, easily out-shouting the 2,000 travelling Reds, and the visitors were forced to dig deep to secure a blank scoresheet with Mark Wright, in particular, outstanding at the heart of the defence.

Evans took his team home in good spirits but, writing in the match programme for the Anfield leg, he warned: 'The game is not a foregone conclusion. We are starting from scratch and the Danes will come here with a positive plan. There are no favourites.' Had Ian Rush's 'goal' after 70 seconds not been ruled offside, perhaps the shape of the game might have been different but, as it was, Brondby defended stubbornly, restricting the home side mainly to half-chances. The Danes had their moments, too, when defensive lapses allowed them openings and Kopites were fidgeting nervously as the game approached its final phase. Sure enough, just 12 minutes from time, Brondby plunged Anfield into dismay by snatching the decisive goal, centre-half Dan Eggen rising above the home rearguard to head in from a corner.

Thus Roy Evans' hopes of a confidence-boosting run in Europe were dashed and Liverpool were left to reflect on a surprise defeat by a team which, though workmanlike, were not by any standards the mightiest of Continental opposition. As John Barnes put it: 'We were outclassed at Anfield by Genoa and Spartak Moscow in recent times, but not by Brondby. It was a disastrous result. Going out of Europe hurts.' To emphasise the scale of the setback, Liverpool had become the first English team to lose to a Danish side in European competition, and they had only themselves to blame. Despite overwhelming superiority in terms of possession, the Reds seemed incapable of mounting prolonged periods of incisive attack. In truth, the performance offered an apt illustration of the team's chief

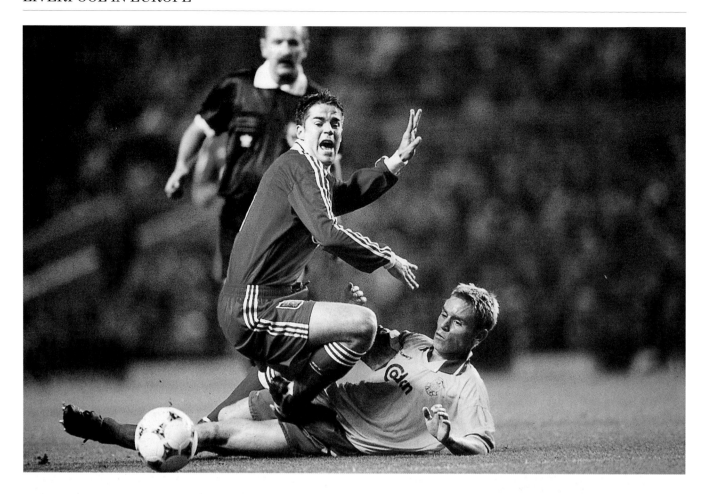

Above: Jamie Redknapp is grounded by a heavy challenge against Brondby at Anfield. The gifted midfielder's career was blighted by injuries when he should have been in his prime.

failing. The defence was generally sound and the midfield was capable of delightful and often exhilarating football. But whereas their chief Premiership rivals, the Uniteds of Manchester and Newcastle, were consistently putting sides to the sword, making their dominance count, the Reds' play often seemed precious by comparison and a frequent criticism was that the team 'passed itself to death.'

Although plenty of admirable reconstruction work had been completed, Evans and his aides, Ronnie Moran and Doug Livermore, knew there was still much to accomplish. Defeat at the hands of a vibrant Newcastle in the Coca-Cola Cup and a disappointing Premiership run-in which saw the team trail into third place could have been forgotten had they managed to defeat their most bitter antagonists, Manchester United, in the FA Cup Final. In many ways this occasion marked a pivotal moment in the public perception of New Liverpool. The sight of the team parading in white Armani suits on the Wembley pitch before the kick-off was one which lingered long and painfully in the minds of Anfield diehards, even more so than the match itself, which proved to be largely sterile and a disappointing spectacle. Eric Cantona's late winner, which sealed a second League and FA Cup double in three years for the Mancunians, could almost be seen as a merciful release for long-suffering Scousers who were sickened by their side's lacklustre display. That particular collection of vastly remunerated young sportsmen had been dubbed 'The Spice Boys' by the scathing media and, however unfair the moniker might have been, it was a tag which would stick like mud on the aforementioned white linen.

One of the great beauties of football is that once the season ends the slate is wiped clean. After a summer break, optimism returns unbounded and before the big kick-off in 1996 Roy Evans reflected: 'We look back with a tinge of under-achievement although I think we gave value for money. Everybody wanted to watch us.' With Patrik Berger the only major summer acquisition, Liverpool took their place in the European Cup Winners' Cup – as beaten FA Cup finalists, Manchester United having entered the Champions League – rather than contest the UEFA Cup, a competition for which they were eligible through their third-place League finish. At this stage, the European trophy for which the Reds were bidding was not held in high esteem in all quarters. Certainly Richard Pedder, chairman of the Liverpool Supporters Club, was rather less than enamoured. He explained: 'I heard one of the commentators put it this way. The Champions League is for champions, the UEFA Cup for the teams that finished second and third while the Cup Winners' Cup is really the Cup Losers' Cup. It seems there are about a dozen sides in it that didn't even win their (domestic) cup competitions.' But the die was cast and an excursion to a far outpost of Finland to face modest opponents in MyPa 47 was negotiated safely with a rejuvenated Stig Inge Bjornebye scoring the only goal on his European debut for the Reds. It was heartening to see the Norwegian international return to consistent first-team duty after breaking his leg at the end of 1994/95. The part-timers of MyPa nursed little realistic expectation of gaining a shock result in the Anfield return, and goals by Berger, Barnes and Collymore duly eased the Reds into the second round. On the domestic front, Roy Evans' men had opened impressively, topping the table until a 1-0 defeat at Old Trafford dented their prospects.

A trip to the unheralded Swiss side, Sion, was the next item on the European agenda. Despite making a terrible start, conceding a goal after 11 minutes when a slip from Matteo allowed Bonvin to take advantage, Liverpool came back strongly through Fowler and Barnes to claim a satisfactory away win. The Reds' positive approach was applauded loudly in Switzerland and Evans was quietly satisfied, paying tribute to his team's professional approach. He could bask deservedly in the praise of the Swiss media, who were impressed that Liverpool were not willing to settle for a draw after their early setback. As *Sport Zurich* put it: 'Swiss supporters are not used to seeing a visiting side play such an offensive game and it was very thrilling to watch. It was a very special game and I know the people of Sion were honoured to see such a performance.' Perhaps such a bouquet was a trifle over the top, and arguably that fulsome summation of events might have been applied to the

Back on track: Robbie Fowler after notching the equaliser which set Liverpool on the victory trail in Switzerland.

On a funny old night at Anfield,
Robbie Fowler, Patrik Berger
and John Barnes celebrate the
sixth goal against Sion.

second leg at Anfield, where it was the plucky Swiss who showed their mettle in attack.

Indeed, in a game which produced nine goals, the hosts' nerves were often stretched to breaking point. Arriving with seemingly little hope of holding Liverpool on their own turf, Sion motored into a 2-0 lead inside 23 minutes with strikes from Chassot and Bonvin. Although the Reds calmed matters by bouncing back with goals from McManaman and Bjornebye, the indefatigable Swiss capitalised once more on Liverpool's frailty to put themselves 3-2 ahead on the night. At that point Roy Evans' side was facing the hitherto unthinkable possibility of elimination on the away-goals rule, but then Barnes back-heeled an equaliser and when Robbie Fowler poached two goals in a minute, poor Sion were flattened. Berger added a sixth, but nothing could disguise the truth that it had been a mighty uncomfortable night. After the match Roy, though visibly relieved at booking a place in the quarter-finals in March, tempered his joy with a note of caution: 'With half an hour to go we were under pressure, but our response was magnificent. We are such a talented bunch on the attack, but we can't afford to do this week-in and week-out.'

Come the spring, a kind draw saw the Reds paired with SK Brann of Norway, who would be playing their first competitive match since their winter break. Liverpool took an early initiative through a brilliant Robbie Fowler goal but the Norwegians refused to buckle, with the tall striker Tore-Andre Flo causing the visitors particular problems. Brann gained just reward for their efforts with an equaliser just after half-time, but few were backing them to win through at Anfield. Certainly the spectre of Brondby lurked large in Merseyside minds and Roy Evans underlined the need for defensive stability without detracting from his customary attacking policy: 'It's pointless trying to get a 0-0 draw out of it. That's suicidal. You could end up with a Brondby situation where someone gets a late goal and you're out.

We have to try to win the game from the start but we must be sensible about it. We can't leave ourselves wide open against any team who can go to PSV Eindhoven and put two goals past them. Brann have to be respected.'

Scandinavia is a hotbed of Liverpool support and among the 200 or so Norwegian fans travelling to Anfield was Roger Dahl, a self-employed computer technician and membership officer and accountant for the Scandinavian branch of the Liverpool Supporters Club. This was no one-off occasion for Dahl, who had been a season ticket holder for six years, with a treasured seat on the Kop. He was accustomed to flying in for a Merseyside weekend at a cost in travel alone of around £350 each time. 'I do have a girlfriend,' he said, 'but she doesn't think I'm mad. She comes with me sometimes. She likes shopping in Liverpool.' It is not recorded whether the lady picked up any bargains on this latest excursion but the Reds, at least, could be happy with their night's work. Despite Evans' pre-match caution, they cruised comfortably to a 3-0 win. A quartet of top-drawer names went into the hat for the semi-finals, Liverpool's coming out alongside that of Paris St Germain, leaving Barcelona and Fiorentina to do battle for the other final berth. The French side boasted an array of top talent, including the Brazilians Leonardo and Rai, and also the striker Patrice Loko (PSG's version of Stan Collymore?) whose much-publicised mental turmoil had seen him head for the psychiatrist's couch. However, the Liverpool boss was well aware of the potential threat posed by the 27-year old Frenchman, whose hat-trick had destroyed AEK Athens on their own ground. 'French football is going through a renaissance and to get a result like they did in Greece is no mean feat.' Both teams had suffered from poor domestic form in the run-up to the first leg at the Parc des Princes, but the hosts rose impressively to the occasion, overwhelming a disappointing Liverpool to the tune of 3-0. David James' uncertainty between the posts was to play a part in the first two goals, the hapless custodian failing to claim crosses which allowed Leonardo and Cauet to score. In fairness, the Reds poured forward in the second half and were a much more threatening outfit, but when Leroy struck for PSG six minutes from time it left the shell-shocked visitors facing a gigantic task in the second leg.

After much thought, manager Evans decided a high-tempo approach was needed to unsettle the French and skipper John Barnes was dropped for the first time in his decade on Merseyside. In fact, he was not even on the bench, instead watching the action from the

The white-shirted Jason McAteer tussles for the ball with Benoit Cauet on the way to a demoralising defeat in Paris.

Mark Wright's soaring header rekindles hope of a dramatic turnaround against Paris St Germain at Anfield. Alas, although some dignity was salvaged by a valiant 2-0 triumph on the night, the task proved too onerous and Liverpool bowed out of Europe.

directors' box. It was PSG who created two early chances, narrowly missed by Loko and Leonardo respectively, but it was Liverpool who drew first blood when Fowler's instinctive left-footer sped past 'keeper Lama. Thus the stage was set for a thunderous match which ebbed and flowed as both teams failed to make the most of their opportunities. When Mark Wright netted with a powerful header from a corner with 11 minutes remaining, it seemed that Liverpool might just force an equaliser and take the match into extra-time. But PSG clung doggedly to their advantage and, despite tremendous pressure, the hosts could not find a way through. At least a measure of pride had been restored by the Reds' feisty second-leg performance, but they had fallen at the semi-final stage and there was no hiding the players' disappointment.

Stig Inge Bjornebye reflected ruefully: 'We needed an early goal and we got it. When we scored the second one I thought we were going to do it and if we had managed to take the game into extra-time we would have been cruising. We lost the game but we should be happy about other things. We showed our pride and played some good football. It was a quality performance.' Now Liverpool needed to put Europe behind them and concentrate on the League, because after defeating Tottenham Hotspur at Anfield they were in second spot in the Premiership and widely fancied to consolidate their position as runners-up, thus gaining a much-coveted place in the Champions League. They needed a mere two points from away matches against Wimbledon and Sheffield Wednesday, but Liverpool's nerve seemed to fail them at the death. Defeat at Wimbledon, where Michael Owen marked his senior debut as substitute with a late consolation goal, was followed by a 1-1 draw at Hillsborough. When the final table was complete, the Reds had dropped to fourth place on goal difference behind both Newcastle United and Arsenal. It was especially hard to bear because all three clubs finished on 68 points, seven adrift of the champions, Manchester

United. This crushing disappointment further escalated doubts that the team had it in them ever to be winners and many disgruntled fans were beginning to question Evans' ability to motivate the unquestioned array of talent under his command. Nevertheless, Roy remained at the helm and the board backed him heavily with cash to strengthen the squad even further in the summer of 1997. Oyvind Leonhardsen, Karlheinz Riedle and, somewhat controversially, Paul Ince were acquired in the belief that they would help turn the 'nearly men' into champions.

The new season had hardly begun when a mouth-watering UEFA Cup first round encounter with Celtic at Parkhead claimed centre stage. With close to 50,000 fans packed into the ground, both teams contributed hugely to a match filled with incident and drama, if rather short of football of the very highest class. Indeed, it was played like a domestic league match, all helter-skelter, rather than in the more cautious, thoughtful manner associated with European competition. Owen's early goal underlined not only his prodigious speed, but also his precocious skill, as he skipped past Alan Stubbs to tuck away his chance. This shifted the onus on to Celtic, who pressurised throughout a hectic first half but always looked vulnerable to rapid counter-attacks. Riedle called forth a point-blank save from 'keeper Jonathan Gould just after half-time, but soon the game was to turn on its head.

First Jackie McNamara fired an unstoppable looping shot past David James to equalise, then Simon Donnelly hit the bar from 20 yards. The home fans, having howled when one penalty appeal had been turned down after Kvarme tussled with Donnelly, were in full voice as Italian referee Graziani adjudged James guilty of a trip on Henrik Larsson in the box. The 'keeper was booked and Donnelly put the Celts in front from the spot. Despite these quickfire setbacks, Liverpool rallied, took the game to their opponents and in the 90th minute an extraordinary goal from Steve McManaman tied the game. From near a touchline, some 15 yards inside his own half, the willowy play-maker and the subject of a possible £12 million transfer to Barcelona, burst forward into the Celtic half with a diagonal run past three defenders before unleashing a perfectly judged drive low into the corner of Gould's net. It was a strike worthy of winning any match, although in this case its value as an equaliser was to prove just as golden.

Anxiety is etched on the faces of Liverpool defenders Jamie Carragher (left) **and Bjorn Tore Kvarme as Celtic's Morton Wieghorst and Craig Burley fail narrowly to convert a cross in the 0-0 draw at Anfield.**

Above: **Liverpool bombard the Strasbourg battlements during the 2-0 victory at Anfield. Sadly the rampant Reds could not quite force the third goal which would have taken the tie into extra time. Pictured straining every sinew in the home cause are, left to right, Michael Owen, Jamie Redknapp, Dominic Matteo and Robbie Fowler.**

Right: **Entente cordiale. The new managerial partnership of Gérard Houllier and Roy Evans pose in front of the portraits of previous legendary Anfield supremos.**

The return encounter at Anfield was held in an atmosphere of mutual *bonhomie* between the two sets of supporters, a far cry from the Cup Winners' Cup semi-final fought out by the two clubs 31 years earlier, when the pitch was littered with bottles after a late Celtic goal was disallowed for offside. The game itself was engrossing and fitfully exciting, but with Liverpool content to control play from defensive positions, the visitors were left to hustle and bustle as best they could. The bluntness of their attack left them unable to force the goal which would have breathed life into the contest, and Liverpool moved into the next round with surprisingly little fuss. When they were paired with Strasbourg, there might have been a tinge of apprehension in the Reds' camp, bearing in mind the awful display in Paris some six months previously. Certainly a 2-0 defeat at the hands of Everton, which saw Liverpool sink to ninth place in the Premiership, was hardly the best preparation for the expedition to France. Strasbourg, who had already disposed of Glasgow Rangers, set about Liverpool from the off. In truth the visitors might already have been two goals adrift when Zitelli stunned David James with a rising volley on 20 minutes, and such was the hosts' dominance that it was almost half-time before 'keeper Vencel was forced to make a save. A second strike from Vitelli just after the hour and a third from Conteh six minutes later left the Merseysiders' hopes in tatters.

Faced with another mountain to climb, one of identical altitude to that demanded by Paris St Germain earlier in the year, even Roy Evans, a man so protective of his charges, let

his frustration pour out. 'It's the same old story,' he groaned, 'and its driving me round the bend. I'm the man in charge, I make the decisions, but I can't go out there and kick the ball for them.' Paul Ince promised the fans that their team would redress the situation: 'We know what we have to do, we will give everything we have, then you never know what might happen,' said the Liverpool captain. Evans echoed his skipper, voicing the rather wistful thought that 'mountains are there to be climbed.'

True to their word, Liverpool set about Strasbourg with a thrilling bombardment of their goal, pinning the visitors inside their own half throughout most of the opening period. Unfortunately, the goal the Reds strove for so passionately failed to materialise until the 63rd minute, when Olivier Dacourt fouled Riedle and Robbie Fowler broke the deadlock from the spot. More relentless pressure brought a second success when Riedle nodded in from close range to set up another last-ditch assault. Sadly, as was the case against the Parisians, the chances just would not fall the way of the home side and so, deflated but unbowed, the vanquished Reds trooped off the pitch to sympathetic applause. The stark truth, though, was that this Liverpool side was not good enough, and it spent the remainder of the 1997/98 season delighting and infuriating the faithful with a series of Jekyll and Hyde performances that can only have increased Evans' frustration. Third place in the Premiership - successful enough for most clubs - was seen as failure by Liverpool fans who had waited with great patience as their heroes had, for the most part, flattered to deceive.

Something had to be done, and executive vice-chairman Peter Robinson moved swiftly when he discovered that Gérard Houllier, the articulate and highly regarded former French team manager, was considering a move back into day-to-day club management from his role with the French Football Association. Robinson stepped in decisively to ensure that the forward-thinking Houllier's expertise would be put to good use at Anfield and not elsewhere. Indeed, Gérard was linked with the hot seat at Sheffield Wednesday and disappointed Celtic at the last moment before, on 16 July 1998, he accepted the challenge of managing Liverpool in a joint capacity alongside Roy Evans. 'I took the job on the condition that Roy stayed,' Houllier explained afterwards. 'There will be shared responsibility and it might take time to get things right, but we will make the best of it.' The doubters, of course, were out in force, being swift to predict that the hastily assembled partnership would not endure; they held the view that Evans would be pushed upstairs after a few poor results and that the Frenchman would assume sole control of team affairs. For Liverpool, their chief ambition for the coming season was clear – qualification for the Champions League, at the very least. 'That's the status of this club,' Evans declared, 'and we could hardly aim for anything less.'

Meanwhile it was back to European business and a visit to Slovakia for the UEFA Cup first-round tie against the champions, Kosice. It turned out to be a comfortable hurdle to clear, the Reds winning 3-0 through strikes by Patrik Berger, Karlheinz Riedle and, most satisfyingly, Robbie Fowler on his comeback. The gifted striker, who had been sidelined for months with a serious knee injury, took just 26 seconds to find the net after rising from the bench as a substitute. The return leg was even more of a stroll for the Reds as Kosice, nicknamed the Tigers, proved to have no teeth whatsoever. Jamie Redknapp and Robbie Fowler bagged a couple of goals apiece and Paul Ince made it 5-0 in a game which proved that, just occasionally, there is such a thing as an easy match in European competition. However, a challenge of an entirely more rarefied order was imminent. Valencia, though languishing in 16th place in the Spanish First Division, provided that old familiar *frisson* of European excitement when they visited Anfield for a tie which was a welcome diversion for the Reds, whose sagging form had seen them without a win in five League matches.

Despite this dispiriting run, Roy Evans was upbeat about the team's chances. 'We would like to be higher in the table but we are starting to get it together. The team spirit and determination is there and, with a bit more luck in front of goal, we will be back on track.' Michael Owen, thus far an ever-present in all senior competitions, was rested, occupying the bench and allowing Riedle to link up with Fowler, but still a below-par Liverpool could not pierce the none-too-distinguished Valencia rearguard. To make matters worse but to be scrupulously honest, if the Spaniards had displayed a tad more ambition and self-assurance, they might have grabbed a priceless away goal, but they seemed more than happy to leave Anfield with a goalless draw.

The intimidating, steep-sided Mestalla Stadium was packed with raucous supporters who waited in anticipation for Valencia to finish the job as the home side threatened to overrun the Reds in a torrid first-half of the second leg. With World Cup stars Ilie and Lopez forming a lethal partnership in attack, Liverpool cracked just before the interval when Lopez crashed home a rebound after Ilie had struck an upright. It seemed only a matter of time before Valencia would extend their lead in the second period, but they were stunned when McManaman grabbed an equaliser. Pressure on the joint management team of Evans and Houllier was further eased when Berger drove in a left-footer to put the Reds ahead. However, with only five minutes to play, any hopes that Liverpool could take the heat out of the game evaporated when both Ince and McManaman were sent off with Carboni following an undignified scuffle. Nerves were further frayed when Lopez struck a free-kick that hit the post and bounced into the net off David James, but the equaliser had arrived too late for the Spaniards, who were eliminated on the away-goals rule. It should be stated that the way in which they regrouped following this reverse, emerging as one of the top sides in Europe and reaching successive Champions League finals, set an uplifting example to any club willing to take notice. So nobody should underestimate the scale of Liverpool's achievement at the Mestalla; they had prevailed over a very good team.

Back on Merseyside, Evans and Houllier prepared their men for a Premiership encounter with Derby County at Anfield in which the Rams inflicted the first home defeat of the season on the Reds. Worse was to follow when Tottenham Hotspur headed north to the one-time fortress for a Worthington Cup meeting. Only 20,772 fans turned out to watch a televised match in which a woeful Liverpool were put to the sword mercilessly. Spurs built a comfortable 3-0 lead before Owen grabbed a late consolation and there was further bitter gall for the Reds as the little jewel of a striker injured himself in the act of scoring. This demoralising defeat brought matters to a head and the following day Roy Evans bravely decided that he should hand over full responsibility for leading the club out of its travail to Gérard Houllier.

On Thursday 12 November chairman David Moores had the poignant task of announcing the departure of the intensely loyal and committed Evans. 'Today is a sad day for Liverpool and for me personally,' Moores said. 'We have agreed by mutual consent that Roy and Doug Livermore, his assistant, are leaving the club. I would like to pay tribute to all he (Evans) has done for the club over 35 years. I offered Roy another position but he has chosen to take a break. I could talk for hours about Roy and my respect for him.' Almost in tears,

Unfazed by the close attentions of Valencia luminary Gaizka Mendieta, Liverpool's Robbie Fowler opts for the spectacular at the Mestalla.

You're off! Paul Ince takes the long walk after his dismissal in the dying minutes of the turbulent encounter with Valencia in Spain.

Evans said: 'I'd like to thank the chairman and the board for the support they have given me. I have felt that over the past three or four weeks things have not been working out. I dispute the theory that my time here has been a failure – fourth, third, fourth and third cannot be termed a failure. That record is second only to Manchester United's.' True enough, but lack of tangible success was ultimately the deciding factor in the board accepting his resignation. For all that, Roy could have been forgiven if he felt that if his players had delivered more when the chips were down, then he would not have had to walk away from the club he loved so dearly.

When new manager Gérard Houllier needed someone with a 'Liverpool heart', Phil Thompson was overjoyed to answer the call.

With Gérard Houllier now in sole charge, and given the surprise installation of the fiercely partisan Phil Thompson – previously axed by Graeme Souness – as his assistant, there would be no hiding place for any malingerers. A delighted but candidly shocked Thompson, still coming to terms with his resurrection from the football scrapheap, laid down an early marker: 'There might be a few hearts getting broken. I've been brought in to provide a kick up the backside to a lot of players. I think most people realise this is one of the greatest days of my life.' A more reflective Houllier observed: 'We need to get some players in to reinforce the team. We are here because the players did not kick the ball in the right way. We cannot kick the ball for the players.'

Still in the immediate after-shock, Liverpool were flying to Spain once again to face League leaders Celta Vigo, a team that had eliminated Aston Villa in the second round. The Reds had never lost a competitive match in Spain before but, despite a first-half strike from Michael Owen, they were sunk by a classy Celta Vigo unit which passed the ball with great aplomb. Truth to tell, there were painful interludes when Liverpool were run ragged by the surprise package of the tournament and three second-half hits by Vigo left the visitors facing an almost certain knockout. Houllier was left to search for some crumbs of comfort before the second match at Anfield. 'The positive thing is that we scored, which will be very important in the return leg,' he mused. 'Celta think the game is finished. They think they have gone through. We don't think so. We have a

Opposite top: **Michael Owen shoots Liverpool into an early lead against Celta Vigo in Spain. However, three goals from the classy hosts put Liverpool's hopes into stark perspective.**

Opposite: **The final nail in the coffin. Danny Murphy (24) and Steve Staunton are helpless to prevent Vigo's Revivo from plundering the only goal of the Anfield return.**

chance.' But Liverpool's already slim prospects were hampered further by the absence of the suspended quartet of Ince, McManaman, Heggem and Redknapp, and Vigo showed no hint of the complacency that Houllier had predicted.

In a cool, damp atmosphere, the supporters were strangely subdued before the kick-off, as if already resigned to their fate. Thus they were prepared for what followed, as Vigo out-manoeuvred a sorry Liverpool in every department, and when Revivo's delightfully taken goal arrived in the 57th minute, it served merely to emphasise just how far behind the Anfield club had fallen in terms of European competition. 'All we can take from the game is that we have lots of young players who give us hope for the future,' remarked Houllier afterwards. 'But hope doesn't make the present. They (Vigo) were better technically and I am disappointed for the 30,000 fans who were behind us and gave everything.'

Gérard was acutely aware of the massive task ahead. He could not countenance the sort of failures that had beset the Reds in recent seasons and only a new footballing edifice built on fresh foundations would set the club on the right path for the future. And sure enough, out of the ashes of defeat by Celta Vigo there arose a new Liverpool, one transformed in mind, body and spirit; a club which soon would take on some of the top names in European football . . . with glorious results.

Round 1 - 1st leg
12 September 1995

SPARTAK VLADIKAVKAZ 1
Kasimov 20

LIVERPOOL 2
McManaman 32; Redknapp 53
H-T 0-0. Crowd 43,000

JAMES
JONES
HARKNESS
BABB
WRIGHT
RUDDOCK
McMANAMAN
REDKNAPP
THOMAS
BARNES
COLLYMORE (FOWLER)

Liverpool made a shaky start on their European return as the Russians of Vladikavkaz gave the Reds' defence a searching early examination. The hosts' seemingly inevitable goal arrived on 20 minutes when Kasimov bamboozled James with a free-kick from just outside the box. But Liverpool responded well and McManaman restored parity in spectacular style, curling in a right-foot shot from the narrowest of angles. Spartak were less of a threat in the second half and Redknapp sealed an ultimately impressive team performance with a long-distance thunderbolt into the top right-hand corner of Khapov's net. Liverpool's distinctly defensive line-up – Fowler was employed only as a late substitute – held the home side comfortably at arm's length to complete a satisfying win.

Round 1 - 2nd leg
26 September 1995

LIVERPOOL 0

SPARTAK VLADIKAVKAZ 0

Crowd 35,042

JAMES
JONES
HARKNESS
BABB
WRIGHT
RUDDOCK
McMANAMAN
REDKNAPP
THOMAS

BARNES
FOWLER (RUSH)

The hard work had been done in Moscow and Liverpool progressed to the next round after an uninspiring Anfield encounter in which clear-cut opportunities were at a premium. Fowler, replacing the unfit Collymore, was lively, but he received little service from a congested midfield. Thomas had the ball in the net on 20 minutes only to be ruled offside, and then both Redknapp and Ruddock failed to convert half-chances before the interval. The Russians made two substitutions at the beginning of the second period and soon fashioned two chances which could have ignited the tie. Even the late introduction of Rush failed to produce a goal and the game drifted uneventfully towards a stalemate on the night.

Liverpool won 2-1 on aggregate.

Round 2 - 1st leg
17 October 1995

BRONDBY 0

LIVERPOOL 0

Crowd 37,648

JAMES
JONES
HARKNESS
SCALES
WRIGHT
BABB
McMANAMAN
REDKNAPP
RUSH
BARNES
FOWLER (THOMAS)

Liverpool needed to be at their most resilient in a Copenhagen cauldron against resourceful opponents spurred on by a passionate home support. Both teams sparred respectfully in the early stages, getting men behind the ball in numbers and releasing them forward only for occasional thrusts. Wright was back to his best form, inspiring the Reds' five-man rearguard with some crisp tackles and timely interceptions. Brondby's main plan revolved around veteran captain Vilfort's dangerous breaks from defensive positions, while Liverpool were more adventurous, with Rush and McManaman carving openings before half-time. The skilful Danes applied more consistent pressure after the break, and following a caution for Jones the visitors were forced to survive a flurry of free-kicks and corners. Late on, James ensured a goalless scoreline with a spectacular diving save to deny the menacing Sand.

Round 2 - 2nd leg
31 October 1995

LIVERPOOL 0

BRONDBY 1
Eggen 78
H-T 0-0. Crowd 35,878

JAMES
JONES (COLLYMORE)
HARKNESS (KENNEDY)
SCALES
WRIGHT
BABB
McMANAMAN
REDKNAPP
RUSH
BARNES
FOWLER

Deep disappointment shrouded Anfield as the immaculately organised Brondby smothered Liverpool's attacking ambitions before stealing a late winner, courtesy of defender Dan Eggen. Yet the outcome might have been different if Rush's near-post effort from Fowler's cross after just 70 seconds had not been ruled offside. Redknapp almost registered on three occasions before the interval as Liverpool continued to surge forward, although not before James' uncertainty saw the Danes go agonisingly close to snatching a 12th-minute lead when the big 'keeper misjudged a cross. He was let off the hook as Sand's header looped harmlessly wide of an unguarded net. As the tension mounted in the second period, Liverpool continued to apply pressure and Scales was denied a goal by Colding's clearance off the line following a corner. It was, however, a Brondby corner which was to prove decisive when Bjur's dispatch was met by Eggen, who rose above a static defence to send the Reds tumbling out of Europe with a powerful header.

Brondby won 1-0 on aggregate.

Round 1 - 1st leg
12 September 1996

MYPA 47 0

LIVERPOOL 1

Bjornebye 61
H-T 0-0. Crowd 5,500

JAMES
McATEER
BJORNEBYE
MATTEO
WRIGHT
BABB
McMANAMAN
COLLYMORE
FOWLER
BARNES
THOMAS

Stig Inge Bjornebye, making his European debut for Liverpool, scored the decisive goal to dispatch the Finnish hopefuls, but the contest was not as one-sided as most pundits had predicted. Certainly the Reds created numerous chances, but profligate finishing meant that their defence endured some anxious moments before the game picked up pace in the second half. The breakthrough came shortly after the hour when McAteer's cross from the right was only half-cleared, enabling the Norwegian international to rifle home a low shot from just inside the box.

Round 1 - 2nd leg
26 September 1996

LIVERPOOL 3

Berger 18; Collymore 59; Barnes 78

MYPA 47 1

Keskitalo 64
H-T 1-0. Crowd 39,013
JAMES
McATEER
BJORNEBYE
MATTEO (RUDDOCK)
WRIGHT (SCALES)
BABB
McMANAMAN
COLLYMORE
BERGER (REDKNAPP)
BARNES
THOMAS

Liverpool created enough scoring opportunities to have buried MyPa 47 comprehensively, but in the end the Finns returned home with a respectable scoreline and a consolation goal. It

seemed only a matter of when, and not if, the opening goal would arrive and, sure enough, Berger delighted Anfield with a glorious strike after nutmegging a defender. Thereafter more chances went a-begging and the fans were getting somewhat restless until Collymore turned his marker and doubled the tally on the hour. Rather than capitulate, My-Pa sent on Keskitalo who, with his first touch, pulled a goal back with a splendid drive from the edge of the box. Barnes restored order some 12 minutes from time, thus wrapping up an efficient rather than an inspired performance.

Liverpool won 4-1 on aggregate.

Round 2 - 1st leg
17 October 1996

SION 1

Bonvin 11

LIVERPOOL 2

Fowler 24; Barnes 60
H-T 1-1. Crowd 16,500

JAMES
McATEER
BJORNEBYE
MATTEO
SCALES
BABB
McMANAMAN
BERGER
FOWLER (REDKNAPP)
BARNES
THOMAS

After carving out a chance in the opening minute, when Berger's shot was deflected for a corner, Liverpool handed the Swiss a gift goal when Matteo's woefully short back-pass was seized upon by Bonvin, who beat James with an exquisite chip. However, the Reds' response was swift and Fowler, returning after injury, claimed an equaliser when he stabbed home a rebound from the post. Liverpool enjoyed the majority of the possession throughout the first half and carried their dominance into the second period with a wonderful goal by Barnes. The midfielder glanced in a header from a corner to leave the home crowd silent. Although McManaman should have added a third following a characteristically dazzling run, Sion still carried a threat and always looked capable of unsettling an uneasy Liverpool defence, as they were to prove when they visited Anfield for the second leg.

Round 2 - 2nd leg
31 October 1996

LIVERPOOL 6

McManaman 28; Bjornebye 54; Barnes 65; Fowler 70, 71; Berger 89

SION 3

Chassot 19, 64; Bonvin 23
H-T 1-2. Crowd 38,514

JAMES
McATEER
BJORNEBYE
MATTEO
SCALES (REDKNAPP)
BABB
McMANAMAN
BERGER
FOWLER
BARNES
THOMAS

What should have been a routine fixture turned into an extraordinary goal-fest at Anfield as the Reds were stunned by Sion's audacity in plundering a two-goal lead after only a quarter of the game. McManaman steadied the ship with a low shot into the corner from McAteer's cross, leaving the outcome in the balance at half-time. Shortly after the interval a 20-yard free-kick from Bjornebye restored Liverpool's aggregate lead, but Chassot stunned the Kop into silence by skipping past Matteo and rounding James to make the score 3-2 to Sion on the night. This provoked a stirring Liverpool revival started by Barnes, who back-heeled the equaliser within a minute, and continued by Fowler, who bagged a quickfire brace courtesy of great play by McManaman. Berger wrapped up a thrilling contest in the final minute, but the Reds had been given the fright of their lives by the plucky and skilful Swiss underdogs.

Liverpool won 8-4 on aggregate.

Above: **Steve McManaman attempts to beguile a Vladikavkaz defender.**

Bottom right: **Stig Bjornebye is tripped by Sion's Frederic Chassot at Anfield.**

Below: **Right shirt, wrong wearer. Dan Eggen, scorer of the winning goal for Brondby, celebrates after the match.**

BRANN 1

Hasund 47

LIVERPOOL 1

Fowler 10
H-T 0-1. Crowd 12,700

JAMES
McATEER
BJORNEBYE
MATTEO
HARKNESS
RUDDOCK
McMANAMAN
BERGER
FOWLER
BARNES
REDKNAPP

The surprise quarter-finalists attracted a UEFA-specified maximum attendance of 12,700 fans to their compact Brann stadium and quickly put the visitors under pressure. Flo nearly scored in the first minute, only to be denied by Ruddock and Harkness, yet despite their shaky opening it was Liverpool who drew first blood with a brilliant individual goal when Bjornebye released Fowler, who flicked the ball over a defender before thumping home. Subsequently Berger wasted an inviting opportunity to double the lead before the interval after a Brann defensive howler. Then the Reds were rocked at the start of the second half when, out of the blue, Hasund scored with a stunning shot from just inside the area. The remainder of the match ebbed and flowed with both sides missing chances, James distinguishing himself ten minutes from time with a superb block from Flo.

LIVERPOOL 3

Fowler 25 (pen), 77; Collymore 60

BRANN 0

H-T 1-0. Crowd 40,326

JAMES
McATEER
BJORNEBYE
HARKNESS
WRIGHT
MATTEO (BABB)
McMANAMAN
BERGER (COLLYMORE)
FOWLER
BARNES
REDKNAPP

Erring on the side of caution, Liverpool took their time to unpick the Brann defence, but in the end they eased their way comfortably into the semi-finals. For the first 20 minutes Brann defended stoutly in the face of Liverpool's intricate passing game, but the Norwegians were undone when Fowler was upended in the box and the prolific striker coolly dispatched the penalty. The hosts continued to dictate, but with no further breakthrough materialising after an hour, they replaced the wayward Berger with Collymore. The move paid off within two minutes when the unpredictable Midlander burst past two defenders and an attempted challenge sent the ball ricocheting into the net from his own ankle. Fowler claimed his second on 77 minutes to put the tie well beyond the visitors' reach.

Liverpool won 4-1 on aggregate.

John Barnes makes a sliding intervention as Dominic Matteo and Brann striker Tore Andre Flo compete for possession.

Above: Jamie Redknapp is a witness as Leroy goes down under challenge from Mark Wright in Paris.

Left: Stan Collymore, who went close in the home encounter with PSG, but not close enough.

Below: Desperation time, as David James surges forward for a corner against PSG in the valiant but vain quest for a third goal at Anfield.

PARIS ST GERMAIN 3

Leonardo 11; Cauet 43; Leroy 84

LIVERPOOL 0

H-T 2-0. Crowd 35,142

JAMES
McATEER
BJORNEBYE
MATTEO
WRIGHT
HARKNESS
McMANAMAN
COLLYMORE (THOMAS)
FOWLER
BARNES
REDKNAPP

Liverpool had only themselves to blame as they sank to defeat in the Parc des Princes with a careless and error-strewn performance, leaving their chances of progressing to the final hanging by a thread. The Merseysiders had an early warning when an effort from Loko was ruled offside, but Leonardo was on hand to turn in Cauet's cross on the far post after James had failed to clear with a weak punch. This setback, however, served only to strengthen the visitors' resolve, with Redknapp and McManaman wresting control of the midfield and quietening the crowd. But all that encouraging work was undone two minutes before half-time when James flapped at another centre and the ball fell to Loko, who headed it back across goal for Cauet to score. Collymore was replaced by Thomas at the interval and immediately the Reds looked a better balanced combination. McManaman's glancing header appeared to have reduced the deficit but was ruled offside and Wright went close with a header just over the bar. However, what was already a torrid evening for the Reds deteriorated further when PSG introduced substitute Pouget, who lost little time in creating a chance for Leroy to tuck home.

Right: Gutted. In the immediate aftermath of elimination by PSG at Anfield, a stricken Neil Ruddock contemplates what might have been.

LIVERPOOL 2

Fowler 11; Wright 79

PARIS ST GERMAIN 0

H-T 1-0. Crowd 38,984

JAMES
McATEER
BJORNEBYE
THOMAS
WRIGHT
RUDDOCK
McMANAMAN
COLLYMORE
FOWLER
BERGER (KENNEDY)
REDKNAPP

Forsaking their customary measured method, the Reds threw everything at PSG in a bold attempt to overturn the three-goal deficit, and the frenzied tempo paid dividends after only 11 minutes. Ruddock's hopeful long pass found Collymore in the area and the ball broke to Fowler, whose left-foot shot angled past Lama into the goal off an upright. Clearly the French were rattled by the home side's commitment in the red-hot atmosphere, but the visitors always threatened on the counter-attack and Leonardo should have equalised before half-time. With the Merseysiders playing towards the Kop in the second half, the PSG goal was placed under siege and both McAteer and Collymore went close before Wright thundered in a header from Bjornebye's corner to set up a nail-biting finale. In the end the holders held firm to book a place in the final against Barcelona, but at least some pride had been restored to the Liverpool ranks by a rousingly passionate display.

Paris St Germain won 3-2 on aggregate.

Round 1 - 1st leg
16 September 1997

CELTIC 2
McNamara 53; Donnelly (pen) 73

LIVERPOOL 2
Owen 6; McManaman 89
H-T 0-1. Crowd 48,526

JAMES
JONES
BJORNEBYE
KVARME
WRIGHT
MATTEO
McMANAMAN
INCE
OWEN
RIEDLE
THOMAS

This was a match in which Liverpool were superior to their opponents but needed a wonder-goal at the death from McManaman to rescue the draw which was the very least their play deserved.

Celtic were on the back foot from the off, and when Owen produced an early trademark strike, Parkhead was hushed. Had McManaman added a second only minutes later when clean through on 'keeper Gould, the tie could have been almost over as the Reds were solid in defence and dangerous on the counter-attack, largely restricting the home side to half-chances. The second-half opened in similar vein, so it was a surprise when McNamara fired a fierce shot past James to equalise. Then Donnelly hit the bar as the home side pressed forward in numbers, gaining a 2-1 lead when Larsson was clipped by James and Donnelly scored from the spot. Despite this setback Liverpool never lost their composure and gained just reward in the dying moments when Riedle passed to McManaman, who set off from 15 yards inside his own half, leaving a string of Celtic defenders in his wake before drilling an unstoppable low shot past the startled Gould.

Round 1 - 2nd leg
30 September 1997

LIVERPOOL 0

CELTIC 0
Crowd 38,205

JAMES
JONES
BJORNEBYE
KVARME
CARRAGHER
BABB
McMANAMAN
INCE
FOWLER (RIEDLE)
OWEN
BERGER

Celtic played with great courage, but were not sufficiently composed to conjure the goal that would have decided the tie in their favour. Over the 90 minutes there was little to separate the two teams, who scrapped tenaciously but without finding the net. A measure of uncertainty between James and his defence gave the Scottish side hope in the first half, when twice the Reds narrowly escaped falling behind. Liverpool gained the ascendancy in the second period as Celtic were forced to commit men forward in search of a goal, leaving McManaman and Ince with chances, but both England men failed to hit the target. The dying minutes provided the most goalmouth excitement as Donnelly stabbed an effort wide and then Liverpool substitute Riedle saw his 88th-minute header cleared off the line.
Aggregate 2-2.
Liverpool won on away goals.

Above: **A goal to grace any occasion. Steve McManaman ghosts through the bemused Celtic rearguard to grab the most sensational of last-gasp equalisers at Parkhead.**

Round 2 - 1st leg
21 October 1997

STRASBOURG 3
Zitelli 20, 63; Conteh 69

LIVERPOOL 0
H-T 1-0. Crowd 18,813

JAMES
McATEER
BJORNEBYE
KVARME
HARKNESS
RUDDOCK (OWEN)
McMANAMAN
INCE
FOWLER
REDKNAPP
LEONHARDSEN

Having been humiliated in Paris only six months earlier, it was a case of déjà-vu for the Reds as they emerged with their egos badly bruised following a 3-0 reverse at the hands of a rampant Strasbourg. Two goals from the impressive striker Zitelli and a third by Conteh hardly did justice to the French team's dominance, which began in the first minute when Arpinon found space in Liverpool's box but failed to control the ball. The visitors' beleaguered defenders were always struggling and Ruddock, in particular, was hard-pressed to subdue the lively Zitelli. The Strasbourg marksman scored the opener with a superb rising volley, then hit the angle of bar and post with a glancing header, before nipping in front of James to put the French side into a two-goal lead. With the exception of a brilliant 40-yard chip from Fowler, crucially saved by Vencel, Liverpool rarely threatened. Their night of woe was complete when Conteh sped past the lumbering Ruddock to drill in a shot which James reached but could not repel, leaving him to watch helplessly as it trickled into the net.

Right: **Karlheinz Riedle goes in where it hurts to bundle the ball over the line, raising slender hopes of late salvation against Strasbourg at Anfield.**

Round 2 - 2nd leg
4 November 1997

LIVERPOOL 2
Fowler (pen) 63; Riedle 84

STRASBOURG 0
H-T 0-0. Crowd 32,426

JAMES
JONES (RIEDLE)
BJORNEBYE (BERGER)
KVARME
MATTEO
LEONHARDSEN
McMANAMAN
INCE
FOWLER
OWEN
REDKNAPP

It was always going to be a monumental task to overturn the 3-0 drubbing of the first leg but Liverpool did not give up without a compelling fight. Indeed, a spellbound Anfield was treated to a frenetic attacking display by the hosts, who carved out enough scoring opportunities to have achieved the seemingly impossible. Fowler's delicious 40-yard chip, turned over superbly by 'keeper Vencel, was the closest the Reds came to gaining the lead in the first half as Strasbourg stood firm. This forced Roy Evans to throw caution to the wind in the second period as Riedle and Berger were pitched into the fray in search of more firepower. The breakthrough came courtesy of a penalty from Fowler after Dacourt brought down Riedle, and more frenzied action followed before the German rose to head home from close range to give his side a faint hope of forcing extra-time. Try as they might, though, they could could not find a way past Vencel and his solid rearguard, but at least they perished gloriously. **Strasbourg won 3-2 on aggregate.**

Below: **How did that one get away? Steve McManaman cannot credit that he hasn't found the net against Strasbourg in France.**

Round 1 - 1st leg
15 September 1998

KOSICE 0

LIVERPOOL 3

Berger 18; Riedle 23; Owen 59
H-T 0-2. Crowd 4,500

FRIEDEL
HEGGEM
STAUNTON
HARKNESS
CARRAGHER
BABB
McMANAMAN (McATEER)
BERGER
RIEDLE (FOWLER)
OWEN
REDKNAPP (LEONHARDSEN)

The Slovakians were completely outclassed by a Liverpool team who put on a fine attacking display in the Locomotive Stadium. Owen was subjected to some brutal treatment, being scythed down from behind repeatedly, and it was yet another bad challenge that enabled the Reds to take the lead, Berger unleashing a fearsome low drive from Staunton's tapped free-kick. Five minutes later Liverpool were two goals up after Riedle registered with a header from six yards out, following a cross by McManaman. The Anfield men maintained their grip in the second half and were buoyed by the return of Fowler following a long injury lay-off. His effect on the match was immediate, as he threaded a delicious through-ball for Owen to exact his revenge on the Slovak defenders with a typically efficient sidefooted finish.

Round 1 - 2nd leg
29 September 1998

LIVERPOOL 5

Redknapp 23, 55; Ince 52;
Fowler 53, 90

KOSICE 0

H-T 1-0. Crowd 23,792

JAMES
McATEER (HEGGEM)
BJORNEBYE
LEONHARDSEN
CARRAGHER
BABB (MATTEO)
REDKNAPP
INCE (STAUNTON)
FOWLER
OWEN
BERGER

Liverpool strolled into the second round in a one-sided contest against an attractive but toothless Kosice side which offered no threat, especially after being reduced to ten men on the hour when Spilar was dismissed for yet another clumsy challenge on Owen. By then the Reds might have been several goals to the good, as Fowler had missed casually from the spot after a 15th-minute foul on Owen, Redknapp had opened the scoring with a low drive following a free-kick, then Berger and Owen had struck post and bar respectively, all before the interval. Such profligacy was stemmed in the second half as three goals came in a four-minute spell, Ince netting from close range, Fowler heading home after the 'keeper had mishandled a Bjornebye cross and Redknapp lashing in a shot from 30 yards. Rarely had the Reds enjoyed an easier night in Europe and Fowler provided the finale, helping himself to a second goal at the death.

Liverpool won 8-0 on aggregate.

Round 2 - 1st leg
20 October 1998

LIVERPOOL 0

VALENCIA 0

Crowd 26,004

JAMES
HEGGEM
BJORNEBYE
McATEER
CARRAGHER
STAUNTON
McMANAMAN
INCE
FOWLER (OWEN)
RIEDLE
BERGER (LEONHARDSEN)

After a saunter through the first round, Valencia presented far tougher opposition at Anfield and they were distinctly unlucky to leave Merseyside without a victory after an enterprising performance which constantly stretched their hosts on the counter-attack. The Reds' favoured option was the high cross towards Fowler and Riedle, while the Spaniards were more cultured in their approach, with Mendieta pulling the midfield strings and Ilie and Lopez dangerous predators up front. Riedle came closest to breaking the deadlock for the Reds, his header being cleared off the line by Popescu, while Roche squandered Valencia's best chance with James stranded and the goal seemingly at his mercy. On the basis of such a performance, few neutrals would have backed Liverpool to make further progress in the tournament.

Top left: **Nap-happy Reds. Jason McAteer, Jamie Redknapp and Paul Ince celebrate one of Liverpool's five goals in the home trouncing of Kosice.**

Below: **Michael Owen and substitute Sean Dundee know the massive value of Steve McManaman's away goal against Valencia.**

Left: **Ready for the fray: Jamie Redknapp leads his troops into battle against Celta Vigo in Spain. At his back can be spotted, left to right, David James, Bjorn Tore Kvarme, Patrik Berger, Stig Inge Bjornebye, Jamie Carragher, David Thompson, Vegard Heggem, Robbie Fowler and Steve Staunton. Michael Owen is obscured.**

Round 3 - 2nd leg
8 December 1998

LIVERPOOL 0

CELTA VIGO 1
Revivo 57
H-T 0-0. Crowd 30,289

JAMES (FRIEDEL)
McATEER
MATTEO
BABB (MURPHY)
CARRAGHER
STAUNTON
GERRARD
THOMPSON (RIEDLE)
FOWLER
OWEN
BERGER

On a damp, cool night on Merseyside, Liverpool's lack of success in Europe throughout the 1990s continued its familiar pattern after Celta Vigo defended their two-goal first-leg advantage with consummate comfort. However, although the patchwork Reds were outplayed and out-thought by Vigo, there was no lack of effort from Gerard Houllier's charges as they worked feverishly to create openings against a sound defence. As in the first leg, Mostovoi was a constant thorn in Liverpool's flesh and James was called upon to rescue a wobbly defence on several occasions. The home supporters had to admire the quality of the Spaniards' play and they offered generous applause to Vigo's goal after another slick move saw Revivo cut through the Reds rearguard, beating Murphy and Gerrard with exquisite skill, then shooting past James. It was a stark lesson for the hosts, but Houllier was already planning major changes to his squad that would see Liverpool return to European competition equipped to compete with the best.

Celta Vigo won 4-1 on aggregate.

Round 2 - 2nd leg
3 November 1998

VALENCIA 2
Lopez 45; James (og) 90

LIVERPOOL 2
McManaman 81; Berger 86
H-T 1-0. Crowd 53,000

JAMES
HEGGEM (DUNDEE)
BJORNEBYE (HARKNESS)
REDKNAPP
CARRAGHER
STAUNTON
McMANAMAN
INCE
FOWLER (McATEER)
OWEN
BERGER

Both teams were in a trough of bad form in their respective leagues and in need of a confidence-boosting result to spark an upturn in their fortunes. In an intimidating atmosphere, the Reds were all but overrun in the opening stages as Valencia set up wave after wave of attacks. The Spaniards were repulsed by an overworked defence until the stroke of half-time when Ilie hit a post, and his lethal strike partner Lopez smashed home the rebound. After the interval there was little respite for Liverpool, who were trying desperately to slow the tempo of the game in the face of quick and nimble Valencia play. But the contest turned on its head in the final ten minutes when McManaman equalised, then Berger crashed in a trademark left-footed strike to give the Reds a shock lead. That was the cue for the high-octane encounter to explode, as Ince and McManaman were sent off with Carboni following an unseemly fracas. Valencia grabbed a last-minute equaliser when a Lopez free-kick struck an upright and bounced in off the unfortunate James, but it was Liverpool who went through to the next round.

**Aggregate 2-2.
Liverpool won on away goals.**

Round 3 - 1st leg
24 November 1998

CELTA VIGO 3
Mostovoi 49; Karpin 56; Gudel 90

LIVERPOOL 1
Owen 35
H-T 0-1. Crowd 24,600

JAMES
HEGGEM
BJORNEBYE
KVARME
CARRAGHER
STAUNTON
REDKNAPP
THOMPSON (RIEDLE)
FOWLER
OWEN
BERGER (BABB)

Having escaped defeat in Valencia, the Reds returned to Spain to face a difficult challenge against the skilful and hugely underrated Celta Vigo. Owen's first-half goal, tucked away in typical fashion after Thompson's glorious defence-splitting pass, furnished the visitors with a precious away strike. But in the end they were comprehensively outplayed by the Spaniards who hit back with three second-half goals. Mostovoi, who was a constant threat, threaded Vigo's first through a crowd of players and Karpin took advantage of a mistake by Heggem to add the second on 56 minutes. Gudel's last-minute strike only confirmed Celta Vigo's superiority on the night and it took two outstanding saves from James to restrict the scoreline to respectable proportions.

Chapter Fourteen

HOU' LET THE REDS OUT?

WHILE the task facing Gérard Houllier after taking lone responsibility for the team was immense, there were many pluses left from the previous three seasons. In particular, Roy Evans had bequeathed a fabulous youth system, guided wisely by Steve Heighway and Hughie McAuley, which enabled the Reds to win the FA Youth Cup in 1996. From that side had emerged Jamie Carragher and Michael Owen and, hot on their heels, a rangy young midfielder named Steven Gerrard would soon be making his presence felt.

Another huge bonus for the new manager was the patience of the fans. Liverpool supporters have always enjoyed a reputation for being among the most sporting and knowledgeable of football followers. Thus, now, they understood that for their team to be a true force again, perhaps there would be short-term disappointments to be suffered as Houllier began his four-year strategy to return the Reds to a place among the elite.

His first concern was to rebuild the team, as he put it 'on foundations of concrete and not straw', and the rest of the 1998/99 season was spent in shoring up the existing edifice while meticulously drawing up a list of materials necessary for a major long-term refurbishment. The club finished in a mildly disappointing seventh place in the Premiership and, perhaps most painfully, suffered a last-gasp defeat at Old Trafford in the FA Cup fourth round, Manchester United coming from behind with two goals in the last five minutes to win a pulsating match. Houllier's promise to the gutted supporters was heartfelt and unequivocal: 'One day we will beat Manchester United.'

Wheeling and dealing began quietly, with Jason McAteer and Steve Harkness the first to leave, but the revolution gathered force during the summer when David James and Paul Ince were among the high-profile departures. The big goalkeeper had ultimately failed to convince. Though he was capable of brilliant saves, of which he made many, there was an underlying frailty about his game. Too often a mistake would appear to undermine his confidence and the knock-on effect on the entire defence was a cause for concern. Although undoubtedly hurt at being transferred to Aston Villa, David took Houllier's decision with admirable dignity and good grace, which is more than can be said for Ince. After signing for Middlesbrough the former skipper did himself little credit with his criticism of his erstwhile boss.

On paper, Liverpool's greatest loss was that of Kop favourite Steve McManaman, who signed for Real Madrid on a Bosman-style free transfer. No one could blame the intelligent Merseysider for bettering himself, and when supporters rounded on him, Gérard Houllier mounted a spirited defence, arguing that as a foreign manager pursuing his career in England, he could hardly complain when McManaman wanted to test himself overseas. There was another dimension to the McManaman deal, too. Naturally it was sad that such a talented performer had gone, yet perhaps Steve's free-spirited style of play had been at the heart of some of the team's recent inadequacies. Without him Liverpool would become stronger and more composed as a unit and not so reliant on flashes of brilliance from one outstanding footballer.

The manager was not blessed with a bottomless pit of money for his transfer dealings and, after failing to secure Sol Campbell from Tottenham Hotspur, he set his sights on foreign stars at less exorbitant prices than those demanded for Premiership men. 'I had a budget of £12 million and I couldn't buy English players for that,' said Houllier. 'I wanted Sol Campbell, but Tottenham wouldn't sell and I can understand that; I wouldn't sell him to me if I was at

Sami Hyypia, the embodiment of Liverpool's new-found defensive stability. The giant Finnish player is that rare individual, a footballing stopper whose fearsome physical presence is matched by his all-round technique.

Vladimir Smicer, whose Liverpool career got off to an uncertain start but who shone frequently during 2000/2001 after he had adjusted fully to the hectic pace of English football. No less a judge than Sir Alex Ferguson has described the Czech international midfielder as a world-class performer.

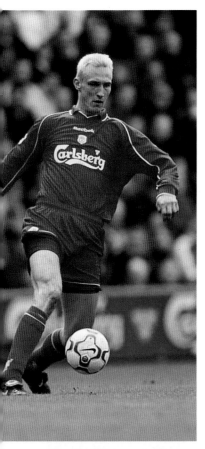

Tottenham. So I went with Stéphane Henchoz and Sami Hyypia, who can both play from the back.'

The towering Hyypia arrived, almost unknown, on 1 July 1999 from Dutch side Willem II for £2.6 million, and the following day the Finn was joined by the accomplished Swiss international, Stéphane Henchoz, a £3.5 million capture from Blackburn Rovers. Already in place behind them was Dutch goalkeeper Sander Westerveld, a £4 million signing from Vitesse Arnhem, and adding to the options in offensive positions Houllier invested in Czech midfielder Vladimir Smicer for £3.5 million from Lens. Also from France came Aboubacar 'Titi' Camara, the exhilarating but unpredictable Guinea-born striker who cost £2.8 million from Marseilles, and reinforcing the strength in depth was the powerful Dutch front-runner Erik Meijer, a Bosman recruit from Beyer Leverkusen. The spending was not yet finished as German international midfielder Dietmar Hamann was then prised from Newcastle for £8 million to add to an extensive squad.

In what was always likely to be a transitional season Liverpool, with no European distractions, were soon gaining admiration for their newly-found commitment and solidity. Their defence was tight, conceding only 30 times in 38 Premiership outings, while their attacking variety was limited by the extended injury-enforced absences suffered by strikers Owen and Fowler, who barely started a game together. Houllier took steps to address that problem by bringing in Emile Heskey from Leicester for a hefty £11 million in March 2000.

For much of that campaign, there were genuine hopes of a top-three finish but, come the climax, the Reds' form tailed off alarmingly. No goals scored in the last five League matches, and defeat to Bradford City at Valley Parade in the final game, saw Liverpool slump to fourth spot and miss out on a Champions League slot at the last gasp once again. In defence of his charges, the manager pointed to the progress made rather than chances missed. 'We finished three places higher and 13 points better than in the previous season and we secured a UEFA Cup place with two matches still to play. So we are on the way to something and we are ahead of schedule,' said a satisfied Houllier. 'One factor that tends to be overlooked is that the average age of our team last season was 23.9 years, the youngest in the Premiership. Manchester United's average was 27.9 years, so there is a four-year gap. Our team needs time to grow and mature together.'

It was, perhaps, that lack of maturity which counted against them when the pressure grew, and Gérard took steps to add experience to his squad by negotiating another Bosman acquisition, that of German international Markus Babbel from Bayern Munich and, in what turned out to be a master-stroke, he enticed the 35-year-old Gary McAllister from Coventry with the offer of an initial one-year contract. Apart from the midfielder's undoubted class, coupled with his eye for goals, Houllier knew it was a chance for his young squad to learn from the Scot's enormous experience and supreme professionalism. While French international winger Bernard Diomède slipped into the ever-expanding squad largely without comment, Houllier's other summer signing arrived with both halves of Merseyside in uproar. Everton midfielder Nick Barmby, having re-established himself in Kevin Keegan's England set-up, rejected all attempts to renew his Goodison contract and the Toffees had little choice but to accept the Reds' offer of some £6 million. Thus the scene was set for what was to prove one of the most thrilling campaigns in the club's history and even fans who thought they had seen it all before would have to think again.

Liverpool set out on the road to their improbable cup treble with a visit to Romania to take on Rapid Bucharest in the first round proper of the UEFA Cup, Houllier giving European debuts to Diomède and the left-sided German international Christian Ziege, recently recruited from Middlesbrough after a protracted saga. Ziege was given plenty of licence to attack in the Giulesti Stadium, but too frequently his enterprising forays left gaping holes at the back. At times the Reds looked impressive, with Barmby's unselfish running and cleverness complementing Hamann's combative tackling in midfield, but although they claimed victory through the ex-Evertonian's well-taken goal, still they could hardly be described as the cream of the European crop.

Anfield was packed for the second leg, though, and the faithful had some cheer before the start with the returns after injury of Gerrard and Fowler, the latter starting for the first time

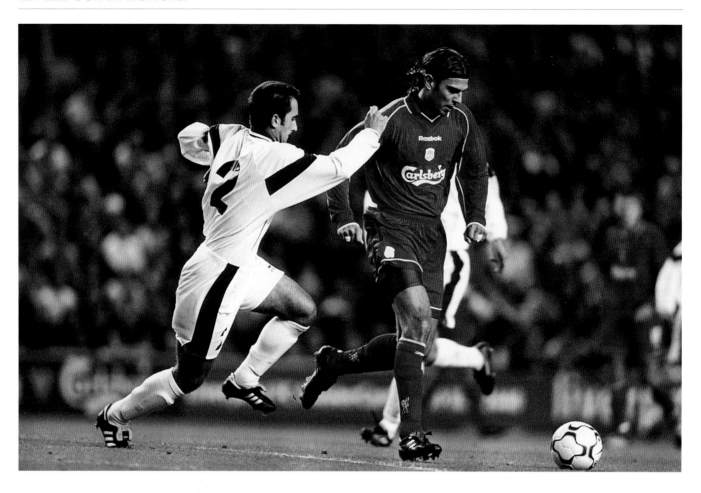

Patrik Berger, always a potential match-winner, lopes past Stanclu of Rapid Bucharest in the goalless draw at Anfield.

after two substitute appearances. 'God is back' adorned one of the many banners, and Robbie was captain, too. His presence represented one of six changes from the weekend's League meeting with Sunderland, the manager feeling confident that he could rest some of his stars. Although regarded only as the third of Bucharest's trio of clubs, Rapid were not to be taken lightly and coach Anghel Iordanescu, who had managed Romania in two World Cup tournaments, was wily enough to employ Daniel Pancu as a lone striker. This formation was effective and the visitors created two first-half chances, but during the second period Houllier brought on Barmby and Ziege, the latter receiving applause almost as rapturous as Fowler's. Immediately the German made his presence felt on the left flank as Liverpool took control, though without being able to find a killer punch to win on the night. Thus, despite a patchy display, Liverpool were through to the second round, while their compatriots, Leicester and Chelsea, found themselves out of the competition at the first hurdle.

The draw was kind to the Reds as the obscure Czech side Slovan Liberec were announced as their next adversaries, and a crowd of just under 30,000 turned up for the Anfield first leg in the hope of more uplifting fare than was offered in the previous round. Sadly, once more Michael Owen was out through injury, this time suffering from concussion after a freak accident against Derby County when he took an inadvertent kick to the back of his head. Certainly Liverpool needed the razor-sharp reflexes and eye for goal of the boy wonder, as his replacement, Robbie Fowler, laboured throughout. During another evening of unconvincing football, Liverpool wasted a catalogue of chances, with Robbie the chief culprit. Such is the affection in which he is held by the Red half of Merseyside that perhaps the gifted striker is allowed a tad more latitude than others when his game is off-song. A missed penalty in the second-half, when he fired the spot-kick into the Kop, summed up his evening, and he must have been grateful that Emile Heskey spared his blushes with a late winner.

Liverpool were still reeling from a careless 4-3 Premiership defeat by Leeds as they headed for the bleak coalfields of Bohemia. Once again the manager rotated his squad, bringing back

Gerrard, Barmby and Fowler to the starting line-up. A shade fewer than 7,000 Liberec fans packed the tiny Mestsky Stadium in the hope of seeing an upset after the Czechs had somehow emerged from their first English examination with a mere one-goal deficit. The temperature rose, metaphorically speaking, after nine minutes when the hosts cancelled out the lead, poor marking allowing Stajner to head in unchallenged. Now the Reds realised they were in for a fight and the Czechs, sensing a famous victory, became ever more physical. Emile Heskey, in particular, received rough treatment, and it was after yet another foul on the England marksman that Ziege flighted a beautiful free-kick from which Barmby netted with a stooping header at the far post. Heskey was enjoying a rich vein of form for the Reds, and now he registered his fifth goal in four matches with a strike on 75 minutes. Seen as something of a gentle giant who didn't always punch his weight, Emile had settled well on Merseyside, and in his unselfish role as a target man he offered the team a much-needed different dimension. In addition, Houllier had worked wonders in boosting the self-belief of the unassuming Leicester lad, thus speeding up the development of his overall game. His maturity was evident in the way he endured some scandalous treatment by the Czechs – the German referee seemed excessively lenient – and his refusal to be intimidated was hugely impressive. Emile reflected: 'I've had a few cuts and bruises in other matches, but the Slovan game was one of the worst. But I am used to it now. It's all about discipline. You don't like to be kicked and kicked and kicked again, but that's the game sometimes and I have to learn to handle it.'

With the Reds 2-1 in front, Houllier took the opportunity to bring on Michael Owen as a late substitute and he took less then 60 seconds to find the net, thus finishing the tie as a contest despite a late goal from Czech substitute Breda, which made it 2-3 on the night. It had been a worrying time for Michael, who had undergone two brain scans following his accident at Derby, and this was just the tonic he needed as he eased himself back into the fray.

A fortnight later the Reds were pitched back into European action against tough, seasoned and accomplished opponents, Olympiakos of Athens. The Greek champions had dropped into the UEFA Cup after being controversially ousted from the Champions League following a

defeat in Lyon. Bookings in that match resulted in the absence of two of their star players, Giovanni and Mantzurakis, both missing through suspension, but Liverpool were more concerned with their own problems. Glaring defensive errors had been costing them dear in the Premiership and Gérard Houllier urged certain senior players to sharpen up their act. 'I am hugely disappointed by the mistakes because I know we can eradicate such things,' he said.' But I do believe that it is practically impossible to stop them through coaching. It is down to individual decision-making, top international players making the right choices. It's not a matter of confidence or ability. It is, in fact, the more high-profile players who are making these mistakes – not the youngsters from whom you might understand it.'

Faced by an intimidating atmosphere, and against a team undefeated at home in 15 Champions League matches, it was clear that Liverpool needed to be at their best to take anything from the away leg. They did not disappoint. Digging deep, the Reds produced a magnificent performance, utterly outplaying their hosts. Steven Gerrard and Danny Murphy gained control of the midfield, thus silencing the home support, and once more Nick Barmby was proving to be Liverpool's European ace in the pack. It was his goal, when he swivelled and hammered a Heskey cross high into the roof of the net, which put the Reds in front before half-time. Thereafter the visitors had more chances to extend their lead before a superb overhead-kick by Alexandris levelled the scores. However, Olympiakos were not given time to celebrate as two minutes later Steven Gerrard headed home majestically from Barmby's corner. Now the Reds were rampant as substitute Steve Staunton curled a free kick against the Greeks' bar, then Vladimir Smicer burst through to shoot against an upright with the home side reeling. Agonisingly, though, in the 90th minute a long cross into Liverpool's penalty area found the ever-dangerous Alexandris, who hit an unstoppable shot past Westerveld, thus preserving the Greeks' proud home record.

Rather disconsolately, the Reds trooped off the pitch feeling that they had let victory slip from their grasp, but in reality they had achieved a tremendous result with a truly top-drawer performance. Gérard Houllier put things into perspective: 'I feel a bit sorry for my players because although this was a great result, they were so close to achieving something exceptional,' said the Frenchman. 'Make no mistake, though. We will not let it slip at Anfield. There is still work to be done but we are determined to finish off the tie. I'm delighted by the way we played and I cannot blame anyone for Olympiakos scoring from the only chances they had. For such a young team, we showed great maturity to take the sting out of them and impose ourselves on a side who have beaten opponents such as Valencia in the Champions League this season.'

Almost unnoticed, the match marked the final appearance for the Reds of Steve Staunton. The modest Irishman had served the club well in two spells since his bargain £20,000 transfer from Dundalk back in 1986. Indeed, it is still a cause of rancour among some Liverpool supporters that Graeme Souness allowed him to move to Aston Villa in the summer of 1991. His unflustered defending and accurate dead-ball skills were sorely missed as he spent the peak years of his career in the Midlands. Since returning 'home' to Anfield in July 1998, Steve had gradually been eased out of the picture by Gérard Houllier's new recruits. However, with Christian Ziege sidelined and young Djimie Traoré suffering from a hamstring strain, Steve – just back from a loan spell with Crystal Palace – rose from the bench at half-time in Athens to play a full part in the draw. Houllier was delighted with the Irishman's performance: 'He has always been fair with us, and the club with him. If an opportunity comes along for him then we will look at it in his own interests.' Staunton was happy to have contributed: 'I knew there were a few injuries in the camp but I wasn't sure whether the club realised that my loan period was up. When they found out, the manager asked me to travel and I was ready for it. I was just delighted for the chance.' However, with Jamie Carragher pencilled in to take on the problematic left-back spot, soon Steve was allowed to rejoin Aston Villa with all parties happy at the outcome.

By the time Olympiakos arrived for the return leg at Anfield, their coach Yiannis Matzourakis had resigned in the wake of their Champions League failure and their poor performance at home to the Reds. Having been showered with abuse by the crowd during the match, he stepped aside for his assistant, Takis Lemonis, to take over. Truly the Olympiakos

away record in Europe was pitiful. Four Champions League campaigns had seen 11 defeats in 15 matches, but still Houllier was guarded about the possible threat: 'I'm aware of their record in Europe and it's true they don't travel well,' he said. 'Even so, it could be fatal to go into what I am certain will be a most demanding fixture believing we've already done enough.'

Before the match there was much speculation as to whether fit-again Michael Owen or Robbie Fowler would partner Heskey up front. In the event, both players watched the kick-off from the bench with Vladimir Smicer operating in a withdrawn role just behind Heskey. Some 3,000 Greek fans packed into a corner of the Anfield Road stand, maintaining a noisy and enthusiastic presence, but in truth their team never posed much of a threat. At less than full throttle, Liverpool eased their way into the last 16 with an efficient victory. Another well-taken goal from Emile Heskey paved the way, but it was Nick Barmby's gem of a second, capping a brilliant individual display, that sent the Reds' fans home happy after a 4-2 aggregate victory. The supporters were eager also for a peek at the latest signing, the tall,

Demonstrating the ability which once made him the most sought-after youngster in English football, Nick Barmby dupes the Greek goalkeeper before clipping an exquisite goal in the 2-0 victory over Olympiakos at Anfield.

Two-goal Michael Owen emerged triumphant from the most rigorous of Roman inquisitions. Here he evades a fierce lunge from Tommasi, with Rinaldi lurking to the left.

powerfully-built midfielder Igor Biscan, purchased from Dynamo Zagreb for around £5 million. Some of Europe's major clubs had been tailing the 22-year-old and it was an indication of Liverpool's rising stock that he chose to come to Merseyside to develop his career. Unfortunately Biscan was not available for selection for European action, having played for his former club earlier in the campaign.

With a break of two months before European action was to resume in February, Liverpool turned their attention to domestic matters and during that interim they secured some notable victories. Danny Murphy's exquisite free-kick saw the Reds triumph over Manchester United at last, and at Old Trafford to boot. When confidence was further bolstered by a 4-0 drubbing of Arsenal at Anfield the following week, the future was looking bright. Although some leading Premiership clubs had chosen not to field their strongest line-ups in the Worthington Cup, Gérard Houllier had always taken the competition seriously, and after a hard-fought 2-1 win at home to Chelsea in round three, Second Division Stoke City were swept away 8-0 at the Britannia Stadium. A classy Fuham, under French coach Jean Tigana, provided stubborn opponents at Anfield in the fifth round before three extra-time goals eased the Reds through to the semi-final against Crystal Palace.

In a torrid first leg at Selhurst Park, Liverpool were often embarrassed and overrun by a Palace side playing without a trace of fear, and with no little skill. Two goals down (and it could have been more), the Reds were grateful for the timely introduction of substitute Jari Litmanen, whose delicious interplay with his new colleagues crafted a vital late goal for Smicer. Beset by injury at Barcelona and unable to force his way back into the star-studded Catalonian side, the Finnish international arrived at Anfield on a free transfer and immediately impressed coaches and players alike with his sophisticated skills and reading of the game. Order was restored in the return at Anfield when the Eagles of South London were put in their place, cruelly and ruthlessly, and although the 5-0 drubbing may have been a trifle unjust, the Reds had booked their place to meet Birmingham City in the final. Meanwhile, the seeds of an FA Cup run were being sown. After plucky Rotherham were dispatched 3-0 at Anfield, Liverpool overcame Leeds United in the fourth round at Elland Road. In a heavyweight contest, the home side were well ahead on points until the Reds delivered a late knockout blow with goals from Barmby and Heskey. At this stage, though, the vision of a cup treble was no more than a pipe-dream, especially as mighty Roma were the next opponents in the UEFA Cup.

Before the first encounter in Rome, Gérard Houllier outlined his feelings about the task ahead. 'Roma are the best side left in the tournament and one of the best sides in Europe right now. So this will be a good test for us. I feel our team is not as strong as Roma's at the moment, but over two legs you never know. I just wish we had our strongest squad available.'

Neither Danny Murphy nor Steven Gerrard was fit to travel, and Emile Heskey failed to shake off an ankle injury, so Houllier pulled a surprise by playing Owen and Fowler up front in a pairing which many critics reckoned to be unworkable. Roma appeared to be ambivalent about the match, their main priority seeming to be maintaining their place at the summit of *Serie A*. Fearsome Argentinian striker Gabriel Batistuta was left on the substitute's bench and the influential midfielder Francesco Totti was rested altogether. Officially he was suffering from flu, but there were murmurs that he was in dispute with the club over a new contract. All this must have been manna from heaven for Houllier, who had been bemoaning the loss of Gerrard, earmarked earlier to shadow the Italian playmaker.

The visit to Rome was one of mixed emotions for assistant manager Phil Thompson. The former Red missed the 1977 European Cup Final after he suffered a knee injury and was forced to undergo a cartilage operation, and in 1984 he was devastated to be left out of the line-up for the final against Roma. Watching the match from the stand that day hurt him immensely, but he was always a fan as much as a player, and he assured the club website: 'No one was more vocal watching the game, I promise.'

The resumption of hostilities with Roma started with an aggressive Liverpool attempting to stamp their physical presence on proceedings. Carragher and Ziege doubled up on the left flank to counter the dangerous Brazilian, Cafu, and the German was distinctly fortunate not to receive a yellow card for a couple of crunching tackles. For all that, the first half was largely uneventful and the Reds must have been surprised at Roma's diffident showing. The hosts were shocked from their torpor immediately after the interval, however, when Rinaldi casually rolled a square pass across the edge of his own area, allowing Owen to intercept. In an instant, the diminutive predator controlled the ball and fired home a low cross-shot past stricken 'keeper Antonioli. Liverpool could hardly believe their stroke of fortune and the fact that it was a precious away goal seemed to increase the home side's frustration. Now Roma pushed forward but without any great penetration, and it was Liverpool who looked more likely to score, Barmby climaxing an incisive counter-attack by driving over following a sweet lay-off from Ziege.

Increasingly desperate, the Italians threw on both Assunção and Batistuta, but it was the Reds who struck again through Owen, who stooped to guide in a far-post header following McAllister's cross. Then Liverpool might have made the tie safe when Barmby found himself clean through, but he shot against Antonioli's legs. Still, a 2-0 victory in Rome was a remarkable achievement and Owen, back on form after months of injury problems, could not resist a pop at his critics. 'Maybe there was the need for me to shut people up, though not the people who matter. The manager and my team-mates have never been the problem.'

Between the two legs, Liverpool shoe-horned a fifth-round FA Cup tie against Manchester City at Anfield, and they ran out 4-2 winners to keep their triple-pronged cup run nicely on the boil. But this match was overshadowed by the thunderous build-up for the showdown with Roma a few days hence. Coach Fabio Capello made noises about 'protecting Roma's reputation' but the absence of Aldair, Cafu, Emerson and Totti (still suffering from his diplomatic flu) could only help Liverpool's chances of reaching the last eight of the competition. With the stadium virtually full and the crowd in fine voice, both teams set about their work with a succession of shuddering tackles and wild challenges. Liverpool were content to defend in depth and were lucky not to go behind when they were caught square by Nakata's through-ball. The Reds' hearts were in their mouths as Delvecchio carefully placed the ball to Westerveld's left but, fortunately for Liverpool, it skidded a hair's breadth wide of the post.

The outcome should have been resolved on the hour when Zebina held back Heskey in the penalty area, but Michael Owen's soft penalty was saved comfortably by Antonioli, diving to his right. Inevitably, this escape roused the visitors, and Capello introduced Batistuta and Guigou to the fray. While all eyes were on the Argentinian legend, it was his fellow substitute who changed the tenor of the contest with a glorious 25-yard strike that screamed past Westerveld. This high-octane encounter exploded again on 77 minutes when Montella's attempted cross into the Liverpool box struck Markus Babbel on the forearm and ran harmlessly into touch. For a moment the Kop fell silent as referee Garcia-Aranda pointed to the spot. However, a Roma player was already preparing artlessly to take the ball for a corner-kick, and this may have swayed the Spanish official as then he pointed towards the corner flag in confirmation. Immediately he was surrounded by a posse of furious Roma players protesting his decision. Farcically, the yellow card was waved in the faces of at least four Italians, and skipper Tommasi appeared to be shown his yellow twice. The referee, however, was unmoved and the corner was cleared, leaving Liverpool to regroup and assume some semblance of control amidst the chaos. Eventually Tommasi was given his just reward, being dismissed for yet another cynical foul, and the Roma captain shook the referee's hand mockingly as he departed. A wave of relief swept around Anfield when the final whistle blew and Liverpudlians knew in their hearts that it had been a mighty close call.

There was no time to celebrate, however, for just three days later the Reds were due to face Birmingham City in the final of the Worthington Cup. It was a wet and overcast Cardiff that welcomed the two sides to the Millennium Stadium, which was packed with 73,500 excited supporters. Any thoughts that the Reds might cruise to victory against their First Division opposition were dispelled as Birmingham rose magnificently to the challenge, taking the Reds every inch of the way in a dramatically compelling match. Robbie Fowler's sublime goal after half an hour, when he volleyed over City 'keeper Ian Bennett from the edge of the box, seemed to put Liverpool in control, but the Blues refused to buckle and gained a deserved lifeline when Henchoz scythed down Martin O'Connor to concede an injury-time penalty. Darren Purse converted nervelessly from the spot to take the match into extra-time, during which it seemed Liverpool's recent European exertions were about to catch up with them. However, the experienced Germans, Hamann and Babbel, steadied the ship, and the game went to a penalty shoot-out. Westerveld excelled himself as Liverpool held their composure to win 5-4 and a relieved Gérard Houllier could celebrate the lifting of his first trophy only 13 months

Robbie Fowler, who contributed fabulous goals in two of Liverpool's three triumphant cup finals during the unforgettable springtime of 2001. Ahead lay the formidable challenge of claiming a regular berth in the Reds' front line.

Above: Anyone for cards? Referee Garcia-Aranda prepares to brandish yellow at Tommasi after the Roma skipper had begged to differ over the outcome of a late and controversial penalty appeal.

Right: Markus Babbel denies space to the dangerous Vincent Candela as Liverpool's Anfield showdown with Roma approaches its chaotic climax.

after taking sole control of the team.

For the Frenchman the satisfaction was immense. Often he had endured a hostile press, as well as criticism from a handful of former Liverpool greats, who had their own opinions on the modern fortunes of their beloved club. That illustrious group had needled the manager, who before the semi-final return against Crystal Palace responded to Ian Rush's comment that Liverpool needed to finish the season with a trophy. Houllier disagreed, and added politely: 'Ian is one of two or three writers who are very nice to us; the rest sometimes make me wish I could be working at other clubs. We know the level of competition is higher and tighter now. You need greater confidence and experience to win things than you did in the past. It took Manchester United three and a half years to win anything (after Alex Ferguson took over); we have been going for two years and a half.'

It had been a breathless time for Liverpool, who had played nine matches in just over a month since beating Crystal Palace, but if the players were tired, they would have little time for recuperation as European action beckoned once again in the form of a quarter-final visit to Porto. The Merseysiders approached the match looking for a repeat of the first leg in Rome, aiming to plunder a goal or two to take back to Anfield. Gérard Houllier was in optimistic mood before flying to Portugal with the team: 'We have a very good strike-force and we have to play on that. There are only five games where we haven't scored this season and we would like to score over there. I believe that the first game of two legs is very important, because it determines what will happen in the tie. Hopefully we can get a goal or two.' As ever, the manager preached a note of caution, commenting on Liverpool's opponents: 'They've beaten Nantes, who are on top of the table in France, and that tells you everything. They are a good passing side, have good skills on the ball and use an unusual system, with two wingers, that suits them. It will not be easy for us.'

Heavy rainfall in the north of Portugal had left the Estadio des Antas pitch saturated but playable, and with the conditions more reminiscent of Merseyside, both sides indulged in their customary passing games. Liverpool were content to let the home side make the running, but Porto were unable to find a way past the Reds' formidable back four of Babbel, Henchoz, Hyypia and Carragher. Indeed, Westerveld had only one save of note to make in the first half. In contrast, his opposite number, Ovchinnikov, had to be alert on a number of occasions to deny both Fowler and Owen. The hosts enjoyed slightly more of the game in the second half, but with the Reds' rearguard again easily rebuffing Porto's often laboured approach, Gérard Houllier, despite his desire for an away goal, could rest relatively satisfied with a 0-0 scoreline. On the other hand, Porto coach Fernando Santos had plenty to muse upon after his side's lifeless display failed to gain them a much-needed advantage to take to Anfield.

Sandwiched between the meetings with Porto, the Reds faced a tricky FA Cup quarter-final against Tranmere Rovers at Prenton Park. Managed by the former Liverpool hero John Aldridge, Tranmere had earned a reputation as giant-killers in recent seasons, and already had chalked up one extraordinary FA Cup triumph. Finding themselves three down to Premiership side Southampton at half-time, Tranmere somehow fashioned a sensational 4-3 victory thanks to a hat-trick from ex-Everton striker Paul Rideout. Liverpool made somewhat hard work of this potential banana-skin, winning 4-2 but at the cost of an ankle injury which was to blight the remainder of Nick Barmby's season.

Back in the Continental arena, Porto coach Santos was in defiant mood as he brought his team to Liverpool, citing Roma's away performance as one his side could emulate. 'After seeing that game, we think victory is possible,' said Santos, who added: 'Liverpool are not a typically English side and they are able to play a very tight compact game, even at home. We would have hoped to win in Portugal and bring something to Liverpool, but I am confident we will not be intimidated by the crowd at Anfield; Porto are a world-class side.' Santos made six changes to his starting line-up but Porto, nicknamed the Dragons, were soon put to the sword by the on-form Reds, who seized command from the off. Danny Murphy, replacing Ziege down the left flank, opened the scoring on 33 minutes when he seemed to control a long, raking cross from Gerrard with his arm before drilling a low shot across the goalkeeper. Murphy's contribution to the cause had been growing as the season progressed. Having started the

Below: **Danny Murphy, who made massive personal strides during Liverpool's treble-winning season, at one point being spoken of as a contender for full England recognition.**

Splashing out: Steven Gerrard, arguably the most complete midfield talent to emerge in the English game for many a long year, makes light of the Portuguese puddles to curl the ball away from the tenacious Pena at the rain-sodden Estadio des Antas.

campaign as a serial substitute, gradually he had become an important member of the side, thanks to his adaptability, industry and willingness to carry out his manager's tactical ploys. The midfielder had faced a bleak future during Houllier's first term in charge, and he was loaned back to his former club, Crewe Alexandra. Happily, the slate was wiped clean for the Chester-born Murphy and he returned to the fold with a new and ultra-positive attitude, blossoming under the manager's watchful eye. Indeed, during the Reds' momentous cup chase, he was unlucky to receive a mid-season injury at a time when there was serious talk of his elevation to the England squad.

Already among the international elite were Michael Owen and Steven Gerrard, and the England pair fashioned a second goal before half-time which virtually settled Porto's fate. Gerrard had already unleashed a dipping 25-yarder which 'keeper Espinha had tipped over, then provided Murphy with his chance to take the opener, when he clipped a first-time curling cross which was headed down and into the net by Owen. Gerrard strode majestically at the hub of the action, dominating proceedings in a manner which had the Liverpool fans practically purring with satisfaction. Despite his appearances being limited by niggling injuries, the still-growing Merseysider evoked memories of no less a giant than the late Duncan Edwards. To be compared to such a magnificent talent was praise of the highest order, but the boy remained unfazed by the adulation. He preferred to let his actions speak for him and his play could hardly have been more eloquent. Strong and clean in the tackle, powerful in the air, a

Above: No respecter of reputations, Jamie Carragher deals summarily with Rivaldo at the Nou Camp.

Right: The Red legions were delighted to be back in Rome, and they showed it.

magnificent passer of the ball and the possessor of a lethal shot from distance, Steven Gerrard has every ingredient necessary to become a genuinely world-class performer. For the present, though, he needs to be nurtured, as his developing body adapts to the tremendous physical demands he places on it. While Gerrard's performance against Porto drew the bulk of the plaudits, the rest of the Liverpool side were not far behind him, and only the overworked Espinha prevented a rout as the Reds sailed towards the semi-finals and a glamour tie with Barcelona.

In truth, the mighty Catalans' reputation somewhat exceeded their recent deeds but, despite a sequence of failures in the Champions League, such attacking riches as Rivaldo, Kluivert, Luis Enrique and Overmars were bound to cause concern to any opponents. Much would depend on whether they could conjure up the sort of form which had seen Leeds hit for four goals, AEK Athens for five, and Atletico Bilbao for seven; or would they turn in the type of meek performances seen against Spanish minnows Numancia and Villarreal? As Barcelona had failed to score at the Nou Camp only twice during the season – once against Milan in the Champions League and on the other occasion in the Spanish Cup when faced by unsung Torrelavega – Liverpool were not underestimating the challenge ahead, but such was the recent improvement in the Reds' defence, Houllier had every confidence that his players would cope. There was one unhappy figure in the Merseyside camp, however. Christian Ziege, having lost his place to Jamie Carragher, had voiced his discontent to the German media after a recent international match and was put firmly in his place by Houllier. In no uncertain terms, the Frenchman told Ziege to shut up and accused him of lacking respect for his team-mates.

Such is the bizarre nature of modern football that the game is ruled by television, and kick-off times are routinely switched to suit the schedules rather than the fans who pay through the turnstiles and travel vast distances to do so. With the BBC paying handsomely to cover the match, Barcelona were only too happy to comply with Auntie's request to delay the start until 8.15 pm. After all, it was to accommodate an event of truly global importance, an extended episode of *EastEnders* with the storyline 'Who shot Phil Mitchell?'

The Nou Camp is one of soccer's cherished shrines, a veritable cathedral of the game, and without doubt every professional would dream of playing in front of the passionate Catalan crowd at some point during their career. Keegan, Clemence, Smith, Callaghan, Toshack . . . they were just a few of Bob Paisley's now-legendary Reds who had pulled off a sensational win back in 1976, on their way to a second UEFA Cup triumph. Now it was time for the class of 2001 to exorcise those revered ghosts, whose memories will be forever treasured but who had weighed heavily on the shoulders of successive Liverpool combinations of more recent vintage.

When the game got under way, Houllier's 4-5-1 formation signalled his intention of not allowing Barcelona the luxury of time and space anywhere across the pitch. Although the home side showed some supple and fluid play, it foundered repeatedly on the rock of Sami Hyypia, who was inspirational at the heart of defence. Even when drawn out of the penalty area to make saving interceptions, his timing was perfect and his tackles shudderingly hard but impeccably fair. Certainly Rivaldo and Kluivert did not relish the physical skirmishes with the giant Finn or his formidable partner, Stéphane Henchoz. Nor did Marc Overmars get much change from Markus Babbel, and eventually the former Arsenal favourite trailed off in dejection, to be replaced by fellow Dutch international flankman Boudewijn Zenden. On the left flank Jamie Carragher proved his mettle yet again, offering no space to Luis Enrique when, for once, a clear opening appeared. Up front, Michael Owen ran his socks off without receiving a ball that utilised his exceptional talents, while Emile Heskey occupied a largely defensive midfield role, except for his occasional forays forward at set-pieces. As a spectacle, it was not pretty, but in Liverpool's disciplined performance on that Nou Camp night, every one of the 14 players who entered the action put in top-quality performances which would have left Shankly, Paisley or Fagan with little cause for complaint.

Once again Houllier had to turn his attentions elsewhere as the team flew back for yet another big match on the following Sunday. Luckily the Reds had drawn giant-killers Wycombe Wanderers in the FA Cup semi final, and though the Chairboys were expertly

Catalonia has nothing on this! The Kop in full voice for the visit of Barcelona.

guided by manager Lawrie Sanchez – the man who, we were told endlessly in the pre-match build-up, scored the winner for Wimbledon against the Reds in the 1988 FA Cup Final – everyone at Anfield had been mightily relieved that both Arsenal and Tottenham had been avoided. In a tense game, Wycombe stretched every sinew, and a below-par Liverpool struggled to gain the ascendancy on a wet and windy Villa Park pitch. Second-half goals from Fowler and Heskey had the favourites coasting to the final until a late reply from Keith Ryan caused yet another few minutes of high blood-pressure for the increasingly edgy Liverpool faithful.

At this stage the Merseysiders' fixture congestion was becoming something of a problem. Starting with the Wycombe game, they were forced to play five crucial matches in 12 days, and they were not happy about it. Despite protests from Gérard Houllier and chief executive Rick Parry, Liverpool had to face Ipswich at Portman Road just 48 hours after the FA Cup semi-final, and it was to their enormous credit that they emerged with a 1-1 draw, before lining up against Leeds United at Anfield three days later on Good Friday. With the third Champions League slot still up for grabs, the Reds were dealt what appeared to be a mortal blow to their aspirations when they were comprehensively outplayed, suffering a 2-1 reverse at the hands of David O'Leary's enterprising young side. Even then Liverpool could not set their sights on the Barcelona return because on Easter Monday they faced Everton at Goodison Park. In yet another incident-packed encounter, the Reds led twice, only to be pegged back by their tenacious local rivals. Both sides needed three points for their respective battles at opposite ends of the table, and with Liverpool reduced to ten men following Biscan's dismissal, it seemed that they were going to have to make do with a point each as the drama stretched into the 93rd minute. Then Gary McAllister, over the ball for a free kick which was sure to be the last action in the match, spotted Everton 'keeper Paul Gerrard standing to one end of his goal. The wily Scot planted a perfect dispatch into the opposite side of the net from fully 40 yards to score perhaps the most sensational winner ever seen in a Merseyside derby. Psychologically it was a massive boost for the Reds, whose dreams of the Champions League were still just alive, and the last-gasp win over the old enemy provided the perfect spur to shrug off the physical tiredness and mental fatigue that might have set in had they been deprived of victory.

Barcelona arrived at Anfield smarting from a couple of 4-4 draws, the second of which, against Zaragoza, ended their chance of winning *La Liga*. But beleaguered coach Llorenc Serra Ferrer but on a brave face before the match: 'I hope my players produce the creativity they are capable of,' he said. 'The supporters will be disappointed if we concede more goals.' Houllier, for his part, was somewhat wearily defending his first-leg tactics to the legion of Spanish journalists who had arrived for the game. 'On their day Barcelona can be awesome. That's why we gave them the respect they deserved in the Nou Camp. The fact that we managed to get a draw keeps our chances open. They have probably one of the best attacking quartets in Europe and they won't change their philosophy at Anfield. They were not happy about the way we played in the first leg but they should take it as a compliment.'

A heaving Anfield was bedecked with flags and banners and tingling with excitement as both teams contested the match with a vigour that befitted the occasion. As Houllier had predicted, Barcelona could not forsake their attacking instincts, and soon the silky skills of Rivaldo were giving cause for concern. In the eighth minute the Brazilian unleashed a dipping shot from 30 yards that brought a superb save from Sander Westerveld, but Liverpool's only other first-half scare came when Overmars, for once escaping Babbel's close attentions, fashioned a clear-cut chance for Luis Enrique. Luckily the Reds escaped punishment as the ensuing shot ran just wide. The game appeared to be drifting goalless to the interval until the Reds forced a corner and Gary McAllister sent in a searching cross looking for the head of Sami Hyypia. Unaccountably Patrick Kluivert panicked and palmed the ball away, leaving Swiss referee Urs Meier with no alternative but to point to the spot. Duly McAllister sent the 'keeper the wrong way with a perfectly executed penalty.

Having gained such a precious advantage, the Reds were not prepared to risk losing their slender lead in the second half. They had a narrow escape ten minutes after the interval when

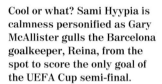

Cool or what? Sami Hyypia is calmness personified as Gary McAllister gulls the Barcelona goalkeeper, Reina, from the spot to score the only goal of the UEFA Cup semi-final.

Dani is desperate but he is beaten by Dietmar Hamann as Liverpool tighten their grip on proceedings against Barcelona at Anfield.

Westerveld, attempting to deal with a back-pass, missed his kick with potentially calamitous consequences. Happily, the Dutchman escaped punishment as Kluivert just failed to reach the ball before it ran over the goal line. Despite the constant promptings of Emmanuel Petit and Josep Guardiola, Barcelona rarely found the time and space to penetrate Liverpool's defensive shield. Steven Gerrard, who was struggling for fitness, was replaced by Danny Murphy and Michael Owen was withdrawn in favour of Patrik Berger as the Reds reverted to the 4-5-1 formation that had served them so well in the first-leg. Emile Heskey's lone presence up front kept the Spaniards' defence occupied, while in midfield Dietmar Hamann and Gary McAllister maintained a vice-like grip. Once again stopper supreme Sami Hyypia, dealt imperiously with everything that came his way, and his partner Stéphane Henchoz was awesome in performing clinical interceptions which left multi-talented but disjointed Barcelona with nothing to feed on. Afterwards Serra Ferrer paid due credit to Houllier's tactical acumen. 'They made us look like a kick-and-rush team,' he admitted. Without undue exaggeration, every Liverpool player was a hero, and the burden of the past had been eased just a little on the current team who, by reaching three finals in the same season, had fashioned their own piece of history. The outstanding Hyypia spoke for his colleagues: 'Every player here is aware of the achievements of the teams of the 1970s and 1980s, and everyone here is determined to do their utmost to match them.'

Houllier refused to bask in the night's glory, however, as he turned his attentions away from the glittering silverware so tantalisingly close at hand, instead mustering his troops for a concerted attack on claiming the Champions League place that had slipped away the previous season. A punishing schedule of five matches in 15 days saw the Reds beat Tottenham Hotspur 3-1, Coventry City 2-0, Bradford City 2-0 and Newcastle United 3-0 before being frustrated by Chelsea at Anfield when the Londoners twice came from behind to force a

2-2 draw. This left just one League match, at Charlton, to complete but by then Liverpool had earned a crucial advantage over their rivals, knowing that triumph at the Valley would guarantee them the much-craved Champions League berth. At the outset of the season this had been the club's main target, and it had been pursued with little short of fanaticism by Gérard Houllier. 'We finished fourth last season, so we want to do better this time around,' he declared.

With the season reaching its pulsating climax, talk among Reds supporters produced contrasting opinions over exactly what constituted success, and there was especially heated debate on the way that every competition had become secondary in importance to the Champions League. Even Manchester United, for so long omnipotent domestically, seemed all-consumed by their desire to add to their single Champions League triumph of 1999. Perhaps it was natural that some Liverpool fans would gladly trade all the cups for a crack at the world's leading club competition, but the more traditional voices were raised in favour of glory now rather than rely on some distant promise in the future. After all, much of the season had been spent in a state of high tension, watching some thrilling football played by a team at long last throwing off the shackles of their recent unsuccessful history. Fortunately, Houllier still had both options to aim at. 'I'm aware that this is just the start,' he said, 'but also I know that this is how Manchester United began their incredible run. They won the FA Cup, the Cup Winners' Cup and then got stronger and stronger before reaching their current position. I hope that what is happening here now is sowing the seeds for our own exciting future.' So, effectively, the Reds faced three cup finals in eight days which would decide everything. Would their tremendous efforts receive tangible reward, or would the campaign be remembered only for what might have been?

Whatever, tired old Wembley was barely given a second thought as Reds supporters descended on Cardiff for the second time in three months, this time to to play Arsenal in the FA Cup Final. On a beautiful sunny day, the Millennium Stadium provided a fabulous stage for the first non-Wembley final (with the exception of one replay) since 1922. One fascinating aspect of the encounter was the collision of the rival managers, Arsène Wenger and Gérard Houllier, two great friends who for this afternoon, at least, would be seeking to upstage one another. At first it seemed as though Wenger would come out on top as, virtually from kick-off, Liverpool were distinctly second-best to an Arsenal side prompted by the imperious Patrick Vieira. Indeed, the Reds were fortunate to escape punishment early on when Thierry Henry's goal-bound shot was deflected wide via the arm of Stéphane Henchoz. The referee waved away appeals for a penalty, but still the sluggish Merseysiders seemed unable to find a way into the match.

Liverpool's goal continued to lead a charmed life, Hyypia clearing from his line on three occasions, and when Fredrik Ljungberg finally made the breakthrough on 72 minutes it seemed that there could be no way back for the Reds. Surely, now, their dream of a cup treble was about to be dashed. However, in the final ten minutes the script was comprehensively rewritten by two flashes of absolute brilliance from Michael Owen. He pounced first on 82 minutes when, following Babbel's knock-down, the instinctive predator swivelled to hit a waist-high, right-foot volley through a crowded six-yard box into the far corner of David Seaman's net. The equaliser seemed to knock the stuffing from the Gunners and they were spiked with just two minutes remaining. Patrik Berger's superb long-distance pass found Owen in full flight and, shrugging off the challenges of Lee Dixon and Tony Adams, the mercurial marksman contrived to squeeze a curling left-foot shot beyond Seaman's despairing dive. The stadium seemed to shake to its very foundations.

True, it could be said that Liverpool were lucky, but they never buckled in the face of Arsenal's territorial dominance and eventually they took their chances while their opponents squandered theirs. Also, it is apposite to recall, there had been previous gala occasions on which the balance of play had been all Liverpool's, only for fate to betray them cruelly. For example, seasoned fans could well remember the misery of losing FA Cup Finals in both 1971 (to Arsenal) and 1977 (to Manchester United) when the rub of the green did not favour the Reds. Quite simply, this time it was their turn. So, with two cups already tucked away safely in the trophy cabinet, it was off to Dortmund for the UEFA Cup Final. Liverpool travelled to

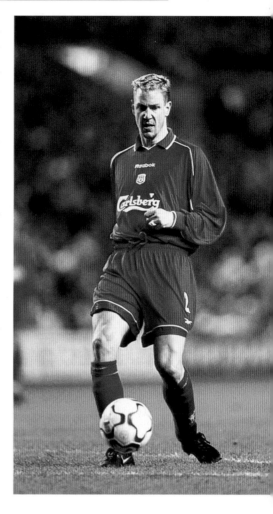

Stéphane Henchoz, who, together with Hyypia, is usually a pillar of unruffled efficiency in defence.

Men of destiny: the starting line-up for the UEFA Cup Final against Alavés. Back row, left to right: Henchoz, Hyypia, Heskey, Westerveld, Babbel, McAllister, Hamann. Front: Owen, Murphy, Gerrard and Carragher.

the Ruhr in Germany's industrial heartland to take on Alavés, the little-known surprise packet of the tournament. The Spanish side had risen swiftly from the third division under the paternal guidance of coach José Manual Esnal, who had skilfully blended a number of players rejected by more glamorous clubs. He had instilled a self-belief and wonderful team spirit that had carried his men all the way to the final. A 9-2 aggregate victory over Kaiserslautern in the semi-final indicated that Alavés were not to be taken lightly and they boasted lethal forwards in Javi Moreno and the young Uruguayan Ivan Alonso.

The atmosphere in the Westfalenstadion was electric with two sets of mercifully good-humoured supporters in full voice, unaware that they were about to witness a sporting drama which would go down in history. The counter-attacking Alavés lined up with an extra defender in a 3-4-2-1 formation, but found themselves behind in the fourth minute when Babbel rose at the far post to head home McAllister's perfectly flighted free kick. The Spanish team seemed to have frozen with fear due to the magnitude of the occasion, and when Owen released Gerrard to put Liverpool 2-0 up in the 16th minute, a rout seemed likely.

Esnal had other ideas and acted swiftly to redress the situation, bringing off defender Dan Eggen and replacing him with forward Alonso, thus reverting to a 4-3-3 formation. It proved to be an inspired substitution because within four minutes the Uruguayan had climbed above Babbel at the far post to head Contra's measured cross past a startled Westerveld. This signalled a period of concerted Alavés pressure and only a succession of last-ditch tackles from Hyypia and company, and some timely saves from Westerveld, prevented the plucky Spaniards from drawing level. Now, though, Alavés found themselves open to the counter-attack. Gary McAllister, having sprung a shaky offside trap, wasted a good opportunity, then five minutes before the break Michael Owen found himself in space on the edge of the box. Goalkeeper Herrera panicked and hauled down the striker, leaving the unflappable 'Macca' to stroke in the penalty.

At half-time, with his side 3-1 to the good, Houllier had time to reorganise and close up the game, but soon his plans were in ruins as the underdogs drew level within six minutes. Full back Contra was again the provider for his team's second, turning Jamie Carragher inside

Left: **Penalty! A split second after this picture was taken, the hurtling Michael Owen was brought down by the hopelessly wrong-footed Alavés 'keeper, Herrera.**

Below: **Gary McAllister seems rather pleased after duly dispatching the spot-kick, thus restoring the Reds' two-goal advantage shortly before half-time in the final.**

Above: **Cometh the hour, cometh the man. After rising from the bench to put the Reds 4-3 ahead with a stunning individual effort, Robbie Fowler gives full vent to his feelings with substitutes Gregory Vignal and Nick Barmby, while Steven Gerrard gets in on the act.**

out before crossing for Javi Moreno to soar over Gerrard and head home. Three minutes later Henchoz fouled Alonso, conceding a free-kick on the edge of the box, and Moreno drilled a low shot under the Reds' defensive wall, past the wrong-footed Westerveld. Houllier reacted smartly, bringing on Vladimir Smicer to replace the struggling Henchoz, with Babbel moving into the centre of defence and Gerrard dropping into the right-back slot. On 65 minutes came two more substitutions which were to have significant ramifications for both sides. The dangerous Moreno was replaced by Pablo Gomez, thereby reducing the Alavés threat, and Robbie Fowler came on for Heskey. Within seven minutes the Kopites' hero had delivered a goal of the very highest quality, taking McAllister's superb through-ball and drifting past several defenders before coolly slotting a low shot into the corner of the net. It was a strike worthy of winning any final, and with Berger brought on to reinforce the midfield in place of

Right: **A sight to make the Reds' blood run cold. Alavés striker Javi Moreno celebrates his equaliser but, rather astonishingly, it wasn't long before the two-goal marksman was substituted by coach Esnal.**

Owen, Gérard Houllier must have been confident that his side could weather the final ten minutes.

Clearly Alavés had not read that particular storyline and with the final minute of normal time approaching, a Pablo Gomez corner was met by Jordi Cruyff, who beat the groping Sander Westerveld at the near post to snatch a dramatic equaliser. Now, as in the Worthington Cup Final, Liverpool found themselves with the prospect of playing extra-time after victory had been snatched away at the death. With the possibility of a golden goal deciding the match, the added period was approached with a caution which had been conspicuously absent during the initial 90 minutes. However, Alavés were living dangerously and as tiredness crept in, so the timing of challenges became increasingly errant, and two of their number were sent off by referee Veissierre. Incidentally, he was the same official who had red-carded both McManaman and Ince in the 1998 fracas with Valencia.

With only four minutes remaining, and the game seemingly heading for a penalty shoot-out, McAllister speared a wicked free-kick into the Spaniards' box and the ball glanced off the head of the wretchedly unfortunate Geli before nestling in the Alavés net. For an almost

Above: **The fateful moment when Geli glanced the ball over his own 'keeper for the decisive 'golden goal.' Had he failed to make contact, though, it should be mentioned that Babbel and Hamann were lurking at the far post.**

surreal fraction of a second, time seemed to stand still, and then came utter pandemonium as McAllister was buried under his team-mates on the touchline. Liverpool had achieved an historic cup treble on a night when football was the winner. Alavés may have lost, but they had won many friends, not only on Merseyside but all across Europe, with their exciting football. Certainly, everyone would know all about the little Basque team from Vitoria now.

For those who preferred silverware on the Anfield table to points in a Champions League table, it was a night to savour. Rick Parry, Liverpool's chief executive, put his finger on what made the club tick: 'We need to be businesslike, but first and foremost we are a football club. Liverpool is about winning trophies. Look at the players and supporters. You don't get celebrations like that for coming third in the Premiership.'

With the cup treble accomplished, the Reds were faced with one final hurdle, a testing match at Charlton, but one with a massive prize on offer, a place in the Champions League. During the first half, the cup kings appeared to be suffering from the cumulative aftermath of their recent toils and were lucky not to be out of contention by the interval. Gérard Houllier restored order at the break, though, and it was a different Liverpool who marched out for the restart. Four second-half goals ensured that the season would end on a rousing note with all their targets achieved. They had played a total of 63 matches, including no fewer than 25 cup ties across the three competitions.

Still, Houllier would be the first to admit that, despite a season of such extravagant success, the job of restoring Liverpool to their previous exalted status was not yet complete. But, crucially, he had taken command of the club and stamped his philosophy on the players. As he put it: 'When I came I was described as a revolutionary with a guillotine. Actually I prefer to convince people rather than dictate. But if I can't convince then I have to dictate.'

Who would have thought that the young French teacher who stood on the Kop to watch the 10-0 massacre of Dundalk in September 1969 would, some three decades later, be setting the football curriculum with a Continental touch at Anfield? *Vive La Revolution!*

Contrasting emotions at the death. Gary McAllister *(above right)* **is mobbed by his team-mates on the touchline, while two Alavés players lie prone in despair and disbelief.**

Round 1 - 1st leg
14 September 2000

RAPID BUCHAREST 0

LIVERPOOL 1
Barmby 29
H-T 0-1. Crowd 12,000

WESTERVELD
SONG
HENCHOZ
BABBEL
ZIEGE (TRAORÉ)
BARMBY
CARRAGHER
HAMANN
DIOMÈDE
OWEN (FOWLER)
HESKEY (MURPHY)

Liverpool's return to European action after a year's absence opened on a positive note with a hard-fought, but deserved, 1-0 win in Bucharest. With Barmby and Owen in outstanding form, the Reds posed plenty of problems for the home side and created enough chances to have wrapped up the game long before the final whistle. Barmby had already hit the angle of bar and post with a 20-yard shot when Liverpool drew first blood. Ziege released Owen on the halfway line and the England striker drove past three defenders into the heart of the penalty area before coolly passing for Barmby to finish. After missing several chances early in the second half, the Reds held off an attempted Rapid comeback late in the game, and it was only resolute defending that ensured a clean sheet.

Round 1 - 2nd leg
28 September 2000

LIVERPOOL 0

RAPID BUCHAREST 0
Crowd 37,954

WESTERVELD
HEGGEM
BABBEL
HYYPIA
TRAORÉ (ZIEGE)
GERRARD
HAMANN
BERGER
DIOMÈDE (BARMBY)
FOWLER
OWEN

Liverpool did enough to move into the next round with a moderate display against Rapid Bucharest at Anfield. With both sides failing to break the deadlock on the night, Barmby's first-leg goal proved enough to settle the tie. To the Scousers' delight, Fowler started his first game of the season but, lacking match practice, he failed to take advantage of the few chances that came his way. With Pancu operating as a lone striker, Rapid gained midfield control as the first half progressed, and, with better finishing, they could have taken the lead before the break. Only when Barmby and Ziege were introduced soon after half-time did the game swing back towards the Reds who, having gained the ascendancy, laid siege to the Rapid goal. Gerrard, Ziege and Owen were all on target with shots, but they were unable to beat Lucescu as an uninspiring game petered out.

Liverpool won 1-0 on aggregate.

Round 2 - 1st leg
26 October 2000

LIVERPOOL 1
Heskey 87

SLOVAN LIBEREC 0
H-T 0-0. Crowd 29,662

WESTERVELD
CARRAGHER
HENCHOZ
BABBEL
ZIEGE
SMICER (BARMBY)
MURPHY (McALLISTER)
HAMANN
BERGER
FOWLER
HESKEY

Against moderate opposition, Liverpool laboured heavily to achieve a slender victory, courtesy of a late goal by Heskey. The Reds created, and missed, a series of chances and Fowler was the chief culprit, spurning several first-half openings. Also he contrived, once again, to miss a penalty, this time in the second period after Hamann was bundled over in the area. Liberec seemed happy to keep Liverpool out, and were barely seen as an attacking force as the home side camped in their half. The palpable frustration of the crowd could be felt as the evening wore on, with Hamann and Berger shooting wide and 'keeper Hauzr making a fine double save from Murphy and Smicer. Heskey's crucial goal, stabbed home after 87 minutes, at least sent the fans home with a win to celebrate, but it had been a hugely unedifying night.

Round 2 - 2nd leg
9 November 2000

SLOVAN LIBEREC 2
Stajner 9; Breda 85

LIVERPOOL 3
Barmby 30; Heskey 75; Owen 82
H-T 1-1. Crowd 6,808

WESTERVELD
CARRAGHER (MURPHY)
BABBEL
HYYPIA
ZIEGE
SMICER
HAMANN (OWEN)
GERRARD
BARMBY
HESKEY
FOWLER (McALLISTER)

Having failed to build a decisive advantage in the first leg, Liverpool were pegged back to level terms after just nine minutes when Stajner raced into the box unmarked to plant a fine header past Westerveld. But Heskey was proving a powerful presence in attack, and after yet another foul on him by the physical Czechs had yielded a free-kick, Ziege produced an accurate cross for Barmby to equalise at the far post. Heskey continued to prove a real handful, hitting an upright shortly before the break, then being frustrated at the start of the second half by a brilliant save from 'keeper Hauzr. The big striker was not to be denied, however, and on 75 minutes he forced home a cross from Smicer. With Liverpool cruising to victory, Owen replaced Hamann and within seconds he rifled a goal with a deflected shot. Liberec brought on substitute Breda who emulated Owen's feat by netting within a minute of his introduction.

Liverpool won 4-2 on aggregate.

Round 3 - 1st leg
23 November 2000

OLYMPIAKOS 2

Alexandris 65, 90

LIVERPOOL 2

Barmby 38; Gerrard 67
H-T 0-1. Crowd 43,855

WESTERVELD
CARRAGHER
BABBEL
HYYPIA
TRAORÉ (STAUNTON)
MURPHY (McALLISTER)
GERRARD
HAMANN
BARMBY
HESKEY
OWEN (SMICER)

After making heavy weather of progressing through the first two rounds, Liverpool faced a stiff task against an Olympiakos side boasting a proud home record of 15 Champions League matches without defeat. Although they embellished this sequence courtesy of an injury-time equaliser by Alexandris, the Greeks were outplayed by a vibrant Liverpool side who silenced the home support for long periods. Barmby stunned Olympiakos with a fine opportunist's goal on 38 minutes after Heskey had flicked on Carragher's throw, and the former Evertonian hit the woodwork early in the second half before the Greeks regrouped and grabbed an equaliser via an overhead kick by Alexandris. The home supporters erupted, but within minutes Liverpool were back in front when Gerrard powered in a header from Barmby's corner. Although Babbel's rare slip allowed Alexandris in for that late leveller, the Reds left the Olympic Stadium confident of finishing the job at Anfield.

Round 3 - 2nd leg
7 December 2000

LIVERPOOL 2

Heskey 28; Barmby 60

OLYMPIAKOS 0

H-T 1-0. Crowd 35,484

WESTERVELD
BABBEL
HENCHOZ
HYYPIA
CARRAGHER
BARMBY
GERRARD (McALLISTER)
HAMANN
MURPHY (ZIEGE)
SMICER
HESKEY

Liverpool demonstrated the striking riches at their disposal by resting both Owen and Fowler, leaving Heskey to spearhead the attack, yet still they seemed capable of playing for long stretches at less than full throttle. Nevertheless, they established early control and after Gerrard's thunderous shot had been splendidly tipped over by Eleftheropoulos, Barmby broke the Olympiakos offside trap to release Heskey, who tucked away his chance with great confidence. In the second half a goalbound header from Hyypia was cleared off the line before the Reds effectively wrapped up the tie with a goal of the highest class by Barmby.

Sent clear on the overlap by Murphy's pass, the England man skipped round a desperate lunge by the 'keeper, then dispatched a left-footer from an acute angle that clipped the near post before nestling in the opposite side of the net. Some 3,000 Greek fans, who had supported their team noisily throughout, finally fell silent and were largely unmoved when a seemingly legitimate appeal for a penalty against Westerveld at the Kop end was waved away.

Liverpool won 4-2 on aggregate

Round 4 - 1st leg
15 February 2001

ROMA 0

LIVERPOOL 2

Owen 46, 72
H-T 0-0. Crowd 59,718

WESTERVELD
CARRAGHER
BABBEL
HYYPIA
HENCHOZ
BARMBY
HAMANN
McALLISTER
ZIEGE (SMICER)
OWEN (LITMANEN)
FOWLER

Rome revisited, and the resilient Reds gained an unexpected and momentous victory that, at long last, stirred echoes of their glorious past. The game began fitfully with the Roma defence largely untroubled by the pairing of Owen and Fowler up front. McAllister and Hamann worked tirelessly in midfield to keep an unusually subdued home side in check as the first half passed largely without incident. The match came alive moments after the break when Rinaldi's casual crossfield pass was intercepted by Owen, who needed no invitation to drive low past Antonioli to give the Reds a precious lead. Liverpool were steeling themselves for a Roman assault but the Italians seemed unable to rouse themselves to a concerted response and Barmby might have doubled the score after Ziege's neat lay-off. Roma sent on Batistuta in the hope of rescuing the game, but it was Owen who had the final say, heading in McAllister's low cross to seal an improbable opportunistic victory for Liverpool.

Top left: **Liverpool's Djimi Traoré tangles with Daniel Christa of Rapid Bucharest.**

Below: **The long leg of the law. Sami Hyypia clears emphatically from Alexios Alexandris of Olympiakos at Anfield.**

Above: Like some gladiator of old, Sander Westerveld hails Liverpool's victory in the Olympic Stadium.

Right: No-go Batigol! Jamie Carragher (left) and Stéphane Henchoz block the way to goal for Roma's Gabriel Batistuta.

Round 4 - 2nd leg
22 February 2001

LIVERPOOL 0

ROMA 1
Guigou 70
H-T 0-0. Crowd 43,688

WESTERVELD
BABBEL
HENCHOZ
HYYPIA
CARRAGHER
BARMBY (FOWLER)
HAMANN
McALLISTER
ZIEGE
HESKEY
OWEN (SMICER)

Any thoughts that Roma were not taking the UEFA Cup seriously were dispelled in the second leg when they set about the Reds with a commitment underlined by a host of yellow cards. With a two-goal advantage, Liverpool were content to defend in depth, and were generally comfortable until Nakata set up a golden chance for Delvecchio, who placed his shot narrowly wide of the post with Westerveld flat-footed on his line. Then the Dutch 'keeper was called on to make a fine save from Montella's free-kick shortly before half-time. The Reds showed more attacking intent in the second half, with Heskey's pace proving troublesome to the visitors' rearguard. Not for the first time, Zebina pulled back the England striker and the referee pointed to the spot. Owen stepped up, but his tame effort was saved easily by Antonioli. This signalled the arrival of Batistuta from the bench, but his contribution was negligible and it was Guigou who crashed a 25-yard drive past Westerveld to wind up the tension. Referee Garcia-Aranda appeared to give a penalty to Roma after the ball was struck against Babbel's arm on the edge of the area but, eccentrically, he changed his mind and awarded a corner. As the match headed hysterically towards the finish, Tommasi shook the referee's hand after being dismissed for yet another cynical foul. In truth, Liverpool had ridden their luck; but Roma were out.

Liverpool won 2-1 on aggregate

Round 5 - 1st leg
8 March 2001

PORTO 0

LIVERPOOL 0
Crowd 21,150

WESTERVELD
BABBEL
HENCHOZ
HYYPIA
CARRAGHER
ZIEGE (MURPHY)
HAMANN
GERRARD
SMICER
OWEN (BARMBY)
FOWLER (HESKEY)

Heavy rain in Portugal left the pitch saturated and it was full credit to both teams that they contrived to play their neat passing football between the puddles of water. Porto pressed forward for much of the first half, but Westerveld was only troubled seriously towards the interval when he was forced to save from Chainho. Indeed, it was the Reds who had the better chances in the opening 45 minutes but both Owen and Fowler failed to convert when well placed. The second half began with Fowler manoeuvring himself into a good position but he couldn't quite find an angle to beat Ovchinnikov, and suddenly it was Porto who looked the more menacing. Certainly the hosts might have scored when Deco's astute pass sent Pena clear, but the striker hurried his shot and it skidded wide. Liverpool's developing side played out the rest of the game showing admirable defensive resilience in pursuit of a goalless draw.

Round 5 - 2nd leg
15 March 2001

LIVERPOOL 2
Murphy 33; Owen 37

PORTO 0
H-T 2-0. Crowd 40,502

WESTERVELD
BABBEL
HENCHOZ
HYYPIA
CARRAGHER
SMICER (LITMANEN)
HAMANN
GERRARD

MURPHY (ZIEGE)
OWEN
FOWLER (HESKEY)

Porto's rather lifeless performance of a week earlier resulted in coach Santos making six changes for his side's visit to Anfield. It was all to no avail, however, as the Portuguese were dispatched by a superlative Liverpool team who mixed incisive attacking with rock-solid defending. The Reds took the game by the throat and it was a surprise that it took 33 minutes to break the deadlock, Murphy firing in following a low, driven cross from Gerrard. The tie was over as a meaningful contest four minutes later when Gerrard fashioned another centre which Owen headed downwards so that the ball bounced at speed past startled 'keeper Espinha. Porto shuffled their pack once more for the second half, but it made little difference as the seemingly omnipotent Gerrard laboured prodigiously in the Reds' cause. Liverpool remained on course for a thrilling cup treble, and now mighty Barcelona were lying in wait.

Liverpool won 2-0 on aggregate.

Semi-final - first leg
5 April, 2001

BARCELONA 0

LIVERPOOL 0
Crowd 90,000

WESTERVELD
BABBEL
HENCHOZ
HYYPIA
CARRAGHER
MURPHY (SMICER)
HAMANN
GERRARD
BERGER (McALLISTER)
HESKEY
OWEN (FOWLER)

With the incomparable Nou Camp stadium filled near to capacity, Liverpool produced the kind of disciplined performance undreamed of in recent seasons as the defence, marshalled superbly by Hyypia, blunted the big-name stars of Barcelona. As a spectacle, the game offered few bright moments, with the fluid movement of the hosts being rebuffed by a sea of white shirts, and only once in the first half did Rivaldo threaten, his long-range drive sailing over the bar. The home fans' discontent was palpable, and Barcelona's laboured efforts to create an opening were greeted by whistles and catcalls from all quarters of the ground. Only twice during the season had the Spanish team failed to score at home and Liverpool's magnificent covering restricted them to a couple of shots by Sergi and Cocu, both of them off target. With sections of the crowd drifting away long before final whistle, the Reds had gained the upper hand in their bid to reach the final.

Above: **We'll meet again. Markus Babbel goes down after a ferocious challenge from Barcelona's Emanuel Petit, who joined Chelsea in the summer of 2001.**

Semi-final - 2nd leg
19 April 2001

LIVERPOOL 1
McAllister (pen) 44

BARCELONA 0
H-T 1-0. Crowd 44,203

WESTERVELD
BABBEL
HENCHOZ
HYYPIA
CARRAGHER
GERRARD (MURPHY)
HAMANN
SMICER (FOWLER)
McALLISTER
OWEN (BERGER)
FOWLER

The purists may have been offended by Liverpool's ultra-cautious display in the Nou Camp, but now the platform was in place for a searching examination of Barcelona's suspect defence. In a game of high passion and aggressive tackling, both teams gave their all. The Spaniards fashioned the best of the early chances,

Rivaldo's 30-yard dipper being turned over the bar by Westerveld and Enrique's shot from an Overmars cross skating inches wide of a post. The hosts had barely threatened in attack, but they were literally handed the breakthrough on 44 minutes when Kluivert, defending a McAllister corner, inexplicably palmed the ball away. The vastly experienced Scot had no hesitation in stepping forward to send a perfect spot-kick low to the 'keeper's left. There was a heart-stopping moment in the second half when Westerveld, under pressure from Kluivert, spectacularly missed a back-pass which rolled past his right-hand post, but having gained a precious lead, the Reds were in no mood to relinquish it. Thus Owen was withdrawn in favour of Berger, who reinforced the midfield as the home side maintained a vice-like grip on proceedings to secure a memorable victory.

Liverpool won 1-0 on aggregate.

UEFA Cup Final in Dortmund
16 May 2001

LIVERPOOL 5
Babbel 4; Gerrard 16; McAllister (pen) 41; Fowler 73; Geli (o.g.) 116

ALAVÉS 4
Alonso 27; Moreno 48, 51; Cruyff 89
H-T 3-1. Crowd 65,000

WESTERVELD
BABBEL
HENCHOZ (SMICER)
HYYPIA
CARRAGHER
GERRARD
HAMANN
McALLISTER
MURPHY
OWEN (BERGER)
HESKEY (FOWLER)

Finally the waiting was over as Liverpool won an enthralling, if error-strewn final against unheralded Alavés to end a barren 17 years without European success, and to complete a unique treble of cup victories in the same season. The match was breathless, with the Reds strolling into a two-goal lead inside 16 minutes, courtesy of Babbel's far-post header and Gerrard's low drive after an interchange of passes with Owen. Already the game seemed lost for the Spaniards, but coach Esnal acted swiftly to bring on striker Alonso, who immediately pulled a goal back with a far-post nod from Contra's accurate cross. For the next ten minutes the Reds wobbled as Moreno and Tellez threatened to equalise, but Liverpool regained the initiative just before half-time when Owen squirmed clear of Herrera on the edge of the box and the hapless 'keeper hauled him down. McAllister stepped up to convert the penalty and the Merseysiders' half-time lead seemed comfortable enough, but two goals in three minutes by Moreno - the first a flashing header and the second a free-kick under Liverpool's defensive wall - levelled the game. Now it was Gérard Houllier's turn to influence the match as first Smicer and then Fowler were introduced. Indeed, the contest seemed to be settled when McAllister played in Fowler for a wonderful individual goal, the striker beating three players across the penalty area before shooting past Herrera. But plucky Alavés were not finished, and with a minute of normal time remaining, Cruyff beat Westerveld at the near post to head home from a Pablo Gomez corner. Extra-time saw Alavés reduced to nine men as two of their number were sent off for fouls and it was from the spot of the second dismissal that McAllister guided a fateful free-kick into the heart of the penalty area, where it was glanced into his own net by the unfortunate Geli. It was a cruel way for Alavés to lose, having played their part in one of the most thrilling and entertaining of all European finals.

4-4 at full time.
Liverpool won on golden goal rule

Right: **Mission accomplished. The beaming Gérard Houllier cradles the UEFA Cup, Liverpool's first European trophy since 1984.**

APPEARANCES AND GOALS: LIVERPOOL IN EUROPE 1964/65 – 2000/01

Player	App	Sub	Gls
Ablett G	6	-	0
A'Court A	1	-	0
Arrowsmith A	1	-	0
Babb P	12	2	0
Babbel M	13	-	1
Barmby N	6	3	4
Barnes J	12	-	3
Beglin J	3	-	1
Berger P	16	3	4
Bjornebye S	16	-	2
Boersma P	13	6	8
Burrows D	11	-	0
Byrne G	22	-	1
Callaghan I	87	1	10
Carragher J	19	-	0
Carter J	0	1	0
Case J	25	6	12
Charnock P	0	1	0
Chisnall P	2	-	1
Clemence R	77	-	0
Cohen A	2	1	0
Collymore S	5	2	2
Cormack P	13	3	2
Dalglish K	46	1	10
Diomède B	2	-	0
Dundee S	0	1	0
Evans A	11	2	7
Evans R	1	-	0
Fairclough D	7	9	4
Fowler R	25	7	11
Friedel B	1	1	0
Gayle H	0	1	0
Gerrard S	10	-	2
Gillespie G	2	1	0
Graham R	13	-	5
Grobbelaar B	37	-	0
Hall B	27	8	2
Hamann D	13	-	0
Hansen A	42	1	3
Harkness S	13	3	0
Hateley A	5	-	3
Heggem V	5	1	0
Heighway S	61	3	11
Henchoz S	10	-	0
Heskey E	8	2	3
Hodgson D	3	4	2
Hooper M	4	-	0
Houghton R	4	-	2
Hughes E	75	-	9
Hunt R	29	2	17
Hutchison D	3	-	1
Hyypia S	11	-	0
Ince P	7	-	1
Irwin C	4	1	0
James D	22	-	0
Johnson D	14	5	8
Johnston C	13	4	2
Jones B	0	1	0
Jones J	12	-	0
Jones R	11	-	0
Keegan K	40	-	12
Kennedy A	34	-	4
Kennedy M	0	2	0
Kennedy R	46	-	12
Kettle B	1	-	0
Kvarme B	5	-	0
Lawler C	66	-	11
Lawrence T	33	-	0
Lawrenson M	26	1	2
Lee S	33	-	4
Leonhardsen O	3	2	0
Lindsay A	31	-	4
Litmanen J	0	2	0
Lloyd L	31	-	1
McAllister G	4	5	2
McAteer J	12	2	0
McDermott T	30	1	12
MacDonald K	3	-	0
McLaughlin J	8	-	0
McManaman S	30	-	5
McMahon S	5	-	0
Marsh M	11	1	1
Matteo D	10	1	0
Milne G	16	-	0
Molby J	7	-	1
Money R	1	-	0
Moran R	4	-	0
Murphy D	6	5	1
Neal P	69	-	12
Nicol S	17	2	2
Owen M	18	3	7
Peplow S	1	-	0
Redknapp J	19	4	3
Riedle K	3	4	2
Robinson M	6	1	2
Rosenthal R	1	3	0
Ross I	5	2	1
Ruddock N	5	1	0
Rush I	35	2	20
St John I	30	2	10
Saunders D	5	-	9
Scales J	4	1	0
Smicer V	6	5	0
Smith T	83	1	8
Song R	1	-	0
Souness	35	1	7
Staunton S	5	2	0
Stevenson W	25	1	1
Stewart P	2	-	2
Storton T	1	1	0
Strong G	16	-	2
Tanner N	6	2	0
Thomas M	10	2	0
Thompson D	2	-	0
Thompson M	0	1	0
Thompson Pe	40	3	6
Thompson Ph	44	3	4
Toshack J	30	6	10
Traoré D	2	1	0
Venison B	0	3	1
Waddle A	0	1	0
Wall P	3	-	0
Wallace G	1	-	2
Walsh P	6	-	3
Walters M	7	1	1
Wark J	9	-	5
Westerveld S	13	-	0
Whelan R	22	1	6
Wright M	17	-	2
Yeats R	36	-	2
Ziege C	6	3	0